DATE DUE

FE 12 '04			
DE _ 8			

DEMCO 38-296

Bike Boys, Drag Queens, and Superstars

Bike Boys

DRAG

Queens

& Superstars

Avant-Garde, Mass Culture,
and Gay Identities in the 1960s
Underground Cinema

Juan A. Suárez

Indiana University Press
Bloomington and Indianapolis

on Permissions constitutes the only exception to this
prohibition.

The paper used in this publication meets the minimum
requirements of American National Standard for
Information Sciences—Permanence of Paper for Printed
Library Materials, ANSI Z39.48-1984.

 TM

Manufactured in the United States of America

Library of Congress-Cataloging-in-Publication Data
Suárez, Juan Antonio.
    Bike boys, drag queens, and superstars : avant-
    garde, mass culture, and gay identities in the 1960s
    underground cinema / Juan A. Suárez.
        p. cm.
    Includes bibliographical references and index.
    Filmography: p.
    ISBN 0-253-32971-X (cl : alk. paper).—
ISBN 0-253-21033-X (pa : alk. paper)
    1. Experimental films—United States—History and
criticism.   2. Homosexuality in motion pictures.
3. Popular culture—United States.   4. Anger,
Kenneth—Criticism and interpretation.   5. Smith,
Jack, 1932– —Criticism and interpretation.
6. Warhol, Andy, 1928– —Criticism and
interpretation.   I. Title.
PN1995.9.E96S82   1996
791.43'653—dc20   95-19742

1 2 3 4 5 01 00 99 98 97 96

A mis padres

CONTENTS

Acknowledgments   ix
Introduction   xi

ONE   **Avant-Garde and Mass Culture:**
            Mapping the Dialectic   1

TWO   **The American Underground as a**
            Cultural Formation: Practices,
            Institutions, and Ideologies   52

THREE   **The 1960s Underground as Political**
            Postmodernism: From the New
            Sensibility to Gay Cultural
            Activism   87

FOUR   **Pop, Queer, or Fascist? The**
            Ambiguity of Mass Culture in
            Kenneth Anger's *Scorpio Rising*   **141**

FIVE   **Drag, Rubble, and "Secret Flix":**
            Jack Smith's Avant-Garde against
            the Lucky Landlord Empire   181

SIX **The Artist as Advertiser: Stardom, Style, and Commodification in Andy Warhol's Underground Films** **214**

Conclusions 260
Notes 265
Filmography 317
Bibliography 321
Index 345

ACKNOWLEDGMENTS

A doctoral fellowship from the Film Studies Program at Indiana University and a grant-in-aid of research from the Indiana University Graduate School were instrumental in writing the first draft of this book. A summer research grant from the Fundación Esteban Romero at the Universidad de Murcia (Spain) helped me complete the last leg of writing and research.

Besides institutions, I owe thanks first of all to Jim Naremore, who steered this work with his characteristic learning, sophistication, enthusiasm, and grace. Over the years, Barbara Klinger has been a stimulating teacher and model of intellectual rigor. Matei Calinescu and Pat Brantlinger shared their wealth of knowledge with me and were encouraging and perceptive readers throughout. Katrina Boyd and Millicent Manglis read parts of this project and provided insightful criticism, not to mention constant support. At the Indiana University Film Studies Program office, Deb Munson helped with film rentals, projectors, VCRs, and other such entanglements. David Frasier, at the Indiana University Library, located obscure 1960s films and publications in the early stages of research. The staff of the Kinsey Institute granted me access to the institute's collection of 1960s experimental films. Neepa Majumdar obtained illustrations. Jonas Mekas graciously allowed me to reproduce some underground film posters, and Roberta Schönemann photographed them. Kenneth Anger provided the still used on the cover. Cristina Guevara Sanz, my research assistant at the Universidad de Murcia, prepared the index.

I am particularly grateful to Joan Catapano, senior editor at Indiana University Press, for her generous interest in this project. I also want to thank John Vollmer for carefully editing the copy.

In addition, John and Roz Moore have always been there, cheering from the sidelines. My parents, Juan Antonio and Maruja, and my siblings, Fernando and Rosaura, have always made themselves near and shown confidence in my efforts. And David Moore has seen me through all this and shared his love, helping me more than I could thank him for.

This book studies the relations between the avant-garde and mass culture in the context of the American underground cinema of the 1960s, particularly in the work of its three most polemical and influential directors: Kenneth Anger, Jack Smith, and Andy Warhol. In contrast to previous writings, which postulate a separation between avant-gardism and the mainstream, it will be my contention that the avant-garde must be understood in relation to dominant modes of artistic and cultural production, which notably include mass culture. My argument requires that we shift attention from textuality and ideology, traditional grounds of inquiry in avant-garde studies, to contextuality and performance. Such a change in focus demands a change in methodology as well—from the analysis of the politics of form, to an examination of how texts circulate in the culture.

Throughout, I will emphasize the dual meaning of "mass culture." On the one hand, the phrase designates the products of what Frankfurt School theorists Max Horkheimer and Theodor Adorno called "the culture industry," that is, advertisements, newspapers, magazines, posters, photographs, recorded music, movies, radio, television, and fashions. All of these forms result from the industrial manufacture of cultural artifacts destined for commercial consumption, and according to Horkheimer and Adorno's analysis, they produce "mass deception." On the other hand such critics as Stuart Hall, Raymond Williams, Dick Hebdige, Pierre Bourdieu, and Michel De Certeau (representatives of what has been named "the cultural studies tradition") have described mass culture in such a way as to include the ephemeral and contingent practices of reading and rerouting through which audiences engage with mass-produced cultural items, often engendering unpredictable, stray significations and desires.

While recent theorists have routinely invoked contemporary urban formations such as punk or hip-hop as sites of oppositional uses of mass culture, they have rarely studied the avant-garde as the front in which such uses first crystallized. In fact, as I will show in the following pages, the avant-garde's identity has always been wrapped up in the self-conscious, often critical activation of mass culture. The conception of mass culture I will be using throughout thus links the Janus-like passive and active faces of the term, its double quality of market circulated consumer *products* and of arenas for popular meaning *production*. Both notions of mass culture are important to the avant-garde, which has constantly oscillated between criticizing mass culture as a dominating force and celebrating its uto-pian potential. As we will see, these two antithetical views often remain suspended in a sort of creative tension as (to paraphrase Adorno) torn halves of a whole to which they do not add up.

For its part, "avant-garde" has sometimes been used as a generic term for a vast range of often short-lived move-ments and artistic practices, beginning in the mid-to-late nineteenth century and continuing into the twentieth, which opposed realistic, representational academicism. This de-finition emphasizes the "shock of the new" in modern artistic production, and it tends to obscure the difference, within the modern aesthetic, between high modernism and the radical "anti-art" practiced by what Peter Bürger and others have termed the "historical avant-garde."[1] The main grounds of distinction between these two modern artistic trends are perhaps their antithetical attitudes towards mass culture. In the face of the stark transformation of daily life brought about by consumer society and the culture industry, high modernist art (represented by such figures as Stéphane Mallarmé, Gertrude Stein, Thomas Mann, Marcel Proust, Henri Matisse, and Arnold Schönberg) withdrew into the realm of autonomous aesthetics; the avant-garde (incar-nated by a long artistic lineage including Tristan Tzara and Marcel Duchamp, and, more recently, Andy Warhol and Joseph Beuys) sought to intervene in everyday life, where it attacked the idea of autonomous art and experimented with the new structures of perception and experience pro-moted by mass culture. I shall be using the term "avant-garde" in this last sense—as a type of subcultural practice that deconstructs "bourgeois" ideas of art while appropri-ating, at the same time, certain images and strategies from the culture industry.

Both the avant-garde and mass culture became significant at roughly the same time—the middle decades of the nineteenth century—as byproducts of the large-scale modernization of daily life. They were characterized by their striving for the new: kitsch depended on planned obsolescence; the avant-garde constantly sought to replace traditional aesthetic tenets with radically new forms of representation. They both addressed society as a non-organic whole made up of multiple constituencies, constantly evolving, and fundamentally unstable. Both tended to perpetuate the fragmentation of personal experience caused by new technologies, by the increased mobility of information, and by modern metropolitan life. And finally, both artistic cultures were marked by deep awareness of the erasure of old forms of community, which they tried to replace with newer ones—whether based on consumer power or style, in the case of mass culture, or on artistic or cultural credos, in the case of the avant-garde.

Similarities between the two cultures have been overlooked by most traditional conceptualizations of the avant-garde, which have tended to focus on textual features rather than on the contextual matrix in which texts operate. Perhaps because our understanding of the present determines the way we see the past, the now-dominant intellectual regime of postmodernism has made us increasingly aware of the avant-garde's tendency to break down distinctions between high and low culture. Since its emergence, the avant-garde has drawn its strength from an attack on traditional cultural hierarchies, an attack differently carried out in the successive waves of cubism, futurism, dadaism, surrealism, *Neue Sachlichkeit,* Soviet constructivism, rayonism, suprematism, (to a much lesser degree) British vorticism, and Bauhaus. These avant-garde explosions can thus be read as foreshadowings of postmodernism: that is, local, incremental rehearsals for the generalized blurring of the categories of high and low which, particularly since the 1960s, has characterized our culture. Study of the early avant-garde productions is, then, indispensable to a better knowledge of present-day cultural politics, and can also add to the debate of whether postmodernism is a radically new paradigm, or merely a replay (albeit on a cyclopean scale) of strategies and conditions already present in earlier historical stages.

A new technological medium identified with popular entertainment and potentially as a purveyor of radically new ways of perceiving and portraying, the cinema was a privileged point of encounter for the avant-garde's fascination with technology, mass cultural forms, and non-traditional modes of representation. The most characteristic early examples of avant-garde cinema included the dadaist movies of Hans Richter, Man Ray, and Marcel Duchamp, and the surrealist films of Luis Buñuel. Meanwhile, the Soviet experiments of Sergei Eisenstein and Dziga Vertov were indebted to Meyerhold's theatrical experiments and to Vladimir Tatlin's constructivism. In the Weimar Republic, the Soviet machine-aesthetic bred with the autochthonous *Neue Sachlichkeit* to produce such films as Walter Ruttmann's *Berlin: Symphony of a Great City.* The futurists shot little footage and what little there was is now lost; however, their film scenarios, theoretical essays, and photographic projects evidence their interest in the medium. Among Bauhaus members, whose main pursuits were architecture and design, there was considerable interest in the cinema, witnessed, for example, by Laszlo Moholy-Nagy's experiments with photography and film. These nervous, often short and ragged films dealing with technology, speed, urban landscapes, or political rebellion were the avant-garde counter-part to the modernist aesthetic of German Expressionism and especially of French Impressionism—which also developed alternative modes of representation but defined themselves as art cinema, in reaction against commercial culture.

The boom of the underground cinema in New York during the late 1950s and early 1960s has consistently been read as an echo of the first wave of avant-garde cinema that took place in Europe in the 1920s and 1930s,[2] yet, at the same time, there were notable differences between the two developments. While the avant-garde cinemas of the 1920s and 1930s arose within wider artistic movements (Buñuel's and Man Ray's films, for example, were framed within the activities of Breton's surrealist group), the American underground was exclusively a film movement, albeit strongly influenced by such contemporary cultural and aesthetic currents as beat literature, pop art, performance, minimalism, the new dance, and assemblages and environments, among others. As an alternative cultural front, the underground lacked the coherence of early avant-garde "movements," a coherence forged through manifestoes, pronouncements, public acts (exhibition openings, movie premieres, scandals), and more or less explicit group rules and hierarchies. At the same time, its dispersion was somewhat kept in check by Jonas Mekas's activities as organizer, programmer, distributor, critic, fundraiser, and filmmaker, to articulate an alternative film front.

Within this rather heterogeneous alternative film front, one can discern the twin tendencies I am describing as modernism and avant-gardism. Filmmakers such as Stan Brakhage, Harry Smith, and Jonas Mekas himself cultivated a difficult, art-for-art's-sake cinema in stark opposition to the commercial Hollywood product. On the other hand, the filmmakers with whom I am mainly concerned—Kenneth Anger, Jack Smith, and Andy Warhol (but also footage-recycler Bruce Conner, Mike and George Kuchar, José Rodríguez-Soltero, Bill Vehr, Warren Sonbert, and Ken Jacobs, among others)—freely borrowed motifs and images from commercial culture, turning their productions into a mixture of parody of and homage to popular icons and myths. The presence of mass culture in this second group of directors is symptomatic of the contemporary erosion of the borderlines between high and low, a development variously named "new sensibility" (in Susan Sontag's phrase) or "pop sensibility" (in Tom Wolfe's). Such mixing and blurring of traditional hierarchies may in turn have been propelled by television and the expanding leisure industries, which had the ability to frame all culture as mass culture. In contrast with the early avant-garde, which coincided with the emergence of the studio film and consumer society, the American underground takes place when mass culture has already "won out" over other cultural modes. As a result, the wholesale permeation of social, cultural, and even subjective life by commodified cultural forms was a pivotal preoccupation in (avant-garde) underground films.

Another link between the three filmmakers I shall discuss is their, for lack of a better term, "gay sensibility."[3] Their reworkings of mass cultural products are most often informed by gay identifications and desires, and by the gay remotivation of cultural artifacts known as "camp." While such subcultural filiation was frequently brought up by 1960s reviewers and critics, it rarely received more than cursory discussion. For the most part, however, this was not so much a consequence of conscious and programmatic homophobia, as of the lack of a critical apparatus that could tie sexuality to textuality and representation. In the intervening years, however, successive waves of variously inflected feminist discourse and, more recently, the development of gay studies have provided conceptual coordinates that can help us make better sense of subculturally anchored textual and cultural strategies. Taking advantage of insights contributed by these critical methods, Anger's taste for ornamentation and stylistic excess, together with his fascination with the hot-rod and motorcycle subcultures; Smith's portrayals of drag queens in *Flaming Creatures,* his threadbare imitations of 1930s and 1940s movie glamour, and his interest in junk and debris; and Warhol's explorations of style, fashion, and (super)stardom will be studied here against the horizon of 1960s gay sexualities, mythologies, and iconographies. In this particular respect, the present project is indebted to Eve Sedgwick's idea, subtending her *Epistemology of the Closet,* that "understanding of virtually any aspect of modern Western culture must be, not merely incomplete, but damaged in its central substance to the degree that it does not incorporate a critical analysis of modern homo/heterosexual definition. . . ."[4] This is particularly true of the sector of the 1960s American underground represented by the Anger-Warhol-Smith triad. In their work, the collusion of experimental avant-gardism, alternative cultural politics and figurations of community and subjectivity, and the fascination with pop culture are strongly mediated, albeit in elusive and circuitous ways, by gay sexualities and social identities.

As can be gathered from what has been said so far, the present project studies the underground cinema as the outcome of a series of intersecting axes: high and low art; avant-gardism and commercial culture; institutional sensibilities and marginal urban subcultures; and avant-garde texts and their activation by specific audiences. The following description of Andy Warhol's 1960s Factory parties provides an emblematic image of the cultural and social hybridity of the movement:

> The silver room was crowded with a-heads, street geniuses, poor little rich girls, the very chic, the desperately unknown, hustlers and call boys, prostitutes, museum curators, art dealers, rich collectors, the best artists of the time, and the worst hangers-on. . . . One senses that, in those days, a thrilling complicity united the artistic and sexual and drug subcultures, that some kind of shared refusal threw together mute *seriosos* like composer La Monte Young with hardened, quick-witted, druggy street performers like Rotten Rita, Narsissy, and Ondine, people living on drugs and their wits, doing their numbers in bars and apartments and lofts. . . . On the one hand, there were the money and established conspicuousness of Pop; on the other, that *really* underground subculture, the transvestites.[5]

Through the layers and nodes of this motley scene circulated the aesthetic credos, styles, reading strategies, allegorical images of modernity, and utopian impulses which shaped the underground.

The critical implications of studying the underground in terms of its complex positioning within this social and cultural scene can be further clarified by defining my argument in relation to two of the most influential and ambitious paradigms in the study of the avant-garde: P. Adams Sitney's history of the American experimental cinema, *Visionary Film: The American Avant-Garde Cinema, 1943–1970,* and the series of writings published in the 1970s by such *Screen* theorists as Peter Wollen, Laura Mulvey, and Stephen Heath. My emphasis on contextuality contrasts with these two conceptualizations of avant-garde cinema, which tended to

favor the textual as object of study, while eliding its historical, social, and cultural backgrounds.

P. Adams Sitney's book is the single most formidable
contribution to the study of the American experimental
cinema, but it is shaped by a romanticism and formalism
that I hope to avoid.[6] Sitney conceived the American avant-
garde cinema in isolation from other areas of the culture,
and in particular from mass culture, which he regarded as
the avant-garde's other. Adopting a stance similar to such
writers as Clement Greenberg, Sitney defined the avant-
garde in completely formalist terms. Hence the rejection of
linear narrative, the elision of causal links, and the penchant for abstraction were the most important features of
the cinematic avant-garde (a label which, in his use, did not
distinguish the avant-garde from modernism). Underlying
Sitney's formalist approach is the assumption (shared by
formalists and new critics alike) that the goal of art is to
enlarge the perceptual idiom, and that such modification
is effected by departing from naturalized, or automatized,
ways of seeing.[7] Thus, Sitney's avant-garde filmmaker generated fresher perspectives on reality through the manipulation of traditional codes of representation, a manipulation
guided by his/her personal genius and intuition.

Sitney's discussion, for all its sophistication and tour-de-
force readings of individual texts, offers few glimpses of the
historical context of the American avant-garde cinema—
its audiences, its channels of dissemination and exhibition,
and its numerous cultural influences. As Dana Polan has
suggested, the American avant-garde cinema and the underground in particular remain, in Sitney's account, timeless
objects, floating in a space of their own, self-propelled
by their own internal artistic momentum.[8] Such aestheticist
isolation in method is the reason for a certain vagueness in

the few historical categories Sitney uses. His characterization of the artist as outsider, for example, lacks nuance and ultimately works toward obscuring important differences between specific artists. As alternative filmmakers, Andy Warhol (commercial illustrator turned pop painter and underground filmmaker, openly gay, and at once voyeur and participant in marginal New York subcultures) and Stan Brakhage (staunch defender of the myth of the independent filmmaker as romantic poet, who lived with his family in bucolic isolation in the Colorado mountains, and who despised urban life and commercial culture) occupy two radically different positions of enunciation and therefore embody two distinct versions of cultural marginality.

Because Sitney never takes such differences into account, his characterization of alternative cinema is surprisingly monolithic. The same can be said, in a more general way, of his notion of the avant-garde itself. From Maya Deren and other "film-poets" to the late 1960s structuralists, the alternative cinema constantly redefined itself against mainstream cultural practices, which were, in turn, evolving across time. The Hollywood popular narrative, the most important discourse against which the avant-garde cinema defined itself, underwent substantial change from the mid-1940s to the 1970s. In the 1940s, the studio system was still in full swing and Hollywood film grammar and genre conventions remained relatively uncontested within the industry; by the late 1960s, on the other hand, classical production systems no longer obtained and commercial films showed the influence of both the European new waves and the underground. The alternative cinemas fashioned themselves in constant dialogue with such changes. In fact, one could conjecture that the assimilative capacity of 1960s popular film, which might have dulled the radical edge of some avant-garde strategies, led to the wholesale rejection of representational codes that characterized structuralist cinema. These, however, are not questions that Sitney's perspective can help clarify.

The critical discourse practiced during the 1970s by the extremely influential British film journal *Screen* can be read as a materialist sublation of the sort of idealism that informs Sitney's work; nonetheless, British writing fell into its own forms of idealism, the most cramping of which consisted in remaining anchored in textual analysis, unable to deal with the concrete materiality of texts' circulation in the culture. *Screen*'s critical enterprise had a double focus. On the one hand, it analyzed classical Hollywood ideology, showing a certain penchant for locating and dissecting places within individual film-systems where this ideology cracked open under its own ill-contained scandals and internal contradictions. On the other, the journal championed the films of such directors as Jean-Luc Godard, Jean-Marie Straub and Danielle Huillet, and Nagisha Oshima, offering them as model counter-cinemas.[9] Despite its interest in this type of alternative filmmaking, *Screen* did not develop a full-fledged theory of the avant-garde; nevertheless, the avant-gardist desire to link innovative textual production and political effect punctuated its most ambitious and influential statements. Hence, Laura Mulvey's "Visual Pleasure and Narrative Cinema" ends with the recommendation that her analysis of Hollywood's gender-pleasure economy be used in the construction of a feminist avant-garde that would redefine such a regime—a project that she herself sought to carry out in her film collaborations with Peter Wollen, such as *Riddles of the Sphinx* and *Panthasilea*. In addition, other programmatic *Screen* texts contemporary with Mulvey's, such as Colin MacCabe's "Realism and Cinema: Notes on Some Brechtian Theses" and Stephen

Heath's "Narrative Space," more or less implicitly argue, in the words of a recent reviewer of their criticism, "for a modernist or avant-garde cinema that would fragment identity and identification, decentering the character, the reader, and the author."[10]

In his important recapitulation of 1970s *Screen* theory, David Rodowick named this sort of avant-gardist aspiration "the discourse of political modernism," which he defined as an alignment of modernist textual practice with postmodern epistemology and leftist politics.[11] The groundwork for this alignment was laid by Louis Althusser's model of ideology.[12] In contrast with much classical Marxism, which regarded structures of ownership of the means of production as the scaffolding of an oppressive social system, Althusser stressed the importance of ideology in the maintenance of existing social relations. Even after a successful revolution, he seemed to argue, an unchanged ideological system would hinder the construction of truly liberated and undistorted social relations. Ideology was for Althusser not a stable body of doctrine manifestly imposed from above; it was a pervasive discourse subtly ingrained in the everyday, determining the structures of social relations and experience. These were in turn channeled by what he called "Ideological State Apparatuses," that is, such institutions as schools, universities, the press, radio, television, the arts and culture, sport arenas, advertisements, and so forth. These institutions perpetuated ideology by enforcing certain structures of subjectivity—by creating and maintaining through a regime of appeal, or "interpellation" in Althusser's phrase, an addressee whose own being was determined by the dominant social machinery.

Subject construction was thus the most pernicious and lasting effect of ideology; invisibly embedded in the social languages constantly mobilized around us, it conditioned even the terms and structures of protest or rebellion. The inescapability of ideology resided precisely in its epistemological constraints, since the subject structures it fostered conditioned our perception and understanding of the world. The escape from the grip of ideology that Althusser envisioned consisted in developing "scientific" analyses of dominant social languages and of their strategies of subject construction. By "scientific" Althusser meant a discourse that would bypass subjectivity, both as a valid standpoint for analysis and as its proposed aim—as in the creation of "more authentic subjectivities." Such critical discourse could help to forge linguistic constructs and social positions that would not posit a subject, a complicit ideological structure immediately entailing subjection (a recurrent pun in Althusser's work). From this perspective, the questioning of received subjective structures and social languages had the political value of questioning existing power structures as well.

As a pervasive and alluring ideological apparatus, the popular cinema had a considerable share in producing and perpetuating ideological subject positions. Through its formal idiom (consisting in centered framing, maximal intelligibility, and clear-cut narrative sequence); identification with individualized character figures; and the physical layout of the screening situation, which placed the spectator as a privileged, phenomenological (all-seeing, centered) eye (I, in a well-worn *Screen* pun), the cinema fostered (through interpellation) a fully ideological subject. From *Screen*'s perspective, any film practice that would displace these traits of the cinematic apparatus was endowed with revolutionary potential, as it obstructed the promotion of ideological subjective positions.

Peter Wollen was the writer associated with *Screen* who most systematically applied the principles of Althusserian ideological analysis to theorizing the avant-garde. In such pieces as "The Two Avant-Gardes," he sought to politicize an area of cultural production that had received, for the most part, largely idealistic appraisals. Opposing romantic characterizations like Sitney's, Wollen proposed to re-read film modernism and avant-gardism as a semiotic inquiry into filmic codes of representation, an inquiry that had ultimately political effects. This recasting of avant-garde formal inquiry as a means of political intervention helped to close the gap between what Wollen considered the "two avant-gardes": a formalist one, identified with abstract cinema and, in the seventies, with the different Co-Op movements; and a more representational, political avant-garde, practiced, for example, from Sergei Eisenstein and Dziga Vertov to Jean-Luc Godard and Jean-Marie Straub. Wollen's argument also posited an implicit analogy between avant-garde or modernist practice and *Screen* criticism, both of which aimed to deconstruct what they postulated as dominant representational codes and pleasures, and to imagine non-repressive (non-ideological, non-subject-based) alternatives.[13]

While avoiding the extreme idealism of Sitney's model, *Screen's* conception of the avant-garde had in common with it its regarding the text as privileged object of inquiry; political significations and tropes of decentering and dissolution were extracted from the stable ground of the text's formal traits, not from the far more volatile dynamics of its circulation. At the bottom of such reduction lay the decision, unwarranted by Althusser's formulations, that ideology was more powerfully operative in texts than in the web of practices which accrue around them. This seemed particularly problematic when applied to one of *Screen's* main objects of study: the popular cinema. In Hollywood films, for example, marketing devices, stars' personae, audiences' exposure to popular genres, and knowledge of inside gossip strongly influence a film's reception, and therefore its ideological effect. With regard to alternative cinemas, the presumably radical effect of non-illusionistic and subject-decentering modes of representation was also context-specific, as demonstrated *de facto* by the development, during the 1980s, of MTV and of certain advertisement strategies which mobilized modernist textual forms in contexts that were far from politically revolutionary. Ironically, *Screen* criticism itself purveyed an example of the power of contextual determinants, since it was the conceptual frame combining sophisticated formal analysis and a leftist political agenda that permitted critics to reactivate the classical cinema as an ideological apparatus, symptomatic of epistemological givens and specific subject constructions and positionings.

While the importance of *Screen* theorists' efforts in endowing modernist formal deviations with a political weight should be kept in mind, I think their text-centered characterizations ought to be complemented with a closer attention to contextual variation and to the *social performance* of avant-garde texts—that is, their *uses* and *effects,* the ways in which they interacted with other texts, were activated by audiences, or functioned (in Fredric Jameson's phrase) as "socially symbolic acts," encoding specific cultural or ideological conflicts. The exploration of these factors with regard to the underground will be the purpose of the present study. In this respect, my work is closer to the general orientation and methodology of two recent and important texts: Lauren Rabinovitz's *Points of Resistance: Women, Power, and Politics in the New York Avant-Garde Cinema, 1943-1971* and David E. James's *Allegories of Cinema: American Film in the 1960s.*[14] Both react to the apolitical romanticism of Sitney, on the one hand, and to the formalist political modernism of *Screen,* on the other, while characterizing avant-garde cinema as an evolving practice in constant negotiation with its social and cultural environments. My own work differs from theirs in that I concentrate on the early 1960s underground, while James and Rabinovitz have broader temporal and generic scopes, and, further, in my attempt to read the underground as the intersection of gay subcultural identities, mass culture, and 1960s avant-gardism.

In order to place the 1960s underground cinema in proper context, chapter 1 maps theoretically and historically the avant-garde's distinctive interaction with mass culture. Chapter 2 characterizes the New York underground as a specific cultural formation. It examines the movement's internal organization, modes of production, showcases, audiences, channels of dissemination, and ideology, stressing an internal split in the movement between a withdrawn, modernist aesthetic, and an avant-gardist one of engagement with mass culture. Chapter 3 explores the underground within the context of the emergent postmodernism reflected in the writings of Susan Sontag, Leslie Fiedler, and Tom Wolfe, and in subcultural popular forms such as comics, film cults, and the camp and gay activation of mainstream texts. I will argue that, in contrast with the apolitical "pop" or "new sensibility" of Wolfe or Sontag, the rejection of modernism and the fascination with mass cultural forms on the part of a sector of the underground must be viewed as a form of subcultural activism linked to the staging of gay identities.

The last three chapters explore how the films of Anger, Smith, and Warhol articulate different relations between avant-garde textuality and mass cultural icons and myths.

The order in which I treat these authors is chronological. I deal with Anger first (chapter 4) because, although he belongs in the same age group as Warhol and Smith, he started making movies in the late 1940s, in the mode of what I will define later as a "gay modernist" aesthetic, and practically stopped producing movies altogether after 1972, when his unfinished *Lucifer Rising* premiered. Anger's oeuvre exemplifies a shift from postwar modernism to early 1960s postmodernism, and shows an ambivalence toward mass culture resulting from the combination of these two contradictory influences. Jack Smith started making films in the late 1950s. His work involves a fascination with drag, Hollywood glamour, and old-fashioned kitsch, together with a rigorous attempt to maintain the critical thrust of alternative culture and to avoid commodification. Warhol comes last because his career extends well into the 1970s and 1980s, when he refashioned himself as a society artist, seemingly questioning his previous underground career. I will show how his underground films transposed into the avant-garde the image-making strategies of fashion and advertisement, blurring, in the process, the distinctions between mainstream and marginal art.

Bike Boys, Drag Queens, and Superstars

Avant-Garde and Mass Culture: Mapping the Dialectic

One

Clement Greenberg's article "Avant-Garde and Kitsch," written in 1939, is often the starting point in discussions of the avant-garde.[1] This famous essay is in many ways symptomatic of late 1930s cultural criticism, especially in its valuation of avant-garde as "authentic" culture in sharp opposition to mass culture or kitsch.[2] Authors such as Theodor Adorno, Max Horkheimer, and Herbert Marcuse in Germany, and Meyer Schapiro and Clement Greenberg in the United States, all of whom wrote about mass culture, modernism, and avant-garde at this time, postulated high modernist and avant-garde aesthetics as antidotes to the spurious and manipulative character shown by mass culture in both democratic and totalitarian regimes.[3]

From this array of influential authors, I choose to start my study with a reevaluation of Greenberg's seminal piece for several reasons. Written and published in the late 1930s, Greenberg's article stands at the end of the most spectacular period of the historical avant-garde and modernism.[4] By the late 1930s, modern artistic tendencies had been fully assimilated into bourgeois culture and were under severe attack from both right- and left-wing political factions. Formal experimentation was being criticized by the left as escapist and isolated from real-life problems at a time when the joint pressure of political conservatism and fascism led left-wing artists and intellectuals throughout Europe to demand an aesthetics of immediate impact and intelligibility that could be used directly in political and social struggle.[5] This tendency was represented in France, for example, by the *Association des artistes et écrivains révolutionnaires* (ADAER), an artistic front seeking to engage art in radical political struggle. With a majority of Communist Party members in its ranks, the ADAER endorsed socialist realism, launched in 1930 by the Second International Congress of Revolutionary Writers, and rejected the avant-gardism of the surrealists, some of whom were members of the organization. In Germany similar debates pitted Ernst Bloch, Theodor Adorno, and Bertolt Brecht, defenders of aesthetic innovation and anti-traditionalism, against George Lukács, one of the leading proponents of the new Soviet realism.[6]

Modern art, as is well known, was not more favorably viewed at this time by the political right. In fascist Germany, artistic movements from Expressionism to *Neue Sachlichkeit* were the object of an exhibition—"Degenerate Art"— where they were exposed as decadent, pathological, and demeaning to the "Aryan race." In France, the right often sought to boycott and prosecute radical artistic expressions, as was the case with Louis Aragon's poem "Front Rouge" and Luis Buñuel's film *L'Age d'or,* both of which appeared in 1930. The reevaluation of avant-garde culture (i.e., modern art, for Greenberg), often modulating into a defense or apology, is therefore a common topic in the cultural criticism of the period. Greenberg, like other of his contemporaries mentioned above, is evaluating both modernism and the avant-garde at a moment when they were besieged by opposite political tendencies. His article reflects the tensions of the moment, and one detects a certain urgency in his defense of experimental art as the only remaining "authentic culture": "Since the avant-garde forms the only living culture we now have, the survival in the near future of culture in general is thus threatened."[7]

Another reason to start my discussion with Greenberg's piece lies in his methodology, which seeks to relate the "aesthetic experience as met by the specific—not generalized—individual, and the social and historical contexts in which that experience takes place."[8] Linking aesthetic experience to social and historical contexts permits Greenberg to theorize avant-garde *and* kitsch as negotiating a similar set of conflicts in the culture. As the title of his article suggests, kitsch is the inseparable double of the avant-garde: "Where there is an avant-garde, generally we also find a rearguard."[9] Hence, despite Greenberg's obvious preference for the avant-garde, he implies the extent to which neither artistic culture can be discussed without reference to the other.[10] This awareness is also the basis of the present chapter, which will recast Greenberg's categorization of these two artistic cultures. In the process it will be shown that, despite the tendency to view avant-garde and kitsch separately, they have been interrelated historically (because of their simultaneous emergence) and structurally (by virtue of their somewhat parallel social vocation). This being the case, there is much to be gained in the understanding of the avant-garde by reevaluating its relations to mass culture.

Greenberg's article is one of the most influential statements on avant-garde culture to be issued in the United States. It was first published in *Partisan Review,* which was perhaps the major vehicle for left (more specifically, Trotskyist) cultural criticism in America during the 1930s and 1940s.[11] *Partisan Review* contributed during its early years to disseminating avant-garde European culture in America, a function that had been carried out in the 1920s by journals such as *The Dial,* Matthew Josephson's *Broom,* and Margaret Anderson's *Little Review,* and would be continued during the 1940s by Charles Henri Ford and Parker Tyler's *View.*[12] Unlike these publications, however, *Partisan Review* tended to foreground the political aspects of modernism and avant-gardism, as can be discerned in Greenberg's piece and in some of his later writing. Greenberg's views must then be framed within the New York-based artistic and intellectual community, which had since the early 1910s been extremely receptive to the European avant-garde.[13] It is important to keep in mind the existence of this tradition in New York, since, as we shall see in later chapters, it was a determining cultural background for successive generations of avant-garde artists, writers, and filmmakers.

By situating Greenberg's text in these contexts, I am trying to show its liminal position in the history of the avant-garde: it is poised between the European and the American avant-gardes; between the historical avant-garde and the so-called neo-avant-gardes of the fifties and sixties;

between the heroic days of the European bohemia and (what Greenberg understood as) the present cultural trivialization brought about by kitsch; and between the Moscow trials and the dissolution of the Popular Front, when many left-wing American intellectuals had become disillusioned with Stalinism, and the onset of the Cold War. Finally, the article summarizes roughly a century of artistic and historical developments, and seeks evaluative criteria that would help us preserve, as he puts it, "whatever living culture we have right now." For all these reasons, Greenberg's piece seems an appropriate starting point for a study which tries to reformulate some of its most influential pronouncements in the context of the American avant-garde cinema of the sixties.

The Greenbergian Paradigm

Greenberg's arguments have been extremely influential, both as a widely accepted critical stance toward both avant-garde and mass culture, and subsequently as a major target of attacks from what we might call postmodern American cultural criticism.[14] The latter type of criticism emerged in the early 1960s when a number of intellectuals began to question high modernist seriousness and elitism. Major representatives of this trend were Marshall McLuhan, Leslie Fiedler, Susan Sontag, and Tom Wolfe.[15] Their celebrations of a cultural logic later tagged postmodernism tended to reject (to borrow Sontag's coinage) Greenberg's "Jewish seriousness" in favor of a purportedly playful and democratic "homosexual aestheticism," to the extent that criticizing Greenberg's piece—implicitly or explicitly—has become a tired move in most contemporary cultural critique. Perhaps for this reason it seems worth reviewing Greenberg's position at the threshold of this study, for his rather categorical (and context-specific) dismissal of mass culture has acted almost as a red flag for his opponents, obscuring other strengths in his arguments.

The "avant-garde" (read, modern art) is, in Greenberg's formulation, a symptom of social and cultural crisis. This crisis is motivated by the ideological relativism that permeated bourgeois culture toward the mid-nineteenth century, when ". . . our present bourgeois social order was shown to be, not an eternal, 'natural' condition of life, but simply the latest term in a succession of social orders."[16] The "relativization" of bourgeois culture led to the emergence of alternative subcultures and ideologies that contradicted bourgeois ways of thinking and doing. Most important among these anti-bourgeois developments were social and political radicalism and avant-gardism.[17] Greenberg described the avant-garde's breakup with the established bourgeois order as the emigration "from bourgeois society to Bohemia." This flight cut the avant-garde off from bourgeois audiences and public life and had the effect of throwing art into the realm of the "merely artistic," which for Greenberg is the formalist exploration of the medium and the rejection of content: "Content is to be dissolved so completely into form that the work of art or literature cannot be reduced in whole or in part to anything not itself." Imitation of external reality is replaced by "the study of imitation" understood, in its Aristotelian sense, as "the disciplines and processes of art and literature themselves."[18] If the basis of all art is mimesis, the avant-garde settles at the center of art by being "the imitation of imitation": imitation turned inward, withdrawn into its own self-referentiality. The result of this inward-turning is an exacerbation of formalism and a sort of art in exile from the values of audiences, that is, an art which seeks to remain untainted by reigning mercantilism and instrumental rationality.

As the avant-garde moves away from its bourgeois audiences, kitsch, in turn, turns these audiences away from the demanding and hermetic art of the avant-garde. Hence, while political pressures threaten the existence of avant-garde culture from the outside, kitsch undermines it from the inside—that is, from the realm of cultural production itself. Kitsch is synonymous with one part of mass culture: the trivial, commodified products of what Max Horkheimer and Theodor Adorno called "the culture industry" and Greenberg described as the "[p]opular commercial literature with their chromeotypes, magazine covers, illustrations, ads, slick and pulp fiction, comics, Tin Pan Alley music, tap dancing, Hollywood movies, etc., etc."[19] As cliché-ridden, predictable, predigested forms, these make for a culture of easy consumption and assimilation; they furnish the appearance of art with none of its intellectual demands.

I have just summarized what I want to call the "formalist argument" in Greenberg's piece: the avant-garde is complex and demanding while kitsch is simplistic and non-demanding. ("Kitsch pretends to demand nothing of its customers except their money—not even their time.")[20] But the formalist argument, like the rigid split between avant-garde and kitsch, has obscured another interesting criterion of value in Greenberg's article—the closeness of cultural forms to the values of audiences. And by this criterion, modernism is seen by Greenberg as somewhat lacking. Modernism is bourgeois art without the bourgeoisie, since its major artists propound bourgeois ideals at a time when these have been rendered empty by an oppressive state and by the culture of consumption. Glossing Greenberg,

T. J. Clark describes this predicament as follows: "They [avant-garde artistic values] are the repository, as it were, of forms of affect and intelligence that once inhered in a complex form of life but do so no longer; they are the concrete form of intensity and self-consciousness, the only one left, and therefore the form to be preserved at all costs and somehow kept apart from the surrounding desolation."[21] Hence while Greenberg defends modernism, he also points out that it is dangerously cut off from its social base, since the only remaining link between bourgeoisie and avant-garde is "an umbilical cord of gold" in the form of the patronage of cultivated bourgeois elites. Greenberg seems doubtful as to the validity of this link, as market relations, characterized by commodification and instrumentalization, cannot replace the former "organic" connections between the bourgeoisie and its artists that reigned when, according to him, art embodied the aspirations and ideals of the rising class; before, that is, this very class betrayed its own ideals.

Art's isolation from the public can be resolved by bridging the gap between art and the experiences, ambitions, and desires of its audiences. Such redefinition of the social place of art is a frequent topic in the critical writings of Leon Trotsky, Walter Benjamin, and Bertolt Brecht, and, as we will see, it constitutes the driving force of what I will describe as the avant-garde in opposition to modernism. The existence of this alternative means that avant-garde culture is different in important ways from high modernism, a difference that Greenberg does not take into account and that will help us reevaluate the relations between avant-garde and kitsch in a more dialectical way. Intent on linking art and daily experience, the avant-garde does not share modernism's relentless hostility toward kitsch. On the contrary, it tries to assimilate critically into its products the iconography, structures of feeling, and forms of practice emanating from mass culture as a means of integrating art into the lives of audiences.

This possible avenue, hinted at but not taken, in the avant-garde and kitsch discussion would soon completely disappear from Greenberg's writings, as he progressively reduced his ideas about the place of art in society to formal arguments. In "Towards a Newer Laocoon," published in *Partisan Review* one year after "Avant-Garde and Kitsch," he reelaborated the contents and general thesis of the latter piece while enhancing the development toward pure form as an autonomous artistic dynamic and eliding the contextual determinations of artistic and cultural develop-ments.[22] Non-specific summations such as "Forces stem-ming outside art play a much larger part than I have room to acknowledge" appear as gestures in this later essay, and because they are just that, they preclude more serious ex-amination of what these forces might be, and how they might operate.[23] The article constitutes a concise yet trench-ant rewriting of the painterly developments of the last two centuries in terms of the emergence of form as the main subject matter of painting. The drift of the piece is, to my eyes, hardly surprising, since its explicit thesis is to demon-strate the superiority of contemporary abstract expression-ism over figurative art. In other words, the rewriting of the past is mediated through the need to justify the present, and this justification seems to demand a certain oblivion toward the social pressures incumbent on art.[24]

Avant-Garde, Modernism, and the Institution of Art

If Greenberg progressively eliminated art's contextual determinations from his arguments, Peter Bürger's *Theory of the Avant-Garde* (1974) emphasized them quite force-fully.[25] Fully inserted in the Marxist tradition of critical theory, Bürger's book approaches the avant-garde from the perspective of its cultural politics, which define in turn its rapport with bourgeois society. Some of Bürger's arguments are already prefigured in Greenberg's piece, but the two authors differ in their conclusions. While Greenberg conflates modernism and avant-garde, much of Bürger's work is taken up by the attempt to differentiate between the two, a difference which is politically marked, as it refers to how each artistic culture operates in bourgeois society.

Like Greenberg, Bürger regards the dominance of form over content as the principal trend in the development of modern art since Romanticism; however, he does not hypostatize such development as art's immanent goal. The increasing importance of form is for him a reflection of art's progressive independence from other realms of value, activity, and rationality. According to his analysis, throughout the eighteenth century, art gradually detached itself from its former patrons, the church and the court, and became closer to the values and aspirations of the rising bourgeoisie. As a result of this independence, art solidified into an institution with its own internal dynamics and sources of value, no longer subordinated to direct patronage, and increasingly reliant on the indirect one provided by the free circulation of works of art in an emergent art market. The aesthetic theories of Kant and Schiller, with their emphasis on the autonomy of aesthetic judgment, reflected the gradual detachment of art from the sphere of life, a development which Bürger dates around the last decades of the eighteenth century.

Aesthetic autonomy, however, is not equivalent to a lack of transcendence in the social realm, and this is a point where Kant and Schiller differ.[26] Contrary to Immanuel Kant's defense of the complete independence of the aesthetic judgment, Friedrich Schiller, in his letters *On the Aesthetic Education of Man* (1801), tries to establish a "social function of the aesthetic."[27] This function consists in restoring the unity of the senses, fragmented by the criteria of rationality, instrumentality, and profit maximization that have come to predominate in everyday life. Art can effect this restoration by virtue of its separation from everyday life. As Bürger summarizes, "It is Schiller's idea that precisely because it [art] renounces all intervention in reality, art is suited to restore man's wholeness."[28] Art's divorce from reality is for Schiller a historical category, not an essential one, and therefore the possibility of a future integration of art and reality is not foreclosed. Because of its separation from life, art remains, for Schiller, the only repository of values—happiness, good, truth, harmony—that remain unrealizable in society. Here lies "the moment of truth" in the autonomy of the aesthetic: a moment that maintains alive the memory of a happiness and integrity permanently exiled from present social conditions. This memory of "goodness" can operate as a critical force by contrasting the limitations of the present with the ideals expressed in art.[29]

The notion of aesthetic autonomy also contains—and here Bürger follows Herbert Marcuse's analysis in "The Affirmative Character of Culture"—a moment of "untruth."[30] This "ideological" moment lies in interpreting autonomy—a historical condition—as an essential characteristic of art. In Bürger's terms, "the category of autonomy does not permit the understanding of its referent as one that develops historically. The relative dissociation of the work of art from the praxis of life in bourgeois society becomes thus transformed into the (erroneous) idea that the work of art is totally independent of society."[31] This ideological moment blunts the critical edge contained in art as bearer of social ideals. In Marcuse's words: "What counts as utopia, phantasy, and rebellion in the world of fact is allowed in the world of art." Artistic productions may then act as safety valves through which radical and rebellious impulses are expressed precisely because they have no consequences in the world of practice: "What occurs in art occurs with no obligation."[32] And from this perspective, all artistic products are ultimately affirmative of the status quo. This is the ideological dead end that threatens the restorative and critical functions of art formulated by Schiller. The autonomy of the aesthetic, concomitant with its institutionalization, is then an intractable quality which gives rise to aporias that are only solvable by symbolically erasing either the social matrix of art (as did modernism) or the art institution itself (as did the avant-garde). Before we turn to examining each of these solutions, we should consider in passing some historical conditions that contributed to the separation of bourgeois art into a realm of action that could be conceptualized as autonomous from other social and political areas of experience.

The affirmative ideology of autonomous art did not become immediately apparent upon art's institutionalization. Both Bürger and Greenberg—and as we shall see a number of other critics—agree on the fact that for a number of decades bourgeois society and its artistic institutions appeared transparent to each other. T. J. Clark describes this period as ". . . a time, before the avant-garde, when the bourgeoisie, like any other normal ruling class, possessed a culture and an art which were directly and recognizably its own." He lists the following examples as illustrations: Hogarth, Chardin, Constable, Géricault, Richardson, Defoe, and Balzac. "The bourgeoisie, we can say, in some strong sense *possessed* this art: the art enacted, clarified, and criticized the class's experiences, its appearance and values; it responded to its demands and assumptions."[33] Independently of its dubious existence, this prelapsarian time "before the avant-garde" has a rhetorical function, as it allows critics such as Greenberg and Bürger to postulate a "historical ground" from which avant-garde culture could emerge. Simultaneously, it operates almost as a utopian memory, and in that respect, a repository of progressive social ideals: it purveys the image of an epoch when the positive values of the enlightenment had not yet been mortgaged to domination and limitless exploitation; when modernity wielded its promise against the oppressiveness of the Old Regime; when culture and society appeared "organically" connected.[34]

The period of harmony seems to end with the Second Empire in France. Throughout the Second Empire, spanning from Louis Napoleon's *coup* in 1848 to the outburst of the Commune in 1871, a rift developed between bourgeois official culture and values and a particular sector of the arts. The beginning of this period witnessed the rise of Gustave Courbet, whom Greenberg considers the first full-fledged avant-garde artist,[35] and of aestheticism, which marked, according to Bürger, the consolidation of art as an autonomous institution.[36] American art critic Meyer Schapiro, a contemporary of Greenberg, also concurred in the existence of a mutual estrangement between art and bourgeois society beginning around these years.[37] In two pieces written shortly before Greenberg's "Avant-Garde and Kitsch," Schapiro links art's alienation and radicalization of style to the self-liquidation of bourgeois political culture that took place after Louis Napoleon's *coup*. When postulating this breach in the relations between bourgeois society and its art, Schapiro, Greenberg, and Bürger leaned on the interpretation of historians and commentators who saw the Second Empire as the bourgeoisie's jettisoning of traditional forms of political culture in order to ensure social control. Karl Marx, witness to these developments, was one of the observers for whom "[t]he defeat of the June insurgents . . . revealed that here *bourgeois republic* signifies the unlimited despotism of one class over the other classes."[38] In these circumstances, the ideals of bourgeois democracy gave way to a reign of absolutism often aided by terror, with politics becoming a simulacrum which betrayed in actuality the intended openness of the public sphere while trying to preserve its appearance: "Society is saved just as often as the circle of its rules contracts, as a more exclusive interest is maintained against a wider one."[39]

The subordination of politics to the "exclusive interests" of a class provoked a separation between private and public realms. Politics became progressively divorced from the real-life contexts of citizens, whose private needs, desires, and claims appeared increasingly estranged from a public sphere controlled by specific class interests. The almost total lack of communication between public and private realms constituted a decisive modification in the bourgeois public sphere, whose classical version was described by Jürgen Habermas in his study *The Structural Transformation of the Public Sphere.*[40] Habermas points out that while the bourgeois public sphere had always been based on a difference between public and private, difference, however, did not entail a complete divorce between the two, but a sort of articulation:

The bourgeois public sphere could be understood as the sphere of private individuals assembled into a public body, which almost immediately laid claim to the officially regulated "intellectual newspapers" for use against the public authority itself. In those newspapers and in moralistic and critical journals, they debated that public authority on the general rules of social intercourse in their fundamentally privatized yet publicly relevant sphere of labor and commodity exchange.[41]

This sense of articulation between public and private is replaced, after the 1848 revolution, by a widening gap, not unlike the one opening between the bourgeoisie and its artists. The unhinging of public and private realms deflated the social and communal aspects of bourgeois existence while intensifying its private traits. Such developments had in turn important consequences for the production and reception of works of art.

The gap opened between public and private experience may have fostered a sense of estrangement from official life among artists. As Thomas Crow writes: "The avant-garde [meaning, in this context, the art of the followers of Louis David: avant-garde because of its anti-traditional form and politically radical content][42] leaves behind the older concerns of official art not out of any special rebelliousness on the part of its members, but because their political representatives had jettisoned as dangerous and obstructive the institutions and ideals for which official art was metaphorically to stand."[43] Cut off from social engagement and public concern, art becomes increasingly privatized. Aestheticism and the *art pour l'art* movements result from the privatization of aesthetic experience. Hence Greenberg writes: "'Art for art's sake' and 'pure poetry' appear, and subject matter or content becomes something to be avoided like a plague."[44] For Bürger, "[a]s long as art interprets reality or provides a satisfaction of residual needs only in the imagination, it is, though detached from the praxis of life, still related to it. It is only in aestheticism that the tie to society still existent up to this moment is severed."[45] In addition to these two critics, Walter Benjamin also understood the emergence of *l'art pour l'art* as a result of the bourgeoisie's seizure "of its own cause from the hands of the writers and the poets": "At the end of this development may be found Mallarmé and the cause of the *poésie pure.* There the cause of his own class has been so far removed from the poet that the problem of a literature without an object becomes the center of discussion."[46]

Aestheticism and art for art's sake made opaque the institution of art and its affirmative ideology by exacerbating the separation between art and life, and by accentuating the lack of consequence of art's artificial paradises. These characteristics make it an early manifestation of modernism, which, following on the tracks of aestheticism, resolved the opposition between the values of the bourgeoisie and those of art by positing aesthetic autonomy as the only realm of transcendence. Such a solution explains modernism's moderate anti-traditionalism: defending the autonomy of art still means accepting art's traditional social place, no matter how critically.[47]

By contrast, the avant-garde defined itself in direct opposition to art's autonomy, to its existence as an institution separate from daily life and practice. In so doing avant-gardists attacked the separation of art from life and the affirmative character that such separation granted cultural products. They resolved the contradiction between the values of mainstream society and those of art by integrating art in the praxis of life, hoping thus to revolutionize the latter. In Bürger's words: "The avant-gardists proposed the sublation of art—sublation in the Hegelian sense of the term: art was not simply to be destroyed, but transferred to the *praxis* of life where it would be preserved, albeit in changed form."[48] The double break enacted by the avant-garde—a break with bourgeois *and* artistic values—explains the virulence of its manifestations.

Bürger's *Theory of the Avant-Garde* provides us with useful coordinates to conceptualize the differences between avant-garde and modernism in terms of how each of them conceives its place within the culture. The usefulness and internal logic of this distinction should not, however, make us lose sight of its heuristic value: neither avant-garde nor modernism can always be separated by neatly laid demarcations. The modernist impulse to withdraw into autonomous art and the avant-gardist desire to fuse art and life can overlap in the same author, even in the same work. Aestheticists and representatives of *l'art pour l'art,* for example, greatly influenced the culture of the avant-garde through such practices as dandyism, anti-bourgeois ideologies, and the formation of subcultural artistic communities. Charles Baudelaire and Oscar Wilde exemplify the overlap of modernist aesthetics and avant-gardist practices. Some artists are easier to classify: Virginia Woolf, Thomas Mann, or Arnold Schönberg can be described as modernist, while John Heartfield, Marcel Duchamp, and Tristan Tzara can be seen as unambiguous representatives of the avant-garde. But how can we classify Picasso, whose work fuses modernist withdrawal and avant-gardist integration of art and everyday life—as in his cubist collages, or in his illustrations for anarchist journals of the 1910s? And how do we explain the fascination with elements of urban mass culture in eminently modernist works like T. S. Eliot's *The Waste Land,* or in James Joyce's *Ulysses?*[49]

Sometimes declaring a work modernist or avant-garde depends on what aspects are actualized through interpretation, rather than on intrinsic qualities of the work itself. Such has been the case with the cubist collages of the 1910s, which were viewed as modernist explorations on perspective and materials until the emergence of pop art in the 1960s helped to reevaluate them as precursors of pop's demystification of art—an avant-gardist aspiration. The opposite is more often the case. In fact, the historical avant-garde has frequently been interpreted as autonomous modernist art, a reading which blunts the former's most radical proposals. As I will try to show in later chapters, the 1960s American underground films were most often decoded as modernist products: as exercises in perception and cinematic codes, withdrawn from the immediate historical and cultural contexts. One of the main goals of the present project is to reevaluate some of the most important examples of the 1960s underground cinema as avant-garde forms. In doing so, I will explore how they relate to other cultural realms—particularly to mass culture—and how these relations define their conflictive insertion in society.

The Avant-Garde and "Integrated Experience" [*Erfahrung*]

To summarize, the avant-garde's attempt (in Bürger's expression) "to organize a new life praxis from a basis in art" and to sublate the division between art and life demands changing art's position in the culture, that is, refashioning art's apparatus rather than merely changing its subject matter or its formal strategies. The goal is therefore to produce art *differently,* not just different art. This difference consists in making art that is more integrated, more relevant, more connected to the lifeworld of its audiences; art that can, in sum, give rise to "authentic experience."[50]

The category of *experience* plays a fundamental role in the critical theory of the Frankfurt School—especially in Theodor W. Adorno's and Walter Benjamin's writings, where it is an important concept for establishing the different orientation of modernism and avant-gardism. It operates in the work of these authors as a hinge between consciousness and world, inside and outside, monadic subject and community. Making experience—concrete doings in life-contexts—a central category of critical discourse is an attempt to avoid at once the excesses of absolute idealism and of empirical materialism, and to sublate both tendencies in an ongoing process characterized by constant negotiations between them.[51]

For most Frankfurt School critics, modernity annihilated the possibilities for integrated experience. Commodification, modern technology—both of which invaded the cultural realm—and changes in political institutions resulted in fragmentation, reification, and the general impoverishment of experience. Thus in the opening of his famous essay, "Some Motifs in Baudelaire," Benjamin dwells on the differences between genuine experience (*Erfahrung*) and subjective experience (*Erlebnis*). The former is organically integrated in historical and communal memory; the latter, a collection of sensations adrift in a subjectivity detached from the continuum of community and history. In Benjamin's words, "Experience [*Erfahrung*] is indeed a matter of tradition, in collective existence as well as in private life. It is less the product of facts firmly anchored in memory than of a convergence in memory of accumulated and frequently unconscious data."[52] And later he adds: "Where there is experience in the strict sense of the word, certain contents of the individual past combine with material of the collective past."[53] Modern forms of socialization, however, produce monadic individuals, thrown into their own subjectivity, exiled from the public realm, and disconnected from each other and from their history. They thus promote *Erlebnis* rather than *Erfahrung*.

According to both Benjamin and Adorno, art had the potential to produce integrated experience, an idea already stated by Schiller in his letters *On the Aesthetic Education of Man*. This assertion, however, is qualified differently by each. For Adorno, art was being invaded in modern times by commodification and by the pervasiveness of the culture industry, and this "invasion" devaluated the experience arising from the aesthetic object. Adorno's solution, like Greenberg's, lay in a withdrawal into the autonomy of the aesthetic. The only type of art that could resist commodification was a demanding modernist art that granted no concessions to the public, and therefore could resist being incorporated into the market. In modernism's disregard for unity and reconciliation, Adorno saw a refusal to appease social contradictions and an implicit criticism of the present: "A successful work, according to immanent criticism, is not one which resolves objective contradiction in a spurious harmony, but one which expresses the idea of harmony negatively, by embodying contradictions pure and uncompromised in its innermost structure."[54] Not surprisingly, he championed twelve-tone music—for him an exemplary artistic practice whose rigorously crafted dissonance encoded a negation of the dominant culture. Furthermore, since modernism exacted from the spectator an active decoding, it could provide a realm for the reconstruction of subjectivity, at present preprogrammed and dissolved into passivity by the culture industry.[55] Such subjectivity would not be integrated in collective life (which is all to the good for Adorno, since collective life in late capitalism took essentially false forms) but in its rootlessness it would constitute instead a critical counterpoint to the existing orders.

If Adorno's ideas were essentially modernist, Benjamin's thought was strongly influenced by avant-garde culture, particularly in his belief that bringing art closer to "the life of the masses" was a means to purvey authentic experience. This, of course, implied refashioning art's social functioning and its relations with audiences, and Benjamin thought the use of technology in cultural production had the potential to effect such changes through the destruction of what he called the "aura" of the work of art.[56] "Aura" is for Benjamin the "unique manifestation of a distance," yet an eminently symbolic one, having to do with the uniqueness of specific creations, artistic genius, or the cult value of art works. The destruction of aura had a democratic potential in so far as it brought cultural products closer to audiences and, at the same time, enabled the use of technology for the exploration of everyday environments and activities.[57] Mechanical reproduction also eliminated the highly introspective reception demanded by bourgeois high art and invited instead reception in distraction. This type of reception was immediate, non-specialized, and collective—as in film, or in the nearly unconscious perception of the architecture in the background of our daily life.

Both the avant-garde and mass culture pioneered the uses of technology in cultural production. Dadaism, for example, incorporated into the realm of art the reception-in-shock imposed by film, a mass culture medium of technological base. Hence, even though Benjamin realized that mass culture was heavily commodified, he regarded it as a form potentially leading to a new, non-bourgeois mode of consciousness. Like other avant-gardists, he saw mass culture as a weapon to be used against art's "disinterestedness" and isolation, and as a terrain for the emergence of a truly democratic art, open not only to experts and specialists but also to amateurs. The avant-garde's main function was then to transpose the culture industry's uses of technology into forms of artistic production endowed with a critical edge. In this respect, Benjamin differed from authors like Greenberg; rather than oppose kitsch and the avant-garde, he defined their relations in a more dialectical way and even stressed the desirability of a constant dialogue between the two.

Understanding and using the progressive potentials embedded in mass culture was for Benjamin an urgent task, since fascism was, at the time of his writing, mobilizing mass cultural forms to create a false sublation between art and life. Parades, uniforms, the mystification of the race, and the cult of leadership were means to aestheticize everyday life, investing it with a "heroic" character. This sublation was false, however, in so far as it led to the annihilation of the subject (not to its autonomous integration in social life), and to destruction, genocide, and war.[58] In the face of these developments, it was the task of the avant-garde and of critical theory to mobilize the potential for change embedded in mass culture with the purpose of liberating history from mythmakers and of creating more harmonious forms of culture and experience.

The Manufacture of Experience by the Public Sphere of Production

During the second half of the nineteenth century, mass culture was the privileged site of a profound reorganization of collective experience. The study of the structures under-lying these massive reorientations of the collectivity is the subject of Oscar Negt and Alexander Klüge's *Öffentlichkeit und Erfahrung* (1972).[59] A brief examination of this work can help us understand the avant-garde's engagement with kitsch as an attempt to mobilize the potentials for inte-grated culture embedded in the latter.

Continuing the debate opened by Habermas's analysis of the structure and function of the public sphere, Negt and Klüge proposed that, through a sort of social homeo-stasis, the gap between public and private opened by the erosion of political life, increasingly subservient to bour-geois self-interest, was overcome at another level by a social mechanism they named the "public sphere of pro-duction"—or production public sphere.[60] In their words, "The traditional public sphere, whose characteristic weak-ness rests on the mechanism of exclusion between public and private, is today overlaid by the *industrialized pro-duction public spheres,* which tend to incorporate private realms, in particular the production process and the life context."[61] In the public sphere of production, experiences and contexts which were formerly private and absent from the public sphere—such as emotions, feelings, fan-tasy images, and modes of personal practice—become now publicly (mass) produced and consumed, among other means, through advertisements, consumer culture, and forms of socialization sanctioned by public powers. While connecting public and private spheres could make public life more responsive to the needs of individual citizens, the sort of link proffered by the production public sphere did not stem from the collectivity, but was a heteronomous, potentially repressive development, which Negt and Klüge labeled a mechanism of "secondary exploitation." By contrast with "primary exploitation" forms, in which people's relations to capital and to apparatuses of production were "externally" enforced by schedules, work discipline, salaries, political repression, and so forth, "secondary exploitation" is "internal" because through it the apparatuses of production infiltrate the most intimate recesses of daily practice, bringing about a wholesale colonization of experience.

According to Negt and Klüge, there are three dimensions in the public sphere of production: (1) the "sensual demonstrative public spheres of banks, factories, urban centers, and industrial zones"; (2) the consciousness industry, including consumption and advertising; and (3) public relations carried out by corporations, political parties, the state, and so forth.[62] Negt and Klüge do not provide any detailed historical examples of the production public spheres, limiting themselves to a rather abstract discussion of their effects. I believe, however, that these three dimensions of the production public sphere can be related to the emergence of three interrelated modern phenomena toward the second half of the nineteenth century: urban reform, the expansion of the commodity market (with the culture industry an important part of it), and the new public relations strategies through which dominant powers tried to compensate for the exclusionary character of public life. These three dimensions can thus be seen as forms of mass culture—in the sense of culture addressed to the masses, seeking to reorganize and structure their experiences by applying industrial modes of production to previously private sensualities.

Negt and Klüge's public sphere of production emerged most clearly in France during the Second Empire in the form of the emergence of a large-scale consumer culture, the "production of the new Paris" by Baron de Haussmann, and the already commented ousting of non-bourgeois interests from political channels.[63] The most common forms of consumer culture were the department store, the popular press (its value as organ of political opinion progressively transmuted into a vehicle for advertisement), the *feuilleton,* the panoramas and dioramas, the bright window displays along the boulevards, and, starting in 1856, the *Expositions universelles* (whose original model was the 1851 British Great Exhibition).[64] The expansion of consumer culture coincided with massive migrations from rural to urban areas, where jobs and resources were increasingly accumulated. For some authors, Greenberg included, the urban concentration of former rural dwellers was the social basis for kitsch, the new "folk culture" of relocated rural workers.

The cultural rootlessness of contemporary city dwellers is structurally homologous to that of Parisians who experienced the remodeling of the city carried out by Baron de Haussmann during the 1860s and 1870s. Old neighborhoods, among them working-class enclaves such as the *faubourg Saint-Honoré,* were transformed after the *image* of a city imposed from above. In the place of the traditional quarters appeared the new boulevards, which replaced a city molded by decades of spontaneous daily practice by one predesigned from above, as it were, according to a rational plan. City as spectacle replaced city as practice. The old communities of the *faubourgs* were substituted in the new boulevards by communities based on acquisitive power, made up of those who could afford the new (substantially higher) rents.

As folk culture and the *faubourg* died out, commodity culture, the remodeled Paris, and the new social bonds brought about by each may have functioned as forms of "secondary exploitation" as Negt and Klüge state; however, they did not simply slip into place, without arousing resistance. In fact, they became terrains of struggle and contestation, inspiring counter-images of urban life and of alternative forms of community. These counter-images surfaced in radical social discourse, mass cultural artifacts, and, more importantly for our purposes, in the avant-garde, most often under the combined influence of the former two.

Counter-Images of Community and the City

As industrialization and modern urban culture erased traditional social formations and created new forms of community based on geographical proximity, work schedules, or purchasing power, the differences between pre-modern and modern forms of social organization were frequent subjects in the work of important turn-of-the-century sociologists. For example, Fernand Tönnier distinguished between *Gemeinschaft,* or organic community, and *Gesellschaft,* a modern social group constituted exclusively with commercial or political ends in sight; Emile Durkheim, between societies based on mechanic or organic solidarity; Georg Simmel, between social groups with and without a developed monetary economy; and Max Weber, between traditional and rationalistic societies. To most of these commentators, the newer forms of social grouping seemed shallow and arbitrary by comparison with the deep-rooted communality of traditional societies, and therefore reinforced the idea that modernity fostered monism and fragmentation. In his *Economic and Philosophical Manuscripts,* Karl Marx had already attributed this monism to the individualized character of labor in capitalist regimes of production. And in one further twist, some critics would later single out such lack of authentic social cohesion as a pre-condition for the insidious work of mass culture.[65]

Given such a broad consensus about the inadequacy of modern social bonds, it is perhaps not surprising that radical social and artistic ideologies seeking to counter the status quo proposed more authentic forms of community as a part of their programs of reform. Utopian socialists like Charles Fourier, Robert Owen, and the Marquis de Saint-Simon, as well as anarchists like Bakunin and Kropotkin, devoted a great deal of attention to designing ideal communities. For some of them, creating new communities was complemented by designing new social spaces, as in the fourierist phalansteries, or Robert Owen's "ideal villages." The fact that the term "avant-garde" was first used by Saint-Simonians in the context of the organization of social life following the dictates of art and science evidences the communal vocation of the concept.[66]

Although avant-garde artists rarely tried to settle into communes the way Saint-Simonians did, they have always shown a strong tendency to form alternative collectives. Louis David and his disciples, predecessors of future avant-garde movements in their uniting social radicalism and artistic experimentation, constituted themselves into a group. They stressed their membership in it by donning ancient Roman costumes and growing beards—which earned them the name of "Etruscans." Similarly, impressionists, cubists, futurists, dadaists, surrealists, and, in a much looser sense, 1960s American underground filmmakers, constituted artistic communities, and much of their cultural activity took place in the frame of the group. In this connection, Raymond Williams has underlined the importance of "cultural formations" in avant-garde culture: these are more or less self-regulated associations of artists and intellectuals that often develop in the margins of official cultural institutions.[67] Rejection of official culture and mainstream social life can be seen as one of the strongest motivations behind the establishment of avant-garde formations. To the arbitrariness of new social links, artists oppose their tight coteries, woven around common aesthetic ideologies.

Alternative communal forms also emerged in the realms of leisure and entertainment, in such manifestations as cabarets, nightclubs, bars, cafés, dances, circuses, and holiday resorts.[68] These were areas of experience exempt from schedules, work, and other means of regimentation, and at the same time, settings for the popular entertainments that frequently attracted the attention of avant-gardists. Regarding such popular forms, Thomas Crow writes, "In their marginality [of popular entertainment] is their secret allure, one which derives less from the promise of pleasure . . . than from the simple existence of a corner of the city which has improvised an appropriate and vivid way to represent itself."[69] They force us to consider kitsch not only in its frozen state (inert, unmovable, and oppressive), as Greenberg, Macdonald, and Adorno and Horkheimer characterized it, but also as prompting forms of practice. Some such forms occasionally entailed strategies of resistance and contestation against the status quo.

Cabarets and *cafés-concerts,* for example, were important arenas for the rehearsal of "popular" identities which performed complex functions of socialization. One of them was the self-identification of audiences as "the people"— the downtrodden and dispossessed—around songs and performances which were often vehicles for virulent attacks on established powers. The vivacity of these manifestations led the public instruction powers in France to monitor closely the lyrics sung in such locales, hunting for both immoral and politically subversive contents.[70] In the words of a historian of the period, "The minister of Public Instruction was quite clear in 1872 that 'the orgy of songs produced during that epoch [the Parisian commune] was partly to blame for the Communards' depravity'; he made it a reason for reimposing censorship on the café-concert, in an effort to prevent such things from happening again."[71]

Given the cabaret's tradition as vehicle for oppositional practice and negation, it is hardly surprising that dadaism stormed into public life as a (quite peculiar indeed) cabaret act.[72] Futurists and dadaists often fashioned their readings after the structure of cabaret shows, with the double purpose of exploiting this form's subversive potential, and of debunking the conventions of the well-mannered *soirées littéraires.* Surrealists were equally responsive to the marginality, rebelliousness, and alternative communities harbored by the cabaret, as the following statement by Louis Aragon bears out: "The persecuted surrealists will be found in *cafés-chantants* taking advantage of the confusion to peddle formulas for infecting images."[73] The American underground directors of my study also clustered around these forms of entertainment: Warhol often recruited his superstars from among the performers he saw in cafes, bars, and nightclubs; and throughout his career Jack Smith alternated filmmaking with stage shows performed in Lower Manhattan clubs and bars.[74]

The modern city was also an area of contestation for avant-gardists, who expressed their opposition to urban spaces in forms that were more local and sporadic than the wholesale reform plans of such utopians as Charles Fourier and Robert Owen. There is in avant-garde culture a high degree of ambivalence toward the modern metropolis, simultaneously an object of fascination and a totalitarian, homogenizing form which must be subverted. Subversion took place through counter-images and forms of practice which involved reading the city "against the grain."[75] In this vein, Fluxus, the New York-based avant-garde group of the mid-1960s, used the streets as a stage, offering concerts, improvisations, happenings, and poetry readings in public monuments, areas designated for transit, or in dead, unused spaces, like empty lots. Their activities had been prefigured by futurists, dadaists, and surrealists, who also used the street as settings for their public manifestations and pronouncements. These activities are reminiscent of acts of social protest, revolt, or celebration, when the streets are occupied by sectors of the population usually forced to invisibility and silence.[76]

Another way to exorcise the city's oppressiveness is by defamiliarizing its spaces. Advertisements, posters, and graffiti perform this function and all of them have been used by avant-garde culture. Italian futurist leader F. T. Marinetti wanted his manifestoes posted on the streets and distributed freely to passersby. Both André Breton's *Nadja* (1925) and Louis Aragon's *Paris Peasant* (1926) contain numerous examples of the surrealists' fascination with the proliferation of disconcerting images that, in the form of posters, bills, signs, and so forth, grow spontaneously in the streets of the city.[77] A few decades later, the French situationists, heavily influenced by surrealism, used posters and graffiti as artistic media and as ways of refashioning urban space according to their desires.[78] The project of refashioning city environments has left its imprint in avant-garde film. Hence, Man Ray's *Etoile de mer* (1927) and Clair/Picabia's *Entr'acte* (1924) playfully defamiliarize well-known Parisian sights (like the *Place de l'Etoile*) by showing them upside down.

Similarly, I think that Andy Warhol's *Empire* (1964), an eight-hour, static camera portrait of the Empire State Building from sundown to sunup, can be read as a mocking defamiliarization of one of the best known symbols of American puissance, especially if we keep in mind the artist's statement that "after looking at things for a very long time, they cease to mean anything, they just become empty."

Lastly, the avant-garde rebels against the homogeneous modern city by rejecting its official, monumental face. As an example, art historian T. J. Clark demonstrates that in the period of Haussmann's reforms artists often concentrated on the unfinished and arbitrary character of Paris, producing non-heroic, deflating depictions of the city's trumpeted reforms.[79] A similar sense of resistance informs much of modern painting, in particular that of the French impressionists. The importance that movement, fleeting surfaces, faint glimmerings, and blurred outlines acquire in their paintings is a way to emphasize the disconnection and shallowness of new forms of life in contemporary cities, qualities that contrast with the solidity and feeling of permanence which new buildings and monuments were meant to evoke. Rejecting the city's official side not only in their art but also in daily practice, avant-garde artists often concentrated in marginal areas like Montmartre or Montparnasse in Paris, or Greenwich Village in New York, where they mingled with bohemians, prostitutes, drug addicts, and other social outcasts. Dadaists, futurists, and surrealists favored seedy bars, cabarets, and old-fashioned restaurants as meeting places, instead of artistic or literary salons. The French surrealists, for example, often met at the cafés around the *Place Pigalle,* part of the "lower depths" of the city, and at the *Café Certa,* in the *passage de l'opéra,* a derelict arcade about to be demolished which housed a brothel, a bathhouse, several old-fashioned stores, and modest restaurants.[80] The surrealists were the first avant-garde group to chronicle extensively their original way of inhabiting the city. They found inspiration in flea markets, in city outskirts, in the old-fashioned arcades, and in out-of-the-way neighborhoods. They seem fascinated with liminal areas, where social classes, architectural styles, or city and countryside appear juxtaposed. These are places of heterogeneity and "otherness," where surfaces and identities shift and blur, contesting the uniformity of the modern metropolis. These sites are themselves a product of modernity—albeit a bastard and involuntary one. They are debris piled up by waves of urban renewal, scars in the face of the city, betraying the dramatic surgery performed on it. In another respect, these inspiring haunts were settings of lifestyles and sectors of the population that the bourgeois transformation of the city had pushed to a marginal existence. Louis Aragon expresses this idea as follows with regard to the Parisian arcades: "Although the life that originally quickened them has drained away, they deserve, nonetheless, to be regarded as secret repositories of several modern myths: it is only today, when the pick-axe menaces them, that they have at last become the true sanctuaries of damnable pleasures and professions. Places that were incomprehensible yesterday and that tomorrow will never know."[81]

Counter-Images of the Commodity Form

From among the three mentioned forms of the public sphere of production (the transformation of the city, the political domination of the bourgeoisie, and the emergence of a large-scale commodity culture) only the latter cannot be imputed to exclusively repressive purposes. Even so, critics and cultural historians from the left and the right concur in regarding the development of the commodity market as a form of *panem et circenses,* a distraction, or a means of hiding the social, political, even intellectual dispossession of the masses under an abundance of goods.[82] Particularly in some leftist critiques, the advance of the commodity market is tied to the bourgeoisie's attempts to consolidate its political monopoly and economic expansionism. However, even if the main function of commodity culture is the maintenance of bourgeois ideology and control, the commodity market cannot be simply explained as a repressive mechanism, a notion which begs the question of its resilience in the face of widespread discontent. The culture of commodities must therefore be accounted for as a system of mediation which somehow compensates for the displacement and uprooting of traditional cultural forms, the narrowing of the public sphere, and the lacks and deficiencies in experience provoked by the very society it seemingly upholds.[83] The commodity market, which Negt and Klüge characterized as a form of secondary, internal exploitation, satisfies desires and needs that have been removed from the public realm, but still survive in private, everyday contexts. For the condemners of the commodity form, these satisfactions are always false and illusory, mere fetishes engendered by the capitalist market in which they are inserted; consumers accept them only because they are ideologically conditioned to do so.

Negt and Klüge revise this classical conceptualization of commodity culture in a way that may help us understand why the avant-garde, an oppositional culture, appears interested in the products of the market and the culture industry. According to Negt and Klüge, commodities are accepted by customers because in them there is a "moment of truth," or what they call a "block of real life." They define this block as needs, real-life contexts, and raw materials of experience that the system tries to manufacture, but in which there is always what Eberhardt Knödler-Bunte, glossing Negt and Klüge, describes as "a residual potential for experience and action which cannot be integrated into the system of profit maximization, but which nevertheless develops in conjunction with the expansion of capitalist profit maximization and the changing composition of capital."[84] This block persists as a structural component of the system based on commodification, in which "[l]ife context is acknowledged in so far as it fits with the realization of capital's interest in exploitation. In the process, . . . capital accommodates itself to real needs, but must, however, simultaneously model all real needs so that it can slot them into its abstract system."[85] The abstraction of "real-life conditions" by the exigencies of the market does not invalidate these raw materials; it simply splits them in two levels: reified forms of experience, circulated and commercialized through the market, and "blocks of real life," where such genuine needs and experiences survive intact. The block of genuine experience (composed of desires, needs, and aspirations unfulfilled by existing social options) is pushed to the margins of the commercial form and the commodification process, where it remains latent, indigestible by the social order, and waiting (in a fairy-tale image) to be awakened for more authentic and participatory forms of cultural and social life—or what is the same, for forms that can project private sensualities and needs onto public discourse and thus palliate the (politically costly) divorce between the two realms. In this narrow space, on the margins of experiences, needs, and fantasies capitalized on by mainstream culture, the avant-garde thrives, seeking to vindicate the utopian potential which the commodity system at once expresses and represses. Ex-

pelled from institutional life due to its alienation from official bourgeois values, and opposed to the affirmative character of autonomous modernism, the avant-garde seems to
have nowhere to go except into the utopian edge of the
commodity form and the spontaneous, sporadic practices
accruing around it.

In my opinion, it would be futile to oppose the positive
characterizations of mass culture implicitly upheld by some
sectors of the avant-garde to the negative views of many of
the high modernists with the purpose of "correcting" and
superseding the latter. Both views should be understood
dialectically, and privileging one over the other would falsify the complex functioning of this phenomenon. I am
trying to show how the avant-garde has tended to be more
open to the liberating character of commodity culture. This
does not mean that it remains oblivious to its negative,
unauthentic, and reified qualities, but it simply seeks to
relate to them differently. In the same way, the staunchest
defenders of modernism—Adorno and Greenberg are two
examples—have also been aware of the utopian promise of
mass culture, yet more doubtful as to the possibility of its
fulfillment.[86]

The notion of an avant-garde exploring the non-reified
potentials of mass culture runs contrary to Greenberg's categorical separation of avant-garde (modern art, at large) and
mass culture. On the other hand, it can help us understand
Bürger's view that mass culture is a flawed form of avant-
gardism in so far as it fulfills, to an extent, the avant-garde's
desire to integrate art and everyday life, but it does so
through the false, standardized, and impoverished forms of
the culture industry.[87] Mass culture has then the appearance
of integration, while leaving untouched one of the most
problematic mechanisms of bourgeois society: the com-

modification of cultural artifacts, conceived as a totalizing phenomenon that preempts any chances for contestation. Bürger's argument that mass culture involves a bad sublation has two contrary implications: it points to the ideological moment of mass culture, yet it also underlines mass culture's closeness to the revolutionary ideals of the avant-garde. I want to study this closeness by exploring three characteristics of mass culture that have proved particularly inspiring for the avant-garde: its utilitarian character, its anti-artistic qualities, and its potentially subcultural style.

The Use Character of Mass Culture   Mass cultural products are destined for use, not for isolated contemplation or autonomous judgment. Popular songs, films, commercial literature, cartoons, news items, films, advertisements, billboards, stars, fashions, styles of decoration, designs—all these mass-produced and mass-consumed artifacts are integrated in the practices of everyday life, and only make "cultural sense" in this context. As entertainment and leisure props, mass cultural items become part of the experiences of consumers, reworked into individual needs and uses, inflected by particular desires and aspirations. Consumption rounds off these artifacts, anchoring them in concrete life-contexts, locating them in the immediate horizon of life. Mass cultural products are thus subject to what Benjamin called a tactile reception: a reception where essence and use are one; where there is a minimal distance between concept and thing.[88] In this way, mass culture is, by its very social function, intent on overcoming the separation between culture and life found at the center of avant-garde ideology, presenting avant-garde artists with an ideal model of reception for artistic products.

In opposition to the modes of consumption demanded by autonomous art, the avant-garde tried to infiltrate the fabric of everyday life rather than the vaults of the museums, and with this purpose it sought to mimic forms and channels of mass culture. The dadaists' use of the newspaper form, posters, leaflets, and photomontage responded to this desire. Richard Huelsenbeck's description of photomontage is almost programmatic of dadaist uses of mass culture.[89] "It [photomontage] is not connected with beauty, nor is it complacently based on inner laws. It has an everyday sober character, it wants to teach and instruct, its rearrangement of parts indicates ideological and practical principles. Thus photomontage is connected to life itself."[90]

Avant-gardists were pioneers in perceiving the artistic potential of illustrations, advertisements, clothing, window dressing, and other mass cultural forms which situate art in everyday contexts. In this respect, they counted the aesthetes among their predecessors. Charles Baudelaire and Oscar Wilde, for example, often wrote about such "trivia" as fashions, styles of decoration, caricatures, and cookbooks.[91] Paradoxically, even an epitome of modernist withdrawal such as Stéphane Mallarmé wrote and edited under a variety of feminine pseudonyms (Marguerite de Pongue was one of them) a review devoted entirely to fashion called *Le Dernier Monde*. The French surrealists rediscovered it and published a selection of articles in the sixth issue of *Minotaure*.[92] Among the surrealists, Salvador Dalí appears the most perceptive to style and its attendant phenomena. In his articles of the 1920s, he often praised fashion and manufactured objects as true expressions of modernity—more suggestive, "lyrical," and "moving" than high-art products. "Modernity," he once stated, "does not mean Sonia Delaunay's canvasses, nor Fritz Lang's *Metropolis*, but English hockey pullovers, anonymously manufactured; it may also mean a mediocre film, which makes us laugh with the most hackneyed pleasantries."[93] Berlin dadaist Raoul Hausmann was also interested in fashions, as he declares in *Dada Courier,* and in this he was following the lead of the Italian futurists, who issued their "Manifesto del vestito anti-neu-trale," in 1912. Signed by Giaccomo Balla and endorsed by his co-revolutionaries, this manifesto is an attack against the neutrality and functionality of bourgeois clothing.[94] Among Soviet artists, Liubov Popova designed factory clothes, fur-niture, and interiors as a means of placing art in contact with the masses.

Another everyday sight which attracted the attention of avant-garde artists was window dressing. In a short piece dated in 1924, Fernand Léger extolled the artistry of window display, "which has assumed increasing im-portance in the last several years. The street has become a permanent spectacle of increasing intensity."[95] The surreal-ists found the juxtapositions of items in window displays extremely inspiring, as can be gathered from Aragon's de-scriptions of the store windows at the *passage l'opéra* in *Paris Peasant.* A prominent member of the surrealist group led by André Breton, Salvador Dalí worked as a window dresser for New York's plush department store Bonwit Teller. This assignment, however, earned Dalí expulsion from the surrealist group in 1938, since Breton regarded it as an out-rageous condescension to commercialism. The American dadaist and surrealist Man Ray was a fashion photographer for *Vogue,* and he also worked during the 1920s for such in-fluential designers as Paul Poiret and Coco Chanel. In a later generation of avant-gardists, the American pop artists of the early 1960s, Jasper Johns, Robert Rauschenberg, and Andy

Warhol worked as window dressers and commercial designers and illustrators.

These avant-garde's attempts to graft art into all areas of daily experience demonstrate that if under mass culture all areas of life can be made into commodities, through the agency of the avant-garde, all contexts of life can be permeated, and thus transformed, by "art." As we will see in a later chapter, Andy Warhol's films offer a rigorous exploration of this dialectic.

Transitoriness and Anti-Artistic Appeal   While modernism strives for a sense of permanence and transcendence based on the redeeming qualities of art, the avant-garde internalizes the fleeting and transitory traits of the commodity. Matei Calinescu points out the proximity between avant-garde and mass culture in this respect: "Even if we accept Clement Greenberg's view that avant-gardism is radically opposed to kitsch, we have to realize that these two extremes are strongly attracted to each other, and what separates them is sometimes much less striking than what unites them."[96] For one, the avant-garde mimes the "planned obsolescence" that characterizes kitsch by striving for the immediate effect ("the shock of the new"), adopting thus a throwaway style of artistic consumption reminiscent of mass culture and opposing art's traditional aspirations to timelessness.[97] The use of newspaper cut-outs—in themselves dated, transient materials—in dadaist collages and photomontages reflects a will to carve the work of art out of the immediate present.

The anti-artistic appeal of mass culture has been a further source of attraction for avant-garde artists and intellectuals. Introducing vulgar, strident, and obnoxiously kitschy elements into artistic creations has been one of the ways in which avant-garde culture has underlined its difference both from modernist aesthetic seriousness and from bourgeois cultural pretensions. The latter were already challenged by Charles Baudelaire, who occasionally extolled non-artistic forms. Hence in "The Salon of 1846," he states how bawdy illustrations and pulp erotic literature "sweep us into enormous drifts of reverie, . . . towards the mystical oceans of the deep," and defends, further on, the "brutal and enormous magic" of dioramas and fake theater sets.[98] In similar fashion, Arthur Rimbaud described the ineffable pleasures he found in "stupid paintings, door panels, stage sets, back-drops for acrobats, signs, popular engravings, old-fashioned literature, church Latin, erotic books with bad spelling, novels of our grandmothers, fairy tales, little books from childhood, old operas, ridiculous refrains, naive rhythms. . . ."[99] Echoing Baudelaire and Rimbaud, the surrealists recorded in their 1920s writings their fascination with the examples of tawdriness, vulgarity, and bad taste they found in flea markets, old-fashioned arcades, and cheap theaters. Their interest in cinema was similarly anti-artistic: they distanced themselves from what was called at the time the "artistic avant-garde film" and championed the popular American cinema and the lurid French film serials of the early decades. The anti-artistic use of kitsch to *épater* the bourgeoisie and the academy extends well into our century (think, for example, of the 1960s pop art movement in America) and cannot be said to have died completely.

These appropriations and rereadings of anti-artistic materials make visible the limits of art, question its principles, and often draw alternatives to them. Under their demystifying action, the realm of art emerges as a code: a system of signification grounded in historical circumstances and subject to change; in sum, a construct which does not emerge from an immutable essence, but from relative social sanctions.

Subcultural Style   According to Andreas Huyssen, the avant-garde's goal of attaining the "psycho-physical unity of human life" led artists to aim for an art "of objects and attitudes, of living and dressing, of speaking and writing."[100] Predating the historical avant-garde, dandies and aesthetes were pioneers in mobilizing style ("objects and attitudes, living and dressing,") in order to infuse art into everyday contexts. Style, in this sense, is an epiphenomenon of art, an example of what Bernard Gendron has called "ancillary aesthetic production."[101] Gendron opposes this concept to "primary artistic products," which he defines as "what the practitioners and/or the art institutions construe as the *real* work—paintings, novels, poems, composed scores and the like." "Ancillary production" encompasses activities like "outrageous public acts, manifestos, public entertainment by artists, the rituals of bohemian leisurely life, and even bohemian clothing style." These do not necessarily crystallize in primary artworks, but when performed by members of the art world, they are attempts to "bring art to bear on the conduct of everyday life," or they "provide a framework for the reception of the primary works themselves."[102]

From Théophile Gautier's famous red vest to Andy Warhol's silver wigs, style is the most visible trait of aesthetes, bohemians, and avant-garde artists; and yet, it has received little scholarly attention. Bohemian style has traditionally had the subcultural function of expressing difference from the mainstream.[103] In the early years of the Second Empire, dandyism became one such subcultural style adopted by aestheticists, bohemians, and proto-avant-gardists like Baudelaire. Dandyism strove for an ideal of re-fined elegance in dress and lifestyle that sought to counter the functionalism and vulgarity of everyday life.[104] The dandy's elegance and fastidiousness resulted from transfer-ring the rigorous criteria of art to the sphere of life.[105] As Oscar Wilde put it: "The arts are made for life, not life for the arts."[106] And elsewhere: "One should either be a work of art or wear a work of art."[107] Dandyism rests on what Ros-alind Williams has called "aristocratic consumption": clothes, decorative items, accessories, and habits are culti-vated by the dandy so long as they are rare and inaccessible to the larger mass of consumers.[108] (One needs only to re-member here Huysmans's "hero" Des Esseintes, with his "perfume organ," his diamond-studded turtle, his medieval manuscripts, and precious dwelling.)[109] However, while the dandy tries to escape the market and mainstream consump-tion, he or she remains paradoxically entangled in it. For one, the external marks of the dandy's spiritual aristocracy have to be provided by the market, yet in lesser amounts and at higher prices than the run-of-the-mill merchandise for the average shopper. Furthermore, the dandy's cult of objects is analogous to the vulgar materialism he or she tries to escape. Despite d'Aurevilly and Baudelaire's claims about the spiritual aristocracy of dandyism, it is through material signs that the dandy expresses his or her aloofness from the rest of mortals, and in this respect, remains tied to a form of conspicuous consumption also shared by the high bour-geoisie, as intent as the dandy in showing status through possessions.

In spite of the aporias dandyism is prey to, it enacts an important function: in Baudelaire's words, that of providing "the last burst of heroism" in the modern age. "Dandyism is a sunset . . . it is glorious, without heat and full of melancholy."[110] The dandy's heroism consists in creating some sense of individualism and difference in times of standardization.[111] In doing this, the dandy marks everyday environments and media—clothing, lifestyle choices, preferred haunts, language—with his or her own protagonism and identity. He or she endows everyday practices such as shopping, dressing, or creating a living environment with a sense of rebellion and with the possibility to encode dissonance and to block the transparency of ideology even inside one of its strongholds: the market.[112]

After the initiatives of dandyism, the Italian futurists ventured into the design of tastes, perfumes, interiors, recipes, and even fashions. Dadaists and surrealists also affected particular ways of dressing and acting. One example is Berlin *Oberdada* George Grosz, who describes in his autobiography how dadaists sported American clothes to signal their alienation from European values, since the looser American fit connoted the new continent's freedom from traditions and expressed a protest against the narrowness of European life.[113] Subcultural style is also distinctive among 1960s American filmmakers. Rather than the exquisite elegance of the dandy, these filmmakers cultivated appearances which drew on several marginal urban groups: gays, bohemian artists, beats, and so forth. At the same time, their work attests to a fascination with styles stemming from the semi-criminal underworld of prostitutes, hustlers, pimps, and drug addicts.

In avant-garde culture, the fastidiousness and connoisseurship of the dandy informed as well the consumption of cultural products. Surrealists treated literary and cultural traditions as commodities at a *grand magasin*. From among the existing "goods" they selected their cult favorites with the same care and premeditation with which a dandy chooses a cravat.[114] In nearly Eliotic fashion, they constructed their own tradition by enlisting such figures as the Count of Lautreamont, Charles Baudelaire, Arthur Rimbaud, Jules Verne, Edgar Allan Poe, Lewis Carroll, and E. T. A. Hoffmann, among others, as surrealists *avant-la-lettre*.[115] Cultural dandyism also operated in their reception of popular culture, as the surrealists become connoisseurs of unabashedly tawdry, lurid, and tasteless movies and plays—such as the play *Les Détraquées* or the film *The Grip of the Octopus*.[116] Their dandy-like appreciation of the excess, artifice, and flamboyance of these "degraded" products is an early form of camp sensibility, quite influential, as will be seen in a later chapter, in the 1960s New York avant-garde. In fact, Susan Sontag conceived "camp" as an updated form of dandyism: "Camp is the solution to the problem: how to be a dandy in the age of mass culture."[117]

Counter-Images of Technology

Technology is a main arena of contact for the avant-garde and mass culture, as it plays an important part in both. For the avant-garde, the artistic application of technology was an important means to enlist art in the transformation of everyday life—through the double attempt to endow art with social purpose and to humanize technique.[118] In this way, the avant-garde tried to counteract the oppressive uses of technology carried out through industrialization and to keep alive its utopian potentials.

An important exponent of these ideas were the writings of Henri de Saint-Simon (1760–1825), for whom scientists, artists, and industrialists together constituted the avant-garde, or leading edge of society.[119] This is the context in which the expression "avant-garde" is first used in its modern sense to designate "various kinds of revolutionary, and therefore future-oriented philosophies" and, I would add, aesthetic programs. The proposals of Saint-Simon and other utopian thinkers attempted an original fusion of technology and art precisely at the time when the split between the two was becoming institutionalized across Europe through the divorce of technical and artistic education, resulting in the creation of engineering schools (like the *Ecole polytechnique* in France) as separate from fine art schools.[120] In the face of such a split, utopian thinkers first and avant-garde artists later on sought to merge the aesthetic potential of science and the social use of art.

As two examples, both Bertolt Brecht and Erwin Piscator incorporated technological innovations such as cinema, photography, and radio into the theater with the purpose of undermining the naturalness of representation and creating the famous alienation effect. Technology had for them the further use of illuminating social relations through scientific means. In Brecht's own words: "I cannot get along as an artist without the help of one or two sciences."[121] From an analogous perspective, avant-garde Soviet directors Dziga Vertov and Sergei Eisenstein allied their faith in technique with the scientific purpose of their work—intended for instruction and reform, not for disinterested contemplation. Thus Eisenstein advocated a ". . . purely intellectual film, freed from traditional limitations, achieving direct forms for ideas, systems and concepts, without any need for transitions and paraphrases. We may yet have a *synthesis of art and science.*"[122]

The progressive (in the sense of future-oriented) conceptions of technology championed by radical utopian thinkers and artists also infused the motif of the man-machine. The equation of people and machines became a popular theme through Julien Offray de la Mettrie's

L'homme machine (1748), a well-read book in its time which argued that human beings are composed of distinct mechanical parts gathered together into a clockwork ensemble.[123] This mechanistic view was meant to dispute the notion that there were such things as "human spirit" or a "soul," metaphysical concepts on which religious and state powers grounded their claims to authority. Against traditional world views, de la Mettrie advocated mechanism and natural science as new paradigms that would supersede metaphysical interpretations of reality and the absolutism legitimated by them.

People-machines are a common motif in the historical avant-garde, where they retain some of the rationalistic thrust of la Mettrie's original conception. Machines are sterile, non-subjective entities, and their celebration constitutes a rejection of romantic subjectivism, emotions, and introspection, all of which are redolent of the art and culture of the past. The futurists expressed these connotations attached to the machine in the manifesto "Geometrical and Numerical Splendor and the Numerical Sensibility" (1914) in terms which are also applicable to many other avant-garde movements: "We are hastening the grotesque funeral of *passéist*[124] beauty (romantic, symbolist and decadent) whose essential elements were memory, nostalgia, the fogs of legend . . . pessimism, phthisis, suicide. . . ." To it all, they opposed "hygienic forgetfulness, hope, desire, controlled force, speed, light . . . the happy precision of gears and well-oiled thoughts."[125] Contemporarily with the futurists' formulations, dada artists produced numerous hybrids of people and machines; some examples were Hausmann's half-mechanical heads; Richter's film *Two-Penny Magic* (1927), which draws comparisons between mechanical and human movements;[126] Marcel Duchamp's enigmatic *ma-*

chines célibataires; Francis Picabia's mechanical portraits; and Fernand Léger's machine paintings, an aesthetic he translated into film in *Ballet mécanique* (1923).[127] And Soviet avant-garde artists like Vladimir Tatlin, Dziga Vertov, Liubov Popova, and Mikhail Larionov, among many others, frequently compared in their art humans and machines. Among American underground filmmakers, Warhol proclaimed his desire to be a machine, thus dispelling the mystique of artistry and genius by comparing artistic and industrial production. He made his art look machine-produced by erasing subjective marks, reproducing images already found in the culture (Campbell soup cans, movie star effigies, Coca-Cola bottles), and practicing seriality. Kenneth Anger presented a peculiar version of the man-machine motif in his films *Scorpio Rising* and *Kustom Kar Kommandos.* Both equate men and machines as objects of erotic contemplation. This notion is reinforced in *Scorpio Rising* by editing images of engines being carefully taken apart, lubricated, and cleaned, to the Ran-Dells hit song "Wind-up Doll": ". . . wind me up, I'll fall in love with you." The homoeroticism of these charged encounters between men and engines playfully exploits the masculine connotations associated with the machine in modernist culture.[128]

The cult of technology brought the avant-garde closer to mass culture, most of which is mediated by technology, or depends on it for its existence. For example, the boom of the department store and the popular press—and, connected to both, the advertisement industry—rested on a developed productive apparatus driven by the latest manufacturing technologies and able to feed a seemingly insatiable market. However clear the technological mediation of mass culture might have been in people's minds, the link between the machine and the product remained initially invisible, since one of the characteristics of the commodity is that it appears abstracted from the means of its production. It was not until the twentieth century that mass culture and technology appeared explicitly wedded in forms of mass entertainment involving the use of electricity, mechanical locomotion, and cinema.

Electricity became almost a harbinger of mass entertainment and leisure around the turn of the century, when street gas lamps were replaced by light bulbs that accentuated the contrast between light and shadow, directed the attention of passersby to window displays, or announced the presence of entertainment at the doors of theaters and cabarets, reinforcing the city's character of an "environment of mass consumption."[129] The futurists were, to my knowledge, the first avant-garde group to celebrate the new face of the city at night. In the context of their enthusiasm for speed, machinery, and progress, they made electric light into a symbol of modernity and opposed it to moonlight, which, in turn, stood for everything *passéist:* "Café-concert performances in the open air on the terrace of casinos offer a most amusing battle between spasmodic moonlight, tormented by infinite desperation, and the electric light that bounces off the fake jewelry, painted flesh, multicolored petticoats, velvets, tinsel, the counterfeit color of lips. Naturally the energetic electric light triumphs, and the soft decadent moonlight is defeated."[130] The spectacle of electric illumination also became the subject of several early avant-garde films, one of the most representative among them is Eugene Deslaw's *La Nuit électrique* (1930).

Electric lighting was extensively used for the first time at a public event in the 1898 *salon de l'automobile.*[131] Hence it can be said that the automobile introduced electricity into social life. Like electricity, motor vehicles were also fetishized by avant-garde groups as motifs of modern life connoting speed, liberation, and progress.[132] The futurists were once more at the vanguard with their famous pronouncement: "A racing car whose hood is adorned with great pipes, like serpents of explosive breath—a roaring car that seems to ride on grapeshot—is more beautiful than the *Victory of Samothrace*."[133] Part of the appeal of motor vehicles resided in the fact that they evidenced the possibility of a pleasant relationship between people and machines in the context of leisure and non-alienated activity.

The avant-garde's fascination with cinema was similarly motivated, since this invention brought together movement, electricity, technology, popular entertainment, and everyday life. Thus Fernand Léger, painter and author of *Ballet mécanique,* eulogized movies from an avant-garde perspective in 1933 in the following terms: "Cinema is thirty years old; it is young, modern, free, and has no traditions. This is its strength. It sprouts in every corner of the district, like the brats of the poor, like the bistros; it is on an equal footing with the street, with life; it is in shirt-sleeves. Mass-produced, ready-made, it is collective."[134] At the same time, the cinema also attracted modern artists for more formalist or aestheticist reasons. According to film historian Standish Lawder, the main reasons were its "kinetic dynamism . . . and its fantasy, that is, the effortless manner of conjuring up a world of strange and unexpected happenings, vividly real and yet without logic or meaning, a world normally accessible only through dreams and hallucinations."[135] Along similar lines, Scott MacDonald has stated in a recent study that the abstract films made in the 1920s by Hans Richter, Oskar Fischinger, Walter Ruttmann, and Viking Eggeling, "focused viewers' attention on shape, motion, rhythm, chiaroscuro, and color, in the hope they could touch the spirit more directly than conventional film-makers can."[136]

From the standpoints offered by these two historians, we can distinguish within experimental cinema between a high modernist and an avant-garde approach to film. The former, practiced for example by the mentioned abstract filmmakers, pursued matters of perception and conscious-ness and distanced itself from contemporary popular cul-ture. On the other hand, the cinematic avant-garde proper was represented in the historical avant-garde period by such dadaist and surrealist films as *Ballet mécanique, Étoile de mer, Chien andalou, L'Age d'or,* or *Entr'acte,* or by the Soviet futurist *Man with a Movie Camera,* to name some of the most representative. These quoted billboard imagery, advertisements, and Hollywood motifs, and characteristi-cally portrayed such emblems of modernity as electricity, speed, machinery, and urban agglomerations.

For its part, this study will focus on the avant-gardist in-volvement with film on the part of 1960s underground artists, an involvement that went beyond the realm of aes-thetics by fusing artistic innovation and the exploration of everyday life, and that found much of its inspiration in com-mercial culture, as well as in the multiple uses, readings, and forms of community and experience directly or indi-rectly prompted by it.

Conclusion

In this perforce schematic detour, I have tried to map theoretically and historically the dialogue between avant-garde and mass culture and to provide a historical di-mension to themes present in the 1960s American under-ground's reception of mass culture. This diachronic view will allow me to characterize the American underground in contrast to the historical avant-garde and to establish historical variations for themes present in different stages of avant-garde film culture. I think it is important to trace these themes to the moment of their emergence because only by understanding their historicity can we understand their changing functions in distinct contexts up to the present. I did not intend to establish definite foundations or to point out unchanging diachronic constants, but tried to explore certain cultural phenomena (counter-images of the city, alternative communities, interest in marginality, subcultural style, and the engagement with technology and science) which, while fashioned anew in each historical context, seem endemic to modernity and post-modernity—to the historical avant-garde and the neo-avant-gardes. All of these themes revolve around the avant-garde's relations to the new character of mass culture in late capitalism. The new mass cultural forms entailed large-scale recenterings and reorientations of public life which affected experience and artistic production.

I have tried to respect the dialectical nature of these developments. Although in many ways they constituted forms of oppression, they also provided grounds of contestation and resistance through counter-images emanating from non-official sites of discourse and practice, such as political radicalism and the life and culture of "the urban masses." And as has been shown here, these counter-images were often appropriated by the avant-garde with the purpose of integrating art and life, of creating more participatory forms of culture, closer to the practice of everyday life.

The American Underground as a Cultural Formation: Practices, Institutions, and Ideologies

Two

This chapter will characterize the American underground cinema as a cultural formation. British cultural theorist Raymond Williams introduced the notion of the cultural formation in his studies on the sociology of culture to designate relatively coherent associations of artists and intellectuals centered around shared social and aesthetic ideologies.[1] As noted in the first chapter, the concept is particularly applicable to the study of the avant-garde, which tends to develop in the context of alternative (and often ephemeral) communities. Williams's idea of the cultural formation stresses the need to examine the productions of these groups in relation to three factors: their internal organization, their ideologies, and their rapport with existing cultural channels. By virtue of their conflictive insertion within the larger society, avant-garde groups are, according to Williams, oppositional formations; they tend to operate in open disagreement with established cultural and social institutions or with the conditions in which such institutions exist. Their conflictive stance often results in a need to forge their own systems of artistic production, exhibition, and dissemination alongside the official culture market.

The American underground film movement is one such oppositional formation. It was a loose group of filmmakers united by a commitment to alternative film production—a commitment that involved rejection of big production values, classical narratives, and all forms of Hollywood professionalism. In their pursuit of experimental film aesthetics, underground filmmakers had to position themselves in the margins of the established film industry. In the following pages, I will demonstrate how this process took place, and how the solutions reached by underground directors were in many ways homologous with those devised by earlier generations of European and American avant-garde filmmakers.

As to their ideologies, 1960s underground filmmakers did not share an orthodoxy or a prescriptive belief system, as was the case, for example, with historical avant-garde collectives; instead, they outlined their cultural politics through spontaneous alliances with and rejections of existing aesthetic and ideological traditions. The underground's oppositional thrust can be associated thematically and ideologically with other waves of dissent of the 1960s, such as youth movements, sexual liberation fronts, civil rights organizations, and the forms of protest and social experimentation often referred to as the "counterculture." In addition, two available traditions were especially important in determining the directions the underground took: the European avant-garde of the 1920s and the American independent cinema of the 1940s and 1950s. The latter was in turn shaped by the cultural politics of American modernism, whose influence persisted in some 1960s underground directors. This influence was not uncontested, however. Modernist ideology, characterized by its defence of "autonomous" art and its opposition to mass culture, was challenged within the underground front itself by such filmmakers as Andy Warhol, Kenneth Anger, and Jack Smith, whose films drew abundantly on familiar images and motifs from commercial entertainment and incarnated a form of postmodernism.

The Underground and the European Avant-Garde

"Underground film" is often used interchangeably with "independent" or "experimental film,"[2] yet as the foregoing remarks suggest, the present study gives the term a more restricted meaning, using it to designate the experimental movies produced in the United States (mostly in New York) by independent filmmakers working outside the movie industry during the early 1960s. Other historians and critics who have used the term "underground" in this fashion tend to disagree as to the exact period and the specific films the term describes. For example, in his recent study of noncommercial American film in the 1960s, David James starts his chapter on the underground by discussing *Shadows* and *Pull My Daisy,* both produced in 1959. In my view, these two films were part of the so-called New American Cinema, which differed from the underground in both its ideology and its modes of production.[3] For French critic and historian Dominique Noguez, author of one of the most thorough histories of the underground American cinema, the beginning and ending dates of the underground are respectively 1962, when Mekas first used the term in his writings, and 1968, the year of Andy Warhol and Paul Morrissey's *Flesh*.[4] My own history will argue that the underground first manifests itself in 1961, with the midnight shows at the Charles Theater—the first more or less regular showcase for underground film—and ends in 1966, with Warhol's *Chelsea Girls*. 1966 is also the year of Tony Conrad's *The Flicker*, a film that signals the shift to structuralist cinema—the predominant mode in experimental film in America and England in the following decade. Of course, the dates I am offering must be taken as provisional reference points, since in any artistic movement several styles coexist side by side. For P. Adams Sitney and Peter Gidal, Warhol's early films, such as *Kiss, Eat,* and *Sleep,* which were produced during the boom of the underground, already contained the seeds of structuralist cinema; on the other hand, aspects of the underground sensibility survive in the Warhol-Morrissey collaborations of the late 1960s and early 1970s and, in more commercialized form, in what Jonathan Rosenbaum and J. Hoberman have called the "midnight movie" phenomenon.

The underground was not unified through manifestoes, devotion to a leader, and group hierarchies, after the fashion of surrealism or futurism. Instead, it constituted an anarchic, motley growth composed of many sensibilities, styles, and modes of production. Underground films range from short, personal, lyrical statements made by one person—exemplified by Marie Menken or Bruce Baillie's film poems—to extremely long films involving a cast and a small crew of technicians, as is the case with Warhol's "epic," *Chelsea Girls*. In terms of style, films like Kenneth

Anger's *Scorpio Rising* and Gregory Markopoulos's *Twice a Man* were highly crafted, carefully edited, and tightly symbolic; at the other extreme, Warhol's films were unpolished recordings, containing long stretches of banal action, no symbolism, and very little editing. Underground filmmakers also differed greatly in age and background: figures like Kenneth Anger, Gregory Markopoulos, Marie Menken, Carmen D'Avino, and Stan Van Der Beek, among others, were veteran filmmakers who in some cases had been producing experimental pieces since the late forties; on the other hand, Jonas Mekas, Jack Smith, Andy Warhol, Mike and George Kuchar, Paul Morrissey, and Ken Jacobs were younger artists with little or no formal film training, who emerged as directors on the eve of the underground boom.

In many ways the underground American cinema of the 1960s is a replay of the avant-garde film aesthetics developed in Europe during the 1920s. Its parallels with the early European "wave" of experimental cinema are numerous. Both the American underground and the European avant-garde film developed as forms of counter-cinema; they sought to establish alternatives to dominant commercial film at the level of aesthetics, production, distribution, and exhibition. Such a vocation makes sense only in the context of highly developed and influential mainstream film industries, such as the ones that loomed in the background of the European avant-garde of the 1920s and the American underground of the 1960s. It is important to note, however, that neither the underground nor the early avant-gardes opposed mainstream entertainment in a simple, categorical manner. As I have shown in the previous chapter, the relations between both cultural practices are at best ambiguous: while the avant-garde may have occasionally held mass culture as an oppressive aesthetic and social other, it has also highlighted the utopian potentials it contained.

European commercial film industries of the 1920s relied on variations of the American studio system of production, characterized by a high degree of product standardization, scientific management, and job specialization. The industry was further supported by firmly established distribution and exhibition channels. As a consequence of their broad popular appeal, the films themselves were surrounded by a dense constellation of extra-textual institutions and practices, such as fan publications, critical journals, trade magazines, and a parallel industry involved in marketing, advertisement, and commercial tie-ins with other manufacturers.[5] Likewise, the American underground developed in the shadow of the all-pervasive Hollywood industry. The most fundamental difference between the contexts of the American underground and the 1920s European avant-garde lies in the fact that classic Hollywood was being displaced in the 1960s by the boom of television and by competition from other mass entertainment forms, which were forcing the industry to undergo severe restructuring. The classical studio picture had become by then a historical object which could be enshrined by film cults and revivals. In spite of its relative decline, however, Hollywood still stood for mainstream taste and filmic values, and was often regarded in the discourse of the underground as foremost cultural adversary.

As to their settings, both the European avant-garde film of the 1920s and the American underground cinema emerged in urban milieus. Metropolitan centers, characterized by intense intellectual activity, wide ranging film programming, and a heterogeneous public, provide the adequate social base for the development of the avant-garde. The avant-garde cinema in turn reflects the fragmentariness, celerity, and sensorial bombardment typical of urban life. The 1920s European avant-garde films portrayed crowds, modern means of locomotion, skyscrapers, and sign-saturated city-scapes, evidence of the avant-garde's fascination with the modern metropolis. The New York underground, less devoted to the city as spectacle, was also the product of distinctly urban sensibilities. It reflects the city as a field of psychological and social experimentation, as a porous ter-ritory where multiple lifestyles, cultural practices, ethnic groups, and their respective sign systems coexist.

The underground developed mainly in New York. If Hollywood was the capital of commercial filmmaking, New York was the center of the art world; it had a large number of resident artists, galleries, museums, and art jour-nals—not to mention a tradition of radical or bohemian culture dating back to the nineteenth century. In the years immediately preceding the boom of the underground, a group of independent directors had turned New York into the capital of the American independent picture. Al-though some underground filmmakers worked out of San Francisco, Los Angeles, and a few other spots between the coasts, New York became the sounding box for their films. New York housed a large number of alternative film venues, the active Filmmakers' Cooperative, and journals like the *Village Voice* and *Film Culture,* from whose pages such critics as Jonas Mekas, P. Adams Sitney, and Ken Kelman trumpeted the cause of the underground.

What follows is an attempt to characterize the under-ground film formation in terms of production, distribu-tion, exhibition venues, advertisement epiphenomena, and ideology. I will establish parallels between the 1960s American underground and the historical avant-garde film formations in order to provide a diachronic dimension to the practices of the underground and to assess its specificity vis-à-vis previous alternative cinema movements.

Production Members of the first wave of the avant-garde were often professionally connected to the commercial film industry. Luis Buñuel, for example, was apprenticed to French art director Jean Epstein and worked as scenarist in *La Chute de la maison d'Usher* (1928). He later abandoned Epstein's team to start his own projects.[6] Among early American experimental filmmakers, Slavo Vorkapich, Gregg Toland, and Robert Florey made *Life and Death of a 9413, a Hollywood Extra* (1927) as a "side project" while employed in Hollywood assignments.[7] More frequent was the crossover in the opposite direction, exemplified by directors like Walter Ruttmann or Oscar Fischinger, who were embraced by the film industry after the commercial potential of their projects became apparent. Hence UFA hired Walter Ruttmann to direct *Berlin: Symphony of a Great City* in 1927, after he had worked as an independent animator for several years. Oscar Fischinger, the German abstract filmmaker and creator of *Diagonal Symphony,* worked in animation departments in Hollywood after leaving Germany in the late 1930s. He even designed a sequence for Disney's *Fantasia,* although his work was considered too abstract by the producers, and was revised by another animator.

Such relations with mainstream commercial industries did not exist among underground directors, nor among their predecessors in the experimental American cinema from the 1940s onward. One reason may be the fact that film equipment became more accessible around World War II, when great amounts of surplus 16mm film stock and portable cameras initially manufactured for the army entered the market. In this situation, it was not necessary for filmmakers to establish symbiotic relations with the industry in order to have access to the medium.

Modes of production in avant-garde cinema are characteristically modest. Small crews were the norm among European and American filmmakers. In the American avant-garde of the 1940s and 1950s and in the 1960s underground, individual methods of production were even more frequent than small crews, as attested by the movies of Joseph Cornell, Stan Brakhage, Kenneth Anger, and Marie Menken. Crews in avant-garde productions were frequently made up of friends of the filmmakers, amateur actors, and spontaneous collaborators drawn from artistic milieus. Hence Jacques Prévert, Salvador Dalí, and Buñuel himself appear briefly in *Chien andalou* (1929); and so does Max Ernst in *L'Age d'or*. The René Clair–Francis Picabia production *Entr'acte* (1926) starred its creators, as well as composer Eric Satie and artists Marcel Duchamp and Man Ray, among others. In the American underground, these types of collaboration abounded—Jonas and Adolfas Mekas, Warhol, Markopoulos, and Jack Smith collaborated in each other's films as performers or technicians.

In spite of the relatively low cost of avant-garde productions, funding was a constant problem for filmmakers. The 1920s avant-garde film always depended on private patronage—except in countries like the Soviet Union, where it was state-sponsored. Perhaps the most remarkable patron of the first wave of the avant-garde was the Vicomte Charles de Noailles, a wealthy French aristocrat who funded Man Ray's *Les Mystères du château de D* (1929), Jean Cocteau's *Sang d'un poète* (1930), and Luis Buñuel's *L'Age d'or* (1930).

The funding of American independent film was equally sporadic and contingent. The creation of a financial infrastructure for experimental filmmakers was one of the main goals of independent American director Maya Deren's continued organizational efforts. One of Deren's initiatives was the creation in 1955 of the Creative Film Foundation, which, under her own direction, granted fellowships to filmmakers between 1955 and 1961. Stan Brakhage, Carmen D'Avino, Stan Van Der Beek, Robert Breer, and Shirley Clarke received CFF fellowships. Other funds sometimes came from private donors and, in the case of Deren, from screenings and lectures. With the success of the New American Cinema in the late 1950s, some private investors often associated with the art world began to provide a modest financial base for avant-garde projects, but this base proved inconsistent and erratic. Frederick Wiseman, a lawyer turned independent film producer (later to become an important documentarist), coproduced with Shirley Clarke her *The Cool World* (1961). This venture seems to have hindered Clarke's control over the film, however.[8] Another of these investors was Emile De Antonio, a part-time art agent and later a filmmaker, who also helped finance some underground films.

In the mid-1950s, more substantial funds became available when corporations began to devote tax-deductible monies to art collections and art projects.[9] The Ford Foundation, for example, started to review grant applications from filmmakers in 1962. Kenneth Anger was one of the first recipients of a Ford grant, which enabled him to finish *Scorpio Rising* in 1963. The general feeling among filmmakers, however, was that corporations were far too timid in their aid to experimental cinema, especially in comparison with the amounts they gave to the other arts.[10] Government institutions like the National Endowment for the Humanities, founded in 1965, made further monies available. In the late 1960s, the boom of film studies in colleges and universities provided a source of employment for filmmakers, and therefore an indirect source of funding for film projects. With academic affiliation came easier access to grant money, access also facilitated by the increased endowment of funding organizations during the late 1960s and into the 1970s.

Exhibition, Distribution, and Audiences   Given its non-commercialism, the avant-garde cinema had to search for alternative channels of exhibition and distribution. The early avant-garde cinema was disseminated mostly through the network of ciné-clubs (or "little cinemas," as they were called in America) that sprouted in metropolitan settings such as Paris, Berlin, London, and New York during the 1920s. Ciné-clubs were instrumental in spreading the notion that cinema was a complex cultural product deserving serious intellectual attention. They were the main showcases for the French art films of Abel Gance, Carl Dreyer, Louis Delluc, Germaine Dullac, and Marcel L'Herbier; the German expressionist films of Robert Wiene, Fritz Lang, Friedrich Murnau, and Wilhelm Pabst; the Soviet films of Sergei Eisenstein, Vsevolod Pudovkin, Alexander Dovjenko, and Dziga Vertov; and the more anarchic, anti-art films of Fernand Léger, Man Ray, Marcel Duchamp, Luis Buñuel, and Hans Richter, among others. Ciné-clubs also functioned as revival houses, including in their programs earlier commercial films of artistic distinction. Besides providing a venue for alternative types of cinema, ciné-clubs organized discussions, lectures, and encounters with filmmakers. Program notes frequently accompanied the screenings; hence film presentations appeared linked to commentary and criticism, and the association favored self-conscious and intellectual spectatorship.

In America, during the same period, "little cinemas" and art museums operated as alternative venues, having a decisive role in forging an audience for non-commercial films. The little cinemas were the American versions of the Parisian ciné-club, as their functioning and fundamental aims were the same: to provide an outlet for non-mainstream cinema. The vogue of the little cinema in America was kicked off on October 29, 1926, by the revival of *The Cabinet of Doctor Caligari* at a small theater, the Fifth Avenue Playhouse, where it ran for six consecutive weeks. *Caligari*'s success proved the economic feasibility of art films and reruns, and started a small yet popular network of showcases for such films.[11]

Museums had an important role as popularizers of alternative cinema, either by distributing experimental films, as did the Museum of Modern Art, or by hosting screenings in their facilities, as at the San Francisco Museum of Art. Instituted in 1935, the traveling film library of the Museum of Modern Art made American and European art films, avant-garde productions, and artistic commercial movies available throughout the country. The films traveled with notes written by Iris Barry, MOMA's film curator, who was also a critic and had been a co-editor of the British avant-garde film magazine *Close-Up.* On the West Coast, Frank Stauffacher and Richard Foster organized in 1947 the San Francisco Museum of Art's series "Art in Cinema: A Symposium on the Avant-Garde Film."[12] The series offered a wide sample of the European and American experimental cinema and was instrumental in stirring the interest of Bay Area intellectuals in independent cinema. San Francisco already counted with some active experimental filmmakers such as Sidney Peterson and James Broughton, who had been making movies both individually and in collaboration since 1945.

Started in 1946 by Amos and Marsha Vogel, Cinema 16 was related to the little cinemas of the mid- and late 1920s. Like the little cinemas, Cinema 16 regularly showed independent and avant-garde films, European art movies, classics, and a wide range of documentaries. Cinema 16 had an indirect influence on the underground by providing a forum where many aspiring filmmakers were able to familiarize themselves with the output of previous experimental directors. (Jonas and Adolfas Mekas, for example, founders of the art film journal *Film Culture* and influential critics and underground filmmakers, claimed not to have missed a single screening at Cinema 16 throughout its existence.) It also hosted the Creative Film Award, given by Maya Deren's Creative Film Foundation, and showed the first movies of what would later be called the New American Cinema— Robert Frank and Alfred Leslie's *Pull My Daisy* (1959), John Cassavetes's *Shadows* (1959), and Jonas Mekas's *Guns of the Trees* (1961).[13]

Given the growing number of experimental movies being produced by the early 1960s, Cinema 16 was no longer sufficient as an exhibition outlet for American avant-garde films.[14] Many new experimental films were rejected by Amos Vogel, who tended to enforce his strict personal criteria in composing Cinema 16 programs. In 1961, a number of small theaters located in the East Village started screening underground movies. The Charles was the first of these theaters, where Jonas Mekas, who was already known by then as a critic and independent filmmaker, began programming underground shows. According to Scott MacDonald, Mekas tried to reformulate the existing patterns of non-commercial film society exhibition at work in Cinema 16: "In place of what he called the 'potpourri' approach to programming standard at Cinema 16 (on any given program, Vogel might present an experimental animation, a scientific documentary, a cartoon, a psychodrama, all by different filmmakers), Mekas established the single film-artist show. . . ."[15] (One must not forget, however, that despite MacDonald's assertion there were also what J. Hoberman called "the salad days" of the underground—in which the only trait common to the rushes, lyrical pieces, abstractions, multimedia shows, and performances crammed by Mekas into an evening was their blatant unconventionality.) The Charles shows were suspended after six months due to managerial changes, but the success of the underground programs helped publicize the existence of a native avant-garde scene.[16] Subsequently, other small cinemas such as the New Yorker, the Bleecker Street Theater, and the Gramercy Arts Center realized the economic potential of the new experimental cinema and continued the tradition of the Charles, almost always under Mekas's guidance.

In Paris during the 1920s, ciné-clubs like Studio 28, Studio de les Ursulines, or the Théâtre du Vieux Colombier had proved stable venues for avant-garde cinema; the New York underground, however, was constantly in search of locales. One problem that discouraged potential exhibitors was the fact that screenings were sometimes interrupted by the police and the movies seized, usually on account of their alleged obscenity. Besides, the unconventional underground cinema seemed to many exhibitors an unreliable investment, given the fact that it was not supported by strong distribution networks, production values, or a well-known star system.[17] As a result of the lack of venues, screenings were often held at museums, art galleries (Warhol's *Blow Job* premiered at the Washington Square Art Gallery in March 1964), and even at a Methodist church on West 4th street. In an attempt to regularize exhibition, Jonas Mekas, assisted by Ken Kelman and Tom Chomont, created in November 1964 a moving program of underground screenings held in theaters all over New York. This moving showcase was called Filmmakers' Cinematheque; it offered weekly and bi-weekly programs, and was hosted by such theaters as the Maidman, Astor Place Playhouse, City Hall Cinema, the Forty-First Street Cinema, Elgin Theater, and Gotham Theater. In addition, the Museum of Modern Art, the Whitney Museum of American Art, and the Jewish Museum also sponsored Cinematheque screenings on several occasions. The Cinematheque's constant relocation ended in the late 1960s with the consolidation of Millennium Film Workshop and the creation of Anthology Film Archives. Millennium, founded in 1966 by Ken Jacobs, offered workshops on 16mm film production and lectures by filmmakers and, after 1968, frequently hosted underground programs. Anthology was an attempt, spearheaded by Mekas, to house the enormous output of the underground as well as previous experimental and art films. Anthology Film Archives also operated (and still does) as a purely experimental theater; it has a screening room, designed by filmmaker Peter Kubelka, for the projection of the collection's pieces.[18]

The theaters where the underground found temporary shelter before taking refuge in Anthology and Millennium deserved some attention in their own right. They were often run-down art or clearance houses in search of enticing fare to boost their limp business. In Manny Farber's essay, "Experimental Movies," the descriptions of two theaters where underground films were being exhibited at the time (Tambellini's Gate and the New Cinema Playhouse) took up as much of the article as commentary on the movies themselves. As the article suggested, the derelict condition of these theaters reinforced the aesthetic marginality of the images on screen.[19]

Besides alternative modes of production and exhibition, the avant-garde also tried to establish its own channels of distribution. In this respect, the American underground was more successful than its early European predecessors. In Europe, distribution had often been directly undertaken by the filmmakers themselves, who rented films to ciné-clubs. Occasionally, avant-garde films were commissioned and distributed by major production companies to be shown with feature films, as was the case with Hans Richter's short *Race Symphony,* commissioned by UFA to accompany a regular production. The eventual success of the ciné-clubs in most European capitals led to the creation of an international art film cooperative located in Paris. This endeavor had been conceived by participants in an international conference of film societies celebrated at Le Sarraz, Switzerland, in 1929, and its goal was to provide distribution outlets for art movies. Despite initial good auspices the cooperative failed due to the success of sound cinema, which made the commercial chances for unconventional silent movies even slimmer. It was finally liquidated in 1931, after ensuring the distribution of some films by ciné-clubs.[20]

In the American underground, the most enduring efforts to create an organism for distributing alternative films were spearheaded by Jonas Mekas, main promoter of the Filmmakers' Cooperative. Founded in January 1962, Mekas's cooperative imitated the initiative of Cinema 16, which had developed a distribution outlet in 1950. Cinema 16 handled a wide variety of films, from the experimental movies of

Maya Deren and Kenneth Anger through European art films such as Bergman's and Antonioni's, to the British Post Office documentaries of the 1930s. According to historian David Curtis, Vogel's continued refusal to distribute underground films, among them Stan Brakhage's *Anticipation of the Night* (1959), spurred Mekas to the creation of the Filmmakers' Cooperative.[21] The Filmmakers' Cooperative developed partly as a response to Cinema 16, some of whose policies it rejected. While the Cinema 16 Library operated for a profit and under the direction of critics and programmers Amos and Marsha Vogel, the Cooperative was a nonprofit venture run entirely by filmmakers. At the Cooperative, rental fees were set by the authors of the movies themselves, who received the entire benefits less handling costs. Unlike Cinema 16, the Cooperative accepted any film submitted for distribution, a practice also applied by Mekas at underground screenings. Lack of selective criteria in screenings and distribution earned Mekas the severe criticism of film critic and writer Parker Tyler and of Amos Vogel himself. Yet despite the polemics surrounding its policies, the Filmmakers' Cooperative served as a blueprint for other experimental film distributors soon to emerge in the United States and abroad.[22]

During the 1920s, audiences of European film societies and ciné-clubs were made up of assorted representatives of the urban intelligentsia and bourgeois in search of thrills.[23] J. Hoberman has described 1960s underground screenings as rallying points for New York bohemia. Underground filmmakers and their collaborators, often friends or fellow filmmakers, were frequently present in the audience, as were other artists including painters, writers, stage directors, dancers, and so on.[24] Commercial illustrator and recent pop art sensation Andy Warhol was one of the artists who regularly attended Mekas's screenings. Stimulated by what he saw at the Charles's late-night shows, he started making his own films, and eventually became the most prolific and famous director of the movement. Underground audiences were predominantly young, and their apparent unconventionality was quickly noted and commented on by the "straight press."[25]

Epiphenomena: Advertisement and Criticism[26]

The advertisement epiphenomena surrounding avant-garde cinema tended to be erratic and slim, especially by comparison with the commercial movie industry. The marketing of underground films was modest, and their publicity consisted mainly of sheets and posters in black and white, often designed by the filmmakers and programmers themselves.[27] Given the fact that most theaters that screened underground movies were located in Greenwich Village, local cafes, taverns, and other hangouts were preferred spots for advertising. In fact, the underground cinema became a feature in the life of the East Village and Soho neighborhoods, one more wave in the long history of downtown bohemianism and radical culture.[28] Periodicals associated with the culture of this area, such as the *Village Voice,* and the underground papers the *East Village Other,* the *Soho Weekly News,* and Ed Sanders's *Fuck You: A Magazine of the Arts,* frequently advertised and reviewed the activities of the underground. The *Village Voice* further emphasized its association with the underground through Jonas Mekas's column "Movie Journal," which ran from 1959 to 1971.

Given the network of artistic discourses surrounding experimental cinema and the intellectual spectatorship fos-

Poster for an early screening of
***Flaming Creatures*, designed by Jack**
Smith. Courtesy of Anthology Film
Archives.

tered in ciné-clubs and film societies, criticism is perhaps
the avant-garde cinema's most important epiphenomenon.
The emergence of the European avant-garde cinema of the

Poster by George Kuchar for
screening of *Born of the Wind* at
the Filmmaker's Showcase.
Courtesy of Anthology Film Archives.

1920s coincided with a great boom in film criticism. In
Paris, for example, film journals such as *Cinémagazine,
Ciné pour tous, Journal de Ciné-club,* and *Cineá* provided a
forum for reviews and theoretical discussions of both commercial and non-commercial film. In addition, following
the example of Guillaume Apollinaire's avant-garde paper

Les Soirées de Paris, artistic and literary reviews customarily published pieces on cinema as part of their advocacy of modern aesthetics. While several journals were particularly sympathetic to the alternative cinemas, no single periodical was identified with the cause of the experimental film.[29]

By contrast, the American underground found its critical voice in a specific journal—*Film Culture,* founded by Jonas and Adolfas Mekas in 1955. *Film Culture* proclaimed itself "America's Independent Motion Picture Magazine." The emphasis on non-mainstream cinema suggested by such a motto was corroborated by Mekas's first editorial: "Cinematic creation tends to be approached primarily as a production of commodities, and large sections of the public—to whom film-going is still merely a form of diversion—remain unaware of the full significance of filmic art."[30] *Film Culture*'s first issue prominently featured an article by the famous dadaist artist Hans Richter, entitled "The Film as an Original Art Form." Richter, at the time a film teacher at City College, further signaled the journal's devotion to film as art and linked it with the European avant-garde tradition. The content of the early issues reveals the art-house bias of *Film Culture:* Hollywood classics (with special issues devoted to *Birth of a Nation,* Von Stroheim, and to Sarris's influential taxonomy of the classical American cinema), European art cinema, and avant-garde films seem preferred topics of publication. In P. Adams Sitney's view, the presence of Andrew Sarris and Jonas Mekas on the editorial board made the journal "schizophrenic" in its dual commitment to Hollywood and to experimental cinema. Yet the writing on these two types of film was couched in the language of auteurism, with its romantic conception of the filmmaker as artist imported from the "legitimate" arts. Due to its interest in art cinema and avant-garde film, the magazine became an apologist, first for the New American Cinema and later on for the underground, of which it became the quasi-official organ.[31]

The Experimental American Cinema, the New American Cinema and the Underground

On January 25, 1962, Jonas Mekas's column in the *Village Voice* bore the title "The Changing Language of Cinema," and it started with an enthusiastic review of the *cinéma verité* documentary *Wasn't That a Time* by Michael and Philip Burton. Despite Mekas's fervor, the film now seems a period piece that very few buffs are likely to remember. Nonetheless, I want to consider this review in some detail, as it provides a schematic account of the underground's formative influences.

In order to provide a background to *Wasn't That a Time,* Mekas begins by surveying recent developments in the vigorous independent cinema of the United States, which he compares favorably to other national cinemas of the time. Downgrading the French New Wave for its relative traditionalism, he defended the new cinematic language "being developed by experimentalists and documentarists in New York, in Boulder, in San Francisco." While the French New Wave and other European art-cinema movements adhered to certain standards of professionalism and some narrative conventions, the American experimental cinema was committed to more radical experiments in film language: "This is what it is all about: new times, new content, new language."[32]

Newness, however, did not mean isolation from historical influences: "The change began with *In the Street,* with James Agee, with Sidney Meyers, with Morris Engel, with Stanley Brakhage" (49). This list alludes to two disparate currents that influenced the underground at different levels: the realistic tradition, which culminated in the late 1950s with the New American Cinema, and the independent lyrical cinema of Stan Brakhage. Mekas considers Agee's documentary *In the Street* (1948), made in collaboration with Helen Levitt and Janice Loeb, a milestone in the development of an alternative cinema based on the language of reality, rather than on Hollywood's standardized plots and artificial sets.[33] This aesthetic was consistent with Agee's film criticism, which favored films conveying close observation of everyday detail—a type of cinema best typified by Italian neo-realism.[34]

For their part, Morris Engel and Sidney Meyers were also part of a realistic tradition in American film, as both had worked during the late 1930s in New York for the leftist documentary collective Frontier Film, collaborating on films such as *Heart of Spain, China Strikes Back,* and *Return to Life.*[35] In the years between Frontier films and the time of Mekas's writing, Meyers had filmed *The Quiet One* (1949), and Engel, together with Ray Ashley, made *The Little Fugitive* (1953). Both movies were shot in documentary style and told intimate stories based on everyday occurrences, two characteristics which foreshadowed the aesthetics of the New American Cinema. Engel and Meyers also helped shape this new trend; their feature, *The Savage Eye,* made with Ben Maddow and Joseph Strick, premiered in 1960 after several years of haphazard shooting schedules. Critics related it to contemporary independent pieces such as Lionel Rogosin's *Come Back, Africa* (1959), John Cassavetes's *Shadows* (1959), and Robert Frank and Alfred Leslie's *Pull My Daisy* (1959)—films that formed the core of the successful New American Cinema movement.

The New American Cinema figures in Mekas's review as the direct predecessor of the underground. "New American

Cinema" was the label first applied by Jonas Mekas and Shirley Clarke to a group of independent filmmakers who worked in New York making low-budget features that recalled in form and spirit the emergent French New Wave. This parallel earned them the name of "American New Wave." The New American Cinema was eminently realistic, and therefore heir to the tradition represented by Agee, Meyers, and Engel. Mekas summarized its aesthetics as follows: "The truth is what matters. The new filmmaker is a child of his times: he has had enough of prefabrication, false intelligence" (49).

The boom of the New American Cinema was kicked off by the commercial and critical success of *Pull My Daisy* and *Shadows*. Both movies stressed factuality and spontaneity, and were implicitly opposed to the carefully crafted Hollywood films. Their narratives seemed, in Jonathan Rosenbaum's words, "almost stumbled upon—one followed thread in a tangle of apparently limitless actuality."[36] Such a "chanced-upon" quality was conveyed by off-center compositions and roaming camera movement, which followed events with "floating attention" and frequently lingered on narratively unimportant details. Both *Shadows* and *Pull My Daisy* established an idiom that combined aesthetic rejection of standard movie grammar with a vaguely defined opposition to "straight society," an opposition informed by the attitudes of the beat subculture. The beat sensibility was present in the free-floating characters that populated these movies (in *Pull My Daisy*, these characters are the beat writers Gregory Corso, Peter Orlovsky, and Allen Ginsberg; Jack Kerouac provides a humorous commentary to the images), in the jazz hipster scenes, smoky bars and parties, carefree attitudes toward sex and romance, pot-smoking, male-bonding, street-roaming, and the general sense of alienation from mainstream America.[37] As Mekas voiced in his writings, the aesthetic gestures of New American Cinema directors were animated by a moral and ethical stance: "During the last few years I have been constantly arguing, often making a fool of myself, over the cause of the new cinema (and the new man)."[38]

The link between ethics and aesthetics was shared by other oppositional movements, such as the beat writers, the French New Wave, and historical avant-garde artists. For most surrealists, for example, their movement was a moral rebellion as well as an aesthetic one; thirty years later, New Wave director François Truffaut echoed this attitude in his famous statement: "The tracking shot is a moral issue."

If the New American Cinema did not entirely bring about the "derangement of the official cinematic senses" Jonas Mekas called for on the eve of the movement,[39] it did foster a sense of community among experimental filmmakers, actors, and producers. This feeling crystallized in the establishment of a group partly inspired by the French New Wave directors and by earlier generations of avant-garde artists and intellectuals. The gatherings of the New American Cinema Group had a precedent in Maya Deren's Film Artists Society, formed in November 1953, whose main purpose had been to establish a support network for independent filmmakers and to "act as a collective to obtain for members bulk purchase rates and discounts, group rentals and insurance rates, and special scaled rates from some trade unions."[40] In like fashion, the New American Cinema collective issued a manifesto ("First Statement of the New American Cinema Group") that defined the group ("Common beliefs, common knowledge, common anger and impatience bind us together . . .") and voiced its goals and claims.[41] Among those who signed this document were Jonas and Adolfas Mekas, Lionel Rogosin, Shirley Clarke,

Emile de Antonio, Peter Bogdanovich, Alfred Leslie, Robert Frank, Ben Carruthers, Gregory Markopoulos, Argus Speare Juillard, and Bert Stein. Some of the group's goals were the creation of a distribution company for alternative film, which later materialized in the Filmmakers' Cooperative, and the establishment of a help fund for filmmakers. This latter idea was also inspired by Maya Deren's Creative Film Foundation grants. The New American Cinema Group's statement emphasized a sense of kinship with other rebellious film movements of the time: "Our colleagues in France, Italy, Russia, Poland, or England can depend on our determination. As they, we have had enough of the Big Lie in life and in the arts." Jonas Mekas, the first reviewer who treated the New American Cinema as a cohesive whole, had already underlined in a 1959 piece the affinities of the New American Cinema with movements like the British Free Cinema and the various European new waves. In this respect, the group showed an internationalist outlook largely absent from the pronouncements of Deren's association, which tended instead to align itself with American artistic trends, such as abstract expressionism.

Alongside the realistic trend, Mekas also singled out the personal cinema of Stanley Brakhage as a fundamental influence on the new experimental film.[42] While Agee, Meyers, and Engel worked with small crews, made feature-length films, and practiced the realistic aesthetics inherited from documentarists and neo-realists, Brakhage shot extremely personal, lyrical statements that flouted realistic conventions. In the words of film historian David Curtis, "[Brakhage's] films have no story, no symbolism, no acting, no posed photographic beauty; the drama is the drama of the skies, light and shadow, movement, trees, windows, people, corners, animals, single blades of grass—in fact the drama of vision, a vision that implies a belief that the first priority is to see and record, the second to structure and interpret."[43] Brakhage's radically personal, almost solipsistic films relate to an important genre in the underground and in earlier experimental American film: the film poem.

The "film poem" had been practiced in the 1940s and 1950s by Marie Menken (*Diaries, Glimpse of the Garden*), Willard Maas (*Geography of the Body*), Kenneth Anger (*Eaux d'artifice*), and Joseph Cornell (*A Legend for Fountains*); and was practiced in the 1960s by Bruce Baillie (*Castro Street, All My Life*), Jonas Mekas (*Diaries, Notes, Sketches*), and Peter Kubelka (*Unsere Afrikanreise*), among others. Brakhage's stylistic link with earlier American experimental filmmakers was accentuated by his association during the late 1950s with American surrealist artist Joseph Cornell, who belonged to an earlier generation of the historical avant-garde. Brakhage had also been a member of the Independent Filmmakers Association until its dissolution in 1961, following Deren's death. His films and writings emphasized the importance of the director's personal vision, and therefore supported an extremely auteuristic view of film. The cult of the artist's vision in opposition to the standardized Hollywood product was one of the ideologies mobilized by underground filmmakers and critics. Part of the modernist heritage of the underground, this emphasis appears paradigmatically embodied in Brakhage's work.[44]

The appearance of Brakhage's name in Mekas's review of *Wasn't That a Time* as one of the forgers of the alternative American cinema seems almost prophetic in view of the fact that both Brakhage's lyricism and his individualistic system of production would become characteristic of a large sector of the underground.[45] Jonas Mekas himself was a symptomatic example of adherence to Brakhage's aesthetics; after *Guns of the Trees,* he made *The Brig* (1964), a recording of the Living Theater's version of Kenneth Brown's homonymous play. *The Brig* is in many ways a transition film that incorporates the individual mode of production and the gestural handheld camera of the underground into an eminently realistic narrative in the style of the New American Cinema. Afterwards, diary films and film poems, such as *Lost, Lost, Lost, Reminiscences of a Journey to Lithuania,* and *Notes, Diaries, and Sketches,* put together in the late 1960s and 1970s out of fragments shot since the 1950s, constituted the bulk of his production. Some of Mekas's statements at the time further reinforced the reorientation of the film community toward the aesthetic of the small, one-person movie: "*Variety* says there are about two hundred low-budget 'art' movies waiting for distribution. I have seen a good number of them, and the best ones are dogs. American cinema remains in Hollywood and the New York underground. There is no American art film."[46]

By the time Mekas wrote these lines, the promise of the New American Cinema to achieve something like an American New Wave—a movement with a certain mass appeal that would be at once independent, artistically bold, and ethically engaged—was bankrupt. John Cassavetes, the most promising of the new directors, was quickly absorbed by Hollywood, where he had a successful career as an actor and director. Bogdanovich also became a celebrated Hollywood director. Many other filmmakers who cosigned the "First Statement of the New American Cinema Group" would not make films of any consequence after 1962. Robert Frank returned to photography after flopping with *The Sins of Jesus;* Rogosin worked mostly in television, and also became a producer and film exhibitor; Edouard de Laurot, Bern Stein, Alfred Leslie, and Adolfas Mekas never repeated the success of their earlier movies. The main exceptions in the group were Shirley Clarke, documentarist Emile de Antonio, who started making films in the 1960s, and Gregory Markopoulos. Clarke produced some of her most ambitious and important films in the mid-1960s, after the initial explosion of the New American Cinema. For their part, de Antonio and Markopoulos, both peripheral to the New American Cinema, maintained their levels of productivity throughout the decade, continuing into the 1970s.

There is therefore a "high moment" of the New American Cinema, extending from 1959 (the year of *Shadows* and *Pull My Daisy*) to 1961 (the year of Clarke's *The Connection*), followed by the emergence of an artisanal underground, which peaks in 1963 with such films as *Scorpio Rising, Flaming Creatures,* the early Warhol movies (*Kiss, Eat, Sleep*), Smith-Jacobs's *Little Stabs at Happiness,* Barbara Rubin's *Christmas on Earth,* the first rushes of Jack Smith's *Normal Love,* and the first screenings of George and Mike Kuchar, to name a few. Straddling the two trends, the work of Ron Rice deserves at least passing mention; his four films, from the minimally narrative feature *The Flower Thief* (1960) to the short, non-narrative psychedelic *Chumlum* (1964), made the year of his death, partake of the stylistic vocabularies of both New American Cinema and underground. These two "modes" differ in methods of production and conceptions of cinema; their difference demands that a distinction be made between them—this distinction, however, is rarely made or, when made at all, is inconsistently maintained. It should be kept in mind, however, that such inconsistency often responds less to the whims of historians than to the uncertain limits of these film trends. Lacking stable and definitive identities, each shows fissures and discontinuities. This is especially true of the underground, which is, as I have indicated, the site of confluence of two opposite artistic ideologies: American modernism and an emergent avant-gardist pop sensibility.

The Underground and the Ideology of American Modernism

The pre-1960s history of the term "underground" reflects the plural cultural inheritance of the 1960s avant-garde film formation. The term is not consistently used by Mekas to refer to the experimental American cinema of the early 1960s until 1962.[47] On September 27, 1962, he argued in his "Movie Journal" column in the *Village Voice* ("About the Changing Frontiers of the Cinema") that the label "New American Cinema" should be abandoned. The so-called New American Cinema, he wrote, was not so new anymore, but part of an outdated impulse to create a homegrown "New Wave." The underground, on the other hand, was "the living, exploring, changing frontier, the Vietnam of cinema."[48] The term "underground" had great critical fortune, due to its descriptive power and its cultural history, which pointed to both the modernist and the avant-gardist components of the movement.

Writing in 1976 for the catalogue of a New York independent cinema retrospective at Paris's Centre Georges Pompidou, Mekas dates the origin of the expression to 1961, to a speech delivered by Marcel Duchamp at the Philadelphia Museum of Art, in which the French artist lapidarily stated that "the only solution for the artist of tomorrow is to go underground."[49] This prestigious antecedent highlighted the connections between the current experimental cinema and its roots in the European historical avant-garde. Yet besides its ties to the European anti-art tradition represented by Duchamp, the expression "underground" had its own history in American culture, a history intimately connected to the evolution of the American intelligentsia in the postwar decades.

The metaphor of the underground links the 1960s experimental cinema to the culture of dissent in postwar America. The notion of an "underground scene" had been put forward by some of the beats themselves—notably, by Jack Kerouac in his novel *The Subterraneans*—and upheld by popular representations of "the scene," such as the film of the same name produced in 1960 by MGM. This bohemian milieu had been, in fact, the setting of many beat novels and poems. Implicit in the term is a certain glamorization of marginality, a desire to thrive outside (or underneath) the mainstream that seemed inherent to earlier waves of radical culture. As Andrew Ross comments, "the impulse to go underground [among the beats] had as much to do with the recent McCarthyist victimization of the identifiable left as it had to do with a romantic infatuation with the nihilistic vanguardism of Dostoyevski's *Notes from the Underground.*"[50] The notion of "being underground," that is, of living as a disaffected exile from the larger society, was not exclusive to radical bohemia; it had always been close to the self-image of the "above-ground" modernist intelligentsia.

The beat "underground" is actually the radicalization (and spectacularization) of a conception of the intellectual developed by *Partisan Review* writers at the time of their complete breakup with the Communist Party and the Popular Front. The late 1930s writings of Philip Rahv and William Phillips, editors of *Partisan Review,* characterized the American intellectual as profoundly alienated from mainstream values. Having severed ties with the traditional left in part because of the myopia of the Communist Party in cultural matters, and uneasy about allying themselves with middle-class values, intellectuals seemed fated to take refuge in the cultivation of their craft.[51] Artists opposed to reigning social mores make up the intelligentsia, conceived by Rahv and Phillips as a separate class, potentially radical in its opposition to society and devoted to the development of genuine culture, which for the *Partisan Review* writers meant high modernism—the innovative and demanding art of such icons as T. S. Eliot, James Joyce, Gertrude Stein, Pablo Picasso, Arnold Schönberg, or Henri Matisse.

Before the emergence of the underground, American experimental filmmakers had perceived themselves as representatives of the alienated intelligentsia. In the 1953 statement of the goals and identity of the Film Artists Society, Deren compared the situation of American experimental filmmakers to that of abstract expressionist painters, who typified the artist's conflicted relation to the rest of society: "Whether factually or not, the abstract expressionists thought of the artist as a solitary individual, forced into isolation not so much by desire, as by the insensitivity of an ill-informed public."[52] Several years later, another experimental filmmaker, Stan Van Der Beek, published a manifesto/collage—"The Cinema Delimina: Films from the Underground"—which drew on analogous ideas to describe the situation of independent filmmakers: "But now the most revolutionary art form of our times is in the hands of entertainment merchants, stars, manufacturers. . . . Meanwhile, what of the artists, poets, experimenters in America, who must work as if they were secret members of the underground."[53] Van Der Beek's use of the term "underground" in this particular context adds overtones of guerrilla warfare and clandestinity to the idea of a marginalized film intelligentsia.

Two ideological motifs strengthen the parallels between Van Der Beek's underground film artists and the modernist intellectuals. The first is resistance to mainstream culture, or to what modernist intellectuals described as "kitsch." The *Partisan Review* writers rejected kitsch as a form of cultural absolutism which threatened to drown the sophisticated modernist art in an ocean of mediocre sludge. This stand was reinforced by their opposition to the Communist-inspired Popular Front, which valued traditional popular and mass culture forms as models for a politically effective art of broad popular appeal. For *Partisan Review* critics, kitsch was the cultural counterpart of political absolutism, most visibly incarnated in the Stalinist regime, which the Popular Front openly supported. The modernist critique of mass culture had its most influential formulations in Clement Greenberg's "Avant-Garde and Kitsch" and Dwight Macdonald's "A Theory of Mass Culture." As we have seen, both pieces juxtaposed authentic art or modernism to kitsch or "masscult." Van Der Beek's persistent allusions to "the vistavisionaries of Hollywood, with their split-level features and Disney landscapes" sound akin to Macdonald's and Greenberg's indictments. His animadversion was shared by many underground filmmakers, and lies at the center of some of Van Der Beek's own films, like the witty satire *Science Friction* (1958). The second important parallel between Van Der Beek's underground cinema and modernist cultural politics is the notion that the "inner self" provides the only realm of authenticity in a morally corrupted environment. A characteristic statement of this view was penned by Samuel Kootz, influential art critic and curator, who in 1949 hailed the work of the first-generation abstract expressionists as a new trend he named "the intrasubjectives": "The intrasubjective artist creates from an internal world rather than an external one. He makes no attempt to chronicle the American scene, exploit momentary political struggles, or stimulate nostalgia . . . he deals, instead, with inward emotions and experiences."[54] A few years later, Lionel Trilling's conclusion to a famous essay on the relations between literature and Freudian psychology similarly affirmed: "The function of literature has been to make us aware of the particularity of the selves and the high authority of the self in its quarrel with its society and its culture."[55] The artist's alienation from the mainstream appears, in these formulations, a wellspring of creativity and a guarantee of the authenticity of his or her insights. For Van Der Beek, the rejection of dominant society and of the culture it fosters goes hand-in-hand with the emphasis on subjectivity. As the abstract expressionists had done in their time, some underground film directors rejected the banality of the surrounding world and turned their inner visions into main subjects of their art: "It is part of the interesting intrigue of art that . . . with the perfection of a means to exactly capture perspective and realism, the artist's visions are turning more to his interior, and in a sense to an infinite exterior. . . ."[56]

There was also an earlier use of the term "underground" by film critic Manny Farber which signaled a quite different attitude toward mass culture, an attitude characterized by the sort of immersion in popular artifacts that shapes the avant-garde sensibility. In his famous essay "Underground Films" (1957), Farber passionately defended the low-budget, action B-movies produced in Hollywood from the early 1930s to late 1950s. These thrived underneath glossy, big-budget Hollywood, forming an almost subterranean world made up of the "male-action soldier-cowboy-gangster" films of such directors as Raoul Walsh, William Wellman, Howard Hawks, pre-*Stagecoach* John Ford, William Kieghley, and Anthony Mann. Farber chose the label "underground" to refer to such movies because their directors "hide out in sub-surface reaches of [their] work," and because these films found their "natural home in caves: the murky, congested theaters, looking like glorified tattoo parlors on the outside, and located near the bus terminal in big cities."[57] He defended the lack of artistic pretensions of "underground" action films, together with their fast-paced, simple narratives and their sharp perception of everyday detail. By contrast, glossy Hollywood productions often flaunted their artiness and seriousness, reaching for mid-brow acceptability and artistic conformity. This commercial underground played a subversive, anti-art role, reacting against mainstream Hollywood's cultural legitimacy. As film critic and historian David James has suggested, the 1940s "B" action film contested Hollywood from within the industry, just as the 1960s avant-garde underground did from the outside.[58]

It is especially suggestive to the subject of my study that the history of the term "underground" should reveal the double allegiance of the movement—to both modernist aestheticism and postmodern pop savvy. From another point of view, Farber's defense of the Hollywood underground is symptomatic of the intellectuals' increasing appreciation of mass culture, manifested in the 1960s pop—or new—sensibility, one of the background forces which shaped the underground cinema. For these reasons, his text provides a fitting transition into the next chapter, which will study the underground in relation both to the changing attitudes of 1960s intellectuals toward mass culture and to the emergence of various forms of subcultural activism—emanating particularly from the gay community—that coalesced around the products of the culture industry.

Three

**The 1960s Underground as Political
Postmodernism: From the New
Sensibility to Gay Cultural Activism**

The underground cinema
is one of many facets of American avant-gardism in the
early 1960s. Other manifestations of the experimental culture of the time include happenings, junk and assemblage
art, pop art, off-off-Broadway theater, and "the new dance."
These currents reacted against modernism's climate of elitism and withdrawal by attacking the autonomy of art, and
by trying to close the gap between art and the practice of
everyday life. Their ideological stance led to the production
of ephemeral forms that could not be collected or commodified and existed only as performances and happenings—
placing art in traditionally non-artistic contexts such as
streets and public spaces, and underplaying the artist's

uniqueness, stressing amateurism and spontaneity (as in John Cage's creative use of randomness, improvisation, and untutored technological experimentation). At the same time, these alternative forms incorporated the idiom of commercial culture into their texts, thus questioning the strict separation between high and low culture defended by modernism since the late 1930s. They were, in this respect, symptomatic of an emergent cultural regime later called postmodernism, which has been characterized by the progressive erosion of the great divide between high and low art, and by the ubiquity of a new electronic culture.

The shuffling of high and low forms taking place in the alternative avant-garde circuits was on a continuum with similar developments in other realms of the culture. Modern art had been popularized during the 1940s and 1950s not only through galleries and museums, but also through paperbacks, recordings, and photographic reproductions—channels of the culture industry which thinkers like Theodor Adorno and Clement Greenberg regarded as potentially destructive of autonomous art. As it became widespread, modernism was canonized in academia, thus forfeiting part of its early marginality and rebelliousness. On the other end of the cultural spectrum, the mid-to-late 1950s and early 1960s witnessed the increasing visibility of popular forms which captured some of the adversarial ethos of contemporary aesthetics in more immediate, everyday media such as street culture, entertainment, or subcultural style.[1] In this context, the rejection of modernism (the established high culture of the time) by contemporary avant-garde artists was allied to the latter's fascination with the popular media and oppositional subcultures.

This chapter will study the underground in the context of an emergent postmodernism, reflected in the writings of

Susan Sontag, Leslie Fiedler, and Tom Wolfe, and in sub-cultural and popular forms such as comic books, rock and roll, film cults, camp, and gay sensibilities. This approach seems to me a necessary corrective to the official reception of the underground by critics of the day, who tended either to defend it as high modernism, or else to condemn it for its presumed affinity with mass art. Furthermore, I will show how the fascination with mass culture characteristic of some underground directors (especially Jack Smith, Kenneth Anger, and Andy Warhol) must be related to the articulation of gay subcultural identities, desires, and fan-tasies. In this respect, the underground cinema created a politicized and embattled version of postmodern aesthetics which differs from the apolitical views held by the most famous defenders of the "pop" or (in Susan Sontag's phrase) "new sensibility."

Dwight Macdonald Meets Andy Warhol

A piece entitled "The American Stasis," published in *Esquire* in August 1964 by the well-known essayist Dwight Macdonald (at the time *Esquire*'s habitual film reviewer), aptly illustrates the erosion of clear-cut distinctions be-tween traditionally separate artistic cultures.[2] Since the early 1930s, Macdonald had been writing cultural criticism for left-oriented journals such as *Partisan Review, Politics, Dissent,* and *Commentary,* from whose pages he had vigor-ously condemned mass culture or kitsch as a threat to authentic art. "The American Stasis" opens with his reflec-tions on the stagnation of contemporary American film. He regards both the recent New American Cinema and the latest generation of commercial filmmakers, represented by Sidney Lumet, Arthur Penn, John Frankenheimer, and Robert Mulligan, as failed promises since they were unable to revitalize the film scene. Lacking direction, American film culture appears radically pluralistic, splintered into multiple cults, aesthetics, and tastes. Such lack of consensus, Macdonald argues, can be seen in the simultaneous success of two disparate films: Robert Wise's *The Sound of Music,* and Andy Warhol and Ronald Tavel's *Harlot.* These movies seemed to Macdonald "connected, in one way antithetical, in the other complementary." They represented two opposite conceptions of cinema: one is a well-made, glossy, big-budget picture, a perfect exponent of Hollywood professionalism; the other, an avant-garde film, quickly shot and cheaply produced, technically raw and unpolished.

Warhol's film is an emblematic example of the paradoxical connection between commercial and marginal cinema noted by Macdonald. *Harlot* is made up of two unedited thirty-minute takes—one per reel. Warhol's static camera, unchanging composition, and spare action and decor suggest a minimalist aesthetic characteristic of much European modernism—the tradition, for example, of Adolf Loos, Bauhaus, and De Stijl. The blocking, costume, lighting, and grainy black and white photography, however, evoke "an old movie still"—an allusion that brings up pop art's immersion in consumer culture. The title, Macdonald rightly speculates, may be a pun on Harlow's name, and the soundtrack is a mostly improvised dialogue in which a man explains to two others why his marriage to a screen queen has failed—perhaps an allusion to the tempestuous marriage of Jean Harlow and Paul Bern. The "protagonist"—a drag queen in a platinum-blonde wig—further suggests Jean Harlow, who was at the time the object of a cultist revival spurred by the publication of a best-selling biography. *Harlot* is therefore a hybrid piece that combines elements of high modernism with elements of mass culture. In previous decades Macdonald would have been able to neatly separate these two domains, yet in the 1960s, the borders between them seem to dissolve. Warhol's film exemplifies how mass culture jumps over the divide between high and low art and infiltrates the former, which had been conceptualized by American critics, notably by Macdonald himself, as a fort from which to repel the advances of the culture industry.

Modernist Criticism on the Underground: The Underground as Mass Culture

The irruption of pop forms into 1960s experimental American film presented an interpretive problem for reviewers schooled in the ideologies of postwar modernism, which stressed clear-cut cultural divisions such as Greenberg's distinction between kitsch and avant-garde, or Macdonald's parallel distinction between mass-cult, midcult, and high culture. Being such an intractable cultural object, the underground drew negative reviews from such modernist intellectuals as Macdonald, Parker Tyler, and Amos Vogel.

At the same time, however, their attacks on the new avant-garde were surprising, since all of these critics in previous decades had been reviewers, advocates, and programmers of experimental cinema. Dwight Macdonald, who belonged to the generation of James Agee, William Phillips, Philip Rahv, and William Dupree, among other left-oriented writers and critics, had written during the 1930s in defense of the Soviet avant-garde cinema, which incarnated for him a model fusion of radical politics and revolutionary artistic form.[3] Parker Tyler also belonged to Macdonald's generation. Together with Charles Henri Ford, he had been the founder and editor of *View* (1940–1947), one of the "little magazines" that took the relay from *Broom,* the *Little*

Review, or *The Dial* as a showcase of the avant-garde in America. If Macdonald defended a certain form of avant-garde cinema, Tyler could be said to practice an avant-garde criticism. His playful and often elusive essays in *View* were surrealist imaginings and digressions based on Hollywood films, but his later criticism adopted more formalist criteria as bases of judgment.[4] Amos Vogel was a programmer and exhibitor who in 1946 founded the New York-based Cinema 16, an important venue for the American and European experimental cinema. In addition to his activities as exhibitor, Vogel penned program notes for Cinema 16 screenings and occasional film criticism for various literary and artistic reviews.

These critics' attitudes toward the underground were mediated by their rejection during the 1930s of the Communist Party cultural politics—whose sphere of influence extended beyond party organs, molding decisively the aesthetics of the Popular Front. Their relations with Party politics operated almost like a structuring absence, shaping their confrontation with the 1960s underground. Of course, from both an aesthetic and political perspective, the underground was quite distant from prewar left radicalism; yet for Macdonald, Vogel, and Tyler, there were certain similarities between the two—especially in the style of political criticism used by the underground. The older generation of modernists frequently noted that advocates of the underground conflated the films' social and political agendas and their aesthetic merits. Defense of the new experimental cinema often focused on ideological values (such as vague notions of "beauty," "freedom," "spontaneity," and so forth), bypassing careful examination of form. In Macdonald's view, an example of such critical "slackness" was Jonas Mekas's writings, since Mekas's defense of the underground was based almost exclusively on its ethos of rebellion rather than on aesthetic considerations. To modernist critics, this attitude was too close to the tendentious ideological criticism practiced by Communist Party intellectuals in the 1930s. During this time, Stalinist critics had favored texts which in their judgment advanced the proletarian cause, regardless of any particular aesthetic value. In this climate, reviews like *The Anvil* and the *New Masses,* or leftist groups like the League of American Writers, under the aegis of the Communist Party, extolled Jack Conroy's proletarian novels, while regarding the innovations of T. S. Eliot, James Joyce, or the anti-art experiments of dadaists and surrealists as decadent and politically ineffectual products of bourgeois culture.[5]

While the cultural organs of the Communist Party focused on contextual and ideological values, *Partisan* writers based their critical judgments on formal and textual ones, suggesting, however, an indirect link between modernist textuality and anti-bourgeois politics. To critics like Macdonald and Parker Tyler, strongly invested in the text-centered advocacy of modernism, Mekas's ideological defenses of the underground were too evocative of the "party line" excesses perpetrated in the name of proletarian art. Tyler explicitly draws this connection in his essay attacking the underground, "Is Film Criticism Only Propaganda?": "I argue that the context of this situation is the modern milieu of social-political-economic protest rather than any drive made by purely artistic protest; the implied logic: artists, too, ought to have jobs—it's too much the unionizing spirit of the old WPA on the rampage."[6]

Although the new avant-garde's fascination with mass culture was never pointed out by Macdonald, Vogel, or Tyler as an argument for rejecting the underground, they berated it for being, in their opinion, akin to commercial culture. They labeled it a "smart novelty," or "new vogue," which Tyler flippantly compared to the mass appeal of the miniskirt: "The avant-garde [cinema] today is like the miniskirt. It's new and it shows things. But some knees are beautiful and some are not."[7] And later on, he continued: "What strikes me in this respect is the fact that if commercialism doesn't suck gifted filmmakers into its own art-annihilating system, it creates what medical scientists call an 'antibody' [i.e., the underground], which, to be effective, it seems, has to be as all-encompassing, as uncritical, overtolerant, and fashion-mongering in its own way as Hollywood is in its way."[8] In much the same way, Macdonald attributed the European success of the New American Cinema and the New York underground to the filmmakers' ability to activate "chic stimuli."[9] Amos Vogel, for his part, deplored that the New York underground had become—crime of crimes—"fashionable."[10] To summarize, these critics assimilated the underground to mass culture: the contemporary New York avant-garde was, according to them, a passing fashion characterized by a shallowness and lack of artistic standards common to the products of the culture industry.

The Baudelairean Cinema:
Between Modernist Withdrawal and
the Exploration of Popular Culture

Less judgmental than Vogel, Macdonald, or Tyler, Andrew Sarris described, in his brief essay "The Independent Cinema" (1966), the underground's interest in star cults and Hollywood fantasies (exemplified, as we have seen, by *Harlot*) as a radical reorientation of American experimental film aesthetics: "Where the mystique of Independent Films was once realistic in seeking the reality beyond conventional movies, Independent Films are now more fanciful in tracing the fantasies of a culture oriented toward conventional movies."[11] According to Sarris, the avant-garde cinema in America had tended to act as a critical negation or even a corrective to the "Hollywood hallucinations," focusing either on a postulated truth of the soul, as in the modernist films of earlier experimental directors such as Maya Deren, or on social truth, as in the 1930s independent political documentaries. In opposition to these traditions, the films of directors Mike and George Kuchar, Kenneth Anger, Andy Warhol, Warren Sonbert, Jack Smith, Ken Jacobs, Bill Vehr, and José Rodríguez-Soltero, to name a few, flaunted their immersion in Hollywood myths and showed little preoccupation with the poetry of dreams or the intricacies of subjectivity.

The departure from the subjectivism that dominated experimental cinema in the 1940s and 1950s is evidenced by the fact that none of the films made by Warhol, Smith, or Anger during the high years of the underground were framed as dreams or psychodramas. In terms of style, they rarely used point-of-view shots or such devices as anamorphic lenses, dissolves, and superimpositions, all of which had been widely used by experimental filmmakers during the previous decades to connote individual perception.[12] By contrast, these underground filmmakers shot in fairly straightforward ways. Anger's fast montages and Smith's long handheld takes, for example, did not function as markers of narrative subjectivity. Warhol's static camera and long takes, portraying exasperatingly banal actions, incarnated the most extreme departure from the subjective mode.

Even enthusiastic defenders of the underground, including such critics as Jonas Mekas, Ken Kelman, and P. Adams

Sitney, failed to examine thoroughly the relations between the films and the contemporary pop sensibility. For the most part, they interpreted the underground in terms of a modernist ideology of authenticity and alienation that had flourished around the work of abstract expressionists and, as we saw in an earlier chapter, of experimental filmmakers in previous decades. Hence, Ken Kelman, regular contributor to *Film Culture* and *The Nation,* and one of the most perceptive writers on the underground, noted in an article from 1964 that "mythically oriented works and directors" made up an important trend in the early 1960s experimental cinema. These works wanted to create "out of a need to fill our rationalistic void, those actual inner worlds which fall within the realm of myth." Within this category he collapsed *Scorpio Rising* together with films like Brakhage's *Anticipation of the Night* and *Window Water Baby Moving,* Markopoulos's *Twice a Man* and *Serenity,* and Charles Boultenhouse's *Dionysus.* Yet Markopoulos, Boultenhouse, and Brakhage are more interested in the poetics of the personal than in the exploration of popular mythologies, which is in turn the main purpose of Anger's film. In the same fashion, Kelman categorized the films of Jack Smith and Mike and George Kuchar as "films of liberation, which suggest, mainly through anarchic fantasy, the possibilities of the human spirit in its socially uncorrupted state." In so doing, Kelman overlooked the fact that these films were mostly concerned with parodying commercial B-movies and turning Hollywood myths on their head. He reads them instead as explorations of "the human spirit," a phrase that evokes the modernist interest in the complexities of the artist's psyche.[13]

Another critic who disregarded the traces of mass culture in the text of the underground is P. Adams Sitney, who had

been involved in the New York underground as programmer, activist, and critic since its early days. Editor of the
short-lived *Filmwise,* which he founded in 1962, Sitney
was, in addition, a frequent contributor to *Film Culture.*
During the early 1970s, in the twilight of the underground
boom, he wrote *Visionary Film,* a monumental survey of the
postwar American experimental cinema that read its laby-
rinthine and fragmentary history through the metaphor of
the artist as visionary. This notion was a touchstone of romantic poetics, and Adams Sitney acknowledges his debt to
Harold Bloom's study of romantic poetry *The Visionary
Company,* alluded to in the very title of his survey.[14] Being
part of the visionary Romantic tradition, American experimental film sinks its roots deep in the soil of high culture.
Sitney's critical and historical project was very much in
keeping with the legitimating spirit of Anthology Film
Archives, where he was a curator: it sought to justify the
avant-garde cinema as a serious, worthwhile cultural tradition deserving a niche in museums, galleries, and university curricula.

Sitney's high art approach to the underground was manifested in the fact that he regarded the work of filmmakers
influenced by mass culture as part of the visionary tradition,
and therefore more indebted to high culture than to popular
practices. For him, the films of a director like Kenneth
Anger, for example, signaled a new phase in the American
avant-garde, a phase characterized by what he calls "mythopoesis." These films were primarily engaged in the
elaboration of myths whose richness and significance stood
in contrast to banal mass-produced fantasies. Sitney singled
out Anger's *Scorpio Rising* and Brakhage's *Dog Star Man* as
the most impressive works in this trend. Yet by grouping
them together, Sitney dissolved the important differences

between the two films: Brakhage's *Dog Star Man* shows a withdrawal into nature and the interiority of the film's "protagonist"; Anger's film, on the other hand, plunges into pop culture imagery and undermines any access to an inner self while emphasizing style and surface. While Brakhage's film was indeed influenced by romantic notions of the unique poetic vision, *Scorpio Rising*'s sources stem from popular art: B-movies (particularly the "criminal youth" subgenre), Hollywood myths, male homoerotic photography of the sort popularized during the 1950s by Bob Mizer's *Physique Pictorial,* and the gay-camp reception of mass culture icons. In other words, *Dog Star Man* and *Scorpio Rising* typify the two antithetical tendencies of experimental cinema: modernist subjectivism and avant-gardist involvement with mass culture, respectively.[15]

Together with Kelman and Sitney, Jonas Mekas was the most influential advocate and exegete of the underground. His label "the Baudelairean Cinema," coined in a review published in the *Village Voice* in May 1963, was designed to establish the high art descent of the New York underground. Mekas's label initially designated the films of Ron Rice, Jack Smith, Bob Fleischner, and Ken Jacobs (the label may have been suggested by Jacobs's film *Baudelairean Capers*), but it was later extended to directors Andy Warhol and Kenneth Anger. According to Mekas, the Baudelairean films "marked a turn in the New York realist school [represented by *Shadows* and *Pull My Daisy,* among others] . . . toward a cinema of disengagement and a new freedom." The works of the Baudelairean directors, he announced, "make up the real revolution in cinema today." They portray "a world of flowers of evil, of illuminations, of torn and tortured flesh; a poetry which is at once beautiful and terrible, good and evil, delicate and dirty."[16] Along with Baudelaire,

Mekas places these films in the tradition of such *maudits* as de Sade, Lautreamont, and Rimbaud, and of turn-of-the-century currents such as aestheticism, symbolism, and *l'art pour l'art*—all of them respected, if somewhat unorthodox, milestones of the modernist canon.[17]

From a different perspective, the Baudelairean element gestures to the influence of mass culture on the underground via Walter Benjamin's essays on Charles Baudelaire.[18] For Benjamin, Baudelaire's importance lies in the fact that his poetry, criticism, and commentaries on contemporary life made visible a series of changes regarding the social situation of the artist and the status of culture at large. These changes were in turn brought about by late capitalism, characterized by industrialization, the spectacle of urban agglomerations, the erasure of pre-modern cultural forms and communities, and the commodification of culture. Out of these factors, which modified and, to a great extent, imperiled traditional conditions for the production and reception of art, Baudelaire fashioned aesthetic forms designed to break through the hardened sensitivities of modern readers and to capture what he called "the intermittent heroism of modern life"—fleeting lyrical moments and shocking juxtapositions purveyed by the heterogeneous life of contemporary cities.

If we view these films in light of Benjamin's exegesis of Baudelaire, I think that Mekas's label is highly suggestive. If Baudelaire carved his poetry from the landscape of modernity, Warhol, Anger, and Smith did the same in the landscape of postmodernity—characterized by a highly developed culture industry which disseminates its products through electronic media. Their films probed into ephemeral objects of commercial culture—fashions, advertisements, songs, comic books, stars, movies, pornography—

from which they extracted new aesthetic structures and tropes. Like Baudelaire, underground filmmakers made marginal social figures the subject matter of their art. They often featured in their projects members of what 1960s sociological parlance described as "deviant groups"—criminals, transvestites, addicts, and gays. Out of these influences, Warhol, Anger, and Smith fashioned their ambiguous artifacts, which stood in unstable relation to their parent cultures—the mass culture of late capitalism and the tradition of modernism.

As we have seen, the hodgepodge of "degraded" influences that came together in the underground appeared terribly disconcerting to most critics, who, in coping with it, systematically erased part of its complex cultural identity, assimilating it to modernist high culture or to kitsch. The underground cinema signaled the inadequacy of previous critical models for dealing with contemporary cultural developments. Such a crisis was not confined to discussions of experimental cinema; it affected all areas of cultural criticism and was ultimately symptomatic of a paradigmatic shift in cultural theory which can be summarized as the shift from critical modernism to postmodernism.

Critical Modernism and the New Sensibility

The two poles involved in this shift were best represented by Irving Howe and Susan Sontag. Their writings of the 1960s embodied the dominant (yet receding) critical modernism and the emergent new sensibility, respectively; or to cast the debate in Susan Sontag's terms, Howe represented "Jewish moral seriousness," while she stood for the "homosexual aestheticism"—a term she had employed in relation to camp, and which connoted the valuation of ephemeral, seemingly banal cultural forms and styles proclaimed by the new sensibility. This comfortable opposition must be qualified, however. As Howe himself observed, there was more "moral seriousness" in Sontag than her "new sensibility" stance suggested. Moreover, Sontag's "orthodox" avant-garde leanings and her position as co-editor of and frequent contributor to *Partisan Review* situated her in relation to the modernist New York intellectuals—a tradition to which Howe himself belonged.[19] For his part, Howe was receptive to the new sensibility, or at least had helped to publicize it; his journal *Dissent* had published during the late 1950s Norman Mailer's influential essay "The White Negro," which Howe considered a milestone in the emergence of the new sensibility.

The term "new sensibility" was first used in Sontag's piece "One Culture and the New Sensibility," which closes *Against Interpretation* (1966).[20] In this essay, Sontag describes a contemporary shift from an Arnoldian conception of culture, based on critical judgment guided by rigorous moral standards, to a culture based on pleasure, brought about by the artistic "representation of new modes of vivacity" (302). The primacy of pleasure dissolves the traditional separation between high and low cultures: "If art is understood as a form of discipline of the feelings, and a programming of the sensations, then the feeling (or sensation) given off by a Rauschenberg painting may be like that of a song by the Supremes. Budd Boetticher and Dionne Warwick may be appreciated as pleasurable and complex, and without condescension" (303). Another division bridged by the new sensibility is the one between art and science. Since the goal of art is the enlargement of the idiom of pleasure and feeling, and the building of ever newer models for aesthetic apprehension, art displays an exploratory zeal reminiscent of experimental science. The historical avant-garde's dream of linking art and scientific experimentation is realized now on an impressive scale by the emergent new sensibility, which converts this fusion into the dominant mode of cultural production. As Sontag stated in the closing of her essay, the new sensibility enthroned a democratic equality among cultural artifacts, whose provenance in the cultural hierarchy did not necessarily determine their expressiveness and intellectual richness: "From the vantage point of this new sensibility, the beauty of a machine or of the solution to a mathematical problem, of a painting by Jasper Johns, of a film by Jean-Luc Godard, and of the personalities and music of the Beatles, are equally accessible" (304).

Irving Howe's "The New York Intellectuals" offers a thorough critique of the new sensibility from the modernist perspective.[21] After assessing the intellectual contributions of leftist criticism during the 1940s and 1950s, Howe examines the characteristics of the new sensibility, represented not only by Sontag, but also by such older figures as Norman O. Brown, Herbert Marcuse (whose inclusion in this list seems to me rather problematic), and Marshall McLuhan.[22] Howe objects to what he regarded as the new sensibility's impatience with structures of complexity and coherence; its naive adherence to untrammelled instinctual satisfaction; and its rather erratic politics—or rather, *style*— of rebellion.[23] Echoing the opinions of modernist film critics, Howe argues that because of the vulgarization of modernist aesthetics brought about by the new sensibility, "in place of the avant-garde idea we now have the style of fashion" (258). In this respect, "alienation has been transformed from a serious revolutionary concept into a motif of modern culture; and the content of modernism into the decor of kitsch" (276).

Howe's position is symptomatic of many other modernist American intellectuals confronted with new cultural phenomena which seemed to undermine some fundamental tenets of modernism. More original than his views on the failure of contemporary culture to uphold high modernist ideals are his observations about the changes occurring in the paradigms of critical thought. Agreeing with Sontag on the fact of change, if not on its evaluation, he claims that the new sensibility rejects all ideas of depth. "Where Marx and Freud were diggers of the intellect, mining deeper and deeper into society and the psyche, and forever determined to strengthen the dominion of reason, today the favored direction of search is not inward but sideways . . . " (273). The sideways search abandoned hierarchical models of thought for models where different approaches coexist as equally valid attempts at explanation. Truth and untruth are not ultimate criteria of judgment any more, being replaced now by criteria like novelty or originality. As Leslie Fiedler contended at about the same time, criticism and literature appear interchangeable.[24] The same democratic liberalism that Sontag incarnated in the realm of aesthetics pervades also the realm of criticism. As a result, criticism abandons its former role of "moral journalism"; it seeks to hitch the aesthetic vocation of literature to the exploratory impulse of science, while reporting on the culture rather than passing judgment on it.

Fiedler's notion was of course mere fancy; whether new-sensibility or modernist, criticism still passed judgment, took positions in intellectual disputes, and maintained hierarchies, however transvalued their content. Nonetheless, it seems quite significant that at this point in American cultural history, some critics diagnosed or even advocated the emergence of a judgment-free criticism—a notion which vaguely echoes the 1950s paeans on the end of ideology— as response to a host of phenomena that seemed to question dominant intellectual paradigms. In this diagnosis, modernist culture, governed by divisions between high and low, hierarchies, and systems of truth, is superseded by the logic of postmodernism, characterized by "aesthetic" criticism, lack of hierarchies, and a sense of the universal equality of cultural artifacts. What was missing from this picture was the fact that the popular phenomena celebrated by the new sensibility carried strong social and political overtones, and connoted, among certain audiences, a rupture of the consensus forged and strenuously kept in place by 1950s culture and politics.

Most detractors and advocates of the new sensibility missed the embattled aspects of the emerging popular forms. Susan Sontag's criticism is a case in point. Her writings, like those of her contemporaries Leslie Fiedler, Tom Wolfe, or Marshall McLuhan, offered a view of new cultural developments that was remarkably free of conflict. Echoing the pluralistic liberalism espoused during the 1950s by critics such as Daniel Bell, David Riesman, Edward Shils, Talcott Parsons, and Arthur Schlesinger, Jr., Sontag conceived the new sensibility as a democratic celebration of the multiple productions of different subcultural groups, status groups, and social formations. These forms offered options based on taste, i.e., on a type of judgment that, like Kant's aesthetic judgment, is disembodied and disinterested, resting on the ultimately ineffable pleasures generated by artistic forms. As a detached cultural observer and liberal intellectual, Sontag sought to do justice to increasingly visible popular forms hitherto exempt from serious critical consideration due to their accessibility and their association with the culture of leisure and consumption. Because of her emphasis on taste, however, she highlighted the erotics of play and enjoyment and failed to notice other social dynamics at work in popular phenomena. In fact, some of the popular forms Sontag wrote about operated less as challenges to, or expansions of, modernist academic tastes, than as rallying points, cries of protest, and embattled cultural expressions for subaltern and underrepresented groups. This fact became more and more blatant as the decade rolled on. In the increasingly explosive atmosphere of the late sixties, the songs of the Supremes or Dionne Warwick—not to speak of more politicized African American musicians like Marvin Gaye, James Brown ("Say it Loud, I'm Black and I'm Proud"), or the Sly Stone of *Riot*—and the amiable ironies of camp, were not adventures in taste as much as war cries, expressions of protest from communities actually claiming social and cultural spaces forcibly denied to them. At that time, even the professedly apolitical theories of Marshall McLuhan covered urgent political impetus when put to use by Yippies Abbie Hoffman and Jerry Rubin, and by other radical insurgents.

The Postmodern Moment: Emergence of Popular Styles

Leslie Fiedler and Irving Howe are among the first writers to use the term postmodernism in American cultural criticism.[25] I do not intend to study the uses they made of the concept, since these have already been widely discussed. Instead, I want to focus on the generally accepted notion that one of the main characteristics of the cultural logic of postmodernism is the blurring of distinctions between high and low. In the previous pages, I have surveyed how high cultural discourses such as critical modernism and the new sensibility reflected such shifts. In the present

section, I want to explore the other side of the reconfigura-
tion of high and low: the emergence of popular styles and
practices, and their break into intellectual discourse.

The emergence of pop styles has many interlocking
causes and an extremely overdetermined status in any account of 1960s culture. The 1960s writings of Tom Wolfe,
the earliest and perhaps most brilliant chronicler of the
pop scene, offer perceptive clues about the reasons for
such an explosion. As he points out in *The Kandy-Kolored
Tangerine-Flake Streamline Baby*, a compilation of articles
written for *Esquire* between 1962 and 1964, the flourishing
postwar economy and a high rate of youth employment
in the 1950s created a community of consumers "whose
styles of life had been practically invisible," and who had
now "the money to build monuments to their own styles."
Some of these ephemeral monuments were associated with
music and fashion—"the twist, the jerk, the monkey, the
shake, rock music generally, stretch pants, decal eyes";
while others entailed whole ways of life, as was the case
of car customizing, surfing, drag racing, and demolition
derbies.[26] Wolfe continued, "All these teen-age styles of
life, like Inigo Jones's classicism, have started having an influence on the lifestyle of the whole community" (xiii).

One example of this influence was "New York's Pop society," whose most visible representative was, for Wolfe,
"Girl-of-the-Year" Baby Jane Holzer, a rich socialite who
merged with "prole" rock artists like the Rolling Stones,
avant-gardists like Jonas Mekas and Andy Warhol, and with
the demimondaines who orbited around "the Warhol
group." Baby Jane Holzer's lifestyle symptomatically reflected the attraction that new popular styles held for people
of high social standing and cultural capital like herself.
Wolfe's articles, Sontag's "Notes on Camp," Fiedler's "The

New Mutants"—a notorious and often misunderstood reflection on the counterculture—pop art, and underground
films are further examples of the reach of the new styles
among the intellectual community, which reacted with a
mixture of puzzlement and fascination. As Wolfe stated in
his introduction to *The Kandy-Kolored Tangerine-Flake
Streamline Baby,* ". . . I didn't know what to do with it [the
Hot Rod & Custom Car show which *Esquire* had commissioned him to report on]. It was outside the system of ideas I
was used to working with, even though I had been through
the whole Ph.D. route at Yale, in American studies and
everything" (xi). All these writers and artists plunged into the
maelstrom of youth cultures and subcultural styles, not, for
the most part, as protagonists, but as fascinated observers,
plunderers, and publicizers.

The attraction exerted by marginal, "low" styles led to
the redefinition of the game of taste and to the expansion
of critical parameters, which, it was felt, ought to account
for the emergent formations. But what exactly put such formations in the orbit of intellectual discussion? A possible
cause might be the large circulation of glossies and periodicals which, geared up to glut a highly increased readership, scouted all corners of the culture in search of writable
material. A staff writer for *Esquire,* Tom Wolfe was one of
those scouts. Yet something in the quality of the new popular forms captured the imaginations of writers and filmmakers in ways that cannot be explained as fashion or as
the latest news scoop.

I think that the newly earned protagonism of popular culture in intellectual discourse must be understood
alongside the academic entrenchment of high modernism.
Modernism, once a rebellious artistic culture that expressed
radically new and disruptive sensibilities and often operated

outside established institutions, became during the late forties and fifties a linchpin of official culture. The hostility of modernist American intellectuals during the late 1930s and early 1940s toward pro-Soviet left radicalism facilitated a reading of modernism as inimical to political totalitarianism. This reading of modernism was enforced by institutions like MOMA and Peggy Guggenheim's Art of This Century Gallery, which, in concert with state agencies, used modernist literature and art (particularly abstract expressionism) as conduits of Cold War propaganda. In exhibitions in the United States and abroad, modernist art was made symptomatic of consensual and democratic societies—such as the United States; its artistic qualities were defended as far superior to the mediocrity of Soviet kitschy realism, product of a totalitarian regime.[27] Such interpretations turned modernism into an artistic counterpart of status quo politics; erased the leftist affiliations (especially its Trotskyist sympathies) of American modernism; and greatly simplified the ambivalent relationship of this artistic culture to American society and politics. These distortions resulted from a polarized atmosphere, in which anti-Soviet stances could be easily contorted into patriotic affirmations of dominant politics. The "official" reading of modernism did much to blunt the oppositional edge of such art, some of whose manifestations were being used to advertise the United States precisely at a time of virulent political and cultural repression enforced through the anti-communist and anti-gay witch-hunts of the 1950s. The enshrining of modernism in academia can be seen as an indirect consequence of its being regarded anti-totalitarian art. It can also be largely accounted for as a result of its own cultural logic, since modernism was, after all, highly crafted art, full of references to the canon and respectful, if not of traditional culture, of the idea of culture itself.

Intellectuals missing the negative thrust that character-ized radical culture during its "heroic period" in the early decades of the century acknowledged the compromised position reached by modernism. Writing in 1964, Leslie Fiedler drew the balance as follows: "No techniques can be devised these days for which the Literature major . . . is not appallingly well-prepared. . . . Certainly the devices that once characterized [modernist and avant-gardist] art (the fractured narrative line, stream-of-consciousness, insistent symbolism, ironic allusion) seem today more banal than the well-made plot, the set description, the heavy-handed morality that they were invented to displace."[28] Fiedler also suggested in the same piece that modernist (read: non-traditional) artistic features were becoming part of the idiom of mass and popular culture. In the early 1960s, commercial films, for example, started to incorporate stylistic and the-matic taboos which had formerly taken refuge in foreign art films and "ill-lit, low-budget, domestic ones."[29]

Since more than a decade before the liberalization of censorship, and often suffering its rigors, popular culture had progressively appeared as a repository of rebelliousness and unconventionality. I would like to consider four "sites" that exemplified the polemical edge of popular culture, and were especially influential on the underground cinema: comic books, rock and roll, film cultism, and the gay sub-culture. The intellectuals' fascination with these forms may be partly attributed to the fact that they blurred distinctions between high and low culture, contesting the elitism of modernism. Besides, their unconventional subject matter and antisocial attitudes seemed to recreate part of the nega-tive and critical potential that had fueled the historical avant-garde. Such parallels, however, do not grant the exist-ence of a direct influence of the historical avant-garde on popular culture. Popular culture developed to a great extent in isolation from "legitimate" cultural antecedents; yet its strategies of negation and opposition were analogous to those of the historical avant-garde. Popular forms therefore operated as symptoms of dissent within a society which touted its consensual nature. Marginal communities (teenagers, youth groups, ethnic groups, gays, and other urban subcultures) cemented around these forms, clearing up a space of their own within the social practices and rituals accompanying popular music, comics, and film cults.

Comic Books   Comic books had been the object of congressional hearings by the Senate Subcommittee on Juvenile Delinquency since late 1953, following the publication of Frederic Wertham's *The Seduction of the Innocent*. Wertham's book was an exposé of the allegedly antisocial values promoted by the immensely popular E.C. Comics and even by seemingly innocent publications such as *Batman*. E.C. Comics received the brunt of the attacks because of its unorthodox style. E.C. Comics was a publishing company founded by Joseph Gaines in the mid-forties, and transferred in 1948 to his son William M. Gaines, who gave it its characteristic profile. William Gaines's first successes were two well-read series of crime comics called *War against Crime* and *Crime Patrol*. Starting in 1950, Gaines shifted the emphasis of his comics from crime to horror, a genre that became the staple product of E.C. and one of the most distinctive forms of postwar American youth culture. E.C. horror comics were published in series with the ominous titles of *Tales of the Crypt, The Haunt of Fear, The Crypt of Terror,* and *The Vault of Horror.* The content of the comics certainly lived up to the titles of the series: cannibalism, dismemberment, grisly murders, and brutal mutilations were regular E.C. Comics fare.[30] Other comic books like the obscure

Tijuana Papers or the more popular *Mad* cultivated an aggressive black humor and a parodic flair, shown for example in *Mad's* imitations of the covers of such magazines as *Saturday Evening Post, Life, Harper's,* and *Atlantic Monthly.*

It was, however, the grisly side of comics that attracted most unwelcome attention, like Dr. Wertham's polemical response. Wertham's attacks led to congressional hearings, and these to the creation of the Comic Code Authority, whose goal was to curtail the excesses incurred in the comics.[31] The Comic Code Authority eventually hounded E.C. Comics out of existence, making it impossible for the publisher to have his magazine distributed by newsagents, who risked sanctions for peddling outlawed material. E.C. Comics tried to modulate the content of its publications to satisfy the exigencies of the Comic Code Authority, losing as a result its original readership. Some such attempts at compromising were series like *Extra!, Impact, Valor, Aces,* and *Psychoanalysis,* which published edifying stories based on newspaper reporters, sportsmen, war heroes, and doctors. None of these survived past the fifth issue.

Besides the negative reactions aroused in the likes of Dr. Wertham and the Senate Subcommittee, the case of the comic books also elicited responses from some intellectuals who tried to assess the cultural role of these popular forms. Two of the most interesting were Robert Warshaw's "Paul, the Horror Comics, and Dr. Wertham," published in 1954 in *Commentary,* and Leslie Fiedler's "The Middle against Both Ends," which appeared in *Encounter* a year later.[32] Both critics focused on the unruly imagination evidenced by the comics. For Warshaw, the tendency of the humor in some of these comic books was "to reduce all of American culture to indiscriminate anarchy" (200). In another place he states, "*Mad* and *Panic* are devoted to a machine-gun attack on American popular culture, creating an atmosphere of nagging hilarity something like the clowning of Jerry Lewis" (199). The horror comics exhibit in turn "the same undisciplined imaginativeness without the leavening of humor" (200). In any case, the comics' antisocial tendencies were, for these two writers, the main reason for their popularity.

Both Warshaw and Fiedler dwelt on the comics' links to high culture. Warshaw points out how some of the stories published in series like *The Vault of Horror* or *Shock Suspense Stories,* if taken simply in terms of their plots, "are not unlike the stories of Poe or other writers of horror tales" (200). In a similar vein, Fiedler responds to attacks against the comic books as follows: "It has been charged against vulgar art that it is sadistic, fetishistic, brutal, full of terror. . . . About these charges there are two obvious things to say. First, by and large, they are true. Second, they are also true about much of the serious art of our time, especially that produced in America" (543). The reason for such similarities lies, for Fiedler, in the common anti-bourgeois origin of both high and low arts, and in the fact that both these ends plunge into the archetypal and unconscious, while the middle does not. Because of this, both ends of the cultural spectrum can be understood as challenges to the more genteel versions of good taste.

There is in Fiedler's article a tendency to romanticize popular literature audiences, manifested in a sort of Rousseauism which construes pulp readers as closer to the life of the imagination and to archetypal images, and as less squeamish in dealing openly with sexuality and death. Like Warshaw, Fiedler locates in the comics impulses that had emerged earlier in the culture of the avant-garde. The anarchic humor, the obsession with dismemberment, and the gratuitous violence that pervade the E.C. horror comics and *Mad* bring to mind the most strident antisocial and anti-art invectives of dadaists and surrealists. After all, European avant-gardists had celebrated in the 1920s the absurd violence of *Krazy Kat* (a far cry from the gory detail of *Tales of the Crypt*), the anarchic humor of American silent comedies, and the horrors and grotesqueries of popular French film serials like *Les Vampires* or *Fantomas*. Like the historical avant-garde, the American comics of the early 1950s also voiced a negation, a sense of discomfort with dominant culture. They represent a rupture, perhaps the first one manifested in popular culture, of the much-trumpeted postwar consensus, a term which connoted the economic splendor and social stability of the 1950s, and hid the violence of the witch-hunts, inquisitions, and the ever present threat of the bomb. For these reasons the comics can be defined, borrowing Tom Wolfe's phrase, as "an unconscious American avant-garde."

The unconventionality of 1950s comics appealed to some underground directors, such as twin brothers George and Mike Kuchar. Armed with their 8mm cameras, during the early 1960s they shot raucously amateurish potboilers like *I Was a Teenage Rumpot, Born of the Wind, Lust for Ecstasy, Corruption of the Damned,* and *Pussy on a Hot Tin Roof,* to name just a few. For their grotesqueness and occasional violence, usually relieved by humor, some of these stories seem racy versions of E.C. plots. In addition, the posters the Kuchars designed to advertise their films confirmed their debt to the comics. Their fascination with the medium ultimately ran full circle in the early 1970s, when George Kuchar became a part-time comic artist and participant in the active underground comics scene, and published his work in *Short Order Comix* and *Arcade.* His 1973 feature

The Devil's Cleavage, which generously dishes out group sex, murder, dismemberment, and rape, recalls the underground comics' taste for chaos, violence, and sleaze.[33] In comparable fashion to the Kuchars' films, the mixture of violence and stylistic flair in Kenneth Anger's *Scorpio Rising* is indebted to E.C. Comics, and, more generally, to comic book culture—indeed the film quotes certain funny-paper images. For its part, the ornate monsters that populate Jack Smith's unfinished *Normal Love* evoke the decaying creatures from the likes of *The Vault of Horror.*

Rock and Roll   Rock and roll came into existence after the earliest horror comics, becoming, like them, a characteristic form of 1950s youth culture. Like the comics, rock and roll was a popular form that flaunted some avant-garde traits, attracting the attention of new-sensibility intellectuals. In a similar fashion to the historical avant-garde, rock and roll celebrated youth, fun, leisure, and speed. It also shared with the avant-garde an emphasis on performance and an indifference, if not open hostility, toward the social and intellectual establishment, on which both depended, however, for part of their audience and some sort of cultural legitimacy.

Like the historical avant-garde, rock and roll mobilized a rhetoric of currentness. Its sound was dramatically opposed to previous fashions in popular music. Rock and roll's emphatic beat and instrumental simplicity were antithetical to the complexities of big band instrumentation; and its vocal delivery, which copied the throaty sounds from blues performers and often floated barely above intelligibility, directly opposed the articulate Tin Pan Alley vocal styles. Besides, rock and roll was shockingly frank on sexual matters and threatened to break certain racial taboos. As critic Greil Marcus observed, in the first years of desegregation in the South, white teenagers were jumping the color line by dancing to rock and roll hits by black performers such as Chuck Berry, Little Richard, Junior Parker, Bo Diddley, Fats Domino, and Sam Cooke, or by white musicians such as Elvis and Jerry Lee Lewis, intent on copying "black sounds." In Marcus's words: "At the start, Elvis sounded black to those who heard him; when they called him the Hillbilly Cat, they meant the white Negro. Or as Elvis put it, years later: '. . . made a record and when the record came out, a lot of people liked it and you hear folks around town saying, 'Is he, is he?' and I'm going 'Am I, am I?'"[34] The ethnic identity of rock and roll was romanticized (and frequently stereotyped) by white teenage audiences as offering an exciting, rebellious stance, as well as a sense of marginality and disengagement from the dull mainstream. These connotations were also being played out at about the same time in the beats' cult of be-bop jazz and their identification with the black ghetto. The celebration of non-white ethnicities among bohemians and avant-gardists ultimately harked back to the high years of the historical avant-garde—to dadaist Richard Huelsenbeck's *Negergedichte,* Apollinaire's defences of nonwestern art, and Man Ray's and Picasso's portraits of African masks, among others.

The rise of rock music took place during the early sixties, and it was founded on the cultural and commercial avenues opened by 1950s rock and roll. Rock developed from early rock and roll, and was therefore one step further removed from the latter's origins in folk styles, rhythm and blues, and urban electric blues. Rock was a hybrid form which mixed the basic rock and roll forms with strands from other types of popular music, including Tin Pan Alley, which rock and roll had initially purported to reject. The multiple cultural influences of rock made it a highly synthetic form, to some critics as allusive and intertextual as the literary pastiches of Joyce and Eliot.[35] An emblematic expression of the 1960s, rock was another popular manifestation which blurred the line between high and low culture, being hence a paradigmatic example of the new sensibility. Rock demonstrated the commercial potential of some stylistic features of the historical avant-garde. For example, mid- and late-1960s (then so-called) "progressive rock" lyrics were often obscure, full of indecipherable imagery and delirious visions, in the vein of such modern visionaries as Antonin Artaud and Arthur Rimbaud.[36] The music itself was an assault on the audience, similar to the sensorial overcharge aimed at the public in the futuristic *serate,* or at the dadaist Cabaret Voltaire. The psychedelic light shows and Trip Festivals of the mid-1960s, which brought together filmmakers such as Jordan Belson, Ben van Meter, and Roger Hillyard, and acid bands such as the Lovin' Spoonful, the Grateful Dead, and Jefferson Airplane, seemed, except for their higher technological sophistication and their links to the drug culture, inspired by the futurist theatrical manifestoes.[37]

Rock performers made themselves into works of art with the same zeal recommended six decades before by Oscar Wilde. They became, in this way, creators of lifestyles, trend-setters, and idols of consumption. Seeing Jimi Hendrix or Janis Joplin perform in their multicolor beads, gauze scarves, hussar jackets, headbands, and rings, one could wonder what the real spectacle was, the music or the musician. But again, these gestures were already present in the historical avant-garde: dadaist artist George Grosz, to name just an example, had paraded the streets of Berlin as Dada

Death during the late 1910s, covered in a huge black over-coat and a white death's head mask.[38] Rock's avant-garde vocation was further evident in its experimental use of technology, reflected in the music's growing complexity as the decade rolled by. Technical virtuosity and sophistica-tion peaked in 1967 with the celebrated *Sgt. Pepper*. In light of these developments, rock can be said to have popularized, in the words of a historian of 1960s culture, "that complication of awareness and technique that we called modernism."[39]

The inclusion of rock and roll in films by Warren Sonbert, Kenneth Anger, Jack Smith, and Andy Warhol accentuated the unconventionality of the underground and its distance from established culture. Rock may also have brought the underground even closer to youth culture, favoring its cross-over potential and therefore its commercial feasibility. The success of Kenneth Anger's *Scorpio Rising* in the main-stream theater circuit, for example, may have been more directly related to the film's rock sound track than to its themes or style. In a similar fashion, Andy Warhol's involve-ment with the rock band the Velvet Underground may have spurred interest in his films and art among audiences that might otherwise have remained oblivious to them. In their uses of rock tunes, underground films provided subversive readings of the iconography of the song's lyrics. The films of Anger and Smith, for example, played off image and sound-track against each other, creating witty commentaries on the gender assumptions underlying pop lyrics, and exposing the songs' manipulability. Two famous such juxtapositions were the "Blue Velvet" sequence in *Scorpio Rising*, in which Bobby Vinton's song ("She wore blue velvet . . .") is edited to images of muscular men in blue denim and leather; and the final sequence of Jack Smith's *Flaming Creatures*, which uses Gene Vincent's "Be-bop-a-loo-la (She's My Baby)" as background to a party of male transvestites slow-dancing with each other. In these examples the oppositional thrust of pop music is overlaid with a further layer of unconventionality deriving from the gay appropriation of the songs.

Film Cults Nineteen sixties film culture was another terrain where the codes of high and low and the ideologies of modernism and the popular appeared in constant flux. It is almost a truism to say that auteurist criticism was the single most important development in the decade's film culture. Auteurism was officially "imported" to the United States by Andrew Sarris, who flippantly described his intellectual credentials as "I had been taking an evening course in film appreciation at Columbia between meandering through graduate English and malingering in Teachers College."[40] The development of auteurism in the States is well known, as are the polemics it raised, and its eventual triumph, connected to (if not responsible for) the boom of Film Studies as an academic discipline. What particularly interests me about auteurism is the fact, pointed out by James Naremore, that it constitutes another chapter in the emergence of the postmodern new sensibility.[41] In this connection, it deserves examination in light of the crisis of modernism and the rise of popular culture forms which recreated some of the subversive momentum of modernism and the historical avant-garde on the margins of official culture.

The title of Sarris's compilation of his 1960s reviews, *Confessions of a Cultist,* underlines the parallels between auteurism and the passionate, almost religious reception of Hollywood films.[42] Spearheaded by the young French critics associated with *Cahiers du cinéma,* auteurism legitimized the serious discussion of popular film. French critics like André Bazin, François Truffaut, Claude Chabrol, Eric Röhmer, Jean-Luc Godard, and Jacques Rivette discovered their passion for American popular cinema in a postwar market inundated by the Hollywood output. They praised the slickness, visual flair, and technical bravura of American film. These qualities were, according to them, missing in contemporary French productions, which they regarded as too literary and lacking in purely cinematographic sense. The French cinema, especially the "tradition of quality," was judged by critic and filmmaker François Truffaut a cinema of scriptwriters, not of filmmakers.[43] *Cahiers* critics praised directors such as Val Lewton, Sam Fuller, Nicholas Ray, Otto Preminger, William Kieghley, and Raoul Walsh as important artists endowed with marked personal styles and vision.[44] These critics' praise of popular American film over the more "legitimate" French literary adaptations involved a transvaluation of value similar to the one performed by American "new sensibility" intellectuals who favored the vigor of popular forms over the intellectual pretension of midbrow culture.

In a way, French *Cahiers* auteurist critics were simply rationalizing their enthusiasms for certain Hollywood directors. Their critical fervors and their rallying around certain filmmakers and films replicated, on an intellectual level, popular cultist formations—collectivities of viewers cemented around the devotion to certain films, stars, styles, or icons.[45] Popular cultism usually revolves around stars rather than directors-auteurs, and it precipitates in ephemeral forms such as fan mail, fanzines, dress styles, posters, buttons, collecting, and occasionally in viewing practices, as was the case with *Rocky Horror Picture Show* and drive-in movie cults. Intellectual cultists created more enduring forms, due, among other factors, to their higher intellectual status, which granted their products a serious reception, and to their access to means of cultural production. Much of *Cahiers* criticism, like Sarris's, is an example of intellectual cultism.

Cultism is a recurrent phenomenon in the avant-garde tradition, given the avant-garde intellectuals' long-standing fascination with products of mass culture. The film criticism of the surrealists, for example, is full of cultist tributes to their screen idols, most of whom were Hollywood stars and directors, such as Buster Keaton, Charlie Chaplin, Mae Marsh, Mickey Mouse, Pearl White, Mae Murray, Harold Lloyd, and Mack Sennett. A characteristic example of surrealist cultism is Jacques Rigaut's passionate note on Mae Murray, published in 1922 in Breton's journal *Littérature.* It consisted of a lyrical description of the star's screen charms that ended with the emphatic declaration "I'm in love with Mae Murray."[46] More amusing is Luis Buñuel's cultist homage, "Variations on the Moustache of Menjou." Adolph Menjou's moustache eclipses, in Buñuel's eyes, any other elements in his films; this particular part of the actor's anatomy ultimately becomes a category for perceiving the world, as Buñuel classifies Parisian cafés by the number of "Menjou's moustaches" floating in the sea of faces.[47] Underlying these homages is a sort of *amour fou* for movie stars, whose fusion of real personhood, phantasmic screen presence, and erotic qualities proved extremely suggestive for many surrealists.

American surrealist artist Joseph Cornell, who was roughly contemporary with the first generation of French surrealists, was, like them, prey to the fascination exerted by American popular culture. This fascination is reflected in Cornell's own brand of cultism, which serves as a link between early surrealism and the 1960s underground. Cornell wrote the brief essay, "'Enchanted Wanderer.' Excerpt from a Journey Album for Hedy Lamarr,"[48] a sketch in the surrealist tradition of the cultist homage, and made the cultist film *Rose Hobart* (1939). *Rose Hobart,* a pop film *avant-la-lettre,* is Cornell's version of George Melford's melodrama *East of Borneo* (1931), starring Rose Hobart. Cornell shortened Melford's film from feature length to twenty-odd minutes, tinted it red, eliminated its original sound, and added to it a soundtrack of Latin dance music. Cornell's version disregards temporal and spacial continuity, creating an unstable, enigmatic atmosphere where characters, settings, and actions are in constant flux. As its title indicates, the film is a tribute to Hobart's screen presence; it is largely made up of shots of the actress reacting to events off screen, or in earnest conversation with interlocutors who have been edited out. Other devices that accentuate the film's fragmentariness are splicing together shots from different scenes as if they were simultaneous in the film's diegesis, inserting shots right before fadeout, and juxtaposing similar gestures and actions that belong in different parts of the plot (a series of images of Rose Hobart opening doors, or expressing surprise, for example). These procedures isolated and heightened the evocative power of images and moods that are normally swallowed by the flow of a continuous narrative. The principle of composition is homologous with the surrealist practice of walking into and out of film screenings in order to enjoy what Breton called cinema's "power to disorient"—the lyricism and suggestive potential of scenes dislodged from narrative logic.[49] *Rose Hobart* circulated privately for several decades among the artist's friends, and was rediscovered by Ken Jacobs and Jack Smith in the early 1960s; following this discovery, it was often included in underground programs, together with other shorts by Cornell. *Rose Hobart* anticipated the use of found footage by such underground filmmakers as Bruce Conner, Ken Jacobs, and Kenneth Anger. At the same time, Cornell's fascination with Hollywood B-film exoticism foreshadowed Jack Smith's *Flaming Creatures,* which also recreates the textures of Hollywood Orientalia and uses Latin music in the sound track.[50]

Cultism is an important influence on the filmmakers that this book focuses on. Jack Smith expressed his personal devotion to the queen of Hollywood exotica in his article "The Perfect Film Appositeness of María Montez,"[51] a piece that enthroned the magic presence of stars as the central pleasure of cinema and as the basis for a passionately personal relation to film, which he favored over the cold distances of criticism. In fact, many of Smith's films and performance pieces dwelt to some extent on film cultism and the aura of popular screen idols. An ambiguous fascination with stars and star presence is also at the center of many of Andy Warhol's films; for example such pieces as *Harlot* and *Hedy,* made in collaboration with writer Ronald Tavel, are irreverent evocations of Jean Harlow and Hedy Lamarr. But even beyond those films which alluded directly to stars, all of Warhol's work in general can be seen as an attempt to extend the attributes of stardom to anything or anyone placed in front of the camera: "The Empire State is a star!" With obvious irony, Warhol fashioned his Factory workshop as a threadbare version of a Hollywood studio, complete with its own stable of stars, of which he was the head producer. Some of Warhol's stars evoked, whether in name or poise, former Hollywood idols—Eve Sedgwick as a new Garbo, Mario Montez as the magic María Montez or as Jean Harlow, Candy Darling as Kim Novak—or else acted out raunchy street versions of star charisma—as did Brigid Polk or Holly Woodlawn. For his part, Kenneth Anger practiced his own peculiar kind of cultism. As we will see in a later chapter, the two volumes of his *Hollywood Babylon,* a lurid history of Hollywood scandal, recreate the self-destructive underside of star charisma, exploiting the proximity of Hollywood glamour and death.

The films of the mass-cultural underground acknowledged some of the numerous cults thriving in the 1960s. Cultism was facilitated by the floating availability of mainstream Hollywood icons, an availability which had in turn several historical causes. The decline of the Hollywood system turned films of the classical period into objects of playful allusion and nostalgia. Renewed interest in the declining institution accounts for the phenomenon of the revival house, inspired partly by the success of Harvard Square's Brattle Theatre. Revival houses gave viewers the chance to familiarize themselves with the entire career of specific actors, actresses, or directors, and were thus instrumental in supplying cult materials. Two of the most popular 1960s cults to emerge from revival theaters were those of Humphrey Bogart and Jean Harlow.[52]

The main purveyor of film cults, however, was not the revival house, but television. While revival houses recalled the popularity of the 1920s "little cinemas," one of whose functions had been the revival of Hollywood quality films,[53] television was fully of the present. During the mid-1950s, TV stations plundered the Hollywood archives to fill in programming schedules cheaply without resorting to staff, shootings, studios, and technicians. In fact, between 1955 and 1956, as the industry attempted to make up for shrinking profits, all the major studios but MGM sold their backlog of pre-1948 features to distributors, who in turn leased them to TV stations.[54] Television made the whole of the Hollywood past available to consumers in their own living rooms, a fact traditionally regarded as a contributing factor in the decline of the classic studio system.[55] Television may have killed Hollywood in the present, but it mythologized its past; it confirmed Hollywood's current decadence while reviving its past splendors. TV not only replaced the movies as the top entertainment industry; it also radically changed spectators' relations to Hollywood.

It would be very difficult to assess accurately how much television's massive recycling of Hollywood movies actually modified viewing attitudes. Robert Ray states in his study of the classical American cinema that TV's indiscriminate revival of Hollywood films had the effect of laying bare the artificiality and conventionality of the classic plots, myths, and iconographies.[56] The reiteration of Hollywood myths on television showed the changes undergone by the classical paradigm over time and exposed the weaker versions of its myths, with the effect of eroding the sense of inevitability that such myths had rested on. It might have seemed as if TV had plunged Hollywood from nature into history, exposing, at the same time, its mythical core. Such a fall led audiences to develop an increasingly ironic attitude toward Hollywood, which appeared now as a storehouse of outmoded signs available for recycling through quotation, allusion, and appropriation. In fact, these forms of intertextuality became especially characteristic of 1960s films and television series, whose full effect and intelligibility were often dependent on the spectators' recognition of the texts alluded to. This is equally true of the mass-cultural underground, especially since many of the films made by Andy Warhol, the Kuchar brothers, or Jack Smith were made as parodies of mainstream cinema. In addition to irony and allusion, Hollywood's decline and its revival in television also fostered a sense of nostalgia that, combined with irony, lies at the center of film cultism.

As 1930s American film critic Harry Alan Potamkin stated in one of the earliest essays on film cultism, movies, stars, and directors acquire cult status only when they are devalued, estranged from mainstream acceptance or from dominant modes of cultural production.[57] According to this definition, there is in cultism a sense of reaching for objects on the verge of disappearance, temporarily rescued from the inexorable march toward obsolescence imposed by commodity culture. This notion is born out by the films of Jack Smith, Kenneth Anger, and Andy Warhol. Their cult objects are rarely contemporary; they evidence in fact a certain necrophilia, being devoted to stars whose moment in the spotlight is long gone, or else to the output of old-fashioned systems of production, like Poverty Row movies. The nostalgia that reverberates through these homages has to do with the obviousness of the signs mobilized by older films, which, at a temporal distance, often seem to show a quasi-allegorical universe of clear-cut plots and stereotyped characters. It can also be attributed to the identification with transitoriness itself, with the mortality of cultural products. In this respect, underground cultism celebrates what Walter Benjamin called the *faccies hippocratica* (or dying face) of the commodity—the eternally dying as the other face of the eternally new. In the case of directors like Warhol, Anger, and Smith, a further reason for identifying with old-fashioned (hence displaced) cultural objects may reside in their marginal status—as filmmakers whose movies were prosecuted and banned; as artists working outside official cultural institutions, who were often dependent on private funds to finance their projects; as gay filmmakers whose movies abound in expressions of "deviant" desires and sexualities.

Gay Subcultures and the Underground

As critics of the time often noted, underground films combined artistic and sexual transgressiveness. During a discussion of the underground at the 1966 edition of the New York Film Festival, which featured for the first time a special section on the contemporary American experimental cinema, Sarris described this conjunction as follows: "When you get some of these films that deal quite frankly with things like homosexuality, I think the majority of the people are very violently opposed, the majority of the critics are opposed, and that is one of the issues that keeps coming up all the time: subject matter."[58] In the same vein, when Mekas first defined the term "Baudelairean cinema," he warned: "A thing that may scare the average viewer is that this cinema is treading on the very edge of perversity. These artists are without inhibitions, sexual or any other kind. . . . They [their movies] contain homosexual and lesbian elements."[59] Hence besides being part of the history of the American avant-garde cinema, underground films were also part of gay American culture. They fashioned models of subjectivity and desire that reflected the experiences of the (male) urban gay communities of the time.[60] In so doing, they departed from the gender politics of mainstream commercial culture, yet at the same time, they explored the transgressive potential embedded in popular forms.

Despite the homosexual filiation of an important sector of the underground cinema, there is practically no mention of it in the gay and lesbian press of the day (represented by such periodicals as *One, The Mattachine Review, Drum,* and the lesbian-oriented *The Ladder,* among others). These were the organs of opinion of the organized homophile movement, which at the time was trying hard to gain social acceptance for homosexuals by projecting an image of respectability and neatness. Given this assimilationist goal, the scandalous sexuality of many underground films embodied a facet of gay culture that the homophile press may have been eager to disavow.[61] On the other hand, these films probably appealed to the gay component in the beat-artistic-bohemian milieu; or to put it in terms of New York gay geography, they appealed to the 8th Street long-haired crowd, rather than to the blazer-and-tie East 50s middle-class coteries. (Contemporary newspaper accounts and historians of the period report on the following gay areas in late 1950s and 1960s Manhattan: 8th Street, which was bohemian and off-beat, favored by the art crowd; the affluent East 50s; the West 70s, mainly populated by working-class gays and lesbians; and finally, the notorious 42nd Street between Seventh and Eighth Avenues.) In both mainstream and alternative press coverage, this hypothetical fraction of the audience remained invisible, as it was collapsed with the larger crowd of unconventionals. A reason for such invisibility may have been the fact that strict self-definition along lines of sexual behavior apparently was not a pressing issue in the beat-bohemian fringe. In this milieu, fashioning critical attitudes toward the "square" world presumably overrode, to a certain extent, the sexual identity of many gay bohemians, and provided a more valued (perhaps also more brazenly attractive) social identity. Sociologist Ned Polski, author of well-read studies of the beat scene at the time, described homosexual identification in the beat world as follows: "Even beats with numerous and continuing post-adolescent homosexual experiences typically do not feel the need to define themselves as homosexuals and create some sort of beat wing of the homosexual world."[62]

Linked to its unconventional sexuality, the underground's transgressive interest in mass culture was a reaction to the modernist exclusiveness and subjective withdrawal that characterized the experimental cinema of the late 1940s and early 1950s. Films like Kenneth Anger's *Fireworks* (1947), Gregory Markopoulos's *Psyche* (1947), *Lysis* (1948), and *Charmides* (1947–48), Willard Maas's *Images in the Snow* (1948), Curtis Harrington's *Fragment of Seeking* (1946–47), and John Smitz's *The Voices* (1953) portrayed gay scenarios through alternative cinematographic styles that were characteristic of the postwar experimental cinema. They focused on solitary, vulnerable male protagonists undergoing psychological struggles expressed in dreams, visions, and trances. Their plots revolved around the search for identity, a search that, in the logic of the films, entailed the untangling of conflicted sexual desires and fantasies.

Kenneth Anger's *Fireworks* is perhaps the most frequently seen and most typical of these films. It portrays a young man's homoerotic dreams, in which the protagonist cruises in public lavatories, is brutalized by a gang of sailors, and eventually finds some satisfaction in a sailor whose penis becomes a Roman candle. Anger's film weaves together a series of puns and icons popular in the gay community. Hence, shots of night traffic on a freeway intercut with the young man stalking a men's room suggest "cruising"—at the time an expression more restricted to gay milieus than today; the "flaming" sailor can be read as another such pun. At once attractive and brutal, the sailors were explained by Anger as a comment on a popular gay icon: "It's a personal statement about my own feelings about violence and a certain kind of masculinity . . . the sailor then was a kind of sex symbol on one level, and on another level, there was a great deal of ambivalence and hostility, latency and fear in the image. . . ."[63] These references open the film up to the almost clandestine world of bars, gyms, physique magazines, and cruising areas to which the postwar homosexual culture was mostly confined. By positing some sort of continuity between the communal and the individual aspects of homosexuality, *Fireworks* departed from the films cited above, which tended to focus almost exclusively on its subjective side.

Despite its use of popular gay icons, *Fireworks* has been taken to exemplify the sort of withdrawal into psychology and interiority that characterized the films of contemporary experimental directors such as Maya Deren, Stan Brakhage, Sidney Peterson, and James Broughton. Such withdrawal is evidenced in the framing of the film as a dream, with the protagonist's consciousness becoming the privileged point of view through which the narrative is relayed. The focus on the dialectics of consciousness and perception resulted in a style that tried to convey the vagueness of dreams and subjective states by supplanting the rigid rules of the classical continuity system with loose constructions of action and setting. In *Fireworks,* for example, the spatial relations between the "Gents" room, the scene of the beating, and the bedroom where the narrative opens and closes are left unclear. Looseness of construction contained an implicit rejection of commercial film, whose grammar and style were often described by experimental filmmakers as standardized and impersonal, and therefore inadequate to communicate the complexity of personal vision. *Firework*'s art-house style, strongly reminiscent of French Impressionist cinema of the 1920s, and of a type of surrealism best exemplified by Jean Cocteau's *Sang d'un poète,* was therefore allied to the ideology of modernism commented on in the previous chapter, with its dual emphasis on a humanistic conception of art (as expression of unique subjectivity), and on the rejection of mass culture—the dehumanizing product of the late industrial world. The transgressive homosexuality of *Fireworks* combined smoothly with modernist aesthetic ideology. The model of transgressive subjectivity the movie proposes is based on a model of depth which contrasts a spurious, superficial society and a "true," inner self. In this scheme, the external society (portrayed in the figures of the sailors) appears as unauthentic, violent, and insensitive; opposition to it takes place by validating the authenticity and sincerity of the artist's subjective experience. The uniqueness of the artist, excluded from the mainstream by his or her intellect and sensitivity, translates easily into the uniqueness of the homosexual, whose marginal sexuality causes disaffection and alienation from the rest of society.

It is hard to determine how popular these proto-gay modernist films were in the gay milieu of the period. Most of them premiered in Vogel's Cinema 16 film society in New York, and were subsequently exhibited by film societies throughout the country, where they may have garnered a gay following. Due to its mixture of popular and modernist elements, *Fireworks* was better known to gay audiences; it was at the center of a few scandals, and was seized by vice squad officers at screenings in Los Angeles and San Francisco in the late 1940s and 1950s. It seems, however, that mainstream films were indeed far more popular than experimental films among gay audiences, who forged their own meanings and identities in the process of decoding and activating popular forms, rather than through alternative productions.

While the modernist films of the postwar decades drew on the abstraction, symbolism, and rhetoric of subjectivism inherited from the art world to construct models of transgressive sexuality, the 1960s underground was inspired by the gay popular reception of commercial culture. Gay audiences had traditionally operated in dialogical relation with the products of the culture industry, appropriating stars, movies, songs, and images in which they found particular resonances. These plunderings had defamiliarizing effects on the appropriated objects, as they unveiled the complexity of popular texts and the existence of a significant gap between the ideologies encoded into them and the ones actually decoded by specific audiences. Critic and historian Richard Dyer has shown how gay audiences perceived in Judy Garland's screen roles and personae such traits of contemporary gay culture as camp humor, androgyny, and a paradoxical relation to normality.[64] From another point of view, the subcultural reception of commercial forms pointed out the fact that gay sensibilities were already at work in the encoding of such forms, and therefore part of their "multi-accentuality"—their hybrid, plural constitution. In the case of Garland, such elements may have entered her image not only through well-known figures such as gay composer Cole Porter, author of some musicals and songs she popularized; but also through the participation of more anonymous figures—such as gay scenarists, scriptwriters, art directors, and costume designers—in the production of her vehicles.[65]

Gay readings demonstrate the subcultural tendency to appropriate (in Russian critic Mikhail Bakhtin's phrase) "the alien word," a tendency dictated by the need of subordinate groups to append their meanings to available images and channels. In this respect, the gay sensibility bears qualities that stem from its subaltern social position. A minority devoid of institutional support or stable cultural apparati, gays have been adept manipulators of received codes. As Harold Beaver has stated in his famous essay "Homosexual Signs," gay signs show a certain duplicity, since in them mainstream codes appear permeated by the gay idiolect:

> [Homosexuals] must learn to live with ambiguity. . . . Every sign becomes the cause for elaborately inconclusive fantasizing. Every sign becomes duplicitous, slipping back and forth across a wavering line, once the heterosexual antithesis between love and friendship has been crossed. The need to trace a compatible world becomes the urge to control one with an unceasing production of signs (the suede shoes and cigarette holders of the fifties, the leather and chain accoutrements of the sixties, the key rings and pink triangles of the seventies) as if nothing could be determined by trial, except the signature; nothing deduced from content, only hieroglyphs.[66]

Camp constitutes one such double code. Often cited as a strategy of survival, a pervasive institution of pre-Stonewall gay life, the camp sensibility extracted from among the culture's debris artifacts that could be invested with gay resonances. Camp overlaps with cultism in that both construct their pleasures from "degraded" objects of commercial culture; furthermore, in both cases, audiences refashioned and reproduced original objects according to their own expressive needs.[67] Camp is, in fact, a particular type of cultism that selects its fetishes on the basis of gender ambiguity and stylistic excess. Hence, cultist re-elaborations of María Montez, Jean Harlow, or Marlon Brando by underground filmmakers are distinctly camp in so far as they focus on the theatricality, artifice, and role-playing attendant on some gender representations in Hollywood films.[68]

Camp had an important social function as communal cement. As is often the case in the realm of the popular, its idiom spread through ephemeral forms such as gossip, short-lived stylistic fads, or ways of speaking and acting that often went unrecorded, and whose social life and history are therefore quite difficult to map. Despite such impediments, it can be ascertained that two of camp's most important channels of dissemination were movie houses and gay bars. While the former contributed images to be remade or recycled after camp affect, the latter provided a ground for the more or less unhampered display of such recyclings—whether in drag performance, in "verbal" signs of gayness, or in the star photos that were, in pre-Stonewall days, a standard feature of bar decor.[69] An important contemporary arena where camp solidified into more lasting forms was the Caffé Cino, a combination of coffeeshop and performance space located in New York's Greenwich Village. The Cino was part of what Jerry Tallmer, drama critic for the *Village Voice* at the time, labeled the "off-off-Broadway" scene, the unconventional productions and theatrical spaces which purveyed a deranged counterpoint to the lavishness and respectability of Broadway and the modernist seriousness of off-Broadway. On the minuscule stage of the Cino, plays by then unknown authors such as Robert Heide, Robert Patrick, Tom Eyen, Lanford Wilson, and Ronald Tavel, among others, often combined unabashed camp gayness and devotion to American pop schlock with a peculiar avant-gardism. Performances unfolded in a noisy, profane atmosphere closer to that of a drag show than to the respectful silence of conventional theater. These works can be seen as a theatrical version of the sensibility evidenced by the filmmakers of the present study. Indeed, some of the Cino acts later found their way into the underground cinema: Robert Heide's *The Bed* appeared as an episode of *The Chelsea Girls;* Ronald Tavel scripted a number of Warhol's films; and Robert Olivio (Ondine, Cino player and local personality) would later attain Factory superstardom. In addition to leaving its imprint on the underground, the Cino brand of camp resurfaced in the productions of John Vaccaro and Tavel's "Theater of the Ridiculous."[70]

Whether as ephemeral form or as lasting artistic influence, camp provided an alternative public sphere for the emergence of significations that were forbidden elsewhere, and in this respect it operated along similar lines as the popular culture forms (such as comic books, film cultism, and rock) mentioned earlier in this chapter. In turn, by drawing on stylistic resources from the camp sensibility, the underground sought to recreate some of the commonality woven around the gay transgressive activation of popular objects.

Besides adopting popular reading strategies, the models of transgressive (homo)sexuality forged by the 1960s gay underground destabilized the opposition between authentic subjectivity and inauthentic society, an opposition that structures a film like *Fireworks.* Hence, in a number of 1960s underground films the inner self appears shaped by external, public images drawn from commercial cul-ture. Subjectivity in these films is not a self-present, essential entity; it is instead constructed as public spectacle through mimicry and performance of "found roles" purveyed by the media.[71] The most extreme embodiment of decentered subjectivity is the figure of the transvestite, which often crops up in the movies of Jack Smith, Bill Vehr, Warren Sonbert, and Andy Warhol, to name a few. The frequent appearance of these "flaming creatures" underlines the underground's taste for "unnatural" identities, whose secondhand quality was deftly described by Andy Warhol: "Drag queens are ambulatory archives of ideal movie-star womanhood."[72] The transgressive identity of the drag queens of Warhol's and Smith's films does not lie in their opposing a true self against an inauthentic world, but on subverting the very notion of self, which is affirmed instead as copy, artifice, and role-playing. Analogous articulations of subjectivity have been recently elaborated by such theorists as Judith Butler, Diana Fuss, Leo Bersani, and Jonathan Dollimore, to name a few.[73] Three decades before them, at the dawn of the postmodern period, gay underground films thematized models of identity which stressed the discontinuities between gender, desire, and socio-sexual roles, and illustrated the formative influence that mass-circulated images have on molding subjectivity.

Ken Jacobs, Bob Fleischner, and Jack Smith's collaboration *Blonde Cobra* reflects the shift from the modernist preoccupation with personal authenticity characteristic of 1940s and 1950s experimental film to the underground's decentered subjectivity. Shot by Jack Smith and Bob Fleischner in 1959 and edited by Jacobs in 1963, *Blonde Cobra* can be read as a spoof of the trance film.[74] It focuses on two seemingly alienated characters (interpreted by Jack Smith and Jerry Sims) living in a derelict apartment. The crowded, dark, and slightly disturbing interiors where the film takes place connote the personal disintegration which appears to be the driving concern of the film. *Blonde Cobra* features several monologues (written and performed by Jack Smith) which, given the familiar conventions of the trance film, one would expect to express the characters' alienated interiority. Instead, Smith's monologues enact kaleidoscopic shifts between several roles—Madame Nescience, Mother Superior, the lonely little child, and Sister

Dexterity. Because of the thin narrative transitions between them, these roles seem, on first viewing, to metamorphose into each other (with Madame Nescience becoming Mother Superior, whose story merges in turn with the "lonely little boy" episode). While the trajectory of the trance film involved the progressive uncovering of the protagonists' subjectivity, *Blonde Cobra*'s own trajectory multiplies potential subjects, thus denying the existence of a stable self.

The dream frame—typical of trance films—structures Madame Nescience's monologue, during most of which the screen remains black. In this particular case, however, the dream does not portray the character's personal truth, but appears as the site of further confusion and shifting— "Madame Nescience, oh oh, I mean Mother Superior oh I've just come from the girls . . . from the girls' dormitory. Madame Nescience . . . I mean, Mother Superior! you see this is a dream!" Similarly, the earnest homosexuality of 1940s and 1950s films is turned here into passing jokes ("Love is a pain in the ass," moans Smith, as the camera pans up his legs, showing a knife lodged in his butt) or grotesque drag (in Smith's impersonation of Madame Nescience as a besequined queen in gypsy-like bandanna and horribly botched lipstick job). Role changes are accentuated by changes in costume, with the performers impersonating the characters of the stories narrated, or else adopting apparently unmotivated costumes and props, such as the "film noir" fedoras, trench coats, and moody poses in the scene preceding Madame Nescience's monologue. The recurrence in the sound track of Astaire and Rogers's version of "Let's Call the Whole Thing Off," and of Smith's anguished cries, "What went wrong?" underline the provisionality and sense of impending dissolution that pervade the subjective shifts and even the form of the film itself. *Blonde Cobra* conveys the overall impression of a madman's trance. While earlier trance films often traced the movement from a divided consciousness to a more or less united one,[75] no such outcome is apparent in *Blonde Cobra*. Instead, its characters repeatedly adopt precarious fictional identities, producing themselves in the interstices of received roles, images, and motifs most often garnered from commercial entertainment.

The confluence of gay readings of mass culture and decentered models of subjectivity in the underground cinema can be contextualized in relation to the historical situation of the gay community in the 1960s; more specifically, as a reaction against the mainstream press and the psychiatric establishment's contemporary attempts to fix and define homosexuality. The greater visibility of gay communities in the early 1960s, facilitated in part by the relaxation of the gay-hunts of the 1950s, led nationally circulated newspapers and magazines such as *Time, Life, Newsweek, Harper's,* and the *New York Times* to publish stories on "the gay lifestyle," with the desire to capture the subculture for the public eye.[76] Shifting in tone from patronizing tolerance to rabid homophobia, these writings tended to combine the points of view of sociology and clinical psychology. Sociological description offered a typology of the homosexual world (divided, as the press repeatedly reported, between the "swish" in puffy sweaters, tight chinos, and sneakers and the "leather-clad toughs"), and described haunts, neighborhoods, and cruising spots, while giving clues to detect "deviants"—"a look that lingers a fraction of a second too long," shrewdly pointed out the *New York Times*. Psychological discussions pondered the causes of homosexuality ("Scientists search for the answers to a touchy and puzzling question, WHY?," read a *Life* headline) and presented the opinions of experts debating its status as a mental disease. The clinical authorities most often invoked by these articles included Irving Bieber, author of *Homosexuality: A Psycho-*

analytic *Study of Male Homosexuals* (1962) and Charles Socarides, a New York analyst. Both of them regarded homosexuality as an illness caused by faulty familial configuration and hastened to announce the possibility of a cure through psychotherapy.[77] The overt purpose of most of these reviews was, as the *New York Times* put it, to dispel "the mysteries and misconceptions that have grown in the dark." Yet, for all the good that may have come from visibility and open discussion, making the gay community easily identifiable contributed as well to making it controllable.[78] Hence, the amused descriptions of gay styles and behaviors present in these articles take on chilling overtones when contrasted with the end to which some of these knowledges were put: "As part of its anti-homosexual drive, the Los Angeles police force has compiled an 'educational' pamphlet for law enforcement officers entitled 'Some characteristics of the homosexual.'"[79]

When considered against this background, the underground's celebration of a decentered subjectivity based on role-playing and artifice can be read as a maneuver of occultation, governed by the desire to escape the fixity that medical and popular journalistic accounts were trying to enforce. In close relation with the production of decentered subjectivities, the underground's appropriation of mass culture can be read as an analogous tactic of escape. Gay meanings and identities were produced precisely in a terrain where they seemed most irretrievable: mainstream commercial entertainment. In this way, subcultural transgressions were hidden in broad daylight: visible to the trained eye, invisible to the unaware.[80]

This chapter has tried to show that in the context of the 1960s, the shifting relations between high and mass culture appear connected to specific subcultural identities and sexual politics. The underground's critique of modernism and its alliance to popular cultural practices and artifacts must be viewed not as a manifestation of an apolitical new sensibility, but in relation to certain subcultural activism linked to the emergence of gay identities. The following chapters will explore how the films by Anger, Warhol, and Smith articulate different relations between avant-garde artistic forms and specific gay signs, meanings, and social identities.

The films of these three directors are among the most characteristic, influential, and celebrated of the New York underground. Smith, Warhol, and Anger received the *Film Culture* award to the best independent filmmaker of the year in 1963, 1964, and 1969, respectively.[81] In addition, Anger's *Scorpio Rising* and Warhol's *My Hustler* and *Chelsea Girls* had extended runs in commercial theaters. This could also have been the fate of Smith's *Flaming Creatures,* had it not been for the extended legal battles over its presumed obscenity, which kept the film out of the theaters. Yet in spite of its unavailability, *Flaming Creatures* became the *cause célèbre* of the underground, a rallying point for both defenders and attackers.[82]

Either by crossing over into mainstream or art-house distribution, or by being hotly debated, the films of Anger, Warhol, and Smith became much more influential than most other underground movies. Their relative success has been regarded as a symptom of their recuperability and of the crisis the avant-garde undergoes once its artistic idiom enters commercial cinema, the established art world, and the language of advertisement and television. From a different perspective, the popularity of these avant-garde films had to do with their *porosity,* with the fact that they allowed multiple points of entry for audiences. As the next three chapters will show, they do this by gleefully problematizing received meanings, identities, genders, sexualities, and desires, and by functioning as alternative public spheres in a decade of increased cultural activism.

Pop, Queer, or Fascist?
The Ambiguity of Mass Culture in
Kenneth Anger's *Scorpio Rising*

Four

Kenneth Anger's *Scorpio Rising* has often been regarded as the most representative film of the 1960s American underground cinema. Premiered in October of 1963 in the Gramercy Arts Theater, it quickly became a hit in the art cinema circuit, and was one of the very few underground movies to enjoy a successful commercial run.[1] To this day, it remains the most widely seen experimental movie of its time and the most frequently rented title in the repertoire of the Filmmakers' Cooperative. A "documentary" of sorts on the lifestyle of a motorcycle gang, it portrays motorcyclists cleaning and putting together their machines, lying about in their rooms, dressing for and attending a party, riding recklessly, and having an accident. As is the case with many other films by Anger, *Scorpio Rising* is deeply ambiguous, since it both glamorizes the marginal group's rebelliousness and seemingly condemns its self-destructive behavior.

Scorpio Rising consists of thirteen distinct segments scored to hit songs of the years 1961 to 1963. It is studded with pop culture icons and allusions that Anger brings up as sources of the biker subculture or as commentaries on it. At the same time, the film employs many thematic motifs and formal traits of the historical avant-garde, such as a fascination with technology, collage technique, and an interest in the "utopian" possibilities embedded in mass cultural forms. Like many other underground movies, *Scorpio Rising* pays tribute to the forms of mass culture which are the source of its imagery, and can therefore be seen as a self-conscious imitation of popular texts. Anger himself attests to this: "What *Scorpio* represents is me clueing in to popular American culture after having been away for eight years, because I had been living in France for that long."[2] "[C]oming back [to the United States] was like visiting a foreign country."[3]

Given the centrality of pop culture to Anger's film, this chapter will analyze *Scorpio Rising* as a movie about popular forms. In this respect, I intend to expand the critical views on Kenneth Anger's major film, views which have consistently underlined its debt to the European avant-garde cinema (Buñuel and Eisenstein frequently come up as creditors) and overlooked its engagement with the American pop vernacular.[4] This involvement consists primarily in the appropriation of popular youth culture forms from the 1950s and 1960s, such as rock and roll songs, the iconography of the motorcycle cult, comic books, and images of teen idols Marlon Brando and James Dean. Appropriation is dominated by a gay viewpoint that unveils meanings—such as homoerotic plots, or the proximity of eroticism and violence—which tend to remain displaced or muted in the straight uses of these forms.[5] Such gay desublimation of mass culture does not have an unambiguously liberating effect. The subtexts the film uncovers resonate with fascist oppression at the same time that they celebrate subversive pleasures and identities. I will show how such contradictory evaluation emanates from the dual implications of the biker and gay subcultures of the time (from which Anger's film borrowed iconography and point of view, respectively), both of which were widely regarded as "subversive," in a positive sense, and as dangerous or deadly. Ambiguity is also the result of the confluence in the film of two contradictory paradigms of mass culture: modernist condemnation, and pop celebration of its expressive potentials.

Before *Scorpio Rising*

Unlike Jack Smith and Andy Warhol, who started making films in the early 1960s, Kenneth Anger had been an experimental filmmaker since the early 1940s. Born in 1930 in Santa Monica, California, to a family connected to the Hollywood film industry (his grandmother had been a costume designer at Metro Goldwyn Mayer), he started shooting movies at age eleven,[6] and in 1947 became a consecrated director with *Fireworks,* a film whose unabashed homosexuality provided a moment of scandal for the postwar American art cinema. As has been noted in an earlier chapter, *Fireworks* portrays a young man's homoerotic dreams, in the course of which he obtains some sexual satisfaction from a muscular sailor and is later brutally beaten by a gang of the sailor's mates. *Fireworks* is an early compendium of Anger's aesthetics: the fascination with eroticism and death,

Advertisement in *The Village Voice* for Kenneth Anger's
Scorpio Rising. Designed by David Brooks, former
secretary of the Filmmakers' Cooperative.
Courtesy of Anthology Film Archives.

the interest in gay iconography, and the unstable tone—by
turns ironic and serious—recur in all his later films. Unlike
most American experimental movies of the time, *Fireworks*
became a cult piece in Europe; it was enthusiastically received at the 1949 edition of the *Féstival International du
cinéma maudit,* celebrated in Biarritz, France, under Jean
Cocteau's direction. Lured by a fan letter from Cocteau,
Anger left America in 1949 for the supposedly wider social
and intellectual horizons of Paris, repeating in this way an
old gesture of the American intelligentsia.

During his European residency, Anger worked on a
number of projects: among them, a film of Cocteau's ballet
Le Jeune Homme et la mort; a feature-length adaptation
of the French erotic novel *Histoire d'O,* of which only a
few tests were run; and a documentary of Thelema Abbey,

Sicily, place of residence of magus Alistair Crowley, one of Anger's intellectual heroes. These 1950s films are no longer available; they succumbed to bad storage conditions, to Anger's almost nomadic existence, or simply to his waning interest in them.[7] On several occasions, a dearth of funds forced Anger to leave his projects unfinished after filming only some fragments. Two incomplete films from this period are *Rabbit Moon* (1955) and *Puce Moment* (1950). *Rabbit Moon* was initially conceived as a feature-length project. Its characters and motifs derive from the *commedia dell'arte,* particularly as recreated in Marcel Carné's *Les Enfants du Paradis* (1945). The film's setting, an enchanted forest, is a reproduction of the background decor used in Max Reinhardt's version of *Midsummer Night's Dream,* in which Anger acted as the Princeling when he was six.[8] *Puce Moment* is also a fragment from a projected feature film on the everyday life of a retired Hollywood actress, and could almost be termed a failed *Sunset Boulevard,* which coincidentally premiered shortly after Anger stopped working on this film. The extant footage shows a middle-aged woman languishing in a luxurious mansion, applying makeup, dressing up, and taking her hounds out for a walk.

The two 1950s films that Anger managed to complete are *Eaux d'artifice* (translated as *Waterworks*) (1953) and *Inauguration of the Pleasure Dome* (1956, recut several times afterwards). *Eaux d'artifice* shows a masked feminine figure in eighteenth-century costume fleeing through baroque gardens full of streams, ornate fountains, and statues, and bathed in spectral moonlight. At the end of the film the mysterious figure metamorphosizes into a fountain, a change conveyed through a series of dissolves that evoke the fluid passage of flesh into water. According to P. Adams Sitney, the film loosely recreates the final episode of Ronald Firbank's camp classic *Valmouth,* whose overwrought prose Anger conveyed through careful pans and zooms on running water, foliage, and statues.[9] *Inauguration,* shot in Hollywood during a brief stay in the mid-1950s, is a mythological masquerade acted by some of Anger's friends, among them bohemians and socialites Samson DeBrier and Anaïs Nin.[10] The film's dazzlingly arrayed characters incarnate such mythological deities as Isis, Shiva, Kali, Ganymede, and Dionysus, among others. In the film's minimal plot, they solemnly drink and get high, lust after a young apparition (the god Pan, according to Anger's notes), and laugh convulsively in their hallucinations. Sitney has argued that *Inauguration of the Pleasure Dome* occupies an important place in the history of American experimental cinema, since it signals the transition from the trance film, based on subjective impressions and dreams, to mythopoesis: the translation of movements of consciousness into archetypal, mythical forms.[11] From another perspective, however, both *Waterworks* and *Inauguration* belong fully in the tradition of decadentism and aestheticism, whose most important representative at the time was Jean Cocteau; they present precious characters in ornate settings, and evidence a fascination with demonism and artificial states of consciousness. These movies also show a self-conscious camp irony, present mainly in the excessive mise-en-scène, which undermines any pretense of seriousness.

As can be gathered from the foregoing descriptions, *Scorpio Rising*'s plunge into pop culture is a departure from the themes and style of Anger's first phase. At the same time, however, the film replays two salient preoccupations of the early works: the deadly underside of (homo)sexual desire and the fascination with appearance and style.

Scorpio Rising. **Courtesy of MOMA Film Stills Archive.**

   Scorpio Rising's bikers recast the main theme of Anger's first film, *Fireworks:* the mutual implication of desire and death. The sailors in *Fireworks* are ambiguous objects of homosexual desire, whose presence leads first to arousal and then to punishment, intimating that desire yearns for an undoing, an inevitably violent self-shattering.[12] The unsettling mixture of desire and death also shapes Anger's anthology of scandal *Hollywood Babylon.* First published by J. J. Pauvert in France in 1960, *Hollywood Babylon* is a scathing look into the underside of Hollywood's glamour—the unheroic background of domestic violence, addiction, suicide, and unhappiness that surrounded some members of the film community behind the scenes. The book is based on the same duality that informs *Fireworks* and *Scorpio Rising:* stars, objects of desire, are also icons of death and destruction.[13] Like the sailors and Hollywood stars, the bikers in *Scorpio Rising* combine violence and eroticism. Early sequences of the film, such as the one edited to the song "Blue Velvet," spectacularize the bikers, who flex their muscles and pose for the camera in leather and chains. In addition to being objects of the camera's and the spectators' gaze, the bikers appear as objects of desire for each other; a series of eye-line matches construct a homoerotic circuit of looks in which the bikers seem to admire each others' bodies in several stages of dress or undress.[14] Well into the second half of the film, by the time such homoeroticism has been well established, the film starts presenting the bikers as a violent group bent on sadism and self-destruction. This becomes most evident in the sado-masochistic rituals of the song segments "I Will Follow Him" and "Point of No Return" and in the deadly crash of a gang member.

Another concern that connects *Scorpio Rising* to the earlier 1950s films is the emphasis on masquerade and appearances. *Inauguration, Rabbit Moon,* and *Waterworks* consist of loosely connected tableaux that showcase the characters' costumes and balletic movements. In this respect, they are more presentational than representational: rather than depict a narrative, they dwell on the process of staging and on precious settings, textures, surfaces, and gestures integrated into a loose storyline. Likewise, several sequences in *Scorpio Rising* show characters constructing their appearance in front of the camera, turning themselves into spectacles that tend to freeze the narrative flow. Yet while the theatrical excess of *Inauguration of the Pleasure Dome* or *Rabbit Moon* derives from high-culture traditions, such as fin-de-siècle decadentism, the styles portrayed in *Scorpio Rising* derive from popular sources: the motorcycle and gay subcultures, whose respective styles had specific resonances in the postwar social and historical contexts.

Scorpio Rising. Eyeline matches involve spectators
in a homoerotic circuit of looks. Courtesy of
MOMA Film Stills Archive.

The motorcycle phenomenon started in California in the years following World War II and was triggered by the conjunction of a flourishing economy and postwar angst. The former gave working and middle-class youths easy access to employment and disposable income, and with it, the material means to acquire and recycle motorcycles, clothes, music, and other commodities. Angst fed the murmur of discontent that can often be heard in their styles and practices. Hunter Thompson, author of the most thorough and extended study on the motorcycle subculture, characterized its origins as follows,

> The whole thing was born, they say, in the late 1940s, when most ex-GIs wanted to get back to an orderly pattern: college, marriage, job, children—all the peaceful extras that come with a sense of security. But not everybody felt that way . . . there were thousands of veterans who flatly rejected the idea of going back to their pre-war pattern. They didn't want order but privacy—and time to figure things out. It was a nervous, downhill feeling, a mean kind of Angst that always comes after wars . . . a compressed sense of time on the outer limits of fatalism. They wanted more action, and one of the ways to look for it is on a big motorcycle. By 1947 the state was alive with bikes. . . .[15]

Even for the youths who had not fought at the front, the postwar period brought on its own internal tensions, strictures, and regulations from which some escaped riding, forming groups cemented around machines and movement. Movement was a way to reject the reorganization and normalization of life after the war, with its conformist, settled lifestyle. In the social and ideological changes brought about by the end of the war, the bikers' constant drifting internalized the ideological instability and uncertainty of the period.

Bikers are one of the various forms of deviant youth culture that emerged in the postwar climate. As early as 1944, a host of documentaries (like the Time/Life movie *Youth in Crisis*), magazine articles, radio programs, and books (most notably, Robert Lindner's *Rebel without a Cause*), started spreading the impression that something had gone radically wrong with the country's adolescents. As the argument ran, lack of parental guidance and the violent atmosphere created by the war combined to turn juveniles into delinquents, whose lifestyles threatened fundamental American values, such as deferred gratification, cooperation, and family life. In this climate, so-called deviant youth culture consisted of a series of largely spontaneous formations which made visible an undertow of social discontent and expressed itself in violence or stylistic revolt—each acting as harbingers of the other.[16] Oppositional youth style, often allied to violence and delinquency, operated on received commodities, props of everyday common sense, practicality, and rationality. The first symptoms of stylistic rebellion emerged alongside violent resistance to authority in the 1943 zoot suit riots of New York and Los Angeles. In them, ethnic minorities (Hispanics in Los Angeles and blacks in New York) rioted against living conditions and the continued harassment of their communities by police and army personnel. The zoot suit, which young males in these communities had turned into a staple of their style, became, as a result of the riots, associated with protest and rejection of authority. The link between the zoot suit and rebellion was such that, after the riots of June 1943, the Los Angeles city council came close to passing an ordinance outlawing zoot suits citywide. The zoot suit consisted of a long, loose jacket with broad lapels and baggy pants pegged at the cuff, often adorned with a long, dangling watch chain. Both suits and watch chains were everyday commodities that members of these ethnic communities turned into signs of their difference from society. Cultural critic and historian George Lipsitz mapped the significations condensed in the zoot suits: the long, draped shapes and almost feminine ornamentation rejected the sober cut of conventional clothing; the conspicuous watch chain, a mere decorative item, mocked the connections between time and work schedules, discipline, and productivity; and finally, the zoot's sartorial excess (its ample, useless cut and flare) evoked its association with the culture of leisure. The zoot suit provided, in sum, "a means for creating a community out of a disdain for traditional community standards."[17]

The bikers can be seen as successors of the zoot-suiters in their use of style as a mark of outsidedness and dissent. Like other spectacular subcultures, they defined themselves largely through their appearance. And like the excessive figures of Anger's theatrical films, bikers turned "being" into an endless decking out intended to call attention to itself. Such self-reflexivity differed from the functionality and transparency of conventional style. To accentuate their difference from the mainstream, bikers dressed in leather and denim, gear that, besides being eminently practical in case of a wipeout, suggested the "open range" and their being untamed by social and communal ways. Their style was based on their interpretation of an all-American commodity: the motorcycle. Bikers did with motorcycles what hot-rodders and customizers did with cars: both cultures provided versions of their vehicles that contrasted with their "straight" functionalistic shapes. Their activities were centered around racing, riding and modifying their

HE REAPER

Kenneth Anger. Courtesy of Anthology Film Archives.

machines. Sober Detroit designs were transformed by the hands of expert customizers into demented shapes by adding chrome pieces, lowering the body of the vehicle, widening the mudguards, multiplying head and back-lights, molding exhaust pipes into all sorts of shapes, adding tail fins and bubble tops. . . . For their part, motorcycles allowed for a smaller ornamental repertoire. Bikers favored heavy, stolidly built American-made machines such as Triumph, Indian, and Harley Davidson. They stripped these "irons" of much of their weight, added lights, mirrors, and chrome embellishments, and sometimes chopped their front axle to extend its length with the double purpose of defamiliarizing the machines and increasing their speed.

These manipulations were sharply described by Gene Balsey, a student at the University of Chicago who, in 1950, wrote an analysis of hot-rod culture for a seminar conducted by sociologist David Riesman.[18] Balsey interpreted hot-rod culture as an example of the autonomy of the consumer and of his or her ability to modify commodities through consumption, "despite the attempts of mass producers to channel consumption in 'respectable' directions." For Balsey, the souped-up cars of the hot-rodders (and the same could be said of the bikers' machines and style) were spontaneous and ingenious stylistic responses to the narrowness of industrial designs and by extension, of available social and professional options. As we will see, such manipulations of received images and commodities are structurally analogous to *Scorpio Rising*'s gay decodings of everyday mass culture icons.

Rebellious youth styles problematized postwar ideological narratives, which postulated a fictitious national unity in opposition to the alien Communist threat.[19] By opening up cracks within such imaginary unity, oppositional youth cultures complicated the simplistic official dichotomies that pitted the United States against foreign threats. Neither alien invaders nor part of the social consensus, youth and other oppositional cultures presented dominant social ideologies with a limit to their legitimizing and naturalizing power. Many contemporary films, pulp novels, and comic books revolved around these troubling spots, attempting to exploit their energy and unmanageability for commercial profit and to contain their ideological scandals. Such popular forms were a privileged terrain of struggle between ideological containment, which worked to reassert official narratives of power, nationhood, and unity, and the dissonant expressions of youth style and resistance.

One of the best known popular genres where such a tug-of-war took place was the 1950s youth picture. Initially, such films as *The Wild One, The Blackboard Jungle,* and *Rebel without a Cause,* to name the most successful ones, and later whole series of B-pictures on rock and roll (*Rock around the Clock, Jailhouse Rock*), motorcyclists (*Motorcycle Gang*), and delinquency (*High School Confidential*) both glamorized and popularized oppositional youth style and, at the same time, cautioned audiences against it by emphasizing its destructive underside. Hence, while popular films ended up by symbolically "punishing" youth subcultural forms, they also attributed to them a sense of autonomy, risk, and excitement. Popular texts like the motorcycle gang movie and the juvenile delinquent picture were thus internally split between condemning destructive outsidedness and glamorizing difference and transgression.[20] While transgression was expressed mostly through moments of spectacular style, condemnation was encoded in the narrative frames which tried to mediate the ideological threat of the bikers and other dissident subcultures. Attesting to a certain fascination with these popular styles, *Scorpio Rising* adopted, along with style bursting out of narrative bounds, the strategies of containment through which narratives set limits to such exuberant explosions of youth style. Anger's film then reproduced the same mismatch between attempted ideological containment and rebellion (or, in Robert Ray's words, between intent and effect) that characterized many commercial depictions of youth culture.

Bikers and Gays

Besides offering a popular transposition of Anger's modernist concerns, the bikers of *Scorpio Rising* deserve to be interpreted in terms of the filmmaker's interest in the iconography of homosexual desire, an interest already attested to by *Fireworks*. In this sense, *Scorpio Rising* shows Anger clueing not merely into popular culture at large, but more specifically into gay popular culture.

According to Hunter Thompson, the bikers' aura of danger and aggressiveness had made them popular icons in the sadomasochistic circuit.[21] The bikers' leather gear was, along with Nazi uniforms, a characteristic icon of the S&M aesthetic, and Anger's film does evoke such connections. However, the biker aesthetic was also attractive to a much larger sector of the subculture than those directly identified with S&M practices.

Images of bikers started cropping up in homoerotic physique magazines of the 1950s, the most popular of which was *Physique Pictorial*. *Physique Pictorial* started publication in the early 1950s. It was marketed as a physical culture magazine, but the insertion of models in elaborate fetishistic scenarios reveals a libidinal fantasy investment that can hardly be justified as interest in health and body-building alone. The magazine was edited by Bob Mizer, who was also its main photographer and head of the photo studio Athletic Model Guild, source of the most widely disseminated gay erotica of the time. Started by Mizer in 1945 as an outlet of sorts for pictures of male models, the Athletic Model Guild soon found its most faithful constituency: male gay audiences. Guild's pictures were sold by mail order to those responding to advertisements in *Physique Pictorial*.[22] Bob Mizer's photos favored rough-looking, muscular men, many of whom, according to British painter David Hockney, had criminal records and earned their living modeling, sitting for artists, and hustling.[23] Many of Mizer's models were the human debris of the movie industry—handsome men who had moved to the area in search of a Hollywood career, and who, failing to land a job in the industry, ended up trading their beauty in less glamorous markets. For critic and historian Tom Waugh, Mizer's pictures evidence a shift in gay erotica away from the classical Greek decor and motifs which often favored androgynous adolescents as sexual ideals (an aesthetic best exemplified by the pictures of turn-of-the-century German photographers Wilhelm von Gloeden and Wilhelm von Pluschow), and closer to commonplace settings and rougher physical types.[24] Other symptoms of this shift are the works of contemporary gay photographer Al Urban; artist Tom of Finland, whose drawings gained wider circulation in America during the early 1960s; and Jean Genet's writings (first published in the English-speaking world by Grove Press) which also aligned homosexuality with roughness, everydayness, and criminality, and whose plots were often set in jails and the urban underworld. Of course, this gay iconography has an older history which can be seen in Walt Whitman's idolization of soldiers, field laborers, and workers, and, in a more elitist context, in Marcel Proust's character Baron de Charlus's weakness for "rough trade."[25] Both Whitman and de Charlus's tough boys are part of a tradition in gay culture that has received less pictorial representation than its Hellenic counterpart, since it lacked the artistic alibi of Greek classicism and was invested in eroticizing commonplace working-class motifs and milieus.

Mizer's photos often featured motorcycle punks as dominant figures in scenarios of bondage and discipline. While these images may have reflected Mizer's fantasy alone, its continued appearance in other facets of the subculture (in Eagle bars and as models for leather boys and for the 1970s clones) point to their wider gay appeal. Part of this attraction

derived from the fact that the biker image contested conceptions of homosexuality disseminated by the popular culture
of the time. The physicality of the biker contrasted with the
effeminacy, frailty, and neuroticism attributed to homosexuals both in popular representations and medical and
psychological discourses. The bikers also differed from a
more genteel stereotype that emerged from within the subculture and that Richard Dyer has called the "sad young
man": the vulnerable man who suffered helplessly in the
dark, embodied for example, by Dirk Bogarde in the British
film *Victim,* or, in a more closeted fashion, by Montgomery
Clift's pin-ups.[26] The iconography of the "sad young man"
was characterized by chiaroscuro lighting, interiors, averted
gazes, and languid poses, and suggested being overpow-
ered and confined, unable either to strike back or to escape.
One can read in these secretive atmospheres the menace of
the McCarthy gay-hunts, a menace corroborated by visual
echoes from two main "paranoid styles": German expressionism and American film noir. By contrast to the physical
and psychological confinement of the "sad young man,"
the biker imagery evoked movement, speed, and the open
road. The bikers' aggressive stance offered a more em-
powering and affirmative gay icon that borrowed from
spectacular forms of youth rebellion and replaced the besieged, passive look of the sensitive young man with a dire
stylistic attack.

The uniformity, externality, and visibility of the biker
image can be seen as instinctive attempts to form a community around an obvious and confrontational style. Images
of sad young men stressed individuality, alienation, and isolation; they were in tune with contemporary characterizations of homosexuality as individual plight and personal
pathology. By contrast, the biker image stressed a sense

of commonality defined in terms of a shared style and de-emphasized individuation and subjectivism as bases of homosexual identification. *Scorpio Rising* exemplifies this shift; its focus on the group style of its multiple, interchangeable, and almost faceless protagonists is a sharp departure from the individualism and the subjectivism of the early *Fireworks.* Interestingly, this is also the time when sociological studies of deviance began to construct a paradigm of homosexuality that stressed the communal viewpoint and contravened the psychological models' emphasis on individual pathology. Deviance theorists and sociologists like Irving Goffman and Howard Becker took for granted a certain relativism in social and sexual mores. In their view, deviant identities developed as persecuted groups tried to establish their own social spaces and practices under the pressures of an antagonistic society. Homosexuality was not regarded by scholars of deviance as a failure to develop according to a normative oedipal trajectory (as American Freudianism claimed), but as an alternative form of socialization and commonality. Given their relativistic viewpoint, instead of proposing that homosexuals be cured and adjust to some psychologically based notion of "normality," sociologists of deviance advocated more acceptance and flexibility in social mores.[27] Gay-biker imagery encoded in an instinctive, untutored way the affirmation of difference, the depersonalization and de-individuation of marginality, and the stress on community that sociologists of the time were defending against the negative models of homosexuality-as-individual-disease legitimized by the psychological establishment.

Along with the emphasis on group style and the displacement of subjectivism, the hyper-masculine images of bikers implied an ironic detachment characteristic of camp.

Anger's bikers, for example, represent masculinity as stylized drag or cosmetic facade, and therefore as far from natural or organic. The overabundance of phallic symbols in *Scorpio Rising* suggests that the masculinity of the bikers cannot be taken for granted, but had to be produced by insistent fetish-wielding. An example of this is the "Blue Velvet" song segment, in which, after putting on their leather and metal accoutrements, one of the bikers straddles a conical shape that points directly to his crotch. In case bulging muscles and macho poses did not bespeak masculinity strongly enough, it had to be underscored once more through this gesture. From another perspective, the fetishes may be a way to overcompensate for the specularization of the bikers, placed in what Laura Mulvey's characterization of visual pleasure has defined as a feminine position—objects of the camera gaze. In any case, the butch masquerade and fetishistic excess of the bikers' images contain strong doses of self-consciousness and artificiality; they contrast with the moral seriousness of the "sad young man," whose suffering is based on certain notions of authenticity and essentialism.

Scorpio Rising: Reading Mass Culture

Scorpio Rising's immersion in popular culture contrasts with the high cultural concerns and imagery of Anger's previous work. One reason for such a shift, as I have already suggested, is the extraordinary development of mass culture at the time when Anger made his film. *Scorpio Rising* appeared in a phase of American history characterized by the expansion of the electronic mass media and by an economic boom that increased consumer purchasing power across all social strata.[28] This period extends from 1945 to the present, and had one of its early peaks in the early

1960s, when *Scorpio Rising* was made, a time when television had reached near-ubiquity and other sectors of the
media and entertainment industries were experiencing an
enormous growth. Such developments came hand in hand
with the vogue of Keynesianism, the most influential economic ideology of the 1960s, which was endorsed by the
Kennedy administration. In contrast to classical economic
theorists, who stressed production as the basis of economic
growth, British economist Maynard Keynes, who developed
his most important insights during the 1920s and 1930s,
maintained that increasing consumption was key to ensuring a stable economy with high levels of production and
employment.[29] In keeping with these views, manufacturers
developed sophisticated marketing and advertisement departments whose goal was to stimulate consumer demand.[30]
Sharp increase in the quantity and quality of advertisement,
coupled by the expansion of electronic media, made mass
culture more pervasive than ever before. Such pervasiveness is born out by Anger's statement about the origins
of *Scorpio Rising*'s rock music score: "When I came back
[from Europe], I spent the first part of the summer of 1962 at
Coney Island on the beach under the boardwalk. The kids
had their little transistors and they had them on."[31] The ubiquity of portable radios illustrates the extreme permeation of
public spaces by the media and commercial culture. Art
spaces seemed at the time equally permeable to mass culture, as in the early 1960s, some types of experimental art
(pop and assemblage art are two examples) began to introduce popular artifacts into cultural domains like museums
and art galleries, where they had traditionally been barred.
We should also remember that, as was explored in the
previous chapter, popular forms had been, since the early
1950s, enacting some of the most subversive features of the

historical avant-garde and high modernism. As an example, the biker and gay subcultures on which Anger draws in *Scorpio Rising* were interested in stylistic display and sexual ambiguity, issues which Anger had previously explored in modernist forms such as ballet and aestheticized cinema. But besides exploiting the subversive edge of some popular formations and iconographies, Anger's film also underlines their totalitarian menace.

Anger illustrates these paradoxical qualities of mass culture by appropriating popular images and artifacts and relocating them in his film. In doing so, he creates an open text which can be read in two nearly symmetrical, mutually contradictory ways. One of them equates mass culture with domination, and highlights its fascistic overtones; the other, in contrast with the former, stresses the anti-authoritarian openness and malleability of popular meanings—what cultural theorist John Fiske has recently called a popular economy of signification.

Before studying in detail how these two conceptions of mass culture traverse the film, I want to examine a sequence in *Scorpio Rising* that illustrates them both. This sequence corresponds to the fifth and sixth song segments, edited to Elvis Presley's "(You're the) Devil in Disguise" and Ray Charles's "Hit the Road, Jack." It shows a biker (Scorpio, in the film's credits) reclining in bed while reading the comics, and later on putting on his leather gear and preparing to attend a party. In the background, a television shows images of Marlon Brando in *The Wild One.* The walls of the room are crammed with posters, pin-ups, and film stills of James Dean—whose effigy also appears in cutaway shots to a plaque, an ashtray, a fan club diploma, and other star memorabilia. The biker's clothes and gestures mimic those of Dean and Brando, who embodied the ethos of youth re-

Scorpio Rising. **"You're the Devil in Disguise."**
Courtesy of Anthology Film Archives.

bellion in their 1950s films, and provided role models that
oppositional youth subcultures such as the bikers eagerly
identified with.[32] Mass-produced images determine Scorpio's looks, gestures, and stance, and can thus be said to
erase his own identity and authenticity. From another point
of view, these shots extend the gay spectatorial gaze that
structures the film's early sequences to a number of mass
cultural texts ranging from the songs of the soundtrack,
to the comics ("Dondi," "Freckles and His Friends," "Li'l
Abner"), to movie stars (besides the ones already mentioned,
there are quick shots of Bela Lugosi and Gary Cooper). In
this sense, the biker's mimicry should not be read as a blind
reflex conditioned by the media, but as a defamiliarizing
reading that "outs" the repressed homosocial and homoerotic significations of these specific popular texts.

The film maintains this ambiguity at every turn: the juxtaposition of Elvis's words "You look like an angel . . ." to

shots of a tough-looking boy lying in bed conveys the wit and exhilaration of deviant appropriation. But on the other side of wit, the noose hanging from the ceiling, skulls, some of the song's lines ("You're the devil in disguise"), and an insert of a newspaper clipping ("Cycle Hits Hole and Kills Two") suggest danger and violence. This is a paradoxical take: on the one hand, mass culture provides models for the construction of "deviant"—i.e., ideologically unmanageable—identities; on the other, the images appropriated and the process of appropriation itself contain a violence and negativity that recur throughout the film and explode in the Nazi imagery, death, and violence of its final sequences.

Totalitarianism and Mass Culture   The images of Nazism and sadism at the end of *Scorpio Rising* have proved particularly opaque to interpretation. At one level, *Scorpio Rising* suggests the closeness of homosexuality (of a sadomasochistic kind) and Nazism. The association had some historical grounding in the sexual scandals surrounding some high officials in the Nazi party, and was further supported by Nazism's misogyny and emphasis on male fellowship. The link between homosexuality and fascism was reinforced in psychoanalytic quarters by Wilhelm Reich's popular *The Mass Psychology of Fascism.* Although later discredited, Reich's theories influenced to a certain extent such sophisticated explorations of fascism in film as Pier Paolo Pasolini's *Saló* (1975), Luchino Visconti's *La caduta degli dei* (1969), and Bernardo Bertolucci's *Il Conformista* (1970).

The Nazi imagery in the film assimilates the bikers to Nazi troopers on the basis of their violence and gang-like structure. Sociological explorations of youth culture in previous decades have often turned to this comparison. Robert

Lindner, whose influential study of juvenile delinquency, *Rebel without a Cause* (1944), became an obligatory point of reference in subsequent discussions of the topic, regarded criminal youth gangs (with their rigid hierarchies, leader-worship, and lust for violence) as embryonic fascist units. In view of the young outlaws' nihilistic and mutinous behavior, Lindner speculated that should they find a leader, the result might be fascism.[33] Two years after the publication of Lindner's book, the National Delinquency Prevention Society also echoed the concern that totalitarianism might infect the American outlaw youth.[34] The association of fascism and delinquency obeys the logic of postwar paranoia, which translated internal differences (those presented, for example, by gays, communists, and young outlaws) into threats to national boundaries. Hence the domestic problem of youth delinquency was transposed into one of borders and invasion—the threat of America falling prey to alien totalitarianism.

The presence of Nazi imagery and fascist icons in *Scorpio Rising* can be best explained as the film's commentary on mass culture.[35] From this perspective, the film relates the adoration of media and religious icons to the violence of fascism. Its overall trajectory depicts the slippage from the witty appropriation of mass cultural identities (the tough pose and leather gear of Brando on the TV screen) to the final outbursts of Nazi and sadomasochistic violence, which seem to be the result of the bikers' adoption of identities and styles disseminated by the media.

The connection between totalitarianism and kitsch is a recurrent trope in modernist left critiques of commercial culture. As I showed in chapter 1, both Clement Greenberg and Dwight Macdonald condemned kitsch for being a symptom of cultural poverty and a hollowing out of the critical and intellectual faculties which might eventually lead to totalitarianism. In the mid-1950s, Dr. Frederic Wertham based *The Seduction of the Innocent,* his well-known indictment of comic books, on the assumption that mass culture had the power to condition readers and consumers in an absolutist manner, outstripping the influence that schools, family, and other social institutions had over them.

The critique of mass culture as totalitarian force received its most influential and sophisticated formulation in the work of two members of the Frankfurt School: Max Horkheimer and Theodor Adorno. Conceived and written in the United States while in exile from Nazi Germany, Horkheimer and Adorno's *The Dialectic of Enlightenment* was a rigorous attempt to understand fascism within a streak of enslavement and domination intrinsic to the Enlightenment project. Fascism was thus, in their view, a latent condition of enlightened rationality (or in Adorno's terms, its dialectical negative), one that emerged most destructively in the Third Reich, but that could be spotted as well in triumphant moments of Western European Enlightenment. In different chapters of their book, Horkheimer and Adorno traced the undercurrent of Enlightenment-as-domination in the transition from mythic thought to reason, in the establishment of the proto-bourgeois notion of the individual in the myth of Odysseus, in the simultaneous emergence of Kant's enlightened ethics and de Sade's equally enlightened anti-ethics, in the ideology of antisemitism, and in the characteristics and social effects of the culture industry. In Adorno and Horkheimer's well-known formula, the culture industry was "enlightenment as mass deception"; it was based on the application of purposive rationality to the production of a totalitarian notion of culture devoid of real depth and complexity, integrated in the commodity market, and endowed with its own industrial infrastructure.[36]

The industrialization of culture results in three levels of totalitarianism. The first one is product standardization: ". . . culture now impresses the same stamp on everything. Films, radio and magazines make up a system which is uniform as a whole and in every part" (120). Variations of and departures from the norm are not manifestations of creativity and autonomy, Horkheimer and Adorno argue, but commercial gimmicks intended to perpetuate the cycle of buying and selling. Second, the very apparati of culture, that is, the mass media, turn communication into a one-way activity: "The sound film . . . leaves no room for imagination or reflection on the part of the audience, who is unable to respond within the structure of the film . . ." (126). Likewise, "[t]he inherent tendency of radio is to make the speaker's word, the false commandment, absolute" (159). Radio and film interpellate listeners, colonizing their own intimate spaces and precluding any opportunity to respond to the media messages. By analogy, the pervasiveness of television and pop culture icons in *Scorpio Rising* illustrates the oppressive ubiquity of mass cultural forms. Lastly, the culture industry exacerbates the commodity character of art products. Hence, for Horkheimer and Adorno, what is new about the culture industry is not so much its being a commodity, but its deliberate admission of this status (157). While in earlier historical times artists and creators resisted commodification by encoding into the work of art the contradictions between art's exchange value and its purposelessness, in late capitalism every feature of the art product works to facilitate exchange. And exchangeability entails a leveling of hierarchies between images and symbols, whose ability to circulate as commodities eclipses any other intrinsic qualities.

Scorpio Rising's mixture of high and low idols (of historical and mass culture figures) exemplifies the general equivalence and the flattening out of all images enthroned by the culture industry. By juxtaposing images of Hitler and Jesus with popular icons like Brando, Dean, Gary Cooper as the sheriff in *High Noon,* Bela Lugosi as Dracula, and several comic book characters, the film establishes an analogy between media myths and greater historical and religious myths. For example, the segment "He's a Rebel," crosscuts between Scorpio and a religious film on the life of Jesus, while the song's lyrics ("By the way he walks down the street . . .") bind together the two "rebels." The editing of the scene cleverly applies Eisenstein's conflict of directions (both Scorpio and Jesus seem to be walking toward each other) to evoke a western-like showdown and to suggest, tongue in cheek, similarities between the two characters. The conflation of high and low icons in the film is made even more total because the high myths are incarnated in kitsch images (think, for example, of the image of Jesus reproduced in plastic statues, day-glo stickers, plaster busts, low-budget films, and Sunday school posters), which become in this manner as inauthentic and shallow as their mass media counterparts.

Throughout *The Dialectic of Enlightenment,* Horkheimer and Adorno highlight the continuity between the standardizing and de-individualizing work of the culture industry and Nazism. What Nazism does forcefully, the culture industry brings about by coaxing and solicitously recommending, yet the deep structure of domination is the same in both cases. In the context of a discussion on the power of advertisement, Horkheimer and Adorno state: "One day, the edict of production, the actual advertisement (whose actuality is at present concealed by the pretense of a choice) can turn into the open command of the Führer" (160). Fascism is thus the most extreme version of the culture industry and of the society it shapes—it is this society's outer limit and underlying structure.

In Adorno and Horkheimer's analysis, the totalitarian thrust of the culture industry works to eliminate authentic experience and autonomous individuality. In the same way that it colonizes the living space of consumers, the culture industry colonizes their minds, enthroning a false interiority whose points of reference, emotions, and ideas originate in media images. "The most intimate reactions of human beings have been so thoroughly reified that the idea of anything specific to themselves now persists only as an utterly abstract notion" (167). Individuality then becomes a reproduction of received clichés. In Anger's film, the images of the bikers copying each other's and their heroes' dress would seem to bear out Horkheimer and Adorno's critique: ". . . the popularity of the hero comes partly from a secret satisfaction that the effort to achieve individuation has at least been replaced by the effort to imitate, which is admittedly more breathless" (155-56).

In a way, the culture industry's social conditioning prepares the masses of consumers for a totalitarian society, training them to respond in unison and to erase their own individuality. ("Fascism hopes to use the training the culture industry has given these recipients of gifts in order to organize them into its own forced battalions" (161)). The Nazi rally, where the masses are uniformed, lined up, and fully organized, literalizes the standardization imposed by the culture industry. Analogously, the stills of Nazi rallies in the last sections of *Scorpio Rising* are foreshadowed by the bikers' imitation of media images, as their mimicry contains the seeds of fascist uniformity.

The sadomasochism of the last sequences in the film can also be understood as an exacerbation of the violence involved in the adoption of borrowed identities, a violence that emanates from the retranslation and reformulation of subjectivity and experience in terms that are disconnected from community and autonomous thought, based instead on the oppressive flatness and one-dimensionality of the commodified images.[37] Such self-addressed violence is essentially masochistic, and defines for Horkheimer and Adorno the relations between consumers and mass culture.

> The attitude of the individual to the racket, business, profession, or party, before or after admission, the Führer's gesticulations before the masses, or the suitor's before his sweetheart, assume specifically masochistic traits. The attitude into which everybody is forced in order to give repeated proof of their moral suitability for this society reminds one of the boys who, during tribal initiation, go round in circle with a stereotyped smile on their faces while the priest strikes them. (160)

The sadomasochism of the last sequences of *Scorpio Rising* results from projecting introjected masochistic structures onto relations with others.[38] The "Torture" segment (the part of the Halloween party in which the "pledge" is manhandled in a prankish manner and doused with mustard) is a turning point in this respect: it follows Scorpio's ritual dressing in imitation of Brando and Dean and precedes the outright sadistic rituals of the (so-called, by Anger) "Rebel Rouser" scene. The goofy horseplay of "Torture" becomes increasingly sinister in subsequent song segments, which intercut shots of Scorpio desecrating a church with pictures of Hitler, footage of a Nazi rally, Nazi flags and swastikas, and references to sadomasochism—which include, in quick succession, close-ups of metal-studded boots, welts on a bare back, pictures of a suffering Jesus, and almost subliminal shots of the desecrator urinating into his helmet and offering it to someone off screen, in a combination of S&M routine and mockery of the eucharist.

After the sadism of the "Rebel Rouser" segment, masochism and self-immolation are the subject matter of the last section of the film, which features bikers riding at night through a city, scored to the Surfaris' "Wipeout" punctuated by the sound of roaring engines and screeching tires. The cyclists' antics become progressively more dangerous until one of them loses control of the machine and crashes. In these images, the sadism of the previous sequences appears introjected by the group and leads to self-annihilation in the final climactic shattering of man and machine. As an outcome of the erotic tensions built up through contemplation of the bikers' bodies and of ritualized violence, the crash almost has the character of sexual release. These last scenes also desublimate the violence that remained latent throughout the film, yet ready to burst to the surface. Ominous lines in such songs as "Fools Rush In," "My Boyfriend's Back," "You're the Devil in Disguise," and "Torture," together with the skulls that recur throughout the movie, spell a vague menace that takes concrete shape first in the gang's Nazism and sadism, and subsequently, in masochism and self-destruction. The shifts from the masochistic imitation of television images, to the sadistic desecration, and then to final self-annihilation suggest that sadism and masochism are inextricably entangled in the subject's relations with the culture industry and its products.

The Popular Economy   The foregoing reading makes *Scorpio Rising* into a visual counterpart of modernist critiques of kitsch. However, this reading does not resolve the ambiguity of the film, which also depicts mass culture as a site of dispute in which meanings are not fixed or imposed by media producers. While the culture industry's apparati may have totalitarian structure and intent, the texts they disseminate can be inflected and modified by specific audiences.

The use of pop love songs in the film exemplifies the mobility of popular meanings. While many of these songs are interpreted by male singers, and their implied address-ees are women, they are edited to eroticized male images, a juxtaposition that contradicts the heterosexual romance of their lyrics. The opening sequence, cut to Ricky Nelson's version of "Fools Rush In," ends with a forward tracking shot on a muscular male chest encased in a leather jacket, while the singer blares "open your heart my love and let this fool rush in." Similar contrasts between sound and image track are the source of much of the humor in the film. Recall, for example, the well-known sequence edited to Bobby Vinton's "Blue Velvet," in which the velvet of the song transmutes into the blue denim and black leather of the images, while "she" becomes a series of tough-looking motorcyclists putting on their studded leather jackets, belts, chains, shades, and insignia. The section cut to Elvis's "(You're a) Devil in Disguise" can be analyzed along the same lines. Given Elvis's heart-throb status, the referent of such lines as "You look like an angel, you talk like an angel, you walk like an angel . . . but I got wise. You're the devil in disguise . . ." is presumably a woman; however, the image track shows a boy who may be an angel only as a member of the notorious motorcycle club. In the shift, the erotic appeal distilled by the male vocalist is redi-rected to the leather boy. These examples typify the sorts of adjustments that male gay listeners may perform in order to anchor popular culture texts in their circumstances. Hence, rather than standardize listeners' reactions, the songs provide consumers with a chance to produce their own meanings, pleasures, and identities. In the case of *Scorpio Rising,* these pleasures emanate from ascribing gay significations to mainstream songs.

The production of gay subcultural pleasure and meaning then regulates the film's interpretations of popular texts. Through quotation and allusion, the film pulls a host of cultural icons into its own circle of homosexual desire. The insertion of images from *The Wild One,* for example, highlights the underlying homoeroticism of the almost all-male outlaw group in Laslo Benedek's film and Marlon Brando's pin-up appeal. Similarly, Anger underlines Dean's gay interest by placing his image within the regime of homoerotic looks and male display that characterizes the first half of the film. Anger's interpretation made visible the gay community's reception of Dean, whose screen persona as a sensitive, tortured outsider embodied some aspects of the subculture's self-image. In addition, Dean's performance in Nicholas Ray's *Rebel without a Cause,* in which he befriended Plato, arguably a gay character with Alan Ladd pin-ups in his high school locker, must have had enormous resonance with gay audiences.[39] (Perhaps Plato's character was a deliberate attempt to thematize an already palpable gay following garnered by Dean's performance in *East of Eden.*) Finally, rumors about Dean's homosexuality—rumors with which gay audiences of the time may have been familiar—might have furthered his eligibility as gay icon.[40] The brief inserts of comic book panels in the film are also charged with homoerotic connotations that might have remained invisible in a different context. Such is the case with the Li'l Abner cartoon showing two boys with their arms about each other under the title "The Sons Also

Rise" (suggesting, in Ed Lowry's view, "the boys' arousal to erection");[41] or a panel of "Dondi" in which the eponymous character invites a handsome older man to see his room.

Such strategies of appropriation and contextualization illustrate a frequently unmapped force in mass culture: consumer agency. Popular agency operates on patterns of textual reception that both corroborate and modify the fetish structure of listening (and by extension, of popular culture consumption) theorized by Theodor Adorno.[42] As Adorno argued, popular listening is fetishistic—it operates as a transaction between songs and audiences which involves reified, mechanical, frozen musical phrases and lines, as well as contents and meanings that go beyond the merely aesthetic. They have to do with the social value of the cultural products—prestige, personal satisfaction, sense of belonging to the exclusive community of fans and connoisseurs, and so on. Adorno decried these surpluses in musical reception because they detracted from the autonomous character of the art work, and such autonomy was for him the only sphere of resistance to capitalist reification and control. These excrescences (or fetishes, in his terminology) introduced the work of art into the circuit of utility, exchange, and reification; they also occluded the structure (or non-structure, as the case might be) of the artistic whole.

But while Adorno's rejection of the fetishistic instrumentalization of cultural objects might be valid when applied to classical music—the original object of his critique—it cannot be unproblematically transferred to popular culture consumption, as he tried to do in the last part of his "The Fetish Character of Music" and in his writings on jazz. Contrary to Adorno's ideas, the circulation of popular texts is not based on autonomous contemplation but on a social contract based on utility, and utility requires the fetishization of listening (or viewing, or reading)—the reduction of songs and images to tokens for the exchange of (in John Fiske's words) "meanings, pleasures, and social identities."[43] *Scorpio Rising* fetishizes the popular texts it incorporates by subjecting them to a gay reading, but such fetishism does not entail a reduction of their meanings; on the contrary, it multiplies the chances of subordinate groups (the gay community, in this particular case) to express and promote their own pleasures and interests.

Scorpio Rising represents a highly articulate use of what cultural theorist John Fiske has called "the popular economy." A basic tenet of this economy is productivity: the "open" character of texts, which can be filled in, finished off by specific audiences in different contexts and for a variety of purposes. In the volatile economics of popular reception, significations are not stable or definitive; they are a function of the contexts in which they are integrated or of the purposes with which they are decoded. Popular texts act thus as catalysts for meanings and pleasures that audiences actualize according to their needs and desires.[44] In this sense, mass culture can provide an open terrain of contestation and resistance, where meanings are floating and relative, closed only in provisional ways by specific acts of reception. A great part of the exhilaration and wit of Anger's film comes precisely from this mobility of meaning, which allows for the inflection of popular artifacts with gay significations.

Scorpio Rising is therefore a complex, contradictory text: on the one hand it joins in a modernist condemnation of mass culture reminiscent of Clement Greenberg, Dwight Macdonald, Max Horkheimer and Theodor Adorno; on the other, it celebrates popular forms in ways that are characteristic of the subcultural, militant gay postmodernism we examined in the previous chapter. While the film's overall movement reduces popular consumption to uniformity, violence, and death, singular acts of appropriation along the way point to the openness and political potential of popular texts. Such ambivalence toward pop culture extends also to the marginal identities and desires engendered in the act of short-circuiting mass cultural myths and icons; the glamour that characterizes outsider style and stance is at the same time problematized by the violence and negativity attendant on both.

After-Effects

Scorpio Rising's oscillation between the enjoyment of opposition and wariness at its possible failure is a function of its historical context. Poised between oppositional marginality and doom, subcultural and dissident communities of the time shared an analogous ambiguity. The bleakness of the film may have seemed unduly pessimistic in the "explosion of joy" (Tom Wolfe's words) of the early 1960s. However, by the end of the decade, which saw the escalation of the war in Vietnam, student revolts across the country, the violent radicalization of some sectors of the counterculture, and the equally violent right-wing responses to liberal movements (manifested, among other events, in the assassination of leaders like Martin Luther King and Robert Kennedy), the overall trajectory of the film may have seemed an accurate metaphor for the fate of 1960s dissent and rebellion. At that time, *Scorpio Rising*'s transition from the affirmative expression of alienation to violent destruction resonated through many quarters of the counterculture and emerged in a handful of texts that expressed the exhaustion and paranoia of 1960s revolt.

Countercultural paranoia surfaced in such late 1960s commercial films as *Easy Rider*, *The Wild Bunch*, and *Bonnie* and Clyde, and in independent productions such as *El Topo,* a midnight hit of the time. All of these films sympathetically depicted the adventures of a group of outsiders and outlaws who end up being destroyed by repressive social forces. *Easy Rider* and *Bonnie and Clyde* are two cases in point. They signaled the breakthrough into mainstream filmmaking of young actors, directors, and sensibilities close to the counterculture. Both films depict the outlaws' aggressive marginality, estrangement from "straight" society, and subcultural values—associated with the drug world in *Easy Rider* and with crime in *Bonnie and Clyde*—in stories which culminated in their heroes' demise. They were self-conscious genre films which often commented on and revised the traditions they were reworking. *Bonnie and Clyde,* for example, quoted a number of visual motifs drawn from such art films as *Breathless, Citizen Kane,* and *Battleship Potemkin,* and, more important to my argument, from popular ones like *Golddiggers of 1933,* and the gangster genre. In turn, *Easy Rider* was less obviously allusive than *Bonnie and Clyde,* yet it also revised many motifs of popular genres like the Western (not the least of these revisions was reversing the direction of the journey from West to East) and incorporated several avant-garde techniques—the editing, for example, was reminiscent of Gregory Markopoulos and the rock and roll score harked back to *Scorpio Rising.* These quotations pointed to the fact that, as was the case with Anger's film, their sources were already existing narratives and icons. Their attitude toward their popular sources was analogous to *Scorpio Rising*'s: they partook of zest for rebellion encoded in mythologies and images from the media and popular culture, and of the paranoia that viewed destruction as the endpoint of difference and marginality. In this respect, these films were simultaneously an homage and an elegy to popular myths.

In more marginal cultural milieus, *Scorpio Rising*'s view of mass culture as a source of violence and manipulation was also echoed in the late 1960s and early 1970s in leftist ideology, more attuned to modernist suspicion than to the early 1960s paeans to the new sensibility. The mistrust characteristic of left media criticism was exemplified by (ex-leader of Students for a Democratic Society) Todd Gitlin's *The Whole World Is Watching,* and it underlay such political films of the time as Jon Jost's *Speaking Directly,* Robert Kramer's *Ice,* the Newsreel units' alternative media coverage, and Emile de Antonio's documentaries such as *Milhouse* and *In the Year of the Pig.* Across the Atlantic, an analogous animosity toward the established media and pop culture subtended post-May '68 film culture in England and France, spearheaded by Jean-Louis Comolli and Jean Narboni's programmatic "Cinema/Ideology/Criticism," which proposed ideological critique as the way to engage and disarm commercial cinema's complicit pleasures. This critical thrust found its cinematic expression in Chris Marker's documentaries and in the projects of Jean-Luc Godard and Jean-Pierre Gorin's *Dziga Vertov* group.

And yet, in a manner befitting its own contradictions, *Scorpio Rising* also foreshadowed less hostile engagements with mass culture on the part of subcultural, marginal, and/or oppositional groups. Its witty plunderings and outrageous readings of commercial culture texts were echoed in punk and in other style wars of the 1970s.[45] In addition, *Scorpio*'s aggressive style foreshadowed contemporary forms of gay street culture, especially the leather, metal studs, butch posing, and other outer signs of radical gay difference deployed by 1970s clones and by such 1980s collectives as ACT UP and Queer Nation. Anger's influence also surfaces in the recent films and videos of such gay and lesbian artists as John Greyson's *Moscow Does Not Believe in Queers* (1986), *The Acquired Dread of Sex Syndrome* (1987)—an ironic remake of Luchino Visconti's *Death in Venice* in music video format—and *The Pink Pimpernel* (1990); John Goss's *Stiff Sheets* (1988) and *Out-Takes* (1989); Paul Wong's *Confused* (1986); Richard Fung's *Looking for My Penis* (1989); Bruce La Bruce's *No Skin Off My Ass* (1990); Julie Zando's *I Like Girls for Friends* (1987) and *The Bus Stops Here* (1990); Sadie Benning's *Jollies,* (1990); Tom Rubnitz's *Wigstock,* (1987), *Made for TV* (1984), and *Drag Queen Marathon* (1988); and Marlon Riggs's *Tongues Untied* (1989) and *Affirmations* (1989), the latter in music video format. These artists recycle popular images and narratives, imbuing them with subcultural significations. Like Anger's film, their texts freely mix original and borrowed footage and are stylistically heterogeneous, combining storytelling, direct cinema, interviews, mock advertisements, and music video formats. These videos and films partake of both activism and experimental culture. Although they have been screened in museums and galleries, many were originally produced for alternative television stations, such as Toronto's Deep Dish TV or the New York-based Paper Tiger TV, and have been regular fare at gay and lesbian film festivals across the country. These video works focus most often on explorations of gay politics and identities and AIDS-related issues. Their communal vocation is evident in their inventive engagement with commercial culture artifacts, an engagement which blurs politics and play, encoding and decoding, mainstream and marginal, while injecting gay significations into widely disseminated popular texts.

Hence, although Anger has tended to diffuse the gay connotations of *Scorpio Rising*,[46] this text has been an important influence on the cinema and cultural forms that emanated from the post-Stonewall politicization of the gay community. While remaining torn between the positive and negative connotations of the popular forms it assimilates, Anger's main film depicts a gay situationism of sorts, a deviation [*détournement*] or perversion (in both its etymological and sexual meanings) of popular objects that engenders a murmur of dissent. In this sense, its lessons are still used today in many quarters of the community, particularly in forms that try to meld politics with the affirmation of gay subcultural pleasures and identities—both of them perversely retrieved from the mass cultural forms which most often make them invisible.

Drag, Rubble, and "Secret Flix":
Jack Smith's Avant-Garde
against the Lucky Landlord Empire

Five

The set was a huge arrangement of, I have no other word for it, human wreckage: cans, bottles, containers, bits and parts of things. . . . [A] sign, half covered by junk and litter, said **FREE GIFTS**, another said **EXOTIC FRUITS**, . . . still another sign, half buried in the garbage, said **BETTER LIVING**.

—Jonas Mekas[1]

Paradoxically, Jack Smith's influential presence in the New York underground rests on his rarely seen film, *Flaming Creatures*. Shot intermittently during five weeks in the summer of 1962 on top of the now demolished Windsor Theater and put together later that year, the film was shown privately during the early months of 1963 at parties and informal gatherings of Smith's friends and acquaintances, where it garnered its initial following. Jonas Mekas first saw it on one such occasion in late February of 1963, and praised it in his "Movie Journal" column: "Jack Smith just finished a great movie, . . . and it is so beautiful that I feel ashamed to sit through the current Hollywood and European movies. . . . [The film] will not be shown theatrically because our social-moral-etc. guides are sick. This movie will be called pornographic, degenerate, homosexual, trite, disgusting, etc. It is all that and it is so much more than that."[2]

Mekas rightly anticipated the scandal produced by *Flaming Creatures*. Shortly after his review appeared in print, two detectives from the district attorney's office seized the film, interrupting its run (only a few days long) at New York's Bowery Theater, where Mekas had been including it in his independent cinema programs. The law enforcers also confiscated a projector and arrested Ken Jacobs and Jonas Mekas, main organizers of the show. This action, written up in the *New York Times,* started a long line of legal maneuvers, court appearances, appeals, and counter-appeals, culminating in the ban of the film in the State of New York, and in its eventual investigation by a Senate commission.

In avant-garde circles, this repression prompted demonstrations and pronouncements against censorship, but confiscations and arrests continued wherever the film was shown. Such legal actions were due to Mekas's insistence on bringing the film to audiences, and perhaps also to the heightened publicity created by court battles and press reportage. Barely a week after the first arrests, Mekas was apprehended again, also on obscenity charges, this time for showing French writer Jean Genet's *Un Chant d'amour* at a benefit show for the "*Flaming Creatures* Defence Fund."

Throughout 1963–64, other showings of Smith's film in New York, Los Angeles, and Chicago were busted by the police. Campus screenings proved particularly explosive: when the local chief of police tried to confiscate the film at the University of Michigan at Ann Arbor, students blocked the door of the projection booth and later staged a sit-in in the station house; at Notre Dame, students were maced by police when protesting the interruption of a show. Such efforts were of course intended to make Smith's film invisible, but had the opposite effect. From this moment on, repression and scandal became trademarks of Jack Smith's celebrity as filmmaker and performance artist, and the keys to his important influence on New York's alternative and avant-garde subcultures. In other words, Smith's cult status and local fame rested on a paradox: his main film, *Flaming Creatures,* was virtually inaccessible, but the discourse surrounding it was visible everywhere.[3]

This chapter will show how *Flaming Creatures*'s signifying strategies and depictions of sexuality (which were the main grounds for prosecution) oscillate between visibility and invisibility, retrieval and loss, figuration and abstraction, and how these dialectics were the result of Smith's embattled social position as a gay avant-garde artist. Such binaries also define Smith's 1970s and 1980s career as a performance artist; although he gave up filmmaking after 1969, the themes and form of his performances were essentially the same as those of his earlier movies.

"A Sex Thing"

The prosecution of *Flaming Creatures* coincided with that of other underground movies. Kenneth Anger's *Scorpio Rising* (1963) had been charged with obscenity and tried by a court in Los Angeles on the basis of a few frames of an erect penis; Shirley Clarke's *The Connection* (1961) was banned for the naked portrayal of drug use and the repetition of the word "shit" (as slang for heroin); *Un Chant d'amour* (1951, shown for the first time in America in 1963), was also banned for the frontal nude shots of prison inmates. Other titles, such as Barbara Rubin's *Christmas on Earth* (1963) and, later on, Carolee Schneemann's *Fuses* (1967) were targets of occasional attacks by watch groups and authorities, but managed to stay clear of the courts. What was especially conflictive in all these films, with the exception of *The Connection,* was their (by official standards) scandalous attitude toward nudity and sexuality.

The ferocity shown toward Smith's magnum opus was unmatched by the attacks against any of these other titles, and was, at the same time, out of all proportion with *Flaming Creatures*'s depictions of sexuality, vastly outdone, for example, by the eloquent erections and penetrations of *Fuses* or the lengthy close-ups of female genitals in *Christmas on Earth.* By comparison, Smith's film was not particularly graphic, although one would not ascertain so from the description of the film recorded in the *Congressional Report* by the Senate committee investigating the film at the time:

> This home-made film has gained notorious reputation for its homosexual content. It [is] . . . studded with sexual symbolisms . . . a mass rape scene involving two females and many males, which lasts for seven minutes, showing the female pubic area, the male penis, males massaging the female vagina and breasts, cunnilingus, masturbation of the male organ, and other sexual symbolisms [!] . . . lesbian activity between two women . . . homosexual acts between a man dressed as a female, who emerges from a casket, and other males, including masturbation of the visible male

> organ . . . homosexuals dancing together and other discon-
> nected erotic activity, such as massaging the female breasts
> and group sexual activity.[4]

While the *Congressional Report* overdramatizes the film's sexual explicitness, it cannot be denied that sexuality figures prominently in *Flaming Creatures*. The film actually consists of a magnificent transvestite party, in which a woman, a number of men in luxuriant drag, and a few others in costume frolic, pose, dance, recline languorously, flirt, primp up, and display their outrageous selves in various states of undress in front of the camera. As the report notes, a central scene of the film portrays the "rape" of a beautiful dark woman by a horde of epicene characters— evidence, incidentally, that for all its gender-bending and unconventional sexualities, Smith's film is just as prone to aestheticizing violence toward women as more conventional movies.[5] In other shots, drag queens expose their genitals, a woman repeatedly bares a breast, and groups of men (some in drag) and women listlessly kiss and caress each other. The overall tone of the film, however, is not so much prurient as droll. The absurd close-ups of penises, testicles, and breasts; the overacted sensuousness of lipsticked mouths pouting and kissing; or the genteel mien of a few drag queens posing like grand dames, skittering about in summer dresses to the rhythm of a Far-Eastern tune—all of these images are suffused with a sort of pot-induced hilarity and parodic wit that undermines the seriousness usually required by pornography. The main effect of the film, an effect that haunts the senators' report, was the collapse of sexual distinctions as men in drag seemingly rape a woman, drag queens engage in acts of lesbianism, and all characters behave in blissful oblivion of traditional alignments of anatomy and gender roles. Such overall crisis of sexual categories may have been what made *Flaming Creatures,* in the eyes of judges and investigators, more pernicious than any other underground movie—after all, even in the very explicit *Fuses,* or in *Christmas on Earth,* sexual roles and identities remained clear throughout.

Since the nature of the attacks always determines the strategy of the defense, the film's proponents—notably, Jonas Mekas and Susan Sontag—tried to legitimate its sexuality by framing it within the discourse of high art. In a contemporaneous review on the Baudelairean cinema, of which Smith's films were paradigmatic examples, Mekas defended their unconventional sexualities in the following terms: "[These films] contain homosexual elements. The homosexuality, because of its existence outside the official moral conventions, has unleashed sensitivities and experiences which are at the bottom of much great poetry since the beginning of humanity."[6] As art, they lived in a realm above and beyond morality, normality, and law. Mekas reiterated his point in a *Film Culture* editorial on censorship: "Like *Un Chant d'amour, Flaming Creatures* is a work of art and like any work of art, it is above obscenity and pornography, or more correctly, above what the police understand as obscenity and pornography."[7] In what is perhaps the most famous review of the film, Susan Sontag celebrated *Flaming Creatures* as "a triumphant example of an aesthetic vision of the world." And further, "The space in which *Flaming Creatures* moves is not the space of moral ideas, which is where American critics have traditionally located art. What I am urging here is that there is not only moral space, by whose laws *Flaming Creatures* would indeed come off badly; there is also aesthetic space, the space of pleasure. Here Smith's film moves and has its being."[8]

Smith disagreed with the terms of these defenses. Although he remained silent during the heyday of the polemic, in interviews and performances throughout the late 1970s and 1980s he virulently criticized the attempt to accord his film the status of a besieged high art piece. "I started making a comedy about everything that I thought was funny. And it *was* funny. The first audiences were laughing from the beginning all the way through. But then *that writing* started—and it became a sex thing. . . . [And then] there was a dead silence at the auditorium."[9] In Smith's view, interpreting the film in terms of aestheticism and high seriousness, as both Sontag and Mekas did, froze the enjoyment of its early audiences. By contrast, the inarticulate laughter that Smith nostalgically evokes before the fall into seriousness, seems an open and spontaneous response. Smith thus implied that the main effect of his film was its ineffability. Whether because of its floating hilarity or because of its pervasive uncategorizable eroticism, the film resisted being neatly codified or conceptualized.

The film's uncertain setting and time frame add to its conceptual elusiveness. The capers of Smith's creatures take place in an undetermined but exoticized location that combines oriental and Spanish motifs. While the film was shot outdoors with available lighting, oriental vases in the painted backdrops and a Spanish-style wrought iron ceiling lamp connote an interior space, probably of a brothel—frequent setting of old "blue movies"—or a harem, if we follow Michael Moon's productive suggestion that the film can be read as a version of the Scheherezade Party.[10] The soundtrack also fails to provide any fixed clues as to either time or place, since it is a musical collage made up of Spanish tunes of the 1920s and 1930s (including several *pasodobles* and the popular "Amapola"), an Eastern song, and Caribbean rhythms (among them, Ernesto Lecuona's "Siboney").[11] The opening credits are accompanied by Max Steiner-like symphonic swellings and the closing by Gene Vincent's "Be-bop-a-loo-la (She's My Baby)." The moody, grainy black and white of the images, resulting from the sensitive, outdated film stock, and the vintage costumes of the performers connote old movie glamour from an indefinite past, contributing to the film's unspecified temporality.

The chaos of bodies and sexualities portrayed by Smith furthers the confusion promoted by unclear spatial and temporal coordinates. In the early sequences of the film, the camera pans over a true melee of bodies and limbs languidly tangled in what resembles postcoital repose. (Adams Sitney has mentioned that rather than an orgy, a term detractors often applied to these scenes, the film pictures its satiated aftermath.)[12] Out of this maze of anonymous anatomies, the camera selects assorted body fragments, which appear oddly juxtaposed in close-ups of a limp penis nesting coyly on a "creature's" shoulder, a grimacing face emerging from someone's armpit, and a tongue licking wriggling toes, to name a few examples. Such juxtapositions create a feeling of burlesque exaggeration, as in the sequence which shows several men—most of them in drag—applying lipstick, their mouths in extreme close-up, while in the soundtrack a mock radio commercial extols the virtues of a new heart-shaped no-smear cosmetic. At one point a moaning voice interrupts the voluble announcer: "How does a man get lipstick off his cock?" And the announcer, unflappable: "A man is not supposed to have lipstick on his cock." This last statement contradicts the crosscutting throughout the scene between vigorous lipsticking and recumbent penises, which implicitly aligns lipstick, penis, and mouth in roundabout evocations of fellatio. Almost

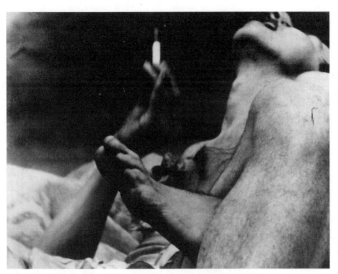

Flaming Creatures. "*Texts of Pleasure.* Pleasure in pieces; language in pieces; culture in pieces." Roland Barthes, *The Pleasure of the Text.* Courtesy of Anthology Film Archives.

miming the promiscuous proximity of its subjects to each other, the camera sometimes hovers so close to the bodies that one can see only fuzzy expanses, gentle slopes, and shady folds of flesh. Intercut with images of hands caressing penises and breasts, these scenes have the effect of indiscriminately eroticizing all body parts. Hence the sexuality that figures prominently in the film is not specifically genital, but polymorphous: not only genitals and breasts, but also feet, navels, beards, gaping mouths, knees, and shoulders are objects of the loving camera gaze and of prodigal caresses. At the same time, gender distinctions cease to obtain—in fact, the most frequently noted feature of Smith's creatures is the gender-blurring enacted by the graceful drag queens, some of whom occasionally lift their skirts to show their penises. As Susan Sontag remarked, in the context of

Flaming Creatures. **Courtesy of Anthology Film Archives.**

the film, a shaken breast and a shaken dick appear nearly equivalent and interchangeable as objects of desire.

Sexuality in *Flaming Creatures* is then an unformalizable element that censors tried to suppress and defenders sought to legitimate by appealing to aesthetic categories. But what sort of sexuality is this, whose mobility so angers the censors and escapes Mekas's legitimating interpretive frame? Male drag, men lying with men, and camp wit confirm Mekas's and the senators' notion that this was indeed a homosexual movie. If so, can we link this attribute to Smith's notion that his work was not a "sex thing" but a comedy? Is there a point at which gay sex, perhaps all sex, becomes a comedy, a form of wit akin to inarticulate laughter? And finally, if we read the film as a parody of sex, or rather, a representation of sex-as-parody, what are the consequences of this characterization for the film's sexual and cultural politics?

With its parodic wit and lightness, *Flaming Creatures* is strikingly different from the considerably gloomier depictions of gayness shown by American avant-garde films of the 1940s and 1950s. In a previous chapter, I took Kenneth Anger's *Fireworks* as the most representative title of an independent cinema subgenre: the proto-gay psychodrama, also cultivated by Gregory Markopoulos, Curtis Harrington, Willard Maas, and James Broughton, among others. In their movies, gayness was aligned to sincerity, subjective truth, and authenticity; the protagonists' homosexuality was the expression of a subjective inner essence repressed in everyday contexts, but released in liminal territories or situations (the countryside, cemeteries, abandoned houses, dreams, and journeys). In *Flaming Creatures,* by contrast, there is no subjective essence to be realized, no interiority where the self's truth lies dormant. Gender-blurring, polymorphous desire, and constant fetishistic substitutions present an unstable sort of sexuality, always *en fugue* through various bodies and body parts, and never incarnated in self-identical images. Moreover, while earlier depictions of gay subjectivity in experimental cinema tended to advance toward some sort of subjective closure, attained in the representation or the unleashing of formerly suppressed desires, Smith's film forbears such trajectory, emphasizing instead the recurrence of fragmentation and dissolution.

Hence, scenes that show whole bodies in long shot, dancing or posing, in full command of their space, are followed by others that portray a rape, an earthquake that turns the brothel-harem into debris, and a scene of vampirism by a Marilyn Monroe impersonator—all of which represent mutilation and fragmentation. Yet even when bodies appear as imaginary wholes, they remain, on another level, subject to symbolic fissures and internal divisions.

Flaming Creatures. **Courtesy of Anthology Film Archives.**

Drag, for example, posits a chasm between anatomy and gender identification; in addition, the floating eroticism that indiscriminately cathects all parts of male and female bodies evidences further discontinuities between gender, identity, and desire. From another perspective, the flaming creatures acquire their identity through mimesis of pre-existent images and icons, emerging from the already-seen, the already-read, the already-done. Their bodies are stages for the reenactment of alien roles. In a way, they are collages made up, like Frankenstein's body, of pre-existing fragments—quotes and images that most often emanate from the stock of Hollywood fantasies. Hence, the blonde figure who emerges from a white coffin after the last trembles of the earthquake have died down has often been referred to as a Marilyn Monroe impersonator, yet since she engages in several acts of vampirism, she also connotes a whole lineage of voracious Hollywood femmes fatales. The dark Spanish lady who appears in the last dancing scene of the movie is also caught in a similarly dense web of allusion: interpreted by Mario Montez, a Puerto Rican drag queen and one of Smith's and Warhol's favorite performers, Mario's name quickly brings to mind late 1940s Universal Pictures star María Montez, about whom Smith wrote several essays; at the same time, the *pasodobles* (bullfight music), the Spanish *mantilla* she wears, and the rose she holds in her mouth evoke at once Mérimée-Bizet's *Carmen* and Marlene Dietrich in Josef Von Sternberg's *The Devil Is a Woman.* Such plurality of allusion evidences that Smith's characters are multilayered constructs whose identities are assemblages of found images. And in connection with this conception of character, it is worth remembering here one of Smith's explanations for his fascination with stars: "[O]f all the things on earth, the most interesting one is that people are other people."[13]

Further examples of the instability of all bodily wholeness in Smith's oeuvre can be found in some passages of his writings, where even María Montez, most often celebrated as emblem of full presence and screen charisma, appears prey to disintegration and decay. Take for example, the opening of "The Memoirs of María Montez": "The dust settled. O finally! María Montez was propped up beside the pool which reflected her ravishing beauty. A chunk fell off her face showing the grey under her rouge."[14]

Because of its insistence on bodily fragmentation, gender instability, and polymorphous desire, Smith's film seems close to recent poststructuralist theories of same-sex desire and subjectivity. In opposition to expressive and essentialist models that propose the definition of a stable gay sexuality as a precondition for gay politics, poststructuralist theorists consider that political action does not necessarily demand the isolation of a discernible "essence" or core of identity.[15] For one thing, the discourse of essences and stable identities is tied to the power-knowledge effects which create, define, and represent the marginal with the purpose of controlling it, a strategy which Michel Foucault described with regard to madness and sexuality.[16] Lack of stability and transparency, on the other hand, hinder the social technologies of institutions which seek to make the marginal concrete with the purpose of better administering it, that is, locating it, knowing it, and subjugating it. Thus in order to avoid power's panoptic gaze, gay desire should emphasize its eccentric, undefinable, undeterminable traits, which plunge into crisis all efforts to define and control such desire "from above," as it were. In the words of Jonathan Dollimore, a recent theorist of gay subjectivity, "queerness" offers "the paradox of a marginality which is always interior to, or at least intimate with, the center," yet itself not fully centered, and because of this, of prime importance in the development of "new strategies and conceptions of resistance."[17]

In the formulation of another important writer, Judith Butler, it is not only gay subjectivity that is fundamentally eccentric and self-split; all subjectivities, desires, and gender constructs are "troublesome"—"performative" rather than "substantive," that is, "with no ontological status apart from the various acts which constitute their reality." Gay desire, not enthroned as mainstream or standard, foregrounds to a higher degree than naturalized heterosexuality the trouble and precariousness attendant on gender definition.[18] For Butler, the main act constitutive of subjectivity and gender identity is the introjection of fantasy images: "Fantasies condition and construct the specificity of the gendered subject. . . ." Subject and gender formation are therefore the product of psychic mimeses or adopted roles that orient and give shape to sexuality, understood as a formless repository of drives and energies. Yet equally important are other not-so-deep mimeses, which are inscribed on the surface of the body through the imitation of external appearances and styles: "If gender is constituted by identification and identification is invariably a fantasy within a fantasy, [the second fantasy being identity itself, subjectivity] a double figuration, then gender is precisely the fantasy enacted by and through the corporeal styles that constitute bodily significations."[19] Smith's film illustrates these conceptions of sexuality and gender identity. In the same way that the characters of *Flaming Creatures* are constituted by imitating or embodying other characters—since people are, according to Smith, other people—sexuality in the film appears as a copy of preexisting models, and for this reason, flouts all notions of primacy or naturalness. Drag represents in emblematic form the mimetic structures which give rise to gender and subjective formations, and in doing so, underscores that mimesis always entails a parodic recoding of seemingly natural gender roles and images. "In imitating gender, drag implicitly reveals the imitative structure of gender itself—as well as its contingency. . . . In the place of the law of heterosexual coherence, we see sex and gender denaturalized by means of a performance which avows their distinctness and dramatizes the cultural mechanism of their fabricated unity."[20]

From the perspective of Butler's theory, which considers sexuality a farce of borrowed identities, both Smith's conception of *Flaming Creatures* as a comedy and the abundance of drag queens in the film obey the desire to posit unstable images of gay sexuality. At the same time, the drag queens literalize the mimetic mechanism subtending all gender identification. This perspective on gay drag as sexual comedy allows us to sublate the opposition between those readings regarding the film as a homosexual movie—"a sex thing"—and Smith's own aspiration that it be taken as a comedy. As a homosexual movie, *Flaming Creatures* was indeed far from clearly nameable, and thus closer to the nonverbal response of laughter. It evoked the crisis of conceptualization that all sexuality entails—and that gay sexuality and male drag, not synonymous but juxtaposed realities in this particular film, trenchantly dramatize. Thus Smith's rejection of Mekas's narrow characterization of *Flaming Creatures* may have been motivated by Smith's view that the film's sexual identity was something of uncertain boundaries that resisted clearcut definition, while its cultural identity was similarly hybrid, cutting across high and popular art. Smith's non-essentialist conception of "gayness" distanced him as well, later on in his career, from Gay Liberation Front–influenced groups and from other forms of militancy informed by more literal conceptions of gay identity than his own.[21] Positing gay identity as a nonidentity, site of mimeses and confusions, is sypmtomatic of the alternation between presence and absence, concealment and unconcealment that structures Smith's work.

Rubble, Human Wreckage

In the same way that individual "characters" are affected by fragmentariness, intertextuality, and impending disintegration, so is the film itself, which Susan Sontag described as a "rich collage of camp lore" which strings together a series of motifs from old-fashioned mass culture: "pre-Raphaelite languidness; Art-Nouveau; the great exotica styles of the twenties, the Spanish and the Arab" and "the repertory of fantasy drawn from corny movies."[22] Accumulation of disparate fragments turns *Flaming Creatures* into an "uncertain body" on the verge of splitting into pieces. In fact, the seven tableaux that make up the film seem separate sequences with no overall pattern. Although one might ascertain in their present arrangement a loose narrative movement from "plenitude" (which, subject to the above mentioned qualifications, appears most evident in the opening poses and makeup sessions), to destruction (in the rape, earthquake, and vampirism scenes), to regeneration (in the upbeat dances at the end), their sequence is, for the most part, arbitrary and mutable; the different plot events do not grow "organically" from each other, as it were, but seem accidentally juxtaposed and give the impression that they could be watched in almost any order.

Smith's fascination with fragments and with provisional, aleatory texts became more and more pronounced in his subsequent work, to the extent that the two films he made after *Flaming Creatures*, (that is, the extremely elusive *Normal Love*, also titled *Secret of Orchid Lagoon* and *The Great Pasty Triumph*, shot between 1963 and 1964; and *No More President*, or *In the Grip of the Lobster*, assembled in 1966) were conceived as image banks rather than as stable texts with fixed boundaries. Smith would thus constantly alter the number and order of their sequences, the music to be played with them, and even their titles, so that no two screenings were ever alike. Exhibition required the presence of the filmmaker, who would often decide on the spot how his fragments would cohere, or how they would be performed.

Due to increasing difficulties in making films, Jack Smith wound up, from the early 1970s on, focusing almost exclusively on performance art. His performances were desultory, freaked-out cabaret acts made up of his own delirious fictional pieces, readings from star biographies, improvisations, autobiographical evocations, lyrical interludes, and abusive diatribes aimed mostly at Jonas Mekas. They mobilized a variety of media, including mime, dance, song, photography, music, and film. Like his mid- and late-1960s films, Smith's performances assembled preexisting pieces under different titles, so that a particular fragment (sketch, mime, or section from a star biography) would often be recycled in different programs and writings. For example, the play *Rehearsal for the Destruction of Atlantis,* a paranoid fantasy of totalitarian control and narcotics use after the style of William Burroughs, premiered at the Filmmakers' Cinematheque on November 7th and 8th, 1965, with a cast that included many participants from the Theater of the Ridiculous (such as John Vaccaro and Joel Marksman) and Warhol's Factory. The script was published in the spring 1966 issue of *Film Culture.* Excerpts of the play would later crop up in various programs, and, in its latest metamorphosis, the whole piece was included, with several other sketches, in a show titled *Lobotomy in Lobsterland,* eventually printed in fictionalized form in a small volume of Smith's writings called *Historical Treasures.*[23] After 1976, the incorporation of slides into performances responded to Smith's desire to create completely open texts; slides allowed for maximal mobility, since he could easily alter their sequence, stringing them through loosely scripted or half-improvised narratives that would metamorphose with each presentation.[24]

Smith thus evolved toward conceiving his works as provisional constructs susceptible of constant reformulation— as processes rather than products. Smith's famous fall-out with Jonas Mekas over *Flaming Creatures* in the late 1970s may have originated in their two divergent conceptions of the text. Mekas understood the movie as a definite whole with an unchangable form; but Smith saw it as an image reservoir to be reshuffled ad infinitum. The actual cause of the fall-out was Smith's desire to retrieve a master copy of his film, owned by Anthology Film Archives, so he could extract, cut up, and reassemble sequences for his performances. Worried about the work's integrity, Mekas refused to comply, claiming Smith was at the time too unstable and might damage the film irreparably.[25]

The fragmentation Smith's work progressively introjected is literalized in his texts through recurring images of rubble, debris, and wreckage. *Flaming Creatures* itself was assembled from what we could figuratively call the scrapheap of mass culture. Actual debris drowns the screen and the revelers halfway through the film, when an earthquake interrupts the rape scene, reducing the setting to shambles. The fascination with ruins already figures in Smith's first movie, *Scotch Tape* (1959), which shows a number of fantastically clad performers doing an extremely slow paced dance among what seems the rubble and twisted steel girders of a demolished building. A few years later, one of Smith's first works for the stage was a "nightclub act," in collaboration with Ken Jacobs, significantly called *The Human Wreckage Review.*[26] Nearly contemporary with this work, *Blonde Cobra* (1963), an aborted collaboration between Smith and Bob Fleischner assembled by Ken Jacobs, takes place in a dark, dingy apartment crammed with useless junk. In this case, not only the setting but the whole movie conveys the overall impression of debris: off-center, poorly lit, and even blank takes seem retrieved from the cutting-room floor; at the same time, mismatches between image and sound track suggest the movie's imminent crumbling away.[27] While the gay overtones of the film, already discussed in a previous chapter, are mostly the result of Smith's text and performance, its trashed-out quality owes much to Ken Jacobs. As evidenced by his early movies *Star Spangled to Death* (1961), *Baudelairean Capers* (1963), and *The Winter Footage* (1965–66), Jacobs shared with Smith an interest in outdated cultural material and literal urban detritus. Part of this devotion to discarded items was Jacobs's occasional use of found footage in his films and even of found footage *as* his films: *Blonde Cobra* was in a way an *objet trouvé,* as was *Perfect Movie,* a reel of TV news footage picked up from a junk bin and shown as found. As Smith continued in his later work his exploration of urban ruins and junk, Jacobs evolved in the late 1960s into structuralist cinema (*Tom, Tom, the Piper's Son*) and multimedia performance.

Like his and Jacobs's 1960s films, Smith's 1970s and 1980s performances used junk and urban debris as decor. Stephan Brecht's reviews, gathered in *Queer Theater,* scrupulously chronicle some of Smith's 1970s shows, and are therefore a rich source of information on the concepts and actual look of the artist's ephemeral work.[28] In his notice of the show *Withdrawal of Orchid Lagoon* (1970), Brecht described the performing area as "a junk heap—metallic and plastic street refuse measuring in the inches and feet . . ." (12). A January 1971 program titled *Claptailism of Palmola Christmas Spectacle* also featured "A center stage filled with junk . . . plastic fish, signs, bottles" (14). And a later piece dating from 1977, *Monty Carlo in The Secret of Rented Island*—a peculiar version of Henrik Ibsen's *Ghosts* in which most of the characters were embodied by stuffed animals and dolls, with Smith playing all the voices—similarly exhibited junk compositions: "The scene on the table and behind the curtain is a terrible mess, indefinitely out of a horror movie—the carton, the leg, black and silver things, the basket and its contents, unidentifiable objects hanging down obscurely from the lamp that Eva has on too much of the time . . ." (173). Occasionally, the junk montages became so overwhelming that, more than mere backdrops to a show, they could almost be regarded as the show itself. Such was the case, for example, with Smith's projected version of *Hamlet,* which was never actually performed, for which he constructed an ornate set in the basement of his apartment building during late 1974 and early 1975. In this case, the locale itself was partially in ruin, so the debris brought in as decor merged with the environment; in Brecht's words: "[The basement] is long and narrow, its walls, scattered scabby irruptions creeping down them, peeling in the most opulent manner imaginable, brittle slats sticking through the soft plaster here and there. . . . The junk has been set up in that inner part of the cellar against the rear wall" (18).

Smith named the project of (anti-)aesthetically redeeming the debris of everyday life the "moldy aesthetic." "I like moldy things because they are imperfect and ugly, and this is very rich material to work with, especially the artifacts of the recent past. I am an antiquarian anyway."[29] The moldy encompassed the old-fashioned, ornamental mass culture material homaged in *Flaming Creatures* as well as the tawdry junk that he used as background in films and performances. These were the quickly churned out, quickly dated products of a culture of consumption and planned obsolescence, and in them Smith saw a potential reservoir of transformative and utopian affects, which seemed exiled from up-to-date products. As he put it in a celebrated statement: "In the middle of the city should be a repository of objects that people don't want any more, which they would take to this giant junkyard. That would form an organization . . . a way that the city would be organized around that. I think that this center of unused objects and unwanted objects would become a center of intellectual activity. Things would grow up around it."[30]

Smith's use of rubble and debris was contemporaneous with the environments and assemblages that such New York-based artists as Claes Oldenburg, Jim Dine, Alan Kaprow, and Robert Rauschenberg had put up in downtown New York alternative exhibition spaces in the late 1950s and early 1960s. These works used as raw materials junk, debris, and even beach-stranded objects randomly collected from the streets and shores of New York City. There are notable differences between Smith's and these artists' use of debris, however. The latter emphasized abstract textures, so that individual fragments and pieces of junk were often thickly painted or plastered over, subordinated to an overall plastic design within which their individuality disappeared. In this way, they attempted to translate into three-dimensional space and concrete everyday material the pictorial concepts of abstract expressionist painting. Smith's constructions, on the other hand, were less abstract; in them, individual junk objects were still recognizable and concrete. In addition, while the cited environment-builders framed their work by reference to recent artistic traditions, Smith's moldy aesthetic was suffused with subcultural significations and camp. The latter was blatant in his taste for kitschy ornamentalism and emotive figurativeness, which contrasted with the more abstract, formalist austerity of Oldenburg, Dine, Kaprow, and others; in fact, Smith's junk assemblages imitated orientalist motifs and baroque Catholic altars, attempting to recreate with indigent materials the intense affects of Yvonne de Carlo's and María Montez's late 1940s technicolor epics and of Latino religious kitsch.

The moldy aesthetic also had a gay inflection. In outdated kitsch, appearances, styles, and gender roles seemed thoroughly artificial, deprived of any overtones of naturalness and normality, and therefore susceptible of being reinvested and revaluated by artists and audiences whose own gender identifications and desires were frequently labeled unnatural and abnormal. Displaced and marginal desires thus found correlative images in materials that had dropped out of the mainstream.

Escaping Lucky Landlord Paradise

In addition to its subcultural context, the recycling of dated kitsch and urban refuse can be projected against its historical and cultural backgrounds: the celebration of "the new," monumentally incarnated by the 1964 New York World's Fair, and, on the other hand, downtown gentrification and the institutionalization of the avant-garde—two developments that gathered momentum after the late 1960s and that Smith linked under the name of "landlordism."

Smith's landscapes of ruins evoke synecdochically the decaying downtown as a devalued territory of boarded-up buildings, junk heaps, shattered sidewalks, and outdated store signs. His insistence on this set of themes contrasts with the waves of suburbanization that led the middle classes to relocate from crowded, aging downtown areas to the orderly suburbs. Such a search for a new environment can in turn be read in relation to the emblematic celebration of the new enacted by the 1964 New York World's Fair. In keeping with the tradition of previous fairs, the 1964 New York World's Fair was a spectacular celebration of commerce and technological development. It occurred at one of the peaks in the expansion of United States–led multinational capitalism, which was propelled by international trade agreements and facilitated by the overdevelopment of communication technologies. At the fair, capital's spread was mapped on to another myth of expansion, the conquest of the "new frontier"—as the Kennedy administration had christened the recently launched space program. Hence the theme of the event was the space age: buildings boasted futurist shapes and designs, and the layout of the enclave was an imaginary map of the cosmos with a "Square of the Planets," a "Fountain of the Universe," and numerous avenues, boulevards, and drives named after galaxies, comets, constellations, and satellites. Celeste Olalquiaga has pointed out that in the wake of the fair, space age aesthetics became a rave, manifested in the temporary reign of hard-edge stylization in furniture; flown, airy shapes in architecture; TV series like *Star Trek* and *Lost in Space* (both of which were optimistic portrayals of a commandable, knowable universe); and shiny fabrics, platform shoes, and technologically inspired accessories in fashion.[31] Against this enthusiasm for futurist styles, Smith's fascination with urban rubble and "moldy," old-fashioned popular imagery could signify a resistance to multinational capital expansion and particularly to its aesthetic limnings. This interpretation seems more likely when one considers that discrepancies between the underground and the World's Fair were not merely aesthetic; with this event and the simultaneous visit of Pope Paul VI, New York authorities undertook a "clean-up" of the city whose effect on avant-garde milieus was the seizure of independent films, the interruption of shows and screenings deemed immoral, arrests of artists, and temporary closedowns of alternative artistic and cultural spaces.

Ironically enough, while the junky, moldy material of Smith's 1960s work stood as a counter-image against suburbanization and the rave for the new, the montages of debris of the late 1970s and 1980s functioned against a certain revaluation of the old that characterized a contemporary mode of urban renewal—gentrification. Hence while Smith's imagery remained largely the same, its insertion in diverse cultural contexts entailed differences in its inflection and meaning. A new trend in consumption, gentrification was based on the revaluation of the historical and cultural connotations of old city areas. According to urban geographer Sharon Zukin, gentrification marketed "values of place"—of locality, of tradition-woven social space—and channeled them into a market-regulated, status-laden landscape of power. To an extent, artists had been to blame for this. The well-advertised antics of local Soho artists throughout the mid and late 1960s, as well as the existence of a lively alternative gallery and performance scene, recreated the image of the neighborhood from working-class, industrial district into a piquant bohemian enclave. This led small-scale developers to refurbish lofts, old tenements, and warehouse spaces in the area, converting them into high-rent apartments for middle-to-high-income occupants with a taste for grungy chic. As a result, the neighborhood was eventually turned into an expensive enclave which the original dwellers could not afford. As in most cases, the gentrification of Soho imposed homogenization as it replaced the class- and ethnically diverse life of the area with more uniform versions of city and community.[32] Gentrification also contributed to replacing a former marginal, noncommercial art life that thrived around alternative exhibition spaces and highly experimental productions (such as the ones developed throughout the 1960s by the avant-garde collective Fluxus) with a more regimented, profit-oriented art market, represented, for example, by the galleries that, since the late 1970s, line West Broadway and adjacent streets. (We will note in passing that this process was often aided by some formerly marginal artists who, acting as curators, gallery owners, or even real estate investors, were now quick to cash in on the market values that, perhaps inadvertently, they had helped to forge.)

Living in Soho since the late 1950s, when zoning laws banned residence in most of the district, Smith suffered the gentrification of the area, which he named "landlordism." Unable to keep up with the constant raises in rent caused by renewal, he was repeatedly evicted in the 1970s, eventually moving from Soho to the cheaper Lower East Side. Stephan Brecht reported on this period of Smith's life as follows: "Jack talks about landlordism. He thinks rent is magic, doesn't understand it—the fact that you have to keep paying: you are paying for time itself, for your very life. Landlordism in his view is the origin of all the current crimes and troubles."[33]

Social and cultural homogenization had a visual counterpart: "[Architects and builders] cling to rectangles because it's the preferred shape of capitalism," stated Jack Smith, implying that a uniform, controllable geometry was capital's main means of penetration through urban tissues.[34] Thus rectangles evoked for him gridlike street layouts, historical harbingers of authoritarian, capital-propelled urban reform from Baron de Haussmann's Paris to the postwar boom of American suburbia—whose local version of Haussmann was real estate baron Robert Moses, incidentally the developer of the 1964 World's Fair grounds and amenities. In this context, the heterogeneity and crazy geometries of rubble and junk assemblages operated as forms of resistance against the smooth uniformity of gentrified urban spaces.

Soho's gentrification provided Smith with a simile for what he saw as the institutionalization of the avant-garde from the late 1960s onward. Emblematic of this development was the refusal on the part of influential film critic, filmmaker, avant-garde programmer, and archivist Jonas Mekas to let Smith repossess *Flaming Creatures,* the film which, in the latter's view, had made an underground cult hit, but from which Smith himself had reaped no benefit whatsoever. While blocking the filmmaker's access to his own product, Mekas (always according to Smith's rather unfair version) had capitalized famously on this and other *succès de scandale,* and these successes had allowed him to rally enough sponsorship to create Anthology Film Archives. These actions turned Mekas into a landlord-profiteer of the avant-garde. In accordance with this characterization, Mekas was the target of colorful abuse in Smith's programs, where he appeared as Uncle Fishook, the Lucky Landlord, or Uncle Pawnshop; in turn, the underground was "the rented world," "rented island," "lucky landlord paradise," "lucky landlord empire," and less salubriously, "rotten lagoon," "rented lagoon," or "the baby poo poo of art." The titles of some performances and never-realized film projects polemically express the artist's view of his position in relation to Mekas's version of the underground: *Sinbad in the Rented World, I Was a Mekas Collaborator, The Horror of Uncle Fishhook's Safe, or Jungle Jack Radio Adventure,* and, to add just another, *I Was a Male Yvonne de Carlo for the Lucky Landlord Underground.* From the last come these lines, which Smith himself enunciated in the first person in the performance: "My dancing and my youth and beauty were exploited by

Uncle Pawnshop to squeeze icing of artcrust over a can of worms of film death of Rented Lagoon. . . . I was manipulated by Uncle Co-Op to run out into the sand dunes when baby filmmakers were parading through the desert of beauty."[35] Smith's notion of "landlordism" was thus a versatile metaphor; close to the Marxian concept of alienation, it designated his lack of control over his own products and the profit they generated, and further connoted powerlessness over how his own works were circulated and even over his own domestic space.

An artist-scavenger of the "rented world," Smith tried to forge two main tactics of escape from the colonization of his productions by capital and landlords: one consisted in stressing the contingency and provisionality of his work while withdrawing it, at the same time, from the usual circuits of cultural exchange; the other, in avoiding the conceptual reification that accompanies capital-mediated cultural production.

In Smith's career, fragmentation, heterogeneity, the recycling of aesthetically disreputable material, and dedication to performance (an extremely fugitive type of production) appear as strategies to hinder commercialization, since as commodities cultural artifacts must have a certain stability so they can be circulated through the market, hung in museums, and be consumed by audiences. Instability was most evident in the shifting boundaries and frequent changes in the length, contents, and titles of Smith's pieces, in the mixture of rehearsal and actual performance, in the fading into and out of his stage spectacles (whose beginnings and ends seemed quite unmotivated and arbitrary), or in the interruption of the action to correct other actors or to discuss with stage assistants the placement of a prop or a light. Performances unfolded in an atmosphere of permanent crisis,

as Smith often forgot his lines, disoriented the other performers with improvisations and contradictory directions,
misplaced the papers from which he read his parts—which
caused much fumbling and rummaging until they were dug
up from under some prop—or lost his place in the text as he
read. As he accentuated these features, his performances
became more and more about the impossibility to stage or
say anything, to the point of dramatizing their own failure,
their own coming undone.

Symptomatically, as the avant-garde film world was
gradually institutionalized (in Anthology Film Archives, for
example) and even made profitable from the late 1960s
onward, Smith burrowed deeper and deeper underground.
While the *Village Voice* often announced some of his shows
cost-free—and most likely without the artist's knowledge or
permission—his programs were, as a rule, poorly advertised, usually in alternative papers with a small readership.
On one occasion, he incongruously advertised one of his
productions in the religious ads of the *Village Voice*—perhaps in an attempt to recruit an unusual cross-section of the
audience or self-consciously alluding to his own cult status.
According to Carel Rowe, desire for anonymity led Smith to
warn Mekas against writing up his shows.[36] The locales that
housed his work were out-of-the-way venues around Soho,
the East Village, Tribeca, or even Smith's own apartment.
The extraordinary length of performances and the frequent
delays in getting them started purported, in J. Hoberman's
words, to "distill audiences to an appreciative core," and
were thus one more means, in addition to the ones already
mentioned, to discourage wide acceptance and to avoid en-
tering the cultural market as a commodity.

The desire to place his work outside the circuits of cultural commerce and to make his pieces fragmentary and

unformalizable was also evident in Smith's resistance to definition or formalization—in sum, to reification.[37] In a way, Mekas's conceptualization of Smith's work as high art and his (perfectly justifiable) desire to maintain the integrity of Smith's films can be seen as a means of instrumentalizing and reifying them with the purpose of facilitating their circulation and possession. The ulterior purpose of both these maneuvers was, in Smith's own reading, exclusively economic. By contrast, Smith's paeans to visual phenomena and his rejection of critics stemmed from the desire to defeat cultural landlordism—not only at the level of money-mediated exchange, but also at the level of the systems of conceptualization required by it.

This attitude informed the rejection of all cultural categories applied to his work, particularly of what he saw as the "crusty" conception of the avant-garde and alternative culture that congealed in the late 1960s around archives, museums, and galleries. It also subtended Smith's defense of visual phenomena that bypass logic or language, a defense articulated in one of his most widely quoted statements: "Film critics are writers and they are hostile and uneasy in the presence of a visual phenomenon." The quote comes from the essay "The Perfect Film Appositeness of María Montez," published in *Film Culture* months before *Flaming Creatures*'s polemical premiere, and appears in the context of a cultist evocation of the faded glamour queen of Universal Pictures exotics.[38] Part of a movie culture that, as he put it, "is all gone with the war years," Montez belongs in the moldy mound of dead commodities: "Universal probably demolished the permanent Montezland sets. Vera West committed suicide in her black mail swimming pool. Montez dead in her bathtub from too much reducing salts. The colors are faded. Reel Art Co. sold all their flix to T.V."

María Montez is a privileged incarnation of the ineffable, uncommunicable, excessive aspects of the film image—of what Ronald Tavel called, in a similar context, the "million emanations of the graphic in the world."[39] Hence, according to Smith, "[Montez's] appeal was on a purely intuitive level. She was the bane of critics—that person whose effect cannot be known by words, described with words, flouts words (her *image* spoke)."

As an unformalizable figure, María Montez was the bearer of a *secret,* part of a group of films and cult figures that Smith regarded in the following terms:

> The whole gaudy array of *secret flix,* any flic we enjoyed: Judy Canova flix (I don't even remember the names), *I Walked With a Zombie, White Zombie, Hollywood Hotel,* all Montez flix, most Dorothy Lamour sarong flix, a gem called *Night Monster, Cat, and the Canary, The Pirate,* Maureen O'Hara Spanish Galleon flix (all Spanish Galleon flix anyway), all Busby Berkeley flix, *Flower Thief,* all musicals that had production numbers, especially Rio de Janeiro pro. nos., all Marx Bros. flix. Each reader will add to the list.

These films' secrecy may reside in their being rallying points for a very small number of fans. At the same time, their secrecy leads back to the realm of undefinable sexualities.

The "secret flix" were also "guilty flix," allied to "guilty pleasures"—"Who would ever admit to having enjoyed a Judy Canova flic?" Smith wonders—and thus evoke the heady mixture of guilt, enjoyment, clandestinity, and duplicity characteristic of a gay institution, "the closet." This particular movie closet is in turn wrapped up in difficulties of definition and expression, as it stands at the crossings of private fantasies and collectively consumed—hence public—texts, of self and other, interior and exterior, authentic subjective expression and ersatz culture, marginality (so long as appropriated by a fringe collective) and mainstream (commercially produced for widespread circulation).[40] As figurative closet props, objects of pleasures that resist formalization, the secret flix bring up once more the terms used earlier to discuss the sexuality of the flaming creatures. If the latter's sexualities circled around unknowable, uncategorizable desires which posed a challenge to censors and controlling institutions, the "secret flix" analogously resisted clear-cut categories. Smith thus suggests that the unformalizable affect attached to the "secret flix" is akin to the fragmentary, decentered, "secret" sexualities of his flaming creatures, and to the disintegrating, desultory form of his performances. Through these sustained analogies and tropes of dissolution, Smith's oeuvre puts forward the notion that only an avant-garde that would prop itself on the "secret" and the ineffable, that refused, in sum, to be located and defined, could avoid reification, or what is the same, being prey to lucky landlords.

Success

Smith's brand of avant-gardism, then, favored marginality and disappearance. In his world, drag, unnameable sexualities, fragmentary bodies, rubble, and junk coexist as means to defeat the stable boundaries demanded by commercial exchange and capital colonization. To them, he opposed the unformalizable and invisible, the negative dialectic moment—the undoing that defied language and could only be experienced as uncodified affect. In this respect, Jack Smith was the photographic negative of his contemporary, Andy Warhol, initially a devoted fan of Smith,[41] whose work addressed the same sort of encroachment of capital on social and cultural life. However, while

Smith went deeper and deeper underground in an attempt to defeat commodification, Warhol fashioned himself into a media celebrity whose work operated, as we will see in the next chapter, in accordance with the semiotics of money-mediated exchange.

Smith's avant-garde idea failed,[42] but that is precisely where it succeeded. Had it become popular and institutionalized, it would have failed, it would have turned—to indulge for a moment in Smith's hyperbolical, alliterative style of abuse—into a crusty, pasty triumph, into rotten refuse for lucky landlords. However, in one more paradoxical twist, because he spectacularly succeeded in failing (that is, in making himself invisible, uncodifiable) he has been variously reified, despite himself, as a myth of alternative culture, as the last garret artist south of Houston street, as the "original" queer performer and activist, predecessor of the stark figurations of otherness furnished by Radical Drag and Queer Nation. To avoid falling into the contradiction of defining an oeuvre which saw its oppositional value in escaping definition, my own analysis has tried to (un)frame Smith in relation to qualities like the secret and the negative, incarnated in the unformalizable textures of rubble and debris, in the visual appositeness of faded glamour, in the ineffable affects of dated mass-culture junk, in the vertigo of sexual identities opened in drag. This has been, in sum, an attempt to map the slidings and analogies that characterize Smith's work, to trace the various ways in which his non-essentialist sexual politics, his fascination with modern ruins, and his critique of capital-mediated, reified culture interacted in the production of . . . "free gifts, exotic fruits, better living."

The Artist as Advertiser: Stardom, Style, and Commodification in Andy Warhol's Underground Films

Six

Duchamp, Warhol, and the Economics of Art Value

From his emergence as a pop artist in 1962, with a show at Eleanor Ward's Stable Gallery, to his death in 1987, Warhol's art has been taken as a symptom of the penetration of the imagery of consumer culture into the avant-garde. There seems to be close to universal agreement on this. Critics with widely divergent ideological agendas—including formalists such as Clement Greenberg or Hilton Kramer; materialists such as Fredric Jameson, Rainer Crone, David James, Jean Baudrillard, Andrew Ross, and Benjamin H. D. Buchloch; and semioticians such as Umberto Eco and Roland Barthes—have concurred on the fact (while disagreeing on its interpretation) that Warhol's art muddled the codes that distinguished autonomous critical art from mass culture.[3] The paintings of Campbell's soup cans, Coca-Cola bottles, Brillo boxes, Marilyns, and Elvises seemed the culmination of the avant-garde's long-standing fascination with mass culture, a fascination that has been traced in an earlier chapter to the very origin of the two artistic cultures, and that had one of its most influential expressions in French artist Marcel Duchamp's ready-mades—i.e., the mass-produced objects he had been signing and placing in galleries and museums since the mid-1910s. Appropriately, dadaism was a constant point of reference in early discussions of pop art, initially called neo-dada, and Duchamp's name was often invoked as Warhol's most direct predecessor. Furthermore, Warhol's emergence as a leading pop artist was probably fostered by the rediscovery of dadaism and of Duchamp in particular, who had two important retrospectives of his work in the United States at the time—at the Pasadena Museum of Art in 1962 and at New York's Museum of Modern Art in 1963.

The juxtaposition of Duchamp's artifacts—such as "Richard Mutt's Fountain" and "L.H.O.O.Q." (the détourné Mona Lisa)—with Warhol's suggested not only similarities but also notable differences between the two artists' approaches to mass culture. Duchamp's recontextualizations of banal, anonymously manufactured objects in gallery spaces had shown that, placed in the right frame, any mass-produced object could be regarded as art. According to this notion, art turned out to be a relative value, a language game, a function of frame and context. Consequently, Duchamp raised the conceptual (or in his own phrase, "non-retinal") aspects of the art work to the level of importance occupied by formal aspects. For his part, Warhol confirmed Duchamp's demystifying strategies, but his own plunder of mass cultural forms had a somewhat different bias. Through shrill, bright colors and billboard imagery, he stressed that art was fundamentally a commodity—merchandise subject to the same publicity strategies and market fluctuations as the soup cans, soap boxes, and movie stars. Moreover, if relocating a soap box into a gallery was an artistic procedure, as Warhol seemed to suggest, perhaps the "art" in the procedure stemmed neither from the materials transposed nor from the spaces connected in the transaction (the supermarket and the gallery, the store window and the museum), but from the process of translation itself. The basic structural procedure in art was therefore translating or recoding—that is, a semiotic transfer which emptied objects of their "originary" or received meaning and reinscribed over them a new set of significations.[4]

This semiotic mimed perfectly the recodings that capital operated on the object world. Capital turned goods into commodities in the market, subject to a price that is their meaning. In his classic dissection of the commodity form, Marx explained this transformation as the process whereby exchange value, artificially determined by market laws of demand and supply, supersedes "natural" use value.[5] In light of this formulation, could not one say that art had been involved in a similar set of transpositions, at least since

Duchamp's ready-mades? Yet while Duchamp had explained his experiments as language games, Warhol defined artistic production as a transcoding structurally equivalent to, and actually interchangeable with, the one performed by capital. "I wanted to be an Art Businessman or Business Artist because making money is art and working is art, and good business is the best art."[6] If art is a means of recoding, so is business, which breaks up the life-world into fragments that it then reframes, packages, revalues, and circulates as commodities. Hence business is analogous with art. Through this syllogism, Warhol declared that the fusion of art and life, millennial aspiration of much radical art and politics, was already accomplished by capital. If social and cultural life in late capitalism were under the sway of the market and if all recesses of experience, including fantasy, dreams, and sexuality, were, thanks to the postwar overdevelopment of the culture industry, mediated as commodities, then *everything* was avant-garde already, that is, everything was transposed, transcoded, and revalued—whether as an art work or as a market product did not matter. After all, the differences between the two in Warhol's (and our own?) world were negligible.

Consequent with this proviso, Warhol projected his avant-gardism into traditionally non-artistic venues and became, besides a painter and sculptor, a rock promoter, a film producer, an advertiser, a magazine owner, a starmaker, and a stargazer. He can be regarded as a non-militant version of what Walter Benjamin called a "producer": a cultural worker who acts not only on artistic content but also on the cultural means of production.[7] Yet while Benjamin envisioned for his "author-as-producer" a role in radical politics, Warhol's intervention in the cultural apparati was that of an entrepreneur: a discoverer, popularizer, and packager of images, sensibilities, fashions, and personalities; he was, in sum, an artist-as-advertiser.[8]

The slippage between art and business shows with admirable coherence (and just as admirable dividends) in his career. As is well known, Warhol started off as a commercial illustrator, became after 1961 a museum and gallery artist and experimental filmmaker, and continued (after a hiatus marked by Valery Solanas's murder attempt and the Factory's relocation from its original address on East 47th Street to more "professional" quarters on Union Square West) as an increasingly commercial artist, film producer, society portraitist, socialite, and owner of *Interview* magazine. This schematic account neatly demarcates Warhol's 1960s avant-gardism from his 1970s and 1980s commercialism.[9] And although this narrative oversimplifies the multiple turns and contradictions within each phase of his career, it nonetheless remains operative even among the most sophisticated of Warhol's critics. To name just two examples, Thierry de Duve distinguishes between Warhol's "great art" of the 1960s and his gimmicky, frivolous social and artistic persona of the 1970s and 1980s: ". . . *career* is truly a bad word, suggesting that the fame that the artist sought and attained also explains and justifies the great artist he was, at least between 1961 and 1968."[10] For his part, Thomas Crow restricts the avant-garde Warhol to 1963 and 1964, the years of the Jackies, Marilyns, and the death and disaster series, which offer a "disabused, pessimistic vision of American life," and implicitly dismisses the rest of his production as commercial, repetitious, and accommodating.[11] It is hard to resist the closure of such a myth, which turns Warhol into a Charles Foster Kane of the avant-garde—a rags-to-riches sellout whose ambition caused his artistic downfall.[12] However, this plot conceals the existence of a factor that binds together the most disparate facets of Warhol's work, from the early commercial illustrations, through the underground movies and pop art, to the concept behind *Interview,* namely, the exploration of the semiotic homology of art and business that I have sketched above.

The Thesis

My purpose in this chapter is to study Warhol's underground films in light of such homology. I am calling "underground" the films he made from late 1963, the year of his debut as a director with *Kiss,* to 1968, the year of *Flesh,* a title which marks his transition to more commercial methods of production. Following the success of *Kiss* and *Sleep* in underground circuits, he launched into an intensive production schedule that yielded a film a week, or according to other testimonies, one every two weeks, until about 1967. Then, the adoption of more sophisticated techniques and equipment and the need to devote more time and energies to distribution and promotion slowed down his frantic pace. Warhol's proclamation, in 1965, that he was abandoning painting for movies makes his underground films especially significant to his overall artistic trajectory; indeed they can be regarded as a privileged arena for exploring the concepts he had so far developed simultaneously in both media.[13]

Warhol's film production seems to recapitulate the aforementioned break in his career between avant-gardism and commercial production. The underground movies, with their bad lighting and sound, their spartan formal qualities (static frame, little or no editing, bare mise-en-scène), their amateurish "acting," and their protracted presentation of unplotted, banal action are particularly impervious to popular pleasure. In this respect, they contrast sharply with Warhol's 1970s consumer products, *Frankenstein, Dracula,* or *Heat,*[14] with enterprises such as *Interview,* and even with his best-known pop imagery, produced contemporaneously with the underground films. And yet, typecasting the underground productions as anti-pleasure and non-commercial poses a discontinuity between them and his pop canvases, and overlooks the artist's suggestion that the shift from paintings to movies was just a change of media, not necessarily of artistic credos or aesthetics. More importantly, such a characterization does not help explain Warhol's interest in stars and stardom, manifest in his creation of superstars, his fashioning of the Factory after a Hollywood studio— a newspaper of the time called him "the L. B. Mayer of the underground"—and in pronouncements such as "Vacant, vacuous Hollywood was all I ever wanted to mold my life into."[15] Even allowing for large doses of cynicism and irony, these statements, together with his parodies of Hollywood, show an ambiguous fascination with the pleasures of commercial cinema and with stardom, celebrities, and fame.[16] My purpose in this chapter will be to explain this fascination in terms of Warhol's equation of art and commodification.

I will maintain that exploring stardom and celebrity status is the main thrust of Warhol's films, and that this interest parallels the equation of art with business that is at the center of his pop art. In this respect, stars are a charged and particularly important preoccupation. They are peculiar incarnations of the commodity form: unlike most other consumer goods, stars offer no concrete, tangible substance to be exchanged; they are representations multiplied and disseminated throughout the media. Lacking concrete substance or instrumentality, their use value is mostly replaced by an overwhelming inflation of exchange value and of its attendant ideologies. Furthermore, in two respects stardom demonstrates the extension of commodification even to the most intimate, personal realms: all aspects of the star personality—from clothing, hair styles, and makeup, to biographical details, tastes, and fantasies—are grist to the commodity's mill, and can be sold as part of the star product; meanwhile, from the audience's point of view, stars catalyze social and libidinal projections and identifications, therefore evidencing the passage of commodities into the fantasy life of social subjects. These traits of star consumption signal the main lines for the ambivalent exploration of the topic that Warhol carried out through his movies and his Factory superstars. Such exploration operated in constant dialogue with the contemporary discourses of fashion and advertisement. At the same time, Warhol's films bring up opacities and unpleasures that resist the dynamics of commodification and exchange. These resistances, however, cannot be understood outside the equation of art and business that Warhol's most commercial productions celebrate; on the contrary, I will try to show that they are the inevitable excesses emanating from such an equation.

Warhol and the Underground

The commercial interests subtending Warhol's films, together with his artistic persona, were initially at odds with the romantic ideologies of the underground. The underground film community fashioned itself as a bohemian group characterized by its unswerving dedication to marginal film production. Jonas Mekas often praised such devotion in such figures as Jack Smith, Stan Brakhage, Harry Smith, and Kenneth Anger, all of whom were close to the idealized image of the romantic artist, striving on their own with little or no financial support to materialize their artistic visions. Warhol was a different social type. He flaunted his bohemian look and his downtown cool as a sort of borrowed cosmetic facade: "I picked up some style from [painter] Wynn [Chamberlain], who was the first to go in for the S and M leather look."[17] His status as one of the best-paid advertisement illustrators in New York set him apart in an artistic medium that avowedly resisted commercialism. As gallery artist turned filmmaker, Warhol appeared close to such underground figures as Robert Frank, Bruce Conner, or Carmen D'Avino; however, the quick success of his pop art and the ambiguity of his imagery—was it critical or celebratory of consumer society?—corroborated the reservations some felt toward him. On a different level, his conceptualism and disregard for subjectivity were further grounds for mistrust in a milieu that favored subjective expression and self-involvement. It is hence not surprising that when Jonas Mekas first mentioned Warhol in his *Village Voice* column, on December 5, 1963, he mused "Anti-filmmakers are taking over. . . . Is Andy Warhol making movies or is he playing a joke on us?"[18] Ronald Tavel, avant-garde playwright and scriptwriter-in-residence at the Factory in 1964 and 1965, described as follows the misgivings of other independent filmmakers toward Warhol: "So I knew all these people with Ron Rice . . . and those are a whole community of underground filmmakers to which, in a sense, Warhol was a Johnny-Come-Lately because . . . he would have entered at almost the last phase of its heyday." Tavel continued that veteran independent filmmakers often resented Warhol because he was exploiting marginal subject matters—such as bohemianism, gay drag, camp, the drug subculture—which they had been the first to explore in their movies.[19]

Perhaps such mistrust, allied with some sense of rivalry, prevented the likes of Jack Smith and Kenneth Anger from regarding Warhol as a fellow practitioner of the "outsider" aesthetic Mekas called "Baudelairean cinema." Instead, it was Mekas himself who legitimated Warhol as an underground filmmaker, and, in doing so, explained him, in terms close to Mekas's own aesthetic, as recorder and redeemer of the everyday.

Warhol's films are eminently devoted to real-time recordings of his performers doing such banal tasks as applying makeup, making coffee, talking on the phone, gossiping, having casual sex, drinking, arguing, kissing, sleeping, and eating. Capturing ordinary, everyday occurrences that seemed too small for Hollywood pictures was a central interest of the underground, an interest that Mekas most consistently articulated in his criticism and films. In Mekas's view, no subject matter seemed so small or unimportant that it could not be transformed by the mediation of film. He once wrote, ". . . whatever happens in man is beautiful if you know how to look at it." This attitude reflected an important impulse in 1960s radicalism, an attitude that historian Stanley Aronowitz described as "The attempt to infuse life with a secular spiritual and moral content, to fill the quotidian with personal meaning and purpose."[20] Mekas's commitment to such ideals is patent in his diary films, which make up most of his production and which he regarded as channels to redeem the everyday by discovering in it, through the technological mediation of the camera, epiphanies and moments of truth and lyricism. Mekas's aesthetic echoes in this respect French critic André Bazin's advocacy of a cinema of "faith in reality." The parallels between both writers are numerous: they shared a religious outlook and saw the phenomenal world as a bearer of transcendence; at the same time, their religious ideology was influenced by the post-World War II vogue of existentialism and socially committed art—a cultural climate responsible, for example, for the critical success of Italian neorealism in Europe and America, and for the enormous impact of Jean-Paul Sartre's *What Is Literature?* Both men were inclined to modify the leftist politics of the neorealists and Sartre with a vague sort of pantheism, arguing for a pure cinema of immediacy and authenticity. These ideas inform Mekas's criticism, in which he praised such filmmakers as Joseph Cornell, Stan Brakhage, Jerome Hill, and Marie Menken, all of whom were devoted to the aesthetic transformation of actuality through recording. "[Joseph Cornell] makes these little, insignificant movies. And ah, and how much love there is in Cornell's movies! Love for people, for flowers, for the summer girls, for the little tree leaning in the dark corner without sun, for the birds in the sad park trees."[21] And in a review on Jerome Hill's *Open the Door:* "Some of the most beautiful movie poetry could be revealed, someday, in the 8mm home-movie footage—simple poetry, with children in the grass and babies on mothers' hands, and with all that embarrassment and goofing around in front of the camera."[22]

Mekas understood Warhol as a further step in this tradition. Hence when *Film Culture*'s Sixth Independent Film Award was given to Warhol in 1964 for his contribution to the independent American cinema—an award that confirmed his status in the underground film community—Mekas introduced him with the following words: "With his artist's intuition as his only guide, [Warhol] records almost obsessively man's daily activities, the things he sees around him. A strange thing occurs. The world becomes transposed, intensified, electrified."[23] Elsewhere, in his "Notes after Reseeing the Movies of Andy Warhol," Jonas Mekas brought Stan Brakhage to his aid in this judgment by re-counting how, on first exposure to Warhol's early films, Brakhage had disparaged them, only to retract his verdict after rescreening them at 16 frames per second instead of at standard sound speed. Mekas reports: "Suddenly, he [Brak-hage] said, when viewed at 16 frames per second, an en-tirely new vison of the world stood clear before his eyes. Here was an artist, he said, who was taking a completely opposite aesthetic direction from his, and was achieving as great and clear a transformation of reality, as drastic and total a new way of seeing reality as he, Stan, did in his own work."[24]

To an extent, Warhol's filmmaking also had as its purpose exploring and transcending the given through the camera's mediation. And yet Warhol's recordings did not yield lyrical epiphanies and elegiac memories (as did Mekas's films) nor visionary illuminations (as did Brakhage's own). While Brak-hage and Mekas's ways of redeeming the everyday were closer to the ideology of American transcendentalism and to a Romantic "natural supernaturalism," Warhol's own way took as its main points of reference the notion of stardom and the discourses of fashion and advertisement. Ultimately, both purveyed the conceptual underpinnings for Warhol's exploration of two different (yet analogous) modes of medi-ation: art and money.

Stars and Superstars

Warhol's difference from the Mekas-Brakhage sector of the underground seems to me most clearly embodied in the issue that *Film Culture* devoted to his film work in the summer of 1967. The issue was edited by Gerard Malanga, Warhol's Factory assistant and star of some of his early movies. George Maciunas, gallery owner and prominent member of the New York avant-garde collective Fluxus, designed the cover—a montage of anonymous faces evoking Warhol's serial portraits. Despite being "his" issue, Warhol is hardly present at all—a significant omission in light of the underground's tendency to inscribe the director's subjectivity as ultimate cause of his or her work. There is a single picture of him, masked and turning away from the camera, as a performer in a movie by Piero Heliczer, and his name crops up in reviews of his recent movies *Chelsea Girls, Hedy,* and *Kitchen.* Otherwise, the issue belongs largely to the superstars, with articles on Edie Sedgwick, the late Fredie Herko, and Ondine, and interviews with Jack Smith and Mario Montez; the tone of these writings oscillates between gossipy chitchat and lyrical evocations of star charisma. The issue is profusely illustrated with film stills, pictures of Factory stars, and with occasional allusions to classical Hollywood glamour—as in several photos of Greta Garbo. It is printed on paper of several colors, and the type set and titles are much more ornate and playful than the sober design of the magazine's regular issues. The Warhol issue clearly tried to imitate the look and tone of a fan magazine. The differences between this issue and a previous one devoted to a compilation of Brakhage's writings, subsequently published as *Metaphors on Vision,* suggests, I believe, the gap between Warhol and the more transcendent sector of the underground. Brakhage's issue is printed on dark sepia paper and sparsely illustrated with abstract stills from his films. It includes numerous pages of scratched, heavily edited typescript and facsimiles of handwritten notes and sketches. Overall, the issue breathes seriousness and emphasizes Brakhage's subjective inscription in his work, an attitude that appears the photographic negative of Warhol's self-erasure and seemingly frivolous plunge into Hollywood glitz.[25]

Another episode pointing to Warhol's fascination with stars took place in the summer of 1965, when Mekas offered him several nights at the Filmmakers' Cinematheque to screen his movies. Warhol immediately suggested a retrospective of his star of the moment, Edie Sedgwick, implying that he conceived his productions as star vehicles rather than as subjective expressions of his sensibility. Due to disagreements between filmmaker and star, the retrospective never took place, and Warhol instead put on several performances of his multimedia show, "Andy Warhol's Up-Tight," later called "The Exploding Plastic Inevitable." The spectacle was Warhol's contribution to the mid-sixties vogue of "Expanded cinema" and multimedia events, triggered by the crossing of late 1950s happenings, Marshall McLuhan's theories, and psychedelic culture. These manifestations tended to be enveloped in a heady countercultural discourse that mixed Oriental spirituality, acid visionarism, and "Global Village" utopian aspirations. Warhol presented his show, however, as another showcase for his stars, featuring the Velvet Underground, the rock band he was managing at the time, with newly discovered model Nico as the band singer, and Factory assistant Gerard Malanga, clad in leather and bondage gear, as a dancer. Occasionally the spectacle also included Mary Woronov, who was then gaining some reputation in avant-garde performance milieus, as a dominatrix who tied Malanga up and flogged him. In addition, Warhol projected fragments of his own films, at times in several layers of superimposition, on the band, the performers, the audiences, as well as on the walls and ceiling of the locale.[26]

Warhol's fascination with his movie stars had Hollywood as a constant point of reference. Acutely aware of the institution's decline at the time, his approach to celebrity and glamour was ridden with self-consciousness and nostalgia.

He noted that his Marilyns and Liz Taylors were homages to a star system that was both figuratively and literally dying—he undertook the Marilyn silkscreens right after her death and while he executed the first of Liz Taylor's portraits ("Liz Taylor as Cleopatra"), the actress was gravely ill and there were rumors about her possible demise.[27] In the void left by the classical star system, Warhol introduced the notion of the superstar, a hyperbole analogous to Baudrillard's hyper-real. In the same way that hyper-reality replaces the real with media-disseminated images of itself, superstars replace the old-fashioned star system with a parodic simulacrum. In this simulacrum anyone could fashion him- or herself into a star: "Friends would stop by and they'd wind up in front of the camera, the stars of that afternoon's reel."[28] And when commenting on Jack Smith's influence on himself, Warhol wrote: ". . . I picked something up from him for my own movies—the way he used anyone who happened to be around that day. . . ."[29] Although superstar recruiting was, as we will see, slightly less casual than Warhol suggested, he seemed invested in underscoring that stardom was an infinitely open condition that could be achieved by anyone. Such a notion extended to his film subjects the democratic attitude toward mass-manufactured objects that informed his own pop artifacts.[30]

At the bottom of the concept of the superstar was the awareness that rather than transmitting a pre-existing "substance"—artistry, beauty, acting skill—the media created stars as an effect, a supplement, of recording apparati and of media circulation. Tally Brown, theater actress and Factory visitor during the high years of underground production, described in the following terms the dominant conception of stardom at Warhol's studio: "[The Factory] was [about] creating a Hollywod outside Hollywood, where you don't have to bother with learning to act, making the rounds, going to agents, getting your 8 X 10 glossy, doing small parts being an extra, and gradually working up to becoming a star. You just got on camera and were a Superstar!"[31] The superstar-effect of Warhol's films then confirmed Walter Benjamin's notion that, while reproduction, or reproducibility, eroded the exclusivity and specialness of the objects reproduced, it paradoxically created, when applied to the human figure, an aura of the personality whose most blatant example was the Hollywood star system.[32] If people only needed to be on film to become celebrities, at least in the restricted underground circles, what superstars might do or say, or how well they could act, was less important than the fact that they were actually doing it on camera. This is born out, for example, by Edie Sedgwick's star-making appearance in *Vinyl,* where she merely sits on a couch, smokes cigarettes, and gazes imperturbably on scenes of violence and torture.

Despite proclaiming the infinite openness of its star system, the Factory did enforce some criteria of selection on its performers. Since, according to screen writer Ronald Tavel, Warhol wanted to base his movies on barely scripted situations rather than on tight plots, he favored spontaneous displays of performers rather than sustained dramatic efforts that require acting expertise.[33] And precisely because of this, there was a definite bias toward flamboyant, loquacious types who were able to improvise on their feet (Ondine, Viva, Ed Hood, or Brigid Polk), and toward figures who simply had an impressive screen presence (Malanga, Sedgwick, or Joe Dallesandro).

Factory superstars had mainly two social provenances: on the one hand, there were (in Warhol's phrase) the "San Remo fags," gay bohemians associated with Greenwich Vil-

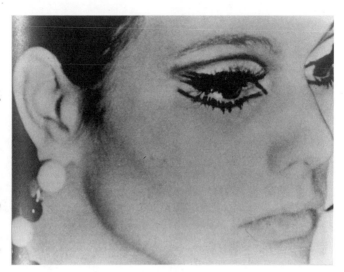

International Velvet in *The Chelsea Girls* (1966).
"You just got on camera and were a Superstar!"

lage and East Village avant-garde subcultures, and whose
main rendezvous was the bar San Remo; on the other, the
Harvard-Cambridge set, young, college-educated, high society dropouts like Edie Sedgwick, Danny Fields, or Chuck
Wein. All of them sought out the mixture of bohemianism
and celebrity status which defined Warhol's circle.[34] As to
their level of professionalism, some in the gay bohemian
sector (figures like Ondine, Freddy Herko, and even filmmaker Jack Smith himself, who acted in a number of
Warhol's films) had been involved in off-off-Broadway productions (such as the ones at the Caffé Cino) or in Judson
Church alternative dance shows. For the most part, however, the performers at the Warhol "studios" had received
little or no formal training as actors. In a piece on Ondine
published in the Warhol issue of *Film Culture,* playwright
and poet H. M. Koutoukas regarded the performer as repre-

sentative of a "New breed of actors who learned their trade not in the academy, but from the late show, the hi-fi, and the music stimuli resulting of varied and unique backgrounds."[35]

Some of the downtown performers—among them Jackie Curtis, Candy Darling, Mario Montez, Mary "Might" Woronow, and Ondine—alternated between Warhol's film productions and those of the avant-garde troupe Playhouse of the Ridiculous or in splinter groups led by John Vaccaro, Charles Ludlam, and Ronald Tavel. Both venues had in common their camp aesthetic and the amateurish and improvisational character of their performances. The exchange was facilitated by Tavel's activity in both groups; besides being the official Factory writer, he would often stage as plays the movie scripts he had originally written for Warhol.

Style: From *Vogue* to Warhol

Both sets of Warhol's performers occupied liminal social positions—as rejects of the entertainment business, as participants in "deviant" urban subcultures (gays, addicts), or as dropouts who rejected the conventions of their class identity. They encoded their liminal status into marginal styles and ways of life, clearing out through these practices social and symbolic spaces for themselves. Drugs and camp fulfilled this function for the San Remo crowd, while adherance to what Tom Wolfe called "pariah styles"—bohemian, low street styles that responded to new society's *nostalgie de la boue*—did so for the Harvard Cambridge set.[36] Warhol's movies matter-of-factly chronicled these marginal fashions and lifestyles, which were read in the counterculture quarters of the time as implicit oppositions to the status quo and as outside cooption from the mainstream. The success of *The Chelsea Girls* and *Flesh,* for example, presumably hung on such mythologies of dissent—also responsible, among other phenomena, for the *Bonnie and Clyde* cult and for the campus revival of Henry David Thoreau's "Civil Disobedience."

It seems to me, however, that what interested Warhol in these marginal social types was not their oppositional stance, but their style, both as a spontaneous aesthetic they bricolaged out of their "outsider" social positions and as catchy visual material he could package and disseminate through the media. In this respect, Warhol's attitude toward his subject matter was more indebted to *Vogue* than to any contemporary counterculture credos. It is symptomatic of his outlook that in his 1960s memoirs, Warhol regards *Bonnie and Clyde* as a fashion statement—"nostalgia fashions"—rather than as an antiestablishment fable amply resonant of the contemporary social and political situation. Hence according to Warhol, what the criminal couple really wanted was to have their picture reproduced and Bonnie's poems printed in the papers; in sum, to be outrageous, aesthetic outlaws and media celebrities.[37]

From a different perspective, Peter Wollen attributed Warhol's fascination with the marginal styles of his superstars to the combined influence of camp and minimalism—two influential aesthetics in the New York avant-garde scene of the time. Both trends stressed recording and theatricalizing the everyday, and exploiting the artistic possibilities of traditionally neglected materials—such as found urban debris, mass-produced kitsch, or subcultural styles and tastes.[38] I want to emphasize in this section that, besides these avant-garde and subcultural discourses, high fashion and style were important influences on Warhol's movies. Like minimalism and camp, fashion also theatricalized the real while linking such theatricalization to the penetration of the commodity form into all realms of experience. In the early 1960s, the most influential venues for high fashion were *Harper's Bazaar* and *Vogue,* along with a host of lifestyle publications such as *Esquire* and the more recent *Mademoiselle* and *Cosmopolitan.* Warhol had worked for all of these periodicals as commercial illustrator and was therefore intimate with their strategies and ideologies. It is therefore not surprising that his movies operated in dialogue with them.

The main goal of fashion magazines was advertising— that is, smoothing the passage of commodities into the everyday world of consumers, which would become in turn transformed by consumption. Fashion consumption in particular purported to aestheticize given environments and situations. One of the ways in which style publications underlined such potential was by bringing fashions and the fashion world into contact with the art world. *Vogue,* for example, would report on art exhibits, artists, or art currents as often as on society and fashions; it also treated art openings as showcases for fashion: reviewers commented on the designs worn for the occasion and photographers took great care to capture the celebrities' wardrobe against the art work.[39] These magazines interspersed in their pages fashion spreads with samples of the "legitimate" arts: for example, in the March 1963 issue of *Vogue,* a Joan Didion short story on childhood vacations by the sea accompanied a swimsuit spread shot on the beach. One month later, a spring collection called "Catalonian white" was photographed against well-known constructions by Catalan architect Antoni Gaudí. A final example: the May 1965 issue of *Vogue* was devoted to the Orient and featured a central spread on a collection called "Scheherazaderie"—"clothes to charm the sheik at home"—sandwiched between an essay on

Jean-Etienne Liotard, an eighteenth-century Swiss orientalist painter, and an interview with Igor Stravinsky that focused on Diaghilev and the Ballet Russes—whose costume and stage designs fostered a vogue for "Oriental" fashions in 1910s Paris.

The juxtaposition of design, literature, and fine art sought to legitimate high fashion by establishing its roots in the "genuine arts" and, at the same time, by comparing style consumption to art consumption. Besides the desire to upgrade the fashion market, such a collage of discourses may have obeyed the desire to gloss over the commercial character of fashion publications, yet it also had the opposite effect—it showed that art could in fact be made into a commodity, or an advertisement for commodities. The blurring of borders between art, fashions, and advertisement was quite familiar to Warhol, who, early in 1962, when still unable to find a gallery willing to exhibit his pop paintings, incorporated some of his early canvases inspired by advertisements and comic book panels into his window displays at Bonwit Teller.

It is interesting to note in passing that fashion, art, and business were rubbing shoulders in the contemporary "social scene" as well. Taste-chronicler Tom Wolfe reported in 1963: "Today in New York, the world of celebrities, the world of society, press agents, gossip columnists, fashion designers, interior decorators, and other hierophants have all converged on Art, now in a special, exalted place." And as Wolfe himself trenchantly described in his pieces of the time, art conferred on the parvenu circles of nouveaux riches and show business and entertainment figures—outsiders in conventional high society—a sense of legitimacy and social status.[40]

Besides proposing consumption as a means to aestheticize the given, lifestyle magazines infused the everyday with the potential to become a sort of catwalk for the display of style and fashion. Since this effect emanated from the application of photographic recording and mass reproduction to everyday experience, Walter Benjamin's ideas provide us here with useful coordinates. In his famous essay on mechanical reproduction, Benjamin stated that in the same way that Sigmund Freud's *The Psychopathology of Everyday Life* uncovered an unconscious of daily behavior, calling our attention to slips, gestures, and coincidences that had previously passed unnoticed, the film camera introduced us to an "unconscious optics," operating a comparable "deepening of apperception": "Evidently, a different nature opens itself to the camera than opens to the naked eye—if only because an unconsciously penetrated space is substituted by a space consciously explored by man."[41] Analogously, fashion and style photography froze the perceptual-experiential continuum into isolated moments and situations that could be turned into arenas for style. This photographic ability might have created, stretching Benjamin's idea, a "deepening of stylistic apperception"—a hyper-awareness of style in areas which had never before been encoded in such terms, and that could now be specularized, packaged in pictures, and circulated through the media.

Fulfilling this notion, sections of *Vogue* and *Harper's Bazaar* recorded styles that seemed to grow spontaneously in the culture and that could be appropriated with the purpose of confirming the magazines' genteel sense of fashion. In the already mentioned Oriental issue of *Vogue*, two articles and photo essays on the Moroccan winter residences of 1960s socialites and aristocrats Tamy Tazi and Anna Maria Cicogna showed how the greenhouse Orientalism of the fashion spread emanated "naturally" from their lifestyle and dwellings. If Orientalist fashions imported an artistic tradition into the everyday of ordinary consumers, the everyday of these socialites was already art. Other issues of *Vogue* contained spreads on such social groups as gallery owners, debutantes, financiers, collectors, aristocrats, designers, or rising artists. Style extended to all realms of the existence of these transformers of the everyday, whose every gesture and attitude seemed immediately photographable, framable, reproducible.

To underscore Warhol's familiarity with these strategies, we need only observe that he appeared in a section that sought to elevate daily life into high style—Ninette Lyon's "A Second Fame: Good Food," a habitual feature of *Vogue*. Lyon's two-page space invited celebrities to discuss food and share their favorite recipes, and it was usually illustrated by a full-page portrait of the guest celebrity (or celebrities) of the day, often by such consecrated photographers as Cecil Beaton or Irving Penn. In different issues, artist Max Ernst, the Duke and Duchess of Windsor, architect Philip Johnson, fashion designer Balenciaga, and choreographer Marques de Cuevas, among others, graced this section. In August 1965, it was Warhol's turn, together with fellow pop artist Robert Indiana, protagonist of Warhol's film *Eat*. Indiana talked about his favorite foods and gave some recipes; Warhol stated "Food does not exist for me. I like candies," and gave no recipes. They were photographed together leaning against the (infamous) Factory couch. Two years before his appearance in Lyon's section, on the edge of his pop art career, Warhol had been commissioned to do a photo essay on art gallery owners and curators for *Harper's Bazaar*. He took photomat pictures of his subjects and then used the results for the magazine layout with very slight modifications. (He repeated this technique in Ethel Scull's portrait, done the same year, and enthroned it later on as a frequent device in *Interview*. Interestingly, the idea has a high modernist source, as Warhol borrowed it from Jasper Johns, who included photomat pictures in one of his *Flag Paintings*.)[42] The portraits turned these figures into instant, if ephemeral, fashion and consumer icons among the magazine's circle of readers, just as Warhol's films made Factory visitors into the short-lived superstars of underground screenings at the Factory or at Mekas's Cinematheque.

Engaged in showcasing spontaneous styles, these sections of style publications were doubly commodified: on the one hand they sold images of the everyday of stylish social groups, demonstrating the magazines' ability to convert nearly every gesture and situation into marketable images through photographic reproduction. On the other, they functioned as potential advertisements of the styles and experiences they portrayed. For example, reportage of early 1960s "Swinging London" made the Carnaby street style, first captured as a street-grown, marginal aesthetic associated with the pop music world, British art schools, and "cult" nightclubs like Ad Lib, into a profitable fashion that flooded the markets on both sides of the Atlantic.

In showcasing his stars' styles, Warhol's movies functioned as street variants of *Vogue* and *Harper's*. Theatricalizing the everyday was the name of the game in both milieus, yet the Factory movies turned the formal traits of fashion magazines upside down: impeccable photographic technique gave way to Warhol's raw recordings, most of the time over- or underexposed, and totally unedited, retaining even sound bleeps and the flare-outs at the end of reels; rich, exotic settings were replaced by the bare interiors of the Factory, dingy hotel rooms, or cold-water East Village walk-ups; designer furniture by ramshackle odds and ends scavenged off the streets; and conventionally beautiful, impersonal models by the street-scarred, intensely personal physiognomies of the likes of Ondine, Ingrid Superstar, or Brigid Polk, to name a few. (In fact, with very few exceptions—Joe Dallesandro may be one—Warhol's superstars could hardly be called beautiful according to traditional canons; even the magnetic physiques of Gerard Malanga or Edie Sedgwick were somewhat idiosyncratic.)

To summarize, in theatricalizing the everyday, *Vogue* and *Harper's* took as their points of reference the fine arts and conventional notions of elegance and style; Warhol's movies, by contrast, were invested in revaluing the marginal, cheap, and (at least by common standards) ugly, incarnated, for the most part, in the "low" styles of his superstars and of other urban subcultures: "The most fashionable girls around town now are the girls of the night."[43] He made similar assertions throughout *POPism:* "The girls that summer in Brooklyn looked really great. It was the summer of the Liz Taylor-in-*Cleopatra* look—long, straight, dark, shiny hair with bangs and Egyptian-looking eye makeup" (29). "Pop Fashion really peaked about now [spring of 1967]—a glance about the Gymnasium [a popular mid-town hangout at the time] could tell you that. It was the year of the electric dress—vinyl with a hip-belt battery pack. . . . There were big hats and high boots and short furs, psychedelic prints, 3-D appliqués, lots of colored, textured tights, and bright-colored patent leather shoes" (208). "These kids [at St. Mark's Dom] really knew how to dress. They just had the right fashion instincts, somehow" (187–88).

Besides his background in fashion and advertisement, I believe Warhol's experience as a gay man must have sharpened his sensitivity toward how marginal groups theatricalized themselves and used style to underline their difference and to identify their peers, or to stake out sporadic, ever shifting "habituses" (in Bourdieu's term) in city spaces. The subcultural styles of Warhol's superstars shaped ways of speaking, dressing, decorating, eating, shopping, walking the streets, or doing one's hair, elevating the everyday into a realm of aesthetic intervention. Style seemed to turn the superstars' whole lives into performances and dissolved traditional boundaries between public and private spaces. The films often thematize this dissolution in sequences where such intimate, quotidian rituals as putting on makeup, bathing, dressing and undressing, or having sex are excuses for on-camera displays. *Village Voice* reviewer Andrew Sarris described this effect as follows: "Warhol's people are more real than real, because the camera encourages their exhibitionism. They are all 'performing' because their lives are one long performance and the party is never over."[44] Warhol himself reinforced the notion that his own field of interest lay precisely at the crossing of public and private when he stated: "I always wanted to do a movie of a whole day in Edie's life. But then that is what I wanted to do with most people. . . ."[45] While he came close to doing this in his *Poor Little Rich Girl Saga,* interrupted by a fall-out between the filmmaker and Sedgwick, he actually fulfilled his desire in a different medium by tape recording superstar Ondine in several marathon sessions during which the performer ate, shaved, shot up, and made his daily rounds, while improvising endlessly (and sometimes brilliantly) a delirious, amphetamine-spiked monologue. Warhol transcribed the material and gathered it into his only novel, *a,* published by Grove Press in 1968.

By making their daily experience into occasions for spectacle, Factory superstars were engaged in constant posing, which Rosetta Brooks described, with regard to art school subcultures in mid-1980s England—subcultures with an obvious debt to Warhol's inheritance—as "the *ne plus ultra* of performing art: street theater extended into continuous performance. Removed from the hallowed context of art, the poser is his/her own ready-made art object, but one whose circulation is not the microcosm of the art world, but the self-consciously constituted clique centered upon (for the moment) *Blitz* [style magazine], and The Hell [then a popular London nightclub]."[46] Changing 1980s London for 1960s New York and The Hell for Cheetah, Max's Kansas City, or the Factory parties, the description fits Warhol's world perfectly. Not surprisingly, the artist and his entourage favored environments where style and art slid into each other—that is, where style became spontaneous street-art and art an excuse for stylistic display. The now-disappeared Max's Kansas City was one of these places. "[It was] the exact place where Pop Art and the Pop life came together in New York in the 1960s . . . [it was] the showcase for all the fashion changes that had been taking place at the art openings and shows: now people weren't going to the openings to show off their new looks. They just skipped the preliminaries and went straight to Max's. Fashion wasn't what you wore someplace. It was the whole reason for going."[47]

Posing actually replaced art in a catalogue edited in 1968 for a Warhol retrospective at Stockholm's Modern Museet. Art and learned commentary took up very little of the thick, vinyl-bound, best-selling book (now a prized collector's item): the art consisted in low-quality black-and-white reproductions of the work and commentary was restricted to a few of Warhol's famous maxims, reproduced in English and Swedish, which opened the volume. The bulk of the catalogue was hundreds of black-and-white snapshots of scenes at the Factory taken by Billy Name and Stephen Shore: images of parties, filmings, art openings, Warhol and Malanga at work screen-printing, the Velvets, visitors, superstars, Warhol inflating his silver pillows. On the pages of this catalogue, as in Warhol's fame, the fleeting, brilliant ephemera of the artist and his entourage overwhelmed the more permanent art.

Style as Commodification: Hustlers, Stars, Warhol

Such ostentatious squanderings of style can be seen as ornamental orgies that fit Georges Bataille's notion of *dépense*—luxurious extravagance that refuses to conform to the restricted economics of a society based on calculation and equitable exchanges.[48] From another point of view—and here is where these street styles come closest to high fashion—some of these displays also obey the dynamics of capital and exchange that Warhol's work mimes so centrally. Taking the commodification embedded in fashion to a logical conclusion, posing and style were a way for the prostitutes, hustlers, models, and drug pushers that populate Warhol's films to advertise themselves as commodities-on-display, whose living depended on their being easily identified as such by prospective customers. *My Hustler* (1965) turns on this notion. Shot in two different locations— a beach and a bathroom—connoting public and private space, the film revolves around the commodity status of the hustler-protagonist. Hired by a rich older man through the "Dial-A-Hustler" service, the protagonist lies on the sand throughout the first reel, basking in the sun, putting on tanning lotion, and sharpening a stick with a penknife, seemingly staging the signifiers of desirability and masculinity that make him attractive to his "john," tartly played by Ed Hood. Throughout the second part of the film, the young hustler primps himself in front of a bathroom mirror; an older colleague tips him, while cruising him mercilessly, on how to best use his style and looks to make money. The last moments of the film underscore this potential, as three characters in succession walk into the frame, making several offers to the young hustler, each attempting to attract him to his or her side: "Do you know the places I could take you? . . . You could have all the money you wanted, cars, travel. . . . I could buy you whatever you want." Their bidding for him as if he were up for auction confirms his commodity status. The interweaving of self-staging, style, and commodification recurs in *Flesh* (1968), a variation on *My Hustler* and the first of Warhol's commercial productions directed by Morrissey. It depicts a day in the life of a hustler, interpreted by Joe Dallesandro, who sells his good looks to customers who pay him to perform a variety of actions—from modeling in the nude, to talking, to having sex. His being a hustler seems to frame everything he does—or could do—as a potential commodity. As one of Joe's tricks (awkwardly) puts it: "Money is all it's about with you, isn't it Joe?" Even in the one scene where Joe gives it away—when he is orally serviced by Geri Miller while drag queens Candy Darling and Jackie Curtis flick through old fan magazines—the conversation is still haunted by the specters of appearance and value: Jackie and Candy discuss star glamour while Geri confers about enlarging her breasts, which might increase her cachet as topless dancer and part-time "girl of the night."

Paul America in *My Hustler* (1965).
The hustler as commodity on display.

Style, self-display, and commodification converge on Warhol's central film interest: stars. Like hustlers, prostitutes, and fashion models, stars are the epitome of the commodification of the body and of personal style, since their whole behavior and looks can be framed as marketable items. In Edgar Morin's words: "The star is a total item of merchandise; there's not an inch of her body, not a shred of her soul, not a memory of her life that cannot be thrown into the market."[49] In *THE Philosophy,* one finds a comparable quote: "Movie stars get millions of dollars for nothing, so when someone asks them to do something for nothing, they go crazy—they think that if they are going to talk to somebody at the grocery store they should get fifty dollars an hour."[50] Not only stars' bodies and personalities, but even their touch has market potential. Since the consolidation of the star system in the mid-1910s, manufacturers cashed in on the stars' Midas-like touch by marketing their styles, the costumes they wore, the props they handled, or the vehicles they drove. Instrumental were the tie-ups and showcasing contracts between manufacturers and studios. Already in the late 1920s, a profitable enterprise like Bernard Waldman's Modern Merchandising Bureau traded sketches of models and accessories to be worn by stars in imminent releases to manufacturers, who in turn tried to market the items in time for the film's opening. Such connections between advertising, merchandising, and stars realized to the maximum the commercial value of cinema, which became, besides an entertainment medium, a conduit for showcasing commodities in libidinally gratifying scenarios.[51]

Lacking the visibility, distribution channels, and budget of commercial Hollywood movies, Warhol's productions could not exploit the superstars' merchandising potential to the same degree as the commercial cinema, yet at the same time, an ironic awareness of this impossibility actually shapes some of his films. Such is the case, for example, with *Kitchen.* Scripted by Tavel, the film was conceived as a vehicle for superstars Roger Trudeau, Rene Ricard, and Edie Sedgwick. Its "plot" develops in a white, impersonal kitchen with run-down furniture that appears as a landscape of dead commodities: a cluttered table, an overbrimming garbage can, and a few shelves with a number of discardable items—old records, paperbacks, and newspapers—figure prominently in the frame. Occasionally a photographer walks into the picture's foreground and takes snapshots of the performance, flaunting the basic mechanism for freezing events into commodifiable images. However, the photographer's presence seems quite tongue-in-cheek, since the movie's merchandising potential can only be evoked as a lack: besides seeming jaded and amateurish, the stars are only known for the most part to an insider group; on the other hand, the objects juxtaposed with them appear to have exhausted their course in the market. The total com-modification of screen space that Hollywood effected exists in some of Warhol's movies as an empty structure.

By contrast, commodification is fully operative with regard to Warhol himself. Aware of his growing media visi-bility, in 1966 he placed the following ad in the *Village Voice:* "I'll endorse with my name any of the following: clothing, AC-DC, cigarettes, small tapes, sound equipment, Rock 'N' Roll records, anything, film and film equipment, Food, Helium, WHIPS, Money; love and kisses Andy Warhol. EL 5-9941."[52] The text of the ad is obviously ironic; think of the capitals, the capriciously assorted items, the blank "anything," the cute specification ("*small* tapes"), or the thin divide between the items of merchandise and the closing salutation "love and kisses"—is he endorsing those too? Warhol seems to be parodying in relation to himself the sort of revaluation that the star touch effects and that he had already represented at the beginning of his career in a sketch titled "Butterfly Crumbled by Greta Garbo." Accord-ing to Bob Colacello, this piece had its origin in a biographi-cal episode sometime in the mid-1950s, when Warhol was invited by actress Mercedes da Costa to a picnic attended also by Greta Garbo. Dumbstruck in the presence of one of his all-time idols, Warhol drew a butterfly with his simple, graceful line, and gave it to the actress. At the end of the picnic, Garbo absentmindedly crumpled the picture and left it behind. Warhol picked it up and framed it, giving it the mentioned title. The aura that the drawing thus acquired owed little to the artist's craft and everything to Garbo's ce-lebrity status.[53]

One could say that throughout his career, Warhol aspired to being Garbo crumbling the butterfly—that is, to bestow-ing value even on what he discarded. This aspiration remits us to his pop art, which transformed everyday objects into art objects, and to his equation of art with business—with creating or increasing value. It was precisely Warhol's ability to bestow value that determined his own functioning as a star. According to Richard Dyer, stars embody ideal images, complexities, and contradictions attendant on being and acting in the world. The three main arenas where they project their influence are notions of public and private behavior, images and attitudes toward sexuality and gender roles, and people's relation to work.[54] In this last realm resides Warhol's star effect. Through his ability to turn marginal performers into superstars, daily objects into art objects, and gestures and styles into media images, Warhol incarnates the absolute producer, able to make the most out of the least, to increase the value of whatever came into his orbit, no matter how banal or inconsequential. In Hollywood's stars-as-advertisers, such potential was the result of fame, beauty, or skill, yet Warhol inverted the terms of this relation, as his fame ultimately resulted from his productive potential. "That's the thing I'm always thinking about: Do you think the product is really more important than the star?"[55] In his particular case, the terms of the question were moot; the star he was eventually became the product he sold, and his particular way of *being* was therefore equivalent to *producing*—even something as untangible as a space, an event, an atmosphere. For example, in 1965 the Philadelphia Institute of Contemporary Art housed a Warhol retrospective, announcing the presence of the artist at the opening. On opening day, there were two thousand people jostling at the door hours before the artist was due. On the inside, the pictures were removed to prevent damage. Warhol arrived surrounded by part of his entourage under flood lights, flashes, and TV cameras to preside over the event: "It was fabulous: an art opening with no art!" As guards were trying to protect the star, fans passed up all sorts of objects to be autographed—shopping bags, soup cans, shirts, matchboxes, train tickets. "We weren't just *at* the art exhibit. We *were* the art exhibit."[56]

Warhol's well-known quip "I want to be a machine" may, in this context, express his desire to equate living with endlessly generating images and commodities—or images as commodities, which he did by appending himself to recording devices. And since everything he touched, did, or witnessed could be frozen into a picture, transvalued, delivered, sold, Warhol's work never stopped—the tape kept running, the polaroids popping, the cameras filming. It was all work. As he himself reminisced to Bob Colacello:

> [In the 1960s] I dragged myself to the office around eleven. Painted. Made movies. Took the kids to dinner. When we had the nightclub [the Dom, on St. Mark's Place], we had to go there until four in the morning. Did the lightshow. Then went to Chinatown for supper. Got home at seven. Crawled into bed. After the nightclub [went out of business], we sat all night in the maze at Max's. It was all work.[57]

In Warhol as emblem of production, enlightened rationalism and archaic myth touched hands. Warhol incarnated a Tayloristic dream, where every gesture and movement were maximally productive. At the same time, and by virtue of such productivity, his was a universe saturated with meaning and without gaps, residue, or gratuitousness: everything Warhol did had a place in the orbits of media circulation and market exchange, where it acquired its value, its meaning. This frenzy of signification, which allowed for no loss, turned Warhol into a near magical decoder or bestower of meaning. In Stephen Koch's words: "He made everybody feel watched. And what is being watched has a meaning, even if it is only the meaning of being watched." And further, "Utterly absorbed and utterly disinterested, he had an almost Satanic power to make their [the superstars' and Factory hangers-on] casual hysteria cohere, signify, become visible."[58]

Capital Overcoding

As I have tried to show in the foregoing sections, the structure of commodity exchange subtends Warhol's activity as an artist, producer, and cultural icon, bringing under its rubric his pop art, movies, and social persona. In all these facets, Warhol enacts the closure of the code of capital. French theorist Jean Baudrillard has argued that capital is a code, since it translates goods into commodities by assigning to them a market value which is their signification. As a code, the study of its functioning belongs to semiotics as much as it does to political economy. In assigning value, capital coding operates what Baudrillard called "a reduction of the symbolic to the semiological"—a formula through which he rewrites Max Weber's modern process of rationalization (or disenchantment, *Entzauberung*) in terms that combine semiology and ideological analysis of commodity fetishism. According to Baudrillard's formula, capital coding translates the complex cultural significations of objects (significations that compound a social symbolic, with its attendant ambiguities, asymmetries, indeterminacies, and confusions) into a perfectly closed semiology that is exempt from ambiguities or gaps because it only takes into account market value. The latter is all-encompassing, since it can apply to any object or experience, and concrete, as it can be quantified and made visible in the form of currency.[59]

Due to the abstraction and flexibility of capital coding, everything can be fragmented, dislodged from the continuum of experience and packaged as a commodity, a process that Warhol frequently describes in his writings: "That screen magnetism is something secret—if you could only figure out what it is and how to make it, you'd have a really good product to sell." And later on, "New York restaurants now have a new thing, they don't sell their food, they sell their atmosphere. . . . They caught on that what people really care about is changing their atmosphere for a couple of hours."[60] Commodification not only informs the themes and structures of Warhol's movies, as we have seen with regard to *My Hustler* and *Flesh,* but it may appear at times as the ultimate goal of his productions, which he often described as advertisements for his stars or for the underground sensibility: "I tried to make [Edie Sedgwick] understand that if she acted in enough of these underground movies, a Hollywood person might see her and put her in a good movie—that the important thing was to be up there on the screen and let everybody see how good she was."[61] Along with isolating marketable material, there is in Warhol a parallel fascination with translating value into quantity, a mechanism that copies the way market value is expressed in units of a given currency: "I always think quantity is the best gauge on anything . . . so I set my sights on becoming a space artist."[62]

Packaging and quantifying replicate the airtight grid that capital imposes on the world. Warhol's interest in these processes is, at bottom, a fascination with "the closed perfection of a system" (Baudrillard's term) which allows for no crevices through which meaninglessness—understood in this context as lack of value—might ooze in, and where everything can find its meaning in the market. In Baudrillard's description: "What is fascinating about money is . . . its *systematic nature,* the potential enclosed in the material for total commutability of all values, thanks to their definite abstraction."[63] Hence under Warhol's paeans to packaging, standardization, and interchangeability, to a world, in sum, where everybody and everything can be translated into something else (commodities into art, personalities into media images), lies his desire to enact, or to *become,* capital, which precisely performs these semiotic maneuvers by recoding all realms of the everyday as commodities.

Melancholia, Violence, and Death

Yet such universal penetration of the codes of capital has consequences that can act as critical counterpoints to the widespread advance of equalization and commodification, and that give rise to three important thematic clusters in Warhol's work: melancholia, violence, and death.

Melancholia, in the sense of estrangement and separation from the given, stems from the mediations that capital introduces in the object world.[64] Capital superimposes on the immanent meanings of things (on their specific cultural and symbolic densities and "use values") a new identity as economic hieroglyphs whose meaning is a function of market exchange. As immanent meanings recede, the world appears an arbitrary, lifeless clutter of objects not unlike the one commented on in *Kitchen.* Capital mediation extends to the body itself, whose commodification and transformation into an economic sign is exemplified in Warhol's movies; as a result, relations with the body are always melancholy—that is, defined by a sense of loss and distance and by a disappearance of organic qualities. These feelings are most apparent in Warhol's representations of eroticism and sexuality. Despite the fact that these are realms seemingly characterized by organic immediacy, Warhol stresses that they are always filtered through multiple levels of mediation.

One such level is the notion that desire does not exist in the proximity of the flesh but is always exiled, as it were, to the cool symbolic distances imposed by signs. "Fantasy love is much better than reality love. Never doing it is very exciting."[65] Such awareness results in Warhol's work in distance from the erotic object, since its inevitable echoing through sign-substitutes condemns one to solipsism—to having relations with ghosts. Contemporary psychoanalysis (notably Lacan) tells us that such is our fate, a fate which remains more or less veiled in human relations. By contrast, Warhol exposes the always removed condition of sexuality, a condition caused by the agency of commodities—items of clothing, styles, or commercialized fantasies. "So if you see a person who looks like your teenage fantasy walking down the street, it's probably not your teenage fantasy, but someone who had the same fantasy as you and decided, instead of being it, to look like it, and so he went to the store and bought the look that you both like. So forget it. Just think about all the James Deans and what it means."[66]

The camera is a further source of mediation; its obtrusive presence frames all sexuality as performance—or second-degree performance, if we take it, as sociologist Erving Goffmann suggests, that everyday life already entails some degree of acting. In Warhol's movies, sexuality is therefore an event that exists not so much in itself as for others, an image inserted within a circuit of alien looks and desires. Perhaps the most representative example in this respect is *Blue Movie* (aka *Fuck*), where two characters carry out such intimate rituals as lounging around the house in the nude, showering, and matter-of-factly performing intercourse. (Such matter-of-factness, by the way, was Warhol's response to the sensationalization of sex in porn movies, which by the late 1960s were breaking into the American market in large numbers.) In the course of the movie, the two protagonists often wink, stare, and nod toward the camera, acknowledging the presence of the mediating apparatus.

Warhol's representations of sadomasochism, whose rituals both turn sexuality into a performance and drain bodies and desires of all organic attributes, function as his most spectacular denial of unmediated, "organic" desires and sexualities. He took up the topic most directly in two films made with Ronald Tavel: *Horse* (1965), a now unavailable recreation of some Western motifs as gay S&M play, and *Vinyl* (1965), a squalid version of Anthony Burgess's *A Clockwork Orange*. *Vinyl*'s protracted depictions of torture show the body of the protagonist J. D. (Juvenile Delinquent), played by Gerard Malanga, connected to harnesses, clasps, cables, tubes, electrodes, and chains. The intangible mediation of desire through signs is literalized here through the mechanical pieces which channel libidinal flows from the discipliner to the disciplined. Both subjects appear as mechanical aggregates, machines connected to other machines, and devoid of any organic qualities. The mask and gag on Malanga's face have precisely such a dehumanizing function. Analogously, the mirroring of his torture in the background of the frame, where two figures silently enact similar bondage and discipline rituals throughout the movie, depersonalizes these actions, suggesting that the protagonist's torture is merely one case among many similar ones— just one link in the institutional chain whose goal is conditioning the criminal. Through such chains run the inorganic, blind desires of the oppressive state-machine, not those of individualized subjects.

Vinyl provides a plot for the violence that underlies most of Warhol's movies. This violence has to do with the mediating function of the camera itself, whose presence seems to

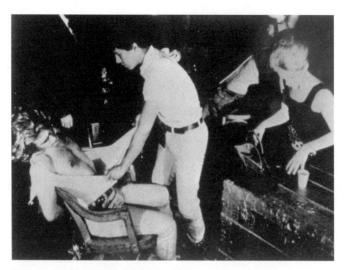

**S&M as denial of unmediated, organic sexuality.
Gerard Malanga, Tosh Carrillo, and Edie Sedgwick
in *Vinyl* (1965), Warhol's version of
Anthony Burgess's *The Clockwork Orange*.**

trigger aggressive reactions. The very act of filming, trans-
forming people into media images, seems the catalyzer of
violence. One can think of the aggressive voyeurism of
Beauty #2, where the director's voice off-screen constantly
coaxes the film's stars "to know each other more intimately";
the abusive, almost sadomasochistic one-on-ones of *Chelsea Girls;* the rape scene of *Lonesome Cowboys;* the yelling
matches between Tavel and his stars in *Life of Juanita
Castro;* the biting mockery of the director of *Screen Test #2,*
which causes Mario Montez to fly off the handle; the concept of *Screen Test #3* (aka *Suicide*): a first-person account
of twenty-odd suicide attempts by the same man, narrated
to the image of his scarred arms; the list could go on.

In Warhol's world, this violence has deadly ramifica-
tions. Warhol's nickname, "Drella"—a combination of
Dracula and Cinderella given to him by some superstars—

expresses the vampirism attached to his activity as image producer and stargazer, the notion that his touch had the effect of draining away the life of his "found personalities." Because of this, the producer and advertiser is simultaneously a life giver and a death agent: his images combine the ability to deliver stars into existence—that is, into the media and the market—and, simultaneously, to start their rapid aging and eventual fading out through repeated exposure. What British critic Dick Hebdige stated in relation to the (Warhol-indebted) British style magazine *The Face* seems thus peculiarly apposite in relation to Factory stars: "Once developed as a photographic image and as a sociological and marketing concept, each group, face, fashion fades out of the now, i.e., it ceases to exist. The process is invariable: caption/capture/disappearance."[67] In this sense, the rapid turnover of superstars at the Factory is a modern form of the medieval dance of death, with Warhol as the universal leveler who allotted almost indiscriminately, along with fifteen minutes of fame (media life), the chance of a much longer death-like oblivion.

Media celebrity thus brings death by the hand as a muffled affect that is seldom openly articulated (with the possible exception of the 1960s "Disaster Series" and the 1980s collection "Skulls") but whose undertow makes itself felt throughout the Warhol text. It appears, for example, in the long line of overdoses, suicides, and accidental deaths among superstars and hangers-on, a roster which the artist himself barely escaped joining. In his films, death emerges more or less mutedly in the pulsating stillness of *Sleep,* in the long interval of *Empire,* in the cool desperation of the superstars, in the uncanny conjunction of documentary immediacy and multileveled mediation, in the absence of the organic, and in the dissolution of temporal progression into futureless seriality.

Melancholia, violence, and death exist in Warhol's films as "scandals" or excesses that escape the neat symmetry and totalizing character of capital coding. Such excesses constitute examples of what Baudrillard calls "symbolic insistence," which "contradicts the duality of economic and sign value to instaurate the unequal balances and discontinuities of signification."[68] In Warhol, these insistences appear as clandestine spinoffs of the dynamics of exchange value. They are the dialectical negative attached to the revaluing, quantifying, and translating into capital that we have located at the center of the artist's enterprise, and they can act as points of leverage for a cultural production that would seek to criticize the advance of capital through the tissue of daily life. They connect Warhol's productions to the critiques of commercial culture carried out by Kenneth Anger and Jack Smith, whose work also explored, most often with clearer oppositional intent than Warhol's own, the desires, separations, and violences that commercial culture tends to sublimate.

Conclusions

The dialectical proximity of the dynamics of value and exchange to resistance to them is potentially one of the most disconcerting—and characteristic—traits of Warhol's films and, by extension, of all of his work. The obstacles to capital exchange and commercial culture that other underground filmmakers and avant-gardists laboriously crafted into their productions appear in Warhol's own as the involuntary shadow thrown by the work of capital. As a result, their critical potential appears unfocused, more often actualized through decoding than explicitly encoded. Capital has then all the roles in Warhol's play: it is the goodies and the baddies; the enemy to be attacked and the purveyor of weapons against it; it generates commodification and market hype and the opposition to both. The unsurpassable horizon of capital and commodity exchange is perhaps the ultimate reason for the irony that pervades Warhol's work, an irony that makes impossible to determine in any unambiguous way whether such work is *either* affirmative *or* critical of the status quo. No easy polarization is possible here, since both aspects are dialectically intertwined as effects of capital coding: the affirmative aspect is an effect of Warhol's empathy with capital value and of his celebratory exploration of its expansion throughout social and symbolic spaces. On the other hand, the critical one is an irreducible excess of such an advance and therefore has no independent existence from it.

Warhol's films and art thus undercut the possibility for a critical avant-garde to exist outside the circuits and the signifying structures of the commodity form. In this situation, avant-garde production rehearses two different ways of inhabiting commodity culture: a critical one and a mimetic one. Balanced against each other in Warhol's work, the two modes have become indeed two more or less distinct courses followed by avant-garde cultural production in the last three decades.

Recognizing that cultural production cannot take place outside the semiotic of money and exchange, a sector of the avant-garde developed a critical way to inhabit the commodity by focusing on "symbolic insistences," that is, on the violence, melancholy, and alienation that both resist capital coding and emerge from it. One could argue, as Rainer Crone has done quite effectively, that Warhol's work enacts one such critical deconstruction of the commodity from within, but as I have tried to show throughout my essay, this proposition only accounts for half the picture, and furthermore, cannot explain the continuities between Warhol's purportedly critical avant-gardism of the 1960s and his later commercialism except by resorting to myths of selling out. Warhol's most politicized progeny exploited the critical possibilities he opened up in his work. Punk, for example, whose debt to the Factory is important, continued in the realm of pop music and street style the investigation of alienation, blankness, and aggressiveness that Warhol articulated in his movies. Practitioners of this (anti-)aesthetic are the early 1980s New York filmmakers Vivienne Dick, Eric Mitchell, Scott and Beth B., and Michael McClard, to name a few, all of whom demystified commercial film culture along lines anticipated by Warhol's underground work—i.e., by parodying commercial genres and showcasing marginal styles. In more established avant-garde gallery circuits, "image scavengers" Cindy Sherman, Richard Prince, Sherry Levine, and Barbara Kruger, among others, follow in the tracks of Warhol's pop art; they explore through recontextualization and pastiche the conditioned, automatized aspects of cultural consumption fostered by the commodification of the art market.

In a second course of action, the avant-garde mimes mass-cultural production to the degree of becoming nearly indistinguishable from it. Avant-garde textual strategies are used in this case to package all areas of experience, even the most marginal and resistant to commodification, as marketable media icons, styles, and fashions. Along with the critical streak discerned by Crone, such an impulse defines Warhol's work right from the beginning and has been the most visible (and for some the most damning) aspect of his 1970s and 1980s production, emblematically incarnated by his magazine *Interview*. As Bob Colacello, his 1970s collaborator and editor of *Interview* stated: "We didn't separate avant-garde culture, rock 'n' roll, fashion, movies, and TV, which were all rising and mixing in the seventies. We mixed and rose with them, little by little."[69] The combination of avant-gardism and commercialism has also provided a blueprint for such style arenas as the 1980s British art school magazines *The Face, i.d.,* and *Blitz,* and even for MTV, where Warhol had had, right before his death, his own space—"Andy Warhol's Fifteen Minutes." Such mapping of capital coding and commodification onto avant-gardism may have been theoretically correct, but it was plagued with ambiguity. For those interested in maintaining the critical thrust of experimental art, Warhol's proposal that the fusion of art and the practice of everyday life was already accomplished by capital seemed monumentally cynical, and his celebrating business as art, a sort of aesthetic alibi for the ruthless entrepreneurship that characterized the (as it turned out) volatile economic high of the Reagan years.

Having made this distinction, I want to conclude by qualifying it once more in order to underline the dialectical interaction between these two halves of Warhol's (and contemporary) avant-gardism. In fact, there might be something suspiciously facile in separating the political engagement with the commodity form and the acritical mimesis with it. As Warhol's oppositional legacy showed, critical art cannot avoid the circuits of exchange, but must find its leverage in them. At the same time, the polemical exploration of melancholia, alienation, and death, can be recoded (and blunted) as mere fashion. Both poles—oppositional and affirmative—can be inverted—or logically exended—into each other, so rather than strict oppositions we have an endless sliding within a sort of Möbius strip, a closed system where each point can take us to any other one.

On this uncertain, slippery terrain Warhol's films are located. If I have portrayed them as accommodating transpositions of stardom and of fashion and advertising strategies into the avant-garde, I have also tried to do justice to the way they open up lines of resistance, opacities, and fissures in the mediation of experience by the commodity form. What they do not show (and this is also the limit of my analysis) is what might be seen through the crevices. But "the beyond" was never Warhol's goal. As always one step ahead of his interpreters, he once said: "If you want to know all about Andy Warhol, just look at the surface of my paintings and films and me, and there I am. There's nothing behind it."[70] I hope I have proved the truth of his statement.

Conclusions

The momentum of the American underground was over by 1968. By then, the alliance of formal innovation, playful/satirical attitudes toward mass culture, and sexual, social, and political protest that converged in the underground had dissolved, but each of these components survived separately in other arenas of discourse. Social protest was mostly channeled through student rebellion and political radicalism; underground gay activism burst into public attention with the Stonewall Inn riots and thrived on in the Gay Liberation Front and its multiple splinter groups; the underground's open depictions of sexuality were outdone in the late 1960s by commercial pornography; and finally, the critical desublimation of pop culture became a highly specialized field of inquiry with university departments, academic journals, and conferences devoted to it.

In the terrain of alternative filmmaking, the underground was superseded at the end of the decade by political film and structuralist cinema. Political film tried to incorporate the formal experimentation and anti-illusionism of the underground into direct documentary. Developed around the short-lived newsreel units that mushroomed at the time in the larger American cities, it had the dual aim of providing alternative media coverage and of criticizing the representational strategies used by mainstream media. However, whether because of its didacticism or its suspicions toward popular culture, late 1960s political cinema had practically no resonance beyond the level of cadres. For its part, structuralist cinema, whose earliest achievements were Michael Snow's *New York Ear and Eye Control* (1964) and *Wavelength* (1967) and Tony Conrad's *The Flicker* (1966), was an inward-turning of the underground, where formal research overwhelmed social and communal concerns. A particularly withdrawn form of modernism, this type of cinema was rarely shown outside museums and galleries, where it was mostly seen by coteries of specialists. While the alternative cinema was becoming increasingly divorced from popular audiences, commercial productions like *Hair, Midnight Cowboy,* and *Easy Rider* started marketing many underground themes and stylistic gestures with singular box office success.

The eventual dispersion of underground styles and impulses calls attention to its composite structure. It is important to keep in mind, however, that the underground did not operate only as an unstable trend threatened with imminent dissolution. On the contrary, its effects emanated from the articulation of the multiple idiolects that compounded it into temporary and strategic wholes. The previous chapters have tried to sketch out this paradoxical, complementary dynamic both by analyzing the underground's components—modernist ideology, transgressive sexual politics, beat bohemianism, and postmodern pop savvy—and by showing their conjoining in an ideological front. Throughout, I have tried to underline the importance of sociological and political factors within this front. I hope to have shown that the underground was not only an artistic formation but also a social one, since it tied artistic exploration and media intervention to the claims and interests of two intersecting constituencies: marginal cultural producers and the gay community. In this regard, it is perhaps more appropriate to speak of an "avant-garde impulse" that mobilizes artistic and social factors under its aegis, rather than of an independent "avant-garde aesthetic," a concept that the historical trajectory of the avant-garde has continuously questioned.

The manipulation of popular materials which I have regarded as the main underground strategy has become an inherent possibility in our culture. With the popularization of videotaping, the accessibility of recording equipment, and, more recently, the computerization of image banks, image production-scavenging has become part of almost everyone's cultural horizon. In this sense, avant-garde strategies of looting and rerouting media images seem now within everybody's reach. They are incorporated within the very apparati of consumption and dissemination, as tape decks allow for sound-assemblages, VCRs for ubiquitous bootlegging, and TV remote controls for endless moving collages. For some critics, this results in the avant-garde losing its role of aesthetic cutting edge, since its artistic strategies

are copied everywhere by popular culture and its consumers. It also results in the liquidation of the avant-garde's
oppositional thrust: if the avant-gardist intervention in the
media is everywhere (in zapping, in video and tape pirat-
ing), its critical power becomes extremely diluted. These
pessimistic views are correct to the extent that the described
means of intervention are largely determined and preempted
by the media themselves. In fact, they are parasitic on them;
what one mixes, bootlegs, and samples is after all determined by what the media make available.

On the other hand, the availability of media and image
banks allows marginal communities to produce local knowledges and histories integrated in their specific horizons of
doing and acting. These local narratives can provide alternatives to mainstream discourses—either by deflating their
effects or by forcing them to accommodate different perspectives. In this context, the notion of the avant-garde as an
aesthetic or political cutting edge can be replaced by the
idea of multicentered cultural fronts which deploy aesthetic
innovation and creative media uses to encode discourses
and interests often excluded from the mainstream. In a way,
this was exactly the ambition of the underground filmmakers whose work I have studied: to propose highly idio-
matic ways of producing and consuming images, ways that
mix popular iconographies and myths with the concerns of
such specific subgroups as the gay community and marginal
artists. As I have pointed out in earlier chapters, a similar
momentum drives contemporary black British film and
video groups such as Sankofa and the Audio-Film Collective;
gay and lesbian video-makers like John Greyson, Richard
Fung, or Marlon Riggs, to name just a few; AIDS artist-
activists; the Hispanic American group Taller de Arte Fronterizo; and even, in more popular quarters, much current

rap music. Rather than dramatize the current impossibility of the avant-garde, I believe these initiatives actualize its utopian potentials in alliance with the present claims of sexual, ethnic, and class formations. As the underground demonstrated in its own time, it is precisely in contact with these claims and in alliance with mass culture that the avant-garde impulse may continue to emerge, as Clement Greenberg wished for modernism, as "the only living culture we have right now."

NOTES

Introduction

1. Peter Bürger, *Theory of the Avant-Garde,* trans. Michael Shaw (Minneapolis: University of Minnesota Press, 1984) and Andreas Huyssen, "The Hidden Dialectic: Avant-Garde—Technology—Mass Culture," *After the Great Divide* (Bloomington: Indiana University Press, 1986). Both of their contributions to theorizing the avant-garde and modernism will be extensively dealt with in the following chapter.

2. See, for a sample of opinions, Lewis Jacobs, "The Experimental Cinema in America," *The Rise of the American Cinema* (New York: Teachers' College Press, 1968); Frank Stauffacher, ed., *Art in Cinema* (New York: Arno, 1947); David Curtis, *Experimental Cinema* (New York: Universe, 1971); P. Adams Sitney, "Introduction," *The Avant-Garde Film: A Reader in Theory and Criticism* (New York: New York University Press, 1978); P. Adams Sitney, *Visionary Film: The American Avant-Garde* (New York: Oxford University Press, 1979); Stephen Dwoskin, *Film Is: The International Free Cinema* (Woodstock: Overlook, 1975); and Malcolm LeGrice, ed., *Abstract Film and Beyond* (Cambridge, MA: MIT Press, 1977).

3. Two influential attempts to define a gay sensibility are Susan Sontag's "Notes on Camp," *Against Interpretation* (New York: Farrar, Straus, and Giroux, 1966), which explores camp as emblematic of "homosexual aestheticism," and George Steiner, "Eros and Idiom," *On Difficulty and Other Essays* (New York: Oxford University Press, 1982), which argues that modernism is eminently homosexual just as classical realism is predominantly heterosexual. More recently, theorists have developed the possibility that a gay sensibility might not be a sensibility in any positive sense, but a place of erasure, a site of confusion that highlights a play of difference where there are no positive terms. See Jonathan Dollimore: "I shall suggest that there is a sense in which the very notion of a homosexual sensibility is a contradiction in terms. I am interested in an aspect of it which exists, if at all, in terms of that contradiction—of a parodic critique of the essence of sensibility as conventionally understood." *Sexual Dissidence: Augustine to Wilde, Freud to Foucault* (New York: Oxford University Press, 1991), pp. 307–308. See also Eve Sedgwick, *Epistemology of the Closet* (Berkeley: University of California Press, 1990), for whom the trope of the closet is the most definitory institution of gay culture, one which permeates the mainstream discourses and categories of experience. Such permeation results at once in a vexing mixture of ubiquity and invisibility; in sum, in a hardly definable web of paradox and difference woven around the (non)figure of the homosexual.

4. Sedgwick, *Epistemology of the Closet,* p. 1.

5. Stephen Koch, *Stargazer* (New York: Praeger, 1973), pp. 4–5.

6. Sitney's work had been preceded by a whole decade of critical writings on experimental cinema, writings which tended to combine formalism and auteurism. Besides numerous articles and reviews published in *Film Culture* throughout the 1960s, some of these writings are: Gregory Battcock, ed., *The New American Cinema: A Critical Anthology* (New York: Dutton, 1967); Sheldon Renan, *An Introduction to the American Underground Film* (New York: Dutton, 1967); Parker Tyler, *Underground Film: A Critical History* (New York: Grove, 1969); David Curtis, *Experimental Cinema* (New York: Universe, 1971); Jonas Mekas, *Movie Journal: The Rise of the New American Cinema, 1959–1971* (New York: Macmillan, 1972); Stephen Dwoskin, *Film Is: The International Free Cinema.*

7. See, for example, I. A. Richards, *Principles of Literary Criticism* (New York: Harcourt, Brace, Jovanovich, 1981 [1930]); V. Shklovsky, "Art as Technique," *Russian Formalist Criticism: Four Essays,* ed. Lee T. Lemon and Marion J. Reis (Lincoln: University of Nebraska Press, 1965).

8. Dana Polan, *The Political Language of Film and the Avant-Garde* (Ann Arbor: UM Research Press, 1985), p. 65. For other powerful critiques, see Constance Penley and Janet Bergstrom, "The Avant-Garde: History and Theories," *Screen* 19, no. 3 (Fall 1979). (See Sitney's lengthy reply to Bergstrom and Penley in *Screen* 20, nos. 3–4 [Winter 1979–80].)

9. *Screen's* agenda was heavily influenced by Jean-Luc Comolli and Paul Narboni, "Cinema/Ideology/Criticism," originally in *Cahiers du Cinéma;* the first English version appeared in *Screen* 12, no. 1 (Spring 1971), pp. 27–36. A random perusal through *Screen* reveals the journal's fetish interests: besides the directors already mentioned, Douglas Sirk, Alfred Hitchcock, Josef von Sternberg, Orson Welles, the 1940s women's film, and film noir.

10. James Naremore, "Authorship and the Cultural Politics of Film Criticism," *Film Quarterly* 44 (Fall 1990), p. 20. Laura Mulvey, "Visual Pleasure and Narrative Cinema," *Screen* 16, no. 3 (Autumn 1975); Stephen Heath, "Narrative Space," *Questions of Cinema* (Bloomington: Indiana University Press, 1981); Colin MacCabe, "Realism and the Cinema: Notes on Some Brechtian Theses," *Screen* 15, no. 2 (Summer 1974).

11. David Rodowick, *The Crisis of Political Modernism* (Urbana: University of Illinois Press, 1988).

12. Louis Althusser, "Ideology and Ideological State Apparatuses," *Lenin and Philosophy,* trans. Ben Brewster (New York: Monthly Review Press, 1971).

13. Peter Wollen, "The Two Avant-Gardes," *Readings and Writings: Semiotic Counter-Strategies* (London: Verso, 1983).

14. Lauren Rabinovitz, *Points of Resistance: Women, Power, and Politics in the New York Avant-Garde Cinema, 1943–1971* (Urbana: University of Illinois Press, 1991); David E. James, *Allegories of Cinema: American Film in the 1960s* (Princeton: Princeton University Press, 1989).

I. Avant-Garde and Mass Culture

1. Clement Greenberg, "Avant-Garde and Kitsch," *Partisan Review* 6, no. 5 (Fall 1939), pp. 34–49. Reprinted in C. Greenberg, *Art and Culture* (Boston: Beacon, 1961) and in F. Frascina, ed., *Pollock and After* (New York: Harper and Row, 1985), pp. 21–33. Page numbers refer to this edition.

2. Like several writers in the Anglo-American tradition, Greenberg uses the term "avant-garde" to designate any form of modern art that opposes traditional modes of representation. His conception of "avant-garde" actually corresponds to what I will call high modernism.

3. These theorists characterized mass culture as intrinsically oppressive. Their contemporaries, Walter Benjamin and Antonio Gramsci, however, argued for shifting the discussion of mass culture from its intrinsic qualities to its uses.

4. Peter Bürger popularized the notion of the historical avant-garde in his *Theory of the Avant-Garde:* "The concept of the historical avant-garde movements used here applies primarily to Dadaism and early Surrealism, but also and equally to the Russian avant-garde after the October revolution. . . . A common feature of all these movements is that they do not reject individual artistic techniques and procedures of earlier art but reject that art in its entirety, thus bringing about a radical break with tradition."

Bürger distinguishes between the historical avant-garde and later avant-garde movements that emerged after World War II. "The concept 'historical avant-garde movements' distinguishes these from all those neo-avant-gardist attempts that are characteristic of Western Europe and the United States during the fifties and sixties." *Theory of the Avant-Garde,* trans. Michael Shaw (Minneapolis: University of Minnesota Press, 1984), p. 109, n. 4.

5. The Soviet writer Ilya Ehrenburgh, a firsthand witness of the cultural polemics of the time, voiced a common left-wing opinion when he deplored the surrealists' lack of interest in social problems, being, as he put it, "too busy studying pederasty and dreams." Ilya Ehrenburgh, *Vues par un écrivain de la URSS,* quoted in Helena Lewis, *The Politics of Surrealism* (New York: Paragon, 1988), p. 122.

6. The main texts of these debates are compiled in Ronald Taylor, ed., *Aesthetics and Politics* (London: New Left Review, 1979).

7. Greenberg, "Avant-Garde and Kitsch," p. 24.

8. Ibid., p. 21.

9. Ibid., p. 24.

10. I am using the term "artistic culture" in the broad sense given to it in James Naremore and Patrick Brantlinger, "Introduction: Six Artistic Cultures," in *Modernity and Mass Culture,* ed. J. Naremore and P. Brantlinger (Bloomington: Indiana University Press, 1991), pp. 1–23. The term signifies both a critical discourse and a group of artistic texts that embody an ideological position and a specific cultural politics.

11. For late-1930s New York Left culture, see T. J. Clark, "Clement Greenberg's Theory of Art," *Critical Inquiry* 9, no. 1 (September 1982), reprinted in *Pollock and After;* see esp. pp. 49–50; Daniel Aaron, *Writers on the Left* (New York: Oxford University Press, 1961); James B. Gilbert, *Writers and Partisans* (New York: Wiley, 1968).

12. See Mark Robinson, "*View:* Parade of the Avant-Garde," *Village Voice Literary Supplement,* Feb. 11, 1992, p. 5.

13. For the early avatars of the avant-garde in New York, see Dickran Trishjian, *Skyscraper Primitives* (Middletown, CT: Wesleyan University Press, 1975); Arturo Schwartz, ed., *New York Dada: Duchamp, Man Ray, Picabia* (Munich: Prestel, 1974); Rudolf Kuenzli, ed., *New York Dada* (New York: Willis, Locker and Owens, 1986). For firsthand accounts see, for example, Matthew Josephson's *Life among the Surrealists* (New York: Holt, Rinehart, Winston, 1962); Man Ray, *Self-Portrait* (Boston: Little Brown, 1963).

14. This shift is not exclusive to America. In Europe critics such as Roland Barthes in France and Umberto Eco and Emilio Garroni in Italy were writing about mass cultural phenomena in a fashion that was far from condemnatory, yet often patronizing. See, for example, Barthes's *Mythologies* (originally published in Paris: Flammarion, 1957), translated by Annette Levers and Colin Smith (London: Cape, 1972); and Umberto Eco's *Apocalitticci e integrati* (Milan: Bompiani, 1961).

15. Andreas Huyssen and Matei Calinescu, authors of two excellent overviews of the history and fortunes of the concept of "postmodernism," understand these writers in this connection. See Matei Calinescu, "On Postmodernism," *Five Faces of Modernity* (Durham, NC: Duke University Press, 1987), pp. 263–312; and Andreas Huyssen, "Mapping the Postmodern," *After the Great Divide* (Bloomington: Indiana University Press, 1986), pp. 178–220.

16. Clement Greenberg, "Avant-Garde and Kitsch," p. 25.

17. As Greenberg himself acknowledges, both alternatives to the bourgeois order are often in narrow interaction with each other: "Nevertheless, without the circulation of revolutionary ideas in the air about them, they [the artistic bohemia] would never have been able to isolate the concept of the 'bourgeois' in order to define what they were *not*" (22). Walter Benjamin makes a similar connection between bohemian artists and political radicals in "The Paris of the Second Empire in Baudelaire," *Charles Baudelaire,* trans. Harry Zohn (London: New Left, 1973), pp. 11–19. On the interrelation of social radicals and modern artists, see also Donald D. Egbert, *Social Radicalism and the Arts* (Princeton: Princeton University Press, 1970), and more recently Jerry Seigel, *Bohemian Paris: Culture, Politics, and the Limits of Bourgeois Life* (New York: Viking, 1986).

18. Greenberg, "Avant-Garde and Kitsch," p. 23.

19. Ibid., p. 25.

20. Ibid.

21. T. J. Clark, "Clement Greenberg's Theory of Art," p. 54.

22. *Partisan Review* 7, no. 4 (July–August 1940), pp. 296–310. Reprinted in *Pollock and After*, ed. F. Frascina, pp. 35–46. References given are from the latter edition.

23. C. Greenberg, "Towards a Newer Laocoon," p. 39.

24. Withdrawing from Marxist-oriented thought to formalist criteria of value was a symptomatic shift among many American art and culture critics during the late thirties and early forties. This shift affected profoundly the cultural politics of the New York avant-garde world, and, as we will see in chapter three, had important resonances within American avant-garde film culture. For a thorough account of this shift, see Serge Guilbaut, *How New York Stole the Idea of Modern Art* (Chicago: University of Chicago Press, 1983).

25. Bürger's book became the object of a lively debate shortly after its publication, provoking a wide range of responses from praise to vigorous attacks. See, for example, W. M. Lüdke, ed., *Theorie der Avant-Garde: Antworten auf Peter Bürgers Bestimmung von Kunst und Bürgerlicher Gesellschaft* (Frankfurt: Suhrkamp, 1976).

26. Although Bürger does not state as much, it seems to me that—accepting the simplification that this implies—Kant's complete isolation of the aesthetic and Schiller's qualified autonomy prefigure two main critical trends in art and literary criticism: formalist approaches versus theories concerned with the social place of art.

27. Bürger, *Theory of the Avant-Garde*, p. 44.

28. Ibid., p. 46.

29. See Fredric Jameson's comments on the value of utopian memories in *Marxism and Form* (Princeton: Princeton University Press, 1974), pp. 83–98.

30. See Herbert Marcuse, "The Affirmative Character of Culture," *Negations* (Boston: Beacon, 1968), pp. 88–133. It is important to point out that Marcuse's concept of "culture" has a wider scope than "art" or the aesthetic.

31. Bürger, *Theory of the Avant-Garde*, p. 46.

32. Marcuse, "Affirmative Character of Culture," p. 114.

33. T. J. Clark, "Clement Greenberg's Theory of Art," p. 53.

34. This assumption is especially pervasive among critics associated with the Frankfurt School. It underlies Jürgen Habermas's writings on the transformation of the public sphere, as well as some later pieces such as "Modernity and Postmodernity," *New German Critique* (Winter 1981), pp. 3–14; see esp. pp. 4–5.

35. Courbet's influence rises with the motif of the "Salon of 1851." Clement Greenberg, "Towards a Newer Laocoon," in *Pollock and After*, p. 39. The authoritative book on Courbet is T. J.

Clark, *Image of the People: Gustave Courbet and the Second French Republic: 1848–1851* (Greenwich, CT: New York Graphic Society, 1973).

36. Although the first manifestations of aestheticism can be dated a little earlier, if we take, as historians usually do, Théophile Gautier's preface to *Mademoiselle de Maupin* (1835) as the manifesto of *l'art pour l'art*. Gautier, however, does not use this expression until later, in his book *L'Art moderne* (1856). Egbert, *Social Radicalism and the Arts*, pp. 151–52. See also Mario Praz, *The Romantic Agony* (New York: Oxford University Press, 1970 [1951]), p. 213ff.

37. Meyer Schapiro, "The Social Bases of Art," and "The Nature of Abstract Art," published in 1936 and 1937 respectively; reprinted in Schapiro, *Modern Art: The Nineteenth and Twentieth Centuries* (New York: Braziller, 1978), pp. 185–211. Schapiro's articles are insightfully commented on by Thomas Crow, "Modernism and Mass Culture in the Visual Arts," in *Pollock and After: The Critical Debate*, pp. 233–66.

38. Karl Marx, "The Eighteenth Brumaire of Louis Bonaparte," *The Marx-Engels Reader*, ed. Robert Tucker (New York: Norton, 1978), p. 602.

39. Ibid.

40. Jürgen Habermas, *The Structural Transformation of the Public Sphere* (Cambridge, MA: MIT Press, 1989).

41. Jürgen Habermas, "The Public Sphere," *New German Critique* (Fall 1974), p. 52ff.

42. The art of David and his followers could add to the examples of "integrated art" listed by T. J. Clark. Since David sought to express the ethos of the French revolution, his art can be said to maintain a harmonious relation with the ideals and aspirations of its social basis.

43. Crow, "Modernism and Mass Culture in the Visual Arts," p. 244.

44. Greenberg, "Avant-Garde and Kitsch," p. 23.

45. Bürger, *Theory of the Avant-Garde*, p. 33.

46. Walter Benjamin, *Charles Baudelaire*, p. 106.

47. In the words of Matei Calinescu, "In France, Italy, Spain and other European countries the avant-garde, despite its own contradictory claims, tends to be regarded as the most extreme form of artistic negativism—art itself being the first victim. As for modernism, whatever its specific meaning in different languages and for different authors, it never conveys the sense of universal and hysterical negation so characteristic of the avant-garde. The anti-traditionalism of modernism is often subtly traditional." *Five Faces of Modernity*, pp. 140–41.

48. Bürger, *Theory of the Avant-Garde*, p. 49.

49. Ultimately, as James Naremore and Patrick Brantlinger state, these texts' belief in the transcendence of art would determine their modernist character: "In English literature the quintessential modernist texts are Joyce's *Ulysses* and Eliot's *The Waste Land*—both of them experimental montages, mixing the artifacts of urban mass culture with fragments of classical literature, encouraging belief in the transcending value of their own sophisticated craft." Naremore and Brantlinger, *Modernity and Mass Culture,* p. 10.

50. See Walter Benjamin, "The Author as Producer," *The Essential Frankfurt School Reader,* ed. Arato and Gebhardt (New York: Continuum, 1982), pp. 254–69. Benjamin adopted this formulation from Bertolt Brecht's ideas. The echo of this (Brechtian/Benjaminian) notion survives in the ideas of several avant-garde filmmakers and critics after May 1968. It underlies, I think, Godard's statements: "Not to make different films, but to make films *differently.*" " Not to make political films, but to make films *politically.*" See Sylvia Harvey, *May '68 and Film Culture* (London: BFI, 1978).

51. For a description of the intellectual position of Frankfurt School critics within these philosophical traditions see Martin Jay, *The Dialectical Imagination* (Boston: Little Brown, 1973), pp. 41–86; Susan Buck-Morss, *The Origin of Negative Dialectics* (New York: Free Press, 1977).

52. *Illuminations,* trans. Harry Zohn (New York: Schocken, 1969), p. 157. The difference between integrated experience and the mere accumulation of sensation underlies much of Benjamin's criticism. The different quality of their experiences separates the novel writer and storyteller, for example. "The storyteller takes what he tells from experience—his own or that reported by others. And he in turn makes it the experience of those who are listening to his tale. The novelist has isolated himself." "The Storyteller," *Illuminations,* p. 87.

53. Ibid., p. 159.

54. Theodor Adorno, "Cultural Criticism and Society," *Prisms,* trans. Samuel and Sherry Weber (Cambridge, MA: MIT Press, 1967), p. 32.

55. See Martin Jay, *The Dialectical Imagination,* p. 187.

56. Benjamin, "The Work of Art in the Age of Mechanical Reproduction," *Illuminations,* p. 258ff. For Benjamin's ideas on the progressive potential of mass cultural forms, see Susan Buck-Morss, "Walter Benjamin's *Passagenwerk,*" *New German Critique* (Spring–Summer 1983), pp. 211–40. Benjamin's redemption of mass culture is also one of the main themes of Buck-Morss's excellent *The Dialectics of Seeing* (Cambridge, MA: MIT Press, 1989).

57. The symbiosis of art and science figures as a prominent ideal in Walter Benjamin's writings. In her reconstruction of Benjamin's *Passagenwerk,* Susan Buck-Morss expresses it as follows: "It could be said that for Benjamin progressive cultural practice entails bringing forth technology and imagination out of their mythic dream states, through making conscious the collective desire for social utopia, and the potential of the new nature to achieve it by translating that desire into the 'new language' of its material forms." S. Buck-Morss, *The Dialectics of Seeing,* p. 125.

58. In the Epilogue of "The Work of Art in the Age of Mechanical Reproduction," Benjamin suggests the closeness between avant-garde attempts to change the forms of everyday life and fascism's mystification of the present. Hence, the futurists' slip into fascism is less an anomaly than a structural possibility embedded in the avant-garde project. It seems to me that many avant-gardist aspirations and tropes have their fascist correlative. Hence the avant-garde's desire to change urban spaces can be related to Albert Speer's totalitarian architecture; its interest in alternative forms of community, to fascism's promotion of forms of collective life; the cult of technology, to the machine-like displays of people in rallies and parades. . . . The list could go on. Fascism is perhaps the outer limit of the avant-garde: the avant-garde institutionalized as state form. This connection seems worth pursuing. Hans Magnus Enzensberger devotes to it some comments in "The Aporias of the Avant-Garde," *The Consciousness Industry* (New York: Seabury, 1974), pp. 22–48.

59. Oscar Negt and Alexander Klüge, "The Public Sphere and Experience," trans. Peter Labanyi, *October,* no. 46 (Fall 1988), pp. 60–82. Selections from *Öffentlichkeit und Erfahrung* (Frankfurt: Verlag, 1972).

60. Peter Labanyi translates the phrase as "production public sphere," while Sara and Frank Lennox prefer "public sphere of production" in their translation of Eberhard Knödler-Bunte's "The Proletarian Public Sphere and Political Organization," *New German Critique* (Summer 1973), pp. 51–75.

61. Negt and Klüge, "The Public Sphere and Experience," p. 71.

62. Ibid., p. 71, n.19.

63. I am focusing on French modernity because these modern developments first became visible in France. France is also the country of origin of the idea of the avant-garde and of its most influential manifestations.

64. The first department store was the *Bon Marché,* opened by Aristide Boucicaut in 1852. See Michael Miller, *The Bon Marché* (Princeton: Princeton University Press, 1981). However,

the arcades—analyzed by Walter Benjamin in his seminal *Passagenwerk*—might be described as the original department store format. On the late nineteenth century press, see Richard Terdiman, "Newspaper Culture," in *Discourse/Counter-Discourse* (Ithaca, NY: Cornell University Press, 1985), pp. 117–46.

65. In his bleak "A Theory of Mass Culture," Macdonald expresses this idea as follows: "There are theoretical reasons why mass culture is not and cannot be any good. I take it as axiomatic that culture can only be produced by and for human beings. But in so far as people are organized as masses, they lose their human identity and quality" (69). In *Mass Culture: The Popular Arts in America,* ed. Bernard Rosenberg and David Manning White (Glencoe, IL: Free Press, 1958), pp. 59–73; originally published in *Diogenes,* no. 3 (Summer 1953). As I will show in this section, "the masses" often do not respond as such to the prompting of mass culture, showing, on the contrary, a remarkable ability to create some forms of community around the culture of consumption.

66. The Saint-Simonians, for example, formed a "family" at the Hôtel de Gesvers in Paris under the leadership of Saint-Amand Bazard and Prosper Enfantin. Later, after a falling-out between the two leaders, part of the community moved to an estate at Mènilmontant where they maintained their collective lifestyle. Egbert, *Social Radicalism and the Arts,* p. 125.

67. Raymond Williams, *Marxism and Literature* (London: Oxford University Press, 1977), pp. 114–20. This concept is further developed in Raymond Williams's "Formations," *Culture* (London: Fontana, 1981), pp. 61–97.

68. See Susanna Barrows's essay in *Paris Pleasures: From Daumier to Picasso,* ed. Barbara Stern Schapiro (Boston: Museum of Fine Arts/David Godine, 1991): "Lodged in dreary, crowded quarters, urban workers could find in cafes the amenities that their domestic surroundings lacked: heat, light, and distraction. Most had been raised in family circles that valued sociability over privacy; once installed in the city, they turned quite naturally to the cafe for their new sense of community," p. 144.

69. Thomas Crow, "Modernism and Mass Culture in the Visual Arts," p. 251. The quote refers to George Seurat's fascination with the poster artist Jules Cheret.

70. For the structure and cultural significance of the cabaret, see Jerry Seigel, "Publicity and Fantasy: The World of the Cabarets," *Bohemian Paris,* pp. 215–42.

71. T. J. Clark, *The Painting of Modern Life* (Princeton: Princeton University Press, 1984), p. 210. Greil Marcus explores the relation between the commune and the famous Parisian singer

Thérèse in "The Dance That Everybody Forgot," *New Formations* 1, no. 2 (Summer 1987), pp. 37–50.

72. Cubists and Russian futurists were also fascinated by the cabaret, café-concert, music hall, and variety theater. See Jeffrey S. Weiss, "Picasso, Collage, and the Music Hall"; Robert Rosemblum, "Cubism and Pop Art"; and John E. Bowlt, "A Brazen Can-Can in the Temple of Art: The Russian Avant-Garde and Popular Culture"; all in *Modern Art and Popular Culture,* ed. Kirk Varnedoe and Adam Gopnik (New York: MOMA, 1990).

73. Louis Aragon, *Paris Peasant,* trans. Simon Watson Taylor (London: Cape, 1971), p. 79.

74. On the favored haunts and night spots of American bohemians and avant-gardists from the abstract expressionists to Warhol, see Ronald Sukenick, *Down and In: Life in the Underground* (New York: Beech Tree, 1988).

75. For an interesting attempt to systematize oppositional uses of urban space, see Michel de Certeau, "Walking in the City," in *The Practice of Everyday Life* (Berkeley: University of California Press, 1986), pp. 90–110.

76. Both the Paris Commune in 1871 and the student revolts of May 1968 opposed "straight" uses of urban spaces as part of their overall rebellion. Popular festivities such as carnivals also involve a symbolic transformation of public spaces for purposes other than everyday business. Gay Pride Parades involve a similar "deviation," to translate the situationist term *détournement,* of straight uses of the street, as the collectivity takes over the city to externalize what is usually forced into the shadows.

77. In an early passage in *Nadja,* Breton recounts the fascination that overtook him one day with the signs of *Vins et charbons.* He also describes a huge advertisement for Mazda as "luminous" and "disturbing." See *Nadja,* trans. Richard Howard (New York: Grove, 1960), pp. 27–28, and 129.

78. See Greil Marcus, *Lipstick Traces: A Secret History of the Twentieth Century* (Cambridge, MA: Harvard University Press, 1989), pp. 378–90, and passim.

79. T. J. Clark, *The Painting of Modern Life,* p. 25ff.

80. Besides the already quoted *Nadja* and *Paris Peasant,* several other personal testimonies are good sources on the haunts of the surrealist group. See, for example, Luis Buñuel, *Mon dernier soupir* (Paris: Gallimard, 1981); Matthew Josephson, *Life among the Surrealists;* Man Ray, *Self-Portrait;* Salvador Dalí's *Oui 1* (Paris: Gonthier, 1971).

For the public life of dadaists, see Richard Huelsenbeck, *Memoirs of a Dada Drummer* (New York: Viking, 1974) and "En Avant-Dada," in R. Motherwell, ed., *The Dada Painters and Poets* (Cambridge, MA: Belknap, 1972); Richard Hausmann, *Courier Dada* (Paris: Terrain Vague, 1958); George Grosz, *A Little Yes and a Big No,* trans. Lola Sachs (New York: Dial, 1947); Hans Richter, *Dada: Art and Anti-Art* (New York: Oxford University Press, 1964); Hans J. Kleinschmidt, "Berlin Dada," in Stephen Foster and Rudolf Kuenzli, eds., *Dada Spectrum: The Dialectics of Revolt* (Madison, WI: Coda, 1979).

81. Louis Aragon, *Paris Peasant,* p. 29.

82. For overviews of negative theories of mass culture, see Leo Lowenthal, *Literature, Popular Culture, and Society* (Engelwood Cliffs, NJ: Prentice-Hall, 1961), and Patrick Brantlinger, *Bread and Circuses: Theories of Mass Culture as Social Decay* (Ithaca, NY: Cornell University Press, 1983).

83. The attempt to understand the culture industry and consumer culture in this dialectical fashion is the underlying motif in several forms of cultural criticism that have emerged since the mid-seventies. Negt and Klüge's *Öffentlichkeit und Erfahrung* is an important predecessor in this respect. In English speaking academia, this emergence has been accompanied by revisions of Adorno and Horkheimer's classic analysis of the culture industry, and the "rediscovery" of the works of Walter Benjamin and Antonio Gramsci. Among the earliest proponents of these views are Fredric Jameson, "Reification and Utopia in Mass Culture," *Social Text* 1, no. 1 (1979), pp. 120–47, and Tania Modleski, *Loving with a Vengeance* (Greenwich, CT: Archon, 1981). In Britain, the most important example of this shift is the work coming out of the Birmingham Center for Contemporary Cultural Studies. Almost programmatic pieces of the work of the center are Stuart Hall's "Encoding/Decoding," *Culture, Media Language,* ed. Stuart Hall et al. (London: New Left Review, 1979), pp. 129–38; and "Notes on Deconstructing the Popular," in *People's History and Socialist Theory,* ed. Raphael Samuel (London: Routledge and Kegan Paul, 1981), pp. 227–39.

84. Eberhard Knödler-Bunte, "The Proletarian Public Sphere and Political Organization," p. 65.

85. Negt and Klüge, "The Public Sphere and Experience," p. 75. Later on they continue, "So the proletarian life-context is split into two halves. One is reabsorbed into the new production public spheres, and participates in the process of industrialization; the other is disqualified in accordance with the systems of production and the production public sphere by which society is determined," p. 76.

86. Greenberg states in "Avant-Garde and Kitsch" that not all kitsch is devoid of merit, and cites the *New Yorker* as an example of "quality kitsch." Adorno's critique of Thorstein Veblen also

shows his awareness of the fact that in acts of consumption there is a claim to happiness and an implicit protest against present conditions. See T. W. Adorno, *Prisms*, pp. 75–94. For his part, Dwight Macdonald, another fierce critic of kitsch, was one of the best critics of American popular cinema during the 1950s and 1960s.

87. Bürger, *Theory of the Avant-Garde*, p. 54.

88. Walter Benjamin, *Illuminations*, pp. 217–53.

89. Hugo Ball, however, criticizes the falsehood inherent in newspaper language. He asserts that sound poetry is a means "to reject the corrupted language made impossible by journalism." Quoted in R. Huelsenbeck, *Memoirs of a Dada Drummer*, pp. 60–61. Hence the dadaist espousal of the newspaper form must be qualified. They accept the directness and immediacy of the medium, while rejecting the ideology of official journalism. Cf. R. Huelsenbeck "En Avant-Dada," passim.

90. Richard Huelsenbeck, *Memoirs of a Dada Drummer*, p. 71. On photomontages, see also Dawn Ades, *Photomontage* (London: Thames and Hudson, 1986), and Douglas Kahn, *John Heartfield: Art and Mass Media* (New York: Tanam, 1985).

91. Charles Baudelaire, *The Mirror of Art*, trans. Jonathan Mayne (New York: Phaidon, 1955); Oscar Wilde, *The Artist as Critic*, ed. Richard Ellmann (New York: Vintage, 1970); and also Wilde, *The Decorative Arts in America* (New York: Brentano, 1909), which contains some pieces not found in Ellmann's collection.

92. Mallarmé's review only lasted six numbers, from September to December of 1874. For some selections, see Marcel Jean, ed., *The Autobiography of Surrealism* (New York: Viking, 1982), pp. 284–86.

93. Salvador Dalí, "Poésie de l'utile standardisé," *Oui 1: La Révolution paranoïaque-critique* (Paris: Gonthier, 1971). "Modernité ne veut pas dire toiles peintes par Sonia Delaunay, ni *Metropolis* de Fritz Lang, mais pull-overs de hockey de manufacture anonyme anglaise; elle veut dire film lui aussi moyenne, qui fait rire avec les plaisanteries les plus connnues," p. 66.

94. The manifesto is printed and translated in Christina Taylor, *Futurism: Politics, Painting and Performance* (Ann Arbor: University of Michigan Research Press, 1979).

95. Fernand Léger, "The Machine Aesthetic." This article was first published in *Bulletin de l'Effort Moderne*, 1924, and appeared in English the following year in *Little Review*. It is reprinted in Léger's *The Function of Painting*, trans. Alexandra Anderson (New York: Viking, 1973), pp. 52–61.

96. Matei Calinescu, *Five Faces of Modernity*, p. 254.

97. Theodor Adorno considers striving for the new an aspect that modernist aesthetics shares with commercial culture. Both of them are deeply aware of their position in time: modernist and avant-garde art see themselves as endpoints of a cultural tradition; the mass cultural product emphasizes novelty as its justification. "The new in art is the aesthetic counterpart to the expanding reproduction of capital in society." *Aesthetic Theory* (Boston: Routledge and Kegan Paul, 1984), p. 31.

98. Charles Baudelaire, "Salon of 1846," *The Mirror of Art,* pp. 70–71. And years later, in "Salon of 1859," he wrote: "I would rather return to the diorama, whose brutal and enormous magic has the power to impose a genuine illusion upon me! I would rather go to the theater and feast my eye on the scenery, in which I find my dream artistically expressed and tragically concentrated! These things, because they are false, they are infinitely closer to the truth; whereas the majority of our landscape painters are liars, precisely because they have forgotten to lie." *The Mirror of Art,* p. 284.

99. Rimbaud, "Alchemy of the Word," a text later canonized by the surrealists. *Complete Works,* trans. Wallace Fowlie. (Chicago: University of Chicago Press, 1970), p. 193.

100. Huyssen, *After the Great Divide,* p. 13.

101. Bernard Gendron, "Jamming at Le Boeuf: Jazz and the Paris Avant-Garde," *Discourse* 12, no. 1 (Fall–Winter 1989–90), pp. 3–27.

102. Ibid., pp. 6–7.

103. On the significance of subcultural style, see Dick Hebdige, *Subculture: The Meaning of Style* (London: Methuen, 1979).

104. Jules Barbey d'Aurevilly, author of a biography of George Brummell, the first study on dandyism, puts it as follows: "It is thus that Frivolity [which he glosses in a footnote: "The hateful name bestowed upon a whole class of preoccupations which are really very legitimate, since they correspond to real wants"], on the one hand, acting on a people who are coarse and utilitarian, on the other Imagination, claiming its rights in the face of a moral law too severe to be genuine, produced a kind of translation, a science of manners and attitudes, impossible elsewhere. And of this Brummell was the final expression and can never be equalled." *Dandyism,* trans. Douglas Ainslie (New York: PAJ Publications, 1988 [1845]), p. 43.

105. The dandy's emphasis on style in appearance must be connected to the role played by literary style in aestheticism and *l'art pour l'art* movements. Patrick Brantlinger connects the importance of literary style to the decadents' rejection of the present: "Out of their impotence and rage in the face of bourgeois hege-

mony, decadent writers sought their revenge by declaring style, that seemingly least powerful value, to be their private monopoly, off limits to the bourgeoisie. Style was a mystery beyond the ken of ordinary mortals." *Bread and Circuses*, p. 126. It is interesting, to my eyes, that the cultivation of literary style, which results in modernist withdrawal, has also an avant-gardist counterpart in the desire to integrate style in everyday life through dress, among other things.

106. In the same piece, Oscar Wilde offers a more extended version of his thesis which emphasizes the desire to make dandyism a generalized social practice: "And finally, there is this to be said: art, it is true, can never have any other aim but its own perfection, and, it may be, that the artist, merely wanting to contemplate and to create, is wise in not busying himself about change in others: yet wisdom is not always the best; there are times when she sinks to the level of common sense; and from the passionate folly of those, and there are many, who desire that Beauty shall be confined no longer to the bric-a-brac of the collector and the dust of the museum, but shall be, as it should be, the natural and national inheritance of all, from this noble unwisdom, I say, who knows what new loveliness shall be given to life, and under these more exquisite conditions, what perfect artist born? *Le milieu se renovellant, l'art se renouvelle.*" "The Relation of Dress to Art," in *The Artist as Critic,* ed. Richard Ellmann (New York: Vintage, 1970), p. 20.

107. Oscar Wilde, "Phrases and Philosophies for the Use of the Young," *The Artist as Critic,* pp. 433–34.

108. Rosalind Williams, "Dandyism," in *Dream Worlds* (Berkeley: University of California Press, 1982).

109. Joris Karl Huysmans, *Against the Grain* (New York: Dover, 1969), passim.

110. Baudelaire, *The Mirror of Art,* p. 56.

111. George Simmel, in his famous "The Metropolis and Mental Life," regards the cultivation of originality in one's lifestyle as a response to the depersonalized environment of the metropolis. "The Metropolis and Mental Life," in *On Individuality and Social Forms,* ed. David Levine (Chicago: University of Chicago Press, 1970).

112. As did the Arts and Crafts movements in late nineteenth-century England. William Morris and his disciples, for example, tried to introduce art in everyday life as a mean to restore the integrity of experience broken down by the advance of industrialization. Naturally, Morris was very close to the utopian socialists in ideology and in the magnitude of his project: the global redesign of everyday life. Morris's was a sort of dandyism, but it differed

from the dandyism of Baudelaire and Wilde, for example, in that it sought to restore past forms of authenticity—medievalism and artisan modes of production. Wilde and Baudelaire, on the other hand, cultivated artificiality and sought to transcend the present by engaging its forms, not by escaping into the past.

113. George Grosz, *A Little Yes and a Big No,* pp. 100–103.

114. The connection between surrealism and dandyism is also pursued, in a somewhat different context, by Alain and Odette Virmaux, "L'heritage du dandisme et le goût de la provocation," in *Les Surréalistes et le cinéma* (Paris: Seghers, 1976).

115. See Anna Balakian, *Surrealism: The Road to the Absolute* (Chicago: University of Chicago Press, 1986 [1970]), esp. the section "The Signal Lights," pp. 37–119.

116. A. Breton, *Nadja,* pp. 37–41. Louis Aragon also wrote on the "Théâtre Moderne," where Breton saw *Les Détraquées:* "Very uneven plays were staged there, *L'École des garçonnes, Ce Coquin du printemps,* and a sort of masterpiece titled *Fleur de Péché:* a model of the erotic, spontaneous, lyrical genre, which we would like our aesthetes to meditate upon when searching for avant-garde ideas." These plays, often merely an excuse for the "dubious trade" that the theater is a setting to, are, for Aragon, "without tricks and truly modern . . . an art as original as the art of the Christian mystery plays of the middle ages." *Paris Peasant,* p. 119ff.

117. Susan Sontag, *Against Interpretation* (New York: Farrar, Straus, and Giroux, 1966), p. 288.

118. As Huyssen states: "Indeed technology played a crucial, if not *the* crucial role in the avant-garde's attempt to overcome the art/life dichotomy and make art productive in the transformation of everyday life." *After the Great Divide,* p. 9.

119. See Donald Drew Egbert, *Social Radicalism and the Arts,* pp. 119–33 for Saint-Simon's ideas on art and his use of the concept "avant-garde." Matei Calinescu, in *Five Faces of Modernity,* corrects Egbert in two details. First, Calinescu states that, although inspired by Saint-Simon, the term avant-garde does not occur in his writings, but in those of his disciples. The first occurrence of the term is thus found in the dialogue "*L'artiste, le savant et l'industriel,*" (1825) written by Olinde Rodrigues, although initially attributed to Saint-Simon. He further shows that, even though the actual term doesn't appear until the dialogue published in 1825, the idea is expressed in its current sense as early as 1820, in the *Lettres de H. de Saint-Simon à Messieurs les Jurés.* See *Five Faces of Modernity,* p. 101. (Cf. Egbert, *Social Radicalism and the Arts,* p. 121).

120. Susan Buck-Morss, *The Dialectics of Seeing,* p. 126.

121. Bertolt Brecht, *Brecht on Brecht,* ed. John Willet (New York: Hill and Wang, 1964), p. 73. Other sections on uses of tech-

nology in stage representation are "The Film, the Novel, and the Epic Theater," and "On the Radio as an Apparatus of Communication."

122. Sergei Eisenstein, *Film Form and the Film Sense,* ed. and trans. Jay Leyda (New York: Meridian, 1964), p. 62. See also Dziga Vertov, *The Writings of Dziga Vertov,* trans. Kevin O'Brien, ed. Annette Michaelson (Berkeley: University of California Press, 1984).

123. See Andreas Huyssen, "The Vamp and the Machine," in *After the Great Divide,* p. 69.

124. From *passé.* In futurist lingo, anything they regarded as outmoded.

125. F. T. Marinetti, *Selected Writings,* ed. R. W. Flint, p. 97.

126. Richard Huelsenbeck considers the dadaists' interest in machines as analogous to their interest in the unconscious, since both are forms of automatism. "Psychoanalytical Notes in Modern Art." *Memoirs of a Dada Drummer,* ed. Hans J. Kleinschmidt, trans. Joachim Neuegroschel (New York: Viking, 1974), p. 95, n. 61.

127. The idea was also pursued outside art in a fashion that was far from radical: with the help of chronophotography, developed by Marey and Muybridge, and film cameras, Frederick Taylor researched the movements of workers, seeking to eliminate unnecessary waste of energy or distractions to convert them into mere pieces of machinery. See Peter Wollen, "Cinema/Americanism/The Robot," in *Modernity and Mass Culture,* ed. Naremore and Brantlinger, pp. 43–70.

128. As maximally functional, soberly designed constructs, machines foreswore ornamental excess and were therefore seen as manifestations of a "masculine principle." Viennese architect Adolf Loos was the author of the most influential formulation of these ideas in his piece "Ornament and Crime," (1908), where he aligned useless flourish, femininity, primitiveness, and crime—for him, mutually implicated concepts. Loos's piece is reprinted in *Programs and Manifestos on Twentieth-Century Architecture,* ed. Ulrich Conrads, trans. Michael Bullock. Cambridge, MA: MIT Press, 1970). See in addition, Peter Wollen's comments on Loos, "Fashion/Orientalism/The Body," in *New Formations* 1, no. 1 (Fall 1988). In addition to the association of machines and masculinity, there is also the counterpoint view that conflated machines and femininity, discussed by Huyssen in "The Vamp and the Machine," *After the Great Divide,* esp. pp. 67–74.

129. R. Williams, *Dream Worlds,* p. 82.

130. F. T. Marinetti, *Selected Writings,* p. 119. One can remember in this connection the delirious futurist manifesto "Let's Murder the Moonshine!" (1909), in Marinetti, *Selected Writings,* pp. 44–54.

131. Williams, *Dream Worlds,* p. 82.

132. See Stephen Kern, "Speed," in *The Culture of Time and Space* (Cambridge, MA: Harvard University Press, 1983), pp. 110–30.

133. F. T. Marinetti, *Selected Writings,* p. 41.

134. F. Léger, "Speaking of Cinema," in *The Function of Painting,* p. 100.

135. Standish Lawder, *The Cubist Cinema* (New York: New York University Press, 1975), p. 20.

136. Scott MacDonald, *Avant-Garde Film: Motion Studies* (New York: Cambridge University Press, 1993), p. 3.

2. The American Underground as a Cultural Formation

1. See Raymond Williams, *Marxism and Literature* (London: Oxford University Press, 1977); and *Culture* (London: Fontana, 1981), especially the chapter "Formations."

2. Two recent examples of this indeterminacy in the use of the term are Richard Dyer and Scott MacDonald. Dyer uses "underground" as synonymous with "experimental American film" in his *Now You See It: Studies in Gay and Lesbian Film* (New York: Routledge, 1990). In his recent *Avant-Garde Film* (New York: Cambridge University Press, 1993), MacDonald writes: "I use avant-garde film as a general term to designate the cinematic terrain that has, at various points in its history, been called 'underground film,' 'New American Cinema,' 'experimental film,' 'experimental avant-garde film,' and so on" (15).

3. David James, *Allegories of Cinema* (Princeton: Princeton University Press, 1989).

4. Dominique Noguez, *Une renaissance du cinéma: le cinéma "underground" américain* (Paris: Klincksieck, 1985).

5. Authoritative works on the classical Hollywood studio system are David Bordwell, Kristin Thompson, and Janet Steiger, *The Classical Hollywood Cinema* (New York: Columbia University Press, 1985); Thomas Schatz, *The Genius of the System* (New York: Pantheon, 1988); Douglas Gomery, *The Hollywood Studio System* (London: Macmillan, 1985). On the French film industry, see Richard Abel, *French Cinema, the First Wave, 1919–1929* (Princeton: Princeton University Press, 1983).

6. Luis Buñuel, *Mon dernier soupir* (Paris: Gallimard, 1981), pp. 65–67.

7. Bodizar Zecevic, "The First of the Independents, or How 'A Hollywood Extra' Was Made," *Framework,* no. 21, Summer 1983.

8. For the Creative Film Foundation and the development of other networks of production and distribution for independent

film, see Lauren Rabinovitz, *Points of Resistance: Women, Power and Politics in the New York Avant-Garde Cinema, 1943–1971* (Urbana: University of Illinois Press, 1991).

9. Corporate sponsorship and corporate collections are a fundamental factor in the expansion of modernist and avant-garde art in America. According to Diana Crane, corporations were the fourth force in the country (after non-academic and academic museums, and art centers) in developing art organizations after the late 1940s. Between 1959 and 1979 the number of corporations with substantial art collections went from 16 to 76. Diana Crane, *The Transformation of the Avant-Garde* (Chicago: University of Chicago Press, 1987), p. 6. See also Dick Netzer, *The Subsidized Muse* (New York: Cambridge University Press, 1978).

10. See Jonas Mekas, *Movie Journal* (New York: Macmillan, 1972), p. 162.

11. Matthew Josephson, "The Rise of the Little Cinemas," in *Spellbound in Darkness,* ed. George C. Pratt (Greenwich, CT: New York Graphic Society, 1973), pp. 483–87. Josephson lists two other little cinema groups active in New York City at the time of his writing: Simon Gould's International Film Arts Guild, which had its screenings at the Cameo Theater, and the Film Associates, directed by Montgomery Smith.

12. See catalogue of the series, *Art in Cinema,* ed. Frank Stauffacher (New York: Arno, 1947).

13. See Stephen Dobi, "Cinema 16: The Largest Film Society in America," unpublished dissertation, New York University, 1983; see also Scott MacDonald, "Cinema 16: An Interview with Amos Vogel," *Film Quarterly* (Summer 1984) and "Amos Vogel and Cinema 16," *Wide Angle,* vol. 9, no. 3 (1987).

14. See Shirley Clarke, Amos Vogel, Bill Kenly, et al. "The Expensive Art—A Discussion," on problems of distribution and exhibition of independent film. *Film Quarterly* 13, no. 4 (Summer 1960).

15. Introduction to "Interview with Jonas Mekas," *The Critical Cinema 2: Interviews with Independent Filmmakers* (Berkeley: University of California Press, 1988), p. 77.

16. J. Hoberman, "The Short Happy Life of the Charles," *American Film* (March 1982), pp. 22, 34.

17. There was, however, a star system of sorts; see Mekas's "Emergence of the Underground Star Cinema," *Movie Journal,* p. 121. (Originally published in the *Village Voice,* Feb. 20, 1964.) *Film Culture* occasionally devoted some of its center photographs to the underground stars. The very first to emerge was perhaps Taylor Mead, who starred in Ron Rice's beat picaresque *The Flower Thief* (1959).

18. On the theaters of the underground, see J. Hoberman and Jonathan Rosenbaum, "The Underground," *Midnight Movies* (New York: Harper and Row, 1983) and Dominique Noguez, *Une renaissance du cinéma: le cinéma "underground" américain,* pp. 203–205. On the foundation of Anthology, see Calvin Tomkins, "All Pockets Open," *New Yorker,* January 6, 1973. For critiques of the politics of Anthology, see Lauren Rabinovitz, *Points of Resistance,* p. 141ff.; David Curtis, "A Tale of Two Co-Ops," *To Free the Cinema: Jonas Mekas and the New York Underground* (Princeton: Princeton University Press, 1992); and Constance Penley and Janet Bergstrom, "The Avant-Garde: History and Theories," *Screen* 19, no. 3 (Autumn 1979). On Millennium, see Scott MacDonald, "The 'Millennium' after Twenty Years: Interview with Howard Guttenplan," and Lindley Hanlon and Tony Pipolo, "Interview with Ken and Flo Jacobs," both in *Millennium Film Journal,* nos. 16/17/18 (Fall–Winter 1986–87).

19. Manny Farber, "Experimental Movies," in *Negative Space* (New York: Praeger, 1971).

20. Richard Abel, *French Cinema,* p. 264ff. See also Léon Mussinac's account of his personal involvement in this venture, *Cahiers du Cinéma,* no. 11 (April 1952), p. 6.

21. In the early 1950s Vogel had clashed with Marie Menken and Willard Maas, leading members of the experimental film collective Gryphon, when refusing to show or distribute their films. These filmmakers then decided to handle distribution themselves. David Curtis, *Experimental Cinema* (New York: Universe, 1971), pp. 51–52.

22. In a few years, there were cooperatives in London, Toronto, Hamburg, Tokyo, and Montreal, which followed the model of the original one. Comparable in policies and scope to the New York-based Filmmakers' Cooperative was Canyon Cinema, located in San Francisco, which was founded in 1966 by filmmakers Bruce Baillie and Larry Jordan, among others. Noguez, *Une renaissance du cinéma* pp. 203–205.

23. Richard Abel, *French Cinema,* pp. 255–56; and Standish Lawder, "The Avant-Garde Film and Its Public," in *The Cubist Cinema,* pp. 183–90.

24. J. Hoberman, "The Underground," in Hoberman and J. Rosenbaum's *Midnight Movies,* esp. pp. 42–44.

25. See, for example, Pete Hamill, "Explosion in the Movie Underground," *Saturday Evening Post,* September 28, 1963; and "Cinema Underground," unsigned note in the *New Yorker,* July 13, 1963, pp. 16–17.

26. This term designates the dense network of discourses that surround films—from promotional to critical, to spontaneous

word-of-mouth commentary. Stephen Heath first used and defined the term in this context: "Film . . . must exist . . . even before we enter the cinema—in a kind of englobingly extensive prolongation. The commerce of film depends on this too, recognized in a whole host of epiphenomena from trailers to remakes, from weekly reviews to star magazines, from publicity stills to mementoes (rubber sharks, tee shirts)." "Screen Images, Film Memory," *Edinburgh Magazine* 1 (1976), pp. 33–42.

27. Some examples of these, showing varying degrees of wit and artistry, were reprinted in Mekas's collection of reviews *Movie Journal.* The compilation of Jonas Mekas's *Village Voice* and *Soho Weekly News* reviews just published (September 1994) by Anthology Film Archives is probably the best source for this material.

28. For an informative and extremely well thought out account of New York bohemia, see Ronald Sukenick, *Down and In: Life in the Underground* (New York: Beech Tree, 1988).

29. Richard Abel, *French Cinema,* p. 245ff; Richard Abel, "The Contribution of the French Literary Avant-Garde to Film Theory and Criticism (1907–1924)," *Cinema Journal* 13, no. 3 (Spring 1975); and Stuart Liebman, "French Film Theory," *Quarterly Review of Film Studies* (Winter 1983), pp. 1–23.

30. Quoted in P. Adams Sitney, *Film Culture Reader,* ed. P. Adams Sitney (New York: Praeger, 1970), p. viii.

31. Alongside its devotion to the underground, *Film Culture* continued publishing critical and historical pieces on Hollywood film—see, for example, the special issue on Hollywood blacklisting (Fall 1970); on commercial cinema of some artistic interest—especially in Herman Weinberg's long-running column "Coffee, Brandy, and Cigars"; and on European art cinema.

32. Jonas Mekas, *Movie Journal,* pp. 48–51; further references are given in the text. Mekas published an extended version of this piece entitled "Notes on the New American Cinema," in *Film Culture,* no. 24 (Spring 1962), pp. 6–16.

33. Mekas points out in a piece parallel to the one I am analyzing here, Agee, Loeb, and Levitt did not shape themselves into a "conscious anti-Hollywood movement. . . . These were single individuals who were quietly trying to express their own cinematic truth, to make their own kind of cinema." "Notes on the New American Cinema," *Film Culture,* no. 24 (Spring 1962), p. 13.

34. See his collected reviews in *Agee on Film,* vol. I (Boston: Beacon, 1968 [1958]).

35. Lewis Jacobs, *The Rise of the American Cinema* (New York: Teachers' College Press, 1968), p. 495ff. For an excellent history of this New York documentary school, see William Alexander,

Film on the Left: American Documentary Film from 1931 to 1942 (Princeton: Princeton University Press, 1983).

36. Jonathan Rosenbaum, "*The Savage Eye, Shadows,*" in *The American New Wave 1958–1967,* ed. Bruce Jenkins and Melinda Ward (Minneapolis: Walker Art Center, 1982), p. 27.

37. See Blaine Allen, "The Hip, the Beat, and the Square," *Film Reader,* no. 5, 1982.

38. See, for example, "On the Changing Language of Cinema," *Movie Journal,* p. 48. The cause of the new *man* reveals a male bias in the New American Cinema and in part of the underground; this bias might be inherited from the beats' somewhat misogynist attitudes. Some practices in the underground film community, such as the tendency to underrepresent women filmmakers in the Anthology Film Archives, reveal that "the cause of the new man" may have been more than careless phrasing. See Lauren Rabinovitz, *Points of Resistance,* p. 178ff.

39. Other films produced under the aegis of the New American Cinema were Jonas Mekas's *Guns of the Trees* (1961); Robert Frank's second film, *The Sin of Jesus* (1961); and Adolfas Mekas's *Hallelujah the Hills* (1962). More interesting are Shirley Clarke's *The Connection* (1961), *The Cool World* (1962), and *Portrait of Jason* (1966); Jonas Mekas's *The Brig* (1964); Lionel Rogosin's *Come Back Africa* (1959); and Robert Young and Michael Roemer *Nothing but a Man* (1964). See *The American New Wave,* ed. Jenkins and Ward.

For contemporary receptions of these films, see Dwight Macdonald, "On the Underground," and "The Above Ground Underground," *On Movies* (New York: Da Capo, 1981); Arlene Croce, "New York Letter," *Sight and Sound* (Spring 1962); Colin Young and Gideon Bachman, "New Wave or Gesture?" *Film Quarterly* 14, no. 3 (Spring 1961); Cecile Starr, "Independents of New York," *Sight and Sound* (Winter 1960–61); and *Film Culture,* 1959–62, passim.

40. Cited in *Points of Resistance,* p. 80. The group changed its name to Independent Filmmakers Association after 1955, and counted an active core of about thirty-three filmmakers.

41. *Film Culture,* no. 22–23 (Summer 1961). Reprinted in *Film Culture Reader,* pp. 79–83.

42. Jonas Mekas's first review of Brakhage's films came out in the *Village Voice* on October 26, 1961: "Brakhage's work is far more advanced cinema, true cinema with a small or capital C, author's cinema, personal cinema—whatever name you choose—than *Hiroshima Mon Amour.*" *Movie Journal,* p. 35.

43. David Curtis, *Experimental Cinema,* p. 130.

44. For an excellent discussion of Brakhage's cinema, see David James, "Stan Brakhage: Filmmaker as Poet," *Allegories of Cinema*, pp. 29–58.

45. Mekas may have been thinking of Brakhage when he wrote on the "new film troubadours": "Every day, young men come into town with movies in their pockets. . . . They screen their films at some friend's loft, or perhaps the Figaro, and then disappear. This is the best thing that has happened to cinema since Griffith shot his first close-up." *Movie Journal*, p. 17. *Village Voice*, October 6, 1960.

46. Mekas, *Movie Journal*, p. 120.

47. On Mekas's sporadic use of the term before this review, see Dominique Noguez, *Une Renaissance du cinéma*, pp. 161–62.

48. Mekas, *Movie Journal*, p. 68.

49. Cited in Noguez, *Une renaissance du cinéma*, p. 162.

50. Andrew Ross, *No Respect* (New York: Routledge, 1989), p. 84.

51. See, for example, Philip Rahv, "Twilight of the Thirties," *Partisan Review* 6 (Summer 1939), p. 6. Cited in James Burkhardt Gilbert, *Writers and Partisans* (New York: Wiley, 1968), p. 212.

52. Cited in Rabinovitz, *Points of Resistance*, p. 80.

53. Stan Van Der Beek, "The Cinema Delimina," *Film Quarterly* (Summer 1961), no page number.

54. Samuel Kootz, catalog for the show "The Intrasubjectives," Kootz Gallery, 1949. Cited in Serge Guilbaut, *How New York Stole the Idea of Modern Art* (Chicago: University of Chicago Press, 1983), p. 178.

55. Lionel Trilling, *Freud and the Crisis of Our Culture* (Boston: Beacon, 1955), p. 33.

56. Van Der Beek, "Cinema Delimina," no page number.

57. Manny Farber, "Underground Films," *Negative Space* (New York: Praeger, 1971); originally published in *Commentary* in 1957.

58. David James, *Allegories of Cinema*, p. 95.

3. The 1960s Underground as Political Postmodernism

1. Recall here Lionel Trilling's remark that the counterculture was "practicing modernism in the streets." Cited in Andreas Huyssen, *After the Great Divide* (Bloomington: Indiana University Press, 1986), p. 190.

2. Dwight Macdonald, *On Movies* (New York: Da Capo, 1981), pp. 36–42.

3. *Partisan Review,* of which he was editor for a time, published his two part analysis of the decline of Soviet cinema. The article was meant as a rebuttal of the cultural politics of the Popular Front and the American Communist Party. Already in 1931 Macdonald had extolled the cinema of Soviet directors Sergei Eisenstein and Vsevolod Pudovkin in an article entitled "Eisenstein and Pudovkin in the 1920s" published in *The Miscellany.* Macdonald's enthusiasms at the time were not restricted, however, to the European avant-garde. Also in *The Miscellany,* he published in 1933 a very "auteuristic" article on his own pantheon of Hollywood directors. All of these pieces are reprinted in Dwight Macdonald, *On Movies.* On the popularity of Soviet montage cinema among the New York intelligentsia, see James B. Gilbert, *Writers and Partisans* (New York: Wiley, 1968), pp. 81, 85.

4. For Tyler's early criticism, see, for example, "Hollywood in Disguise; Gods and Goddesses Paid to Be Alive," *View,* no. 2 (October 1940); "Heroes by Welles and Chaplin," *View,* no. 6 (June 1941); "Dorian Gray, Last of the Movie Draculas," *View,* no. 1 (Fall 1946); "Each Man His Own Private Detective," *View,* nos. 9–10 (December 1941–January 1942)—this last reprinted in View: *Parade of the Avant-Garde: An Anthology of* View *Magazine* (New York: Thunder's Mouth, 1991). See also the essays collected in *The Hollywood Hallucination* (New York: Simon and Schuster, 1970), originally published in the early 1940s. For his later opinions on the underground, see his *Underground Film: A Critical History* (New York: Grove, 1969).

5. See James B. Gilbert, *Writers and Partisans* (New York: Wiley, 1968), and Daniel Aaron, *Writers on the Left* (New York: Avon, 1969).

6. "Is Film Criticism Only Propaganda?" Talk delivered at the Fourth New York International Film Festival in 1966, reprinted in Battcock, ed., *The New American Cinema* (New York: Dutton, 1967), p. 71. In Charles Henri Ford and Tyler's 1930s novel *The Young and Evil* (London: GMP, 1989 [1933]), Karel, a stand-in for Tyler himself, delivers a similar message to a communist audience when deriding the party's conception of art: "I wouldn't take all of twentieth-century poetry for *Romeo and Juliet.* The point is that everyone must have jobs and there are 99 competent milliners to one creative artist" (135).

7. "Is Film Criticism Only Propaganda?" p. 68.

8. Ibid., p. 70.

9. Macdonald, *On Movies,* p. 329.

10. Amos Vogel, "Thirteen Confusions," *Evergreen Review* (Summer 1966); reprinted in Battcock, *New American Cinema,* p. 125ff.

11. Andrew Sarris, "The Independent Cinema," *Motive* (November 1966). Reprinted in Battcock, *New American Cinema,* pp. 51–57.

12. See sections 1 and 2, by Lucy Fisher and Stuart Liebman respectively, in *A History of the American Avant-Garde Cinema,* ed. Marilyn Synger (New York: American Federation of the Arts, 1976).

13. Ken Kelman, "Anticipation of the Light," *The Nation,* May 11, 1964. Reprinted in Battcock, *New American Cinema,* pp. 22–33.

14. P. Adams Sitney, *Visionary Film* (New York: Oxford University Press, 1979 [1974]). See also Sitney's Introduction to *The Avant-Garde Film* (New York: New York University Press, 1978).

15. For analogous critiques of Adams Sitney's approach to avant-garde cinema, see Dana Polan, *The Political Language of Film and the Avant-Garde* (Ann Arbor: University of Michigan Research Press, 1985), pp. 64–66, and Constance Penley's review "The Avant-Garde: History and Theories," in *The Future of an Illusion* (Minneapolis: University of Minnesota Press, 1989).

16. Jonas Mekas, *Movie Journal* (New York: Macmillan, 1972), p. 85. First printed in the *Village Voice,* May 2, 1963.

17. See Carel Rowe, *The Baudelairean Cinema* (Ann Arbor: University of Michigan Research Press, 1983). Rowe studies the films of Smith, Anger, and Warhol as representative of the baudelairean sensibility and explores their indebtedness to turn-of-the-century symbolism and aestheticism. Rowe's book purported "to validate Mekas's somewhat hypothetical nomenclature and make a rigorous attempt to establish a critical context for a group of American avant-garde films." In the process he discovered "a rich system of resemblance between the form and content of these films and the technique and themes of the Decadent/Symbolist movement which had been inspired by the French poet Charles Baudelaire" (xv). Following the orientation of traditional comparative studies, much of the text is devoted to drawing parallels between the themes and styles of both 1960s avant-garde movies and turn-of-the-century symbolism and decadentism. Hence, a theme such as the myth of Persephone, favored by symbolist poets, is also "the elemental material" of Jack Smith's *Flaming Creatures;* a decadentist motif such as the phoenix born from the ashes is "basic" to Kenneth Anger's *Fireworks;* and vampirism is crucial not only to Charles Baudelaire and a Joris Karl Huysmans, but also shapes Andy Warhol's attitude toward his superstars. From a formal point of view, the superimpositions present in the work of nineteenth-century French symbolist painter Gustave Moreau are analogous to those of Anger's *Inauguration of the Pleasure Dome*

and Ron Rice's *Chumlum*. These parallels are quite unmediated and enact a particular form of historical idealism: the belief that gestures, themes, and forms (in this case associated with the ethos of artistic rebellion of decadentism), can jump across time, media, genres, and cultures and reappear elsewhere (in the 1960s New York underground) with the same meaning and impact. Yet at least after structuralism we know that meaning is always differential, a function of insertion within a signifying system. Rowe, however, does not really provide information on the place that stylistic gestures from French decadentism or from the American underground cinema occupy within the range of possibility and variation available in their respective cultures at their specific historical contexts.

18. Walter Benjamin, *Charles Baudelaire,* ed. and trans. Harry Zohn (London: New Left Review, 1973). Dana Polan also mediates his discussion of the American avant-garde through Benjamin's writings on Baudelaire, yet from a perspective different from mine. He draws a typology of avant-garde filmmaking based on the gallery of themes and textual responses Benjamin discerns in Baudelaire. See "Political Vagaries of the American Underground," in *The Political Language of Film and the Avant-Garde,* p. 60ff.

19. For a more comprehensive discussion of Susan Sontag's criticism, see Sohnya Sayres, *Susan Sontag: The Elegiac Modernist* (New York: Routledge, 1990).

20. Sontag, *Against Interpretation* (New York: Farrar, Straus, and Giroux, 1966), pp. 293–304. Further references are given in the text.

21. Irving Howe, "The New York Intellectuals," *Commentary* 46, no. 4 (October 1968). Reprinted in Irving Howe, *Selected Writings: 1950–1990* (New York: Harcourt, Brace, Jovanovich, 1990). Further references are given in the text.

22. Herbert Marcuse's inclusion with Norman O. Brown and Marshall McLuhan seems to be based on the popularity of Marcuse's works on university campuses and also on a selective (and rather perverse) foregrounding of some writings, such as *Reason and Revolution, An Essay on Liberation,* and *Eros and Civilization.* The last volume was somewhat of a "sleeper": published in the early fifties, the emergence of the "sexual revolution" during the polymorphously erotic 1960s gave the book its immense social resonance and linked its destiny to the counterculture. However, if one judges by his 1930s writings (collected in *Negations*), and even his *One-Dimensional Man* (1964), Marcuse's cultural criticism seems closer to modernist thinkers like Irving Howe; like him, Marcuse openly rejects the fascination with mass culture and the rhetoric of instinctual liberation and untrammeled desire that Howe discerned at the center of the new sensibility.

23. "Though linked to New Left politics, it [the new sensibility] goes beyond any politics, making itself felt, like a spreading blot of anti-intellectualism, in every area of intellectual life." Howe, "The New York Intellectuals," p. 267.

24. Leslie Fiedler, "Cross the Border—Close the Gap," *The Collected Essays of Leslie Fiedler* (New York: Stein and Day, 1971), p. 459.

25. Among American critics, Irving Howe first wrote of "postmodern literature" in relation to mass culture in 1959 in his "Mass Society and Postmodern Fiction," in *Partisan Review* 26, no. 3 (Summer 1959). In Howe, "postmodernism" has negative connotations, as a fall from the heights of modernism. Another early use was Harry Levin, "What Was Modernism?" *Massachusetts Review* 1, no. 4 (August 1960). For Leslie Fiedler's use of postmodernism—always as a positive development from modernism—see "The Death of Avant-Garde Literature," and "Cross the Border—Close the Gap," in *The Collected Essays of Leslie Fiedler*, vol. II. In the tradition of American cultural theory, see the more recent formulations by Ihab Hassan, *The Dismemberment of Orpheus* (Madison: University of Wisconsin Press, 1982 [1971]) and Fredric Jameson, "Postmodernism and Consumer Society," in *The Anti-Aesthetic* (Port Townsend, WA: Bay, 1983), later expanded in "Postmodernism, or the Cultural Logic of Late Capitalism," *New Left Review* 146 (July–August 1984) and then into *Postmodernism, or the Cultural Logic of Late Capitalism* (Durham, NC: Duke University Press, 1991). See also Jameson, "Periodizing the 1960s," in *The 60s without Apology,* ed. S. Aronowitz, F. Jameson, S. Sayres, A. Stephanson (Minneapolis: University of Minnesota Press, 1984). Unlike earlier American formulations of the concept, Jameson's writings acknowledge theories of the postmodern emerging from European philosophy and cultural theory, most notably Jean-François Lyotard, *The Postmodern Condition,* trans. Geoff Bennington and Brian Massumi (Minneapolis: University of Minnesota Press, 1984); Jürgen Habermas, "Modernity and Postmodernity," *New German Critique* (Winter 1981), pp. 3–14; and *The Philosophical Discourse of Modernity,* trans. Frederick Lawrence (Cambridge, MA: MIT Press, 1987).

26. Tom Wolfe, *The Kandy-Kolored Tangerine-Flake Streamline Baby* (New York: Noonday, 1965), pp. viii, ix. Further references are given in the text.

27. Serge Guilbaut, *How New York Stole the Idea of Modern Art,* trans. Arthur Goldhammer (Chicago: University of Chicago Press, 1983). Guilbaut's study had been predated by less comprehensive, yet equally effective accounts on the liaisons between modernist ideology, abstract expressionism, and Cold War politics.

See Eva Cockcroft, "Abstract Expressionism: Weapon of the Cold War," *Artforum* 12 (June 1974), pp. 39–41, and Max Kozloff, "American Painting during the Cold War," *Artforum* 13 (May 1973), pp. 43–54, both reprinted in *Pollock and After,* ed. F. Frascina (New York: Harper and Row, 1985). The official acceptance of modernism was not uncontested. Congressman George Dondero, Republican representative from Michigan, started a campaign against communism in the arts in 1953. Predictably, muralists and modernists were Dondero's main *bêtes noires.* See Jane De Hart Matthews, "Art and Politics in Cold War America," *American Historical Review,* 81 (1976), esp. 771–72.

28. Leslie Fiedler, "The Death of Avant-Garde Literature," *Collected Essays,* pp. 455–56.

29. The popularization of taboo themes was due to several court decisions which acquitted previously forbidden work on the grounds of their artistic value. The most famous of these trials were the ones concerning *Tropic of Cancer, Lady Chatterley's Lover,* and *Fanny Hill,* that took place in 1966. See Charles Rembar, *The End of Obscenity* (New York: Leslie B. Adams, 1991 [Random, 1968]), and Felice Flannery Lewis, *Literature, Obscenity, and the Law* (Carbondale, IL: Southern Illinois University Press, 1976). Before these processes, however, underground films had tested the limits of the permissible during the years 1961–1965, and had consequently suffered prosecution.

30. See Mark Ester's informative *A History of the Underground Comic Books* (San Francisco: Straight Arrow, 1974). See also the extremely insightful comments by J. Hoberman and Jonathan Rosenbaum, *Midnight Movies* (New York: Harper and Row, 1983), pp. 114–16. For Hoberman and Rosenbaum, the grim thematics of the horror comics act as a "repressed," and therefore ever-returning, element in American culture.

31. For an extremely well-documented account of the debates surrounding the comic books and for a complex portrait of Fredric Wertham, see James B. Gilbert, "Crusade against Mass Culture," in *Cycle of Outrage* (New York: Oxford University Press, 1986).

32. Both are reprinted in Bernard Rosenberg and David Manning White, eds., *Mass Culture* (Glencoe, IL: Free Press, 1957). Further references are given in the text.

33. J. Hoberman, "Desire Under the El: How the Kuchar Brothers Found Hollywood in the Bronx," *Village Voice,* December 8, 1975; Robert Christgau, "Will Art Spoil the Kuchar Brothers?" *New York World Journal Tribune,* November 20, 1966; Paul Arthur, "History and Crass Consciousness: George Kuchar's Fantasies of Un-Power," *Millennium Film Journal,* nos. 20/21 (Fall–Winter 1988–89); David James, "The Critique of Authenticity:

The Kuchars," in *Allegories of Film* (Princeton: Princeton University Press, 1989), pp. 143–49.

34. Greil Marcus, *Mystery Train*, 3rd ed. (New York: Dutton, 1990), pp. 152–53.

35. See Morris Dickstein, "The Age of Rock Revisited," in *Gates of Eden* (New York: Penguin, 1989 [1977]), pp. 183–213. For the connections between rock and modernism, see also Richard Poirier, "Learning from the Beatles," in *The Performing Self* (New York: Oxford University Press, 1970), and more recently, Simon Frith, "Rock and the Politics of Memory," in *The 60s with-out Apology*, pp. 59–69 and Simon Frith and Howard Horne, *Art into Pop* (London: Methuen, 1987).

36. Such high-art descent of rock visionaries has been noticed in popular representations. In an early scene in Oliver Stone's *The Doors*, a pan of Jim Morrison's apartment in Venice Beach, California, clearly shows, among the room's disorder, copies of the Grove paperback editions of Antonin Artaud's *The Theater and Its Double* and Arthur Rimbaud's *A Season in Hell*.

37. The most exciting account of the origin of the light shows and trip festivals is Tom Wolfe, *The Electric Kool-Aid Acid Test* (New York: Farrar, Straus and Giroux, 1968). See also Eugene Youngblood, *Expanded Cinema* (New York: Dutton, 1970) and David James, *Allegories of Cinema*, pp. 133–37.

38. Greil Marcus, *Lipstick Traces* (Cambridge, MA: Harvard University Press, 1989), pp. 316–17.

39. Morris Dickstein, *Gates of Eden*, p. 189.

40. Andrew Sarris, *Confessions of a Cultist* (New York: Simon and Schuster, 1970), p. 11.

41. What follows is largely inspired by James Naremore, "Authorship and the Cultural Politics of Film Criticism," *Film Quarterly* 44 (Fall 1990). In his piece, Naremore explores the convergence in auteuristic discourse of romanticism, avant-gardism, and modernism, together with a postmodern pop sensibility that embraces popular culture in reaction to the elitism of the high modernist canon.

42. "In the realm of role-playing, I stopped lowering my head at the epithet 'cultist' as soon as I realized that the quasi-religious connotation of the term was somewhat justified for those of us who loved movies beyond all reason. . . . Thereafter I could see that the main difference between a cultist and a careerist is that the cultist does not require the justification of a career to pursue his passion, and the careerist does." Sarris, *Confessions of a Cultist*, pp. 13–14.

43. François Truffaut, "A Certain Tendency of the French Cinema," in *Movies and Methods*, ed. Bill Nichols (Berkeley: Uni-

versity of California Press, 1976). For interesting qualifications of Truffaut's evaluation of the French cinema, see Ginette Vincendeau, "France 1945–1965 and Hollywood: The *Policier* as International Text," *Screen* (Spring 1992), pp. 50–79.

44. Jim Hillier, ed., *Cahiers du Cinéma, The 1950s: Neo-Realism, Hollywood, New Wave* (Cambridge, MA: Harvard University Press, 1985), esp. Jacques Rivette, "Discovering America," pp. 68–72.

45. See Jonathan Rosenbaum and J. Hoberman, *Midnight Movies,* "Cults, Fetishes, and Freaks: Sex and Salvation at the Movies" for an analysis of the ideology and history of cultism. Umberto Eco, "*Casablanca:* Cult Movies and Intertextual Collage," *Sub-Stance,* no. 57 (1985). One of the best and most extended pieces of research on the phenomenon of cultism is Cynthia Erb's "Film and Reception: A Contextual and Reading Formation Study of *King Kong* (1933)" (dissertation, Indiana University, 1991), which contains a detailed study of reading tactics and cultist versions inspired by *King Kong.* Other studies of cultist reading formations are Constance Penley's "Brownian Motion: Women, Tactics, and Technology," in *Technoculture,* ed. Constance Penley and Andrew Ross (Minneapolis: University of Minnesota Press, 1991) and Henry Jenkins, *Textual Poachers* (New York: Routledge, 1992).

46. Paul Hammond, ed., *The Shadow and Its Shadow* (London: British Film Institute, 1978), p. 128.

47. "Variations on the Moustache of Menjou." See "Appendix: Buñuel's Film Criticism," in Francisco Aranda, *Luis Buñuel: A Critical Biography,* trans. David Robinson (New York: Da Capo, 1976), pp. 271–72. See also Salvador Dalí's interview "Luis Buñuel," *Oui 1* (Paris: Gonthier, 1971), pp. 118–20.

48. Joseph Cornell's essay was originally published in *View* in 1941; it is reprinted in Paul Hammond, ed., *The Shadow and Its Shadow.*

49. André Breton's "As in a Wood" contains the famous passages that describe his own and his friend Jacques Vaché's unorthodox filmgoing habits: "I agreed wholeheartedly with Jacques Vaché in enjoying nothing so much as dropping into the cinema when whatever was playing was playing, at any point in the show, and leaving at the first hint of boredom—of surfeit—to rush off to another cinema where we behaved the same way, and so on. . . ." *The Shadow and Its Shadow,* p. 43.

50. See David Ehrenstein's comments on *Rose Hobart* in *Film: The Front Line 1984* (Denver: Arden, 1984), pp. 37–39.

51. *Film Culture,* no. 27 (Fall–Winter 1962–63). Reprinted in Jack Smith, *Historical Treasures* (New York: Hanuman, 1991).

52. On the Harlow cult, see Ronald Tavel, "Banana Diary," *Film Culture*, no. 40 (Spring 1966). The Bogart cult was described by Peter Bogdanovich in his piece "Bogie in Excelsis," *Esquire* (September 1965).

53. Matthew Josephson, "The Rise of the Little Cinema," *Motion Picture Classic* 24, no. 1 (September 1926), pp. 34–35, 69, 82. Reprinted in George C. Pratt, ed., *Spellbound in Darkness* (Greenwich, CT: New York Graphic Society, 1973), pp. 483–88, esp. 486.

54. Erik Barnouw reports "The distributors taking these gambles recouped their investments with astonishing speed. . . . WORT-TV, New York, which in 1954 had had live drama every night, had none two years later. In the fall of 1956 its schedule was 88 percent film, and almost all of it consisted of feature films organized under such titles as *Million Dollar Movie*." *Tube of Plenty* (New York: Oxford University Press, 1975), pp. 197–98.

55. For a more complex view of the relations between television and the Hollywood studios, see Chris Anderson, "Hollywood in the Home: TV and the End of the Studio System," in *Modernity and Mass Culture*, ed. James Naremore and Patrick Brantlinger (Bloomington: Indiana University Press, 1991), pp. 80–102. As Anderson amply demonstrates, far from simply pushing studios out of business, television accentuated a trend in Hollywood history: commercial tie-ins with broadcast media. In this respect, TV provided an open market for television films and serials, which replaced the studio production of moderate and low budget formula films; further, it offered a venue for the promotion of film features. See also Thomas Schatz, *The Genius of the System* (New York: Pantheon, 1988), pp. 463–87.

56. R. Ray, *A Certain Tendency of the Hollywood Cinema, 1930–1980* (Princeton: Princeton University Press, 1985), p. 265ff.

57. Harry Alan Potamkin, *The Compound Cinema* (New York: Columbia Teacher's College, 1977). Quoted in J. Hoberman and Jonathan Rosenbaum, *Midnight Movies*, p. 23.

58. Quoted in Fred Wellington, "Liberalism, Subversion, and Evangelism," *The New American Cinema*, ed. Battcock, pp. 44–45.

59. Mekas, *Movie Journal*, p. 86.

60. The qualification "male" is important, since a full-blown lesbian alternative cinema did not emerge until the early years of the gay liberation movement.

61. On the homophile movement of the early 1960s, see Toby Marotta, *The Politics of Homosexuality* (New York: Houghton Mifflin, 1981); John D'Emilio, *Sexual Politics, Sexual Communities* (Chicago: University of Chicago Press, 1983), pp. 149–75; Eric Marcus, *Making History* (New York: Harper/Collins, 1992), esp.

interview with Barbara Gittings and Kay (Tobin) Lahusen, pp. 103–24; Martin Duberman, *Stonewall* (New York: Plume, 1994), pp. 100–17.

62. Ned Polsky, "The Village Beat Scene," *Dissent* 8, no. 3 (Summer 1961), pp. 347–48.

63. Robb Baker, "The Trials of Lucifer: An Interview with Kenneth Anger," *Soho Weekly News,* October 28, 1976, p. 16. Cited in Robert Haller, *Kenneth Anger* (Minneapolis: Walker Arts Center, 1980), p. 2. For earlier examples of the sailor as a ravishing and at the same intimidating and brutal gay icon, see Paul Cadmus's polemical series of paintings of the 1930s, *The Fleet's In,* and, in a different medium, the episode "Cruising" in Charles Henri Ford and Parker Tyler's gay-modernist novel *The Young and Evil* (London, GMP, 1989 [1933]).

64. Richard Dyer, "Judy Garland and Gay Men," *Heavenly Bodies* (New York: St. Martin's, 1986).

65. As Richard Dyer puts it, "The fact that professional entertainment has been by and large conservative in this century should not blind us to the implicit struggle within it, and looking beyond class to divisions of sex and race, we should note the important role of structurally subordinate groups in society—women, blacks, gays—in the development and definition of entertainment." "Entertainment and Utopia," *Genre: The Musical,* ed. Rick Altman (New York: Routledge, 1981).

66. Harold Beaver, "Homosexual Signs," *Critical Inquiry* (Autumn 1981), p. 105. Other commentators have remarked on this characteristic of gay culture. Since oppression forced gays to communicate indirectly, "[c]ultural objects, items of dress, changing fashions in speech and gesture and even cologne, became protective measures, ways of conveying a man's predilection that didn't put him in legal jeopardy or destroy his status in the eyes of the straight world." Michael Feingold, *Village Voice,* June 14, 1980, p. 77. Quoted in Altman, *The Homosexualization of America* (Boston: Beacon, 1983), p. 151.

67. The recreation of pre-existing texts is, according to Andrew Ross, central to the mechanics of camp: "The camp effect, then, is created . . . when the products of a much earlier mode of production, which has lost its power to dominate cultural meanings, become available, in the present, for redefinition according to contemporary codes of taste." "The Uses of Camp," in *No Respect* (New York: Routledge, 1989), p. 139.

68. On camp generally, see Susan Sontag's essential "Notes on Camp," *Against Interpretation* (New York: Farrar, Straus, and Giroux, 1966). From among the abundant bibliography generated by Sontag's article, two recent and interesting (and fabulously illustrated) studies are Michael Booth, *Camp* (New York: Quartet,

1983); and Philip Core's "encyclopedia of camp," in *Camp: The Lie That Tells the Truth* (New York: Delilah, 1984). More recently, see the collections, *Camp Grounds: Style and Homosexuality*, ed. David Bergman (Amherst: University of Massachusetts Press, 1993) and Moe Meyer, ed., *The Politics and Poetics of Camp* (New York: Routledge, 1993).

69. Michael Bronski, *Culture Clash* (Boston: South End, 1984), p. 92. Occasionally, it seems both movie houses and bars combined their functions when gay bars showed 16mm prints of screen classics. See "Homosexuality in America," *Life,* June 26, 1964; on p. 71 there is a picture taken at one of those screenings.

70. Robert Heide, "Magic Time at the Caffé Cino," *New York Native,* May 6, 1985; Michael Feingold, "Caffé Cino: Twenty Years after Magic Time," *Village Voice,* May 14, 1985; Michael Bronski, *Culture Clash,* pp. 129–30.

71. In his recent study on gay and lesbian film, Richard Dyer remarks on this very mutation in representations of gay subjectivity: "There is a shift from the personality of the filmmaker to the personality of the performer, which is also a shift from personality as an inner reality to be explored to personality as outer surface to be observed" (104). Dyer does not relate the transition from depth to surface to parallel shifts from modernism to postmodernism— which implies the omnipresence of mass culture even in the most subjective recesses. *Now You See It* (New York: Routledge, 1990).

72. Andy Warhol, *THE Philosophy of Andy Warhol* (New York: Harcourt, Brace, Jovanovich, 1975), p. 54.

73. See, for example, Judith Butler, *Gender Trouble* (New York: Routledge, 1990), and "Imitation and Gender Insubordination" in *Inside/Out: Lesbian Theories, Gay Theories,* ed. Diana Fuss (New York: Routledge, 1991); Leo Bersani, *The Freudian Body: Psychoanalysis and Art* (New York: Columbia University Press, 1986), and "Is the Rectum a Grave?" *October,* no. 43 (1987); Diana Fuss, *Essentially Speaking: Feminism, Nature, and Difference* (New York: Routledge, 1989); and Jonathan Dollimore, *Sexual Dissidence* (New York: Oxford University Press, 1991).

74. P. Adams Sitney suggests this possibility when he states that both Ken Jacobs and Jack Smith "hated the trance film." In his notes to *Blonde Cobra,* Jacobs reports that Smith found the end product still "too heavy"—too much like a trance film itself. *Visionary Film,* pp. 370–71.

75. P. Adams Sitney suggests that most trance films often culminate by retrieving lost integrity and redeeming their protagonists. *Visionary Film,* p. 396.

76. "New York's 'Middle-Class' Homosexuals," *Harper's* (March 1963); "Growth of Overt Homosexuality in City Provokes Wide Concern," *New York Times,* December 17, 1963; "City Side,"

Newsweek, December 30, 1963; "Homosexuality in America," *Life,* June 26, 1964; "The Homosexual in America," *Time,* January 21, 1966.

77. See Martin Duberman, *Cures: A Gay Man's Odyssey* (New York: Plume, 1994) for a firsthand account of 1960s psychotherapies used for "curing" gays.

78. In his famous *History of Sexuality,* vol. I (New York: Random, 1979), Michel Foucault explains the emergence of modern homosexual identity as the result of a desire for specification. According to him, institutions of social control did not fight the homosexual as much as made him/her into an identifiable type, a discernible lifestyle with its own unique set of characteristics.

79. "Homosexuality in America," *Life,* June 26, 1964.

80. Invisibility and opacity vis-à-vis public discourse was later recognized by some sectors of late 1960s and 1970s counterculture as a means to evade manipulation and social control. When (un)characterizing the Digger movement in the late 1960s, Abbie Hoffman wrote: "Confusion is mightier than the sword. . . . We [Diggers] cry, 'No one understands us,' while at the same time, we wink out of the corner of our eye, recognizing that if the straight world understood all this Digger shit, it would render us impotent, because understanding is the first step to control and control is the secret to our extinction." *The Best of Abbie Hoffman* (New York: Four Walls, Eight Windows, 1988), pp. 16–17.

81. See "Appendix: The Independent Film Award," in *Film Culture Reader,* ed. P. Adams Sitney (New York: Praeger, 1970), pp. 423–29.

82. For a chronicle of the legal battles surrounding *Flaming Creatures,* see J. Hoberman, "The Big Heat," *Village Voice,* November 12, 1991. Smith remarked disdainfully years later that, intended as a comedy, his film had became "the sex issue of the cocktail world." See his review of John Waters's *Pink Flamingoes:* "*Pink Flamingoes:* Formulas in Focus," *Village Voice,* July 19, 1973.

4. Pop, Queer, or Fascist?

1. J. Hoberman states ". . . so avidly was this film absorbed by the media that one forgets that it was also avant-garde." "Once More with Anger," *Village Voice,* August 13, 1980.

2. "An Interview with Kenneth Anger," conducted by the magazine *SPIDER, Film Culture,* no. 40 (Winter 1966), p. 68.

3. Cited in J. Hoberman and Jonathan Rosenbaum, *Midnight Movies* (New York: Harper, 1983), p. 56.

4. For a sample of such criticism, see the film's first reviews in *Film Culture* (Fall–Winter 1963, and Fall–Winter 1964), especially Ken Kelman, "Thanatos in Chrome," in the Fall–Winter 1963 issue of *Film Culture.* See also Jonas Mekas's enthusiastic note on the film in his *Village Voice* column on November 14, 1963, reprinted in *Movie Journal* (New York: Macmillan, 1972), p. 108. P. Adams Sitney stressed *Scorpio Rising's* place within the tradition of the American avant-garde cinema and within the rest of Anger's oeuvre. Perceptive as his criticism is, Adams Sitney rarely refers to the film's subcultural identity and belabors—too much, in my opinion—Anger's own conception of *Scorpio* as a conjuration of "Magick" (Anger's preferred spelling) forces. See "The Magus," *Visionary Film* (New York: Oxford University Press, 1979). More recent examples of discussions stressing *Scorpio's* avant-garde aesthetics are Carel Rowe's *The Baudelairean Cinema* (Ann Arbor: University of Michigan Research Press, 1983), which dwells on Anger's connections to symbolism and decadentism, and his indebtedness to Eisenstenian montage; and Robert Haller, *Kenneth Anger* (Minneapolis: Walker Art Center, 1980).

5. For interesting discussions of Anger's film as a gay movie, see Ed Lowry's excellent "The Appropriation of Signs in *Scorpio Rising,*" in *The Velvet Light-Trap,* no. 20 (1983), pp. 41–47; the sections on Kenneth Anger in Richard Dyer, *Now You See It* (London: Routledge, 1990), pp. 117–29; and Michael Moon, "A Small Boy and Others: Sexual Disorientation in Henry James, Kenneth Anger, and David Lynch," *Comparative American Identities,* ed. Hortense Spillers (New York: Routledge, 1991).

6. Kenneth Anger, "Filmography," *Film Culture,* no. 31 (Winter 1963–64).

7. Other accounts maintain that *Histoire d'O* was seized by the French government because it featured the daughter of a government official. Robert L. Cagle, "Auto-Eroticism: Narcissism, Fetishism, and Consumer Culture," *Cinema Journal* 33, no. 4 (Summer 1994), p. 33, n.20.

8. Robert Haller, *Kenneth Anger,* pp. 15–16.

9. P. Adams Sitney, *Visionary Film,* pp. 102–103.

10. Samson DeBrier, "On the Filming of *Inauguration of the Pleasure Dome,*" *Film Culture,* nos. 67/68/69 (1979), pp. 211–15.

11. Another key filmmaker whose work also shows a parallel transition was Gregory Markopoulos. In Adams Sitney's scheme, Stan Brakhage's films represent the culmination of mythopoesis, as do Anger's *Scorpio Rising* and his later *Invocation of My Demon Brother* and *Lucifer Rising.* See P. Adams Sitney, *Visionary Film,* passim.

12. Along these lines, see the review by one of *Mattachine Review*'s editors, Richard Howard, "Homosexuality as a Vehicle for Masochism Symbolized in the Film *Fireworks*," *Mattachine Review*, 7, no. 7 (July 1961), pp. 6–9.

13. Kenneth Anger, *Hollywood Babylon* (San Francisco: Straight Arrow, 1975). In order to launch the first edition of his book in America, Anger took to the road with a multimedia "funny Black Mass of a show," which included slides, film clips, music, dramatizations, and Anger's frantic performance as master of ceremonies. See Greil Marcus, "'Hollywood Babylon' on the Road," *Village Voice*, October 13, 1975.

14. As Richard Dyer states, "*Scorpio Rising* is intensely homoerotic but, apart from some lewd horse-play in 'Party Lights,' this is not so much in the form of sex acts as in the way the film invites us to look at these boys, as desirable . . .", *Now You See It* (New York: Routledge, 1991), p. 125. Furthermore, as an avant-garde film, *Scorpio* was marketed and shown as a personal expression of its director; hence awareness of Anger's gender may have emphasized its homoeroticism.

15. Hunter Thompson, *Hell's Angels* (New York: Ballantine, 1981 [1966]). For a study of the British motorcycle subculture that integrates the perspectives of the British cultural studies school, see Paul Willis, *Profane Cultures* (London: Routledge, 1978).

16. "It is unclear what teenagers did in the very early 1950s . . . 'youthville' was absolutely nowhere in 1953. Within two years, things had changed. American youth were headlines uniquely their own: Juvenile Delinquency and Rock 'n' Roll." Richard Staehling's "From *Rock around the Clock* to *The Trip:* The Truth about Teen Movies," in *Kings of the Bs,* ed. Todd McCarthy and Charles Flynn (New York: Dutton, 1975), p. 220. For an excellent study of the social constructions of juvenile delinquency, the discourses surrounding it, and the frequent scapegoating it was subject to in the 1950s, see James B. Gilbert, *Cycle of Outrage* (New York: Oxford University Press, 1986).

17. On zoot suits, see George Lipsitz, *A Rainbow at Midnight* (New York: Praeger, 1981), p. 27, and "Cruising the Historical Block," in *Time Passages* (Minneapolis: University of Minnesota Press, 1987); and Stuart Cosgrove, "The Zoot Suit and Style Warfare," *History Workshop* 18 (Autumn 1984).

18. Gene Balsey, "The Hot Rod Culture," *American Quarterly* (Winter 1950), pp. 353–58.

19. For a reading of postwar culture as a tug-of-war between overall narrative "ideological" mediation and local attempts to escape such narratives, see Dana Polan, "Narrative Limits," in *Power and Paranoia* (New York: Columbia University Press, 1985).

Some other limit cases to the "narrative's powers to naturalize and justify historical tensions" explored by Polan are labor politics, race relations, women's labor, and heterosexual relations.

20. In his study of the classical Hollywood cinema, Robert Ray states that this is a characteristic of the ideology of 1950s films, which evidence a mismatch between intent and effect. Robert Ray, *A Certain Tendency of the Hollywood Cinema, 1930–1980* (Princeton: Princeton University Press, 1985).

21. Hunter Thompson, *Hell's Angels,* p. 114.

22. For a rather schematic history of Bob Mizer's enterprise and for illustrations of his art, see Timothy Lewis, *Physique: A Pictorial History of the Athletic Model Guild* (San Francisco: Gay Sunshine, 1983).

23. Cited in Stuart Timmons, "Wanted: Athletic Models," *The Advocate,* July 30, 1992.

24. For a succinct yet useful essay on American gay iconography, see Tom Waugh, "Photography: Passion and Power," *Body Politic,* no. 101 (February 1984). Representatives of such gay Hellenism in the nineteenth century are, for example, John Addington Symmonds, Oscar Wilde, Walter Pater, Lord Byron, Edward Carpenter, and, a generation later, E. M. Forster. See R. Jenkyns, *The Victorians and Ancient Greece* (Oxford: Blackwell, 1981); and P. Hahn, *Nos ancêtres les pervers* (Paris: Olivier Orban, 1979). On gay Hellenic iconography, see also Bruce Russell, "Wilhelm von Pluschow and Wilhelm von Gloeden: Two Photo Essays," *Studies in Visual Communications* 9, no. 2 (Spring 1983), pp. 57–80.

25. Walt Whitman's "Calamus" is the most openly homoerotic section of *Leaves of Grass,* ed. Malcolm Cowley (New York: Penguin, 1959). *Time Regained* contains some humorous episodes involving de Charlus's fascination with young criminals and street toughs. In Proust, *Remembrance of Things Past,* trans. C. K. Scott Montcrieff and Terence Kilmartin. Vol. 3 (New York: Random, 1982).

26. Richard Dyer, "Seen to Be Believed: Some Problems in the Representation of Gay as Typical," *Studies in Visual Communication* 9, no. 2 (Spring 1983), pp. 2–19.

27. The classic works in this trend are Howard S. Becker, *Outsiders: Studies in the Sociology of Deviance* (New York: Free Press, 1963), and Irving Goffman, *Stigma: Notes on the Management of Spoiled Identity* (Englewood Cliffs, NJ: Prentice-Hall, 1963). For an overview of deviance theory, see Stuart H. Traub and Craig B. Little, eds., *Theories of Deviance* (Itasca, IL: Peacock, 1975). See also John D'Emilio, *Sexual Politics, Sexual Communities* (Chicago: University of Chicago Press, 1983), p. 142ff.

28. This follows the periodization of mass culture in modern America proposed in George Lipsitz, "Popular Culture: This Ain't No Side Show," in *Time Passages,* pp. 6–13.

29. For new-style Keynesian consumerism in 1960s America, see David Horowitz, "Capitalism and the Crisis of Abundance," *In the Marketplace: Consumerism in America* (San Francisco: Canfield, 1972). Christin J. Mamiya, *Pop Art and Consumer Culture* (Austin: University of Texas Press, 1992) is a fascinating study of the relation between pop art and the emergence of Keynesianism as official economic ideology.

30. The adoption of Keynesianism and the development of the advertising industry worked to instaurate Henry Ford's dream of linking mass production to mass consumption. The products of work would be absorbed by the market as props of leisure. This notion seemed to make leisure and consumption necessary to the industrial machine as work itself, and suggested a dissolution of the distinctions between both. David Harvey, *The Condition of Postmodernity* (Oxford: Blackwell, 1989), pp. 125–41.

31. SPIDER, "Interview with Kenneth Anger," p. 69.

32. See Graham McCann, *Rebel Males* (New Brunswick, NJ: Rutgers University Press, 1992). See also Hunter Thompson, *Hell's Angels,* p. 90, where he quotes the responses of some bikers to the film when it first came out: "[*The Wild One* and Marlon Brando's role in it] gave the outlaws a lasting, romance-glazed image of themselves, a coherent reflection that only a very few had been able to find in a mirror. . . ."

33. Interestingly, Lindner attributed youth revolt to rebellion against a father wielding immoderate authority in the eyes of the son. A few years earlier, Adorno and Horkheimer had located the roots of authoritarianism in an opposite but equally problematic development of the father figure in contemporary German society. Writing separately, they argued that the authority of the father had been weakened while that of the state had increased. Concomitantly, the subjects' oedipal investment in the father as figure of opposition and identification was replaced by identification with the state incarnated in the person of the Führer. Consequently, the origin of the superego and of the subject's moral structure lay now not in autonomous familial and interpersonal relations, but in a "collective," "standardized" investment in the image of the Führer. The collective character of this process erases individuation and predisposes individuals to fascist uniformity. See Max Horkheimer, "The End of Reason," T. W. Adorno, "Freudian Theory and the Pattern of Fascist Propaganda." Both in *The Essential Frankfurt School Reader,* ed. Andrew Arato and Eike Gebhardt (New York: Contin-

uum, 1982); and Max Horkheimer, "Authoritarianism and the Family," in *Critical Theory* (New York: Continuum, 1981).

34. See James Gilbert, *Cycle of Outrage,* p. 42. Lewis Yablonsky, "The Violent Gang," *Commentary,* no. 30 (August 1960), pp. 125–30.

35. All other interpretations of *Scorpio*'s Nazi imagery I know differ from mine. P. Adams Sitney states that the film is mythographic; it "self-consciously creates its own myth of the motorcyclist by comparison with other myths: the dead movie star, Dean; the live one, Brando; the savior of men, Christ; the villain of men, Hitler. Each of these myths is evoked in ambiguity, without moralizing. From the photos of Hitler and a Nazi soldier and from the use of swastikas and other nazi impedimenta, *Scorpio* derives a Nietzschean ecstasy of will and power." (P. Adams Sitney, *Visionary Film,* p. 121.) One of the most clairvoyant critics of the film, Ed Lowry, attributes the film's fascism and self-destruction to the repression of the homoeroticism underlying the bikers, comics, Brando and Dean, and the many other icons that populate the film. Repressed homoeroticism thus expresses itself obliquely or else enacts a violent return in sadomasochism and fascism. (Ed Lowry, "The Appropriation of Signs in *Scorpio Rising,*" *The Velvet Light Trap,* no. 20 [1983], pp. 41–47). Richard Dyer sees these icons as "wild, transcendent forces that convention represses. The point is that most people disapprove of them . . . their disapprovableness is a sign of their fitness for Magick invocation" (*Now You See It,* p. 129). Magick is Alistair Crowley's sort of magic, which Kenneth Anger recognizes as one of his major sources of inspiration. Part of the point of the film is to collide images and icons together with the purpose of liberating their latent meanings and identities—roughly, their Magick forces. And to sample one more opinion, David James states in his thorough study of 1960s avant-garde and alternative cinemas: "Though intercut images of Hitler imply that Scorpio's cult is fascist and his command is destructive, in general, the associations that accrue around him are unstable." *Allegories of Cinema* (Princeton: Princeton University Press, 1989), p. 153.

36. Max Horkheimer and Theodor W. Adorno, *The Dialectic of Enlightenment,* trans. John Cumming (New York: Continuum, 1972). Page numbers are given in the text.

37. In other words, mass culture does not falsify a "pure" pristine experience, since all experience only exists as a function of texts, as pure trace of signifiers. What Adorno and Horkheimer call attention to is what type of signifiers are used in making experience visible. The problem does not lie with the process of identity

formation as such, which always entails a betrayal of a hypothetical "real" experience, but with the specific texts and images used in the process.

38. Freud's writings on sadism and masochism evolved, in connection with his views on instincts, from "Three Essays on the Theory of Sexuality" (1905), where he postulates a primary sadism linked to a will to mastery that is later introjected as masochism, to "The Economical Problem of Masochism" (1924), which proposes a primary masochism, residue of the death instincts and later externalized as sadism. Freud's difficulties in establishing the primacy of one or the other signal the fundamental mobility and fluidity of aggressive relations; these characteristics are illustrated by *Scorpio Rising*'s swift transitions between other-directed and introjected violence. "Three Essays on the Theory of Sexuality," *Standard Edition*, vol. VII; "The Economical Problem of Masochism," vol. XIX, trans. James Strachey (London: Hogarth, 1948).

39. The homoeroticism of their friendship was a source of concern for censors. Colonel Geoffrey Stockley, successor of Joseph H. Hays as head of the MPAA Production Code Administration, wrote to Jack Warner: "It is of course vital that there be no inference of a questionable or homosexual relationship between Plato [Sal Mineo] and Jim [James Dean]." Cited in James Gilbert, *Cycle of Outrage*, p. 186. Vito Russo cites Stuart Stearn, screenwriter of *Rebel*, saying that the Alan Ladd pin-ups are meant to suggest to the audience that Plato was "the faggot character." *The Celluloid Closet* (New York: Harper and Row, 1981), p. 110. For a gay reading of the film, see Christopher Castiglia, "Rebel without a Closet," *Engendering Men*, ed. Boone and Cadden (New York: Routledge, 1990), pp. 207–21.

40. Anger expatiates on these rumors in *Hollywood Babylon*.

41. Ed Lowry, "The Appropriation of Signs in *Scorpio Rising*," p. 45.

42. Theodor Adorno, "The Fetish Character of Music and the Regression of Listening," in *The Essential Frankfurt School Reader*.

43. John Fiske, *Television Culture* (London: Methuen, 1988), p. 313.

44. See John Fiske, "Popular Discrimination," in *Modernity and Mass Culture*, ed. James Naremore and Patrick Brantlinger (Bloomington: Indiana University Press, 1991), p. 110. See also "Conclusions" to *Television Culture*.

45. The best analysis of punk along these lines is still Dick Hebdige, *Subculture: The Meaning of Style* (London: Methuen, 1979). See also Stuart Hall et al. *Resistance through Rituals* (London: Hutchinson, 1976); Peter York, *Style Wars* (London: Sedgwick and Jackson, 1980); Dave Laing, *One-Chord Wonders*

(Milton Keynes: Open University Press, 1985); and, on popular and street culture in general, Iain Chambers, *Popular Culture* (New York: Routledge, 1986).

46. On *Scorpio,* he stated: "In that film I'm viewing a certain phenomenon that was happening at that particular time. I don't see the film as a homosexual statement. I see it as a human statement." Cited in Robert Haller, *Kenneth Anger,* p. 6.

5. Drag, Rubble, and "Secret Flix"

1. Jonas Mekas, "Jack Smith, Or the End of Civilization," *Village Voice,* July 23, 1970. Reprinted in *Movie Journal,* 390–91.

2. Jonas Mekas, "*Flaming Creatures* and the Ecstatic Beauty of the New Cinema," *Village Voice,* March 2, 1963. Reprinted in *Movie Journal,* p. 83.

3. For accounts of the vicissitudes of Smith's *Flaming Creatures,* see J. Hoberman, "The Big Heat," *Village Voice,* November 12, 1991; and J. Hoberman and Jonathan Rosenbaum, *Midnight Movies* (New York: Harper, 1983), pp. 59–61.

4. Cited in J. Hoberman, "The Big Heat," p. 61.

5. Misogyny reappears occasionally throughout Smith's work, where women are often grotesque bulldykes or dominant, engulfing mothers: when sexualized, they are made to look preposterous, and when non-sexual, oppressive. The early Jacobs-Smith-Fleischner production *Blonde Cobra,* for example, refers in its monologues to a Mother Superior who disrupts a lesbian orgy in the convent and to a mother who leaves her child alone and deprives him of food.

6. *Village Voice,* May 2, 1963. Reprinted in *Movie Journal,* p. 85–86.

7. Jonas Mekas, "Editorial Statement," *Film Culture,* no. 32 (Spring 1964), p. 3.

8. Susan Sontag, "Flaming Creatures," *The Nation,* March 1964; reprinted in *Against Interpretation* (New York: Farrar, Straus, and Giroux, 1966), p. 231. I am only stressing these two reviews because they set the tone for subsequent discussions of the film, and because Smith also took issue with them in his own writings and interviews. Other interesting contemporary notices are Gregory Markopoulos, "Innocent Revellers," *Film Culture,* no. 33 (1964); Ken Kelman, "Smith Myth," *Film Culture,* no. 29 (1963); and, from a more autobiographical point of view, see Joel Markman (one of the performers in *Flaming Creatures*), "Some Thoughts about Jack Smith," *Film Culture,* no. 32 (Spring 1964).

9. Jack Smith and Sylvère Lotringer, "Uncle Fishhook and the Sacred Baby Poo Poo of Art," *Semiotext(e)* 1 no. 2 (1978), pp. 192–93.

10. Michael Moon, "Flaming Closets," *October,* no. 51 (Winter 1989). For a characterization of the aesthetic of old blue movies, see Tom Waugh, "Homoerotic Representation in the Stag Film, 1920–1940. Imagining an Audience," *Wide Angle* (Summer 1992); special issue on gay and lesbian film and video.

11. On temporal and spatial cueing as a function of film music, see Claudia Gorbman's *Unheard Melodies* (Bloomington: Indiana University Press, 1987), p. 83. Although Gorbman defines the term in relation to narrative film music, I think it can be applied to Smith's film as well, which is amply allusive of narrative cinema and parodically manipulates the conventions of such cueing.

12. P. Adams Sitney provides an excellent description and commentary of *Flaming Creatures* in "Innocence Recovered," in *Visionary Film* (New York: Oxford University Press, 1979). On "the orgy" as a recurrent (and mutating) motif in 1960s cinema that connoted hedonism, sexual liberation, and youth culture, see J. Hoberman, "After the Orgy," *Village Voice,* December 3, 1991. While absent from this discussion, which deals mostly with late 1960s versions of "the orgy" made in the wake of *Blow-Up, Flaming Creatures* is probably the earliest gay version of the motif.

13. Gerard Malanga and Jack Smith, "Interview with Jack Smith," *Film Culture,* no. 45 (Summer 1967), p. 14.

14. Jack Smith, "Memoirs of María Montez, or Wait for Me at the Bottom of the Pool," *Film Culture,* no. 31 (Winter 1963–64).

15. The polemic between essentialist and constructivist models of gayness is, of course, far more complicated and meandering than I am able to suggest here. For a finely tuned, balanced discussion of the issue, see Diane Fuss, *Essentially Speaking* (New York: Routledge, 1989).

16. See, for example, Michel Foucault, *History of Sexuality,* vol. I, trans. Robert Hurley (New York: Vintage, 1980); and *Madness and Civilization,* trans. Richard Howard (New York: Random, 1976).

17. Jonathan Dollimore, "Different Desires: Subjectivity and Transgression in Wilde and Gide," *Genders 2* (Summer 1988), p. 37. For a more extended version of his arguments, see his *Sexual Dissidence* (New York: Oxford University Press, 1991).

18. Judith Butler, "Gender Trouble," *Feminism/Postmodernism,* ed. Linda Nicholson (New York: Routledge, 1990), p. 334.

19. Ibid.

20. Ibid, p. 338.

21. As Smith told Lotringer in an interview, "I took my program [sometime in the late 1970s] to a gay theater and he couldn't understand how it was gay because he was unable to see it in a context. If it wasn't exactly discussing how many inches was my

first lollipop, well, then it wouldn't be anything they would be interested in." Jack Smith and Sylvère Lotringer, "Uncle Fishhook," p. 196.

22. Sontag, "Flaming Creatures," pp. 230–31.

23. Jack Smith, *Historical Treasures* (New York: Hanuman, 1990).

24. For some descriptions of Smith's slide shows, see Stephan Brecht, *Queer Theater* (Frankfurt: Suhrkamp, 1979), pp. 175–77; and J. Hoberman's "The Theater of Jack Smith," *Drama Review* 23, no. 1 (1979). After Smith's death, Hoberman has given some presentations of his slides and fragments of texts at Anthology and Millennium.

25. Paul Arthur reads the Smith-Mekas polemic, accurately in my view, as emblematic of an inevitable conflict in the underground (and almost any other marginal artistic formation) between the anarchic centrifugal tendencies of individual artists and a centripetal need for coordination and stability, which Mekas provided. See Arthur, "Routines of Emancipation," in *To Free the Cinema,* ed. David James (Princeton: Princeton University Press, 1992). For his part, David Ehrenstein fully credits Smith's (doubtlessly biased) version of the affair, "Jack Smith," *Film: The Front Line. 1984* (Denver: Arden, 1984), pp. 16–18. For my part, I am not crediting Smith's narrative, merely reading it for its symptomatic significance with regard to his work, his notions of the avant-garde, and his own position within the independent cinema.

26. J. Hoberman, "The Theater of Jack Smith," p. 4.

27. David James has compared the movie to Yves Tinguely's self-destructing structure, *Hommage à New York. Allegories of Cinema* (Princeton: Princeton University Press, 1989), p. 127.

28. Stephan Brecht, *Queer Theater.* Further references are given in the text.

29. Jack Smith and Gerard Malanga, "Interview with Jack Smith," p. 15. For a photographic translation of the "moldy," see Smith's atmospheric photo essay, "The Moldy Hell of Men and Women," *Film Culture* (Winter 1964), pp. 33–37.

30. Jack Smith and Sylvère Lotringer, "Uncle Fishhook," p. 199.

31. Celeste Olalquiaga, *Megalopolis: Contemporary Cultural Sensibilities* (Minneapolis: University of Minnesota Press, 1991), pp. 25–29.

32. For the history of the neighborhood, see Stephen Koch, "Reflections on Soho" and Lawrence Alloway, "Soho as Bohemia," in *New York, Downtown Manhattan, Soho,* ed. René Block (Berlin: Akademie der Kunste, 1976). For Soho's gentrification, see Sharon Zukin, *Loft Living* (Baltimore: Johns Hopkins University

Press, 1982). On gentrification in general, see R. Deutsche and C. Ryan, "The Fine Art of Gentrification," *October,* no. 31 (Winter 1984), pp. 91–111; and Sharon Zukin, "Gentrification, Cuisine, and the Critical Infrastructure: Power and Centrality Downtown," *Landscapes of Power: from Detroit to Disney World* (Berkeley: University of California Press, 1991).

33. Brecht, *Queer Theater,* p. 18.

34. Smith and Lotringer, "Uncle Fishhook," p. 200.

35. The script of this performance is printed in Uzi Parnes, "Pop Performance, Four Seminal Influences: The Work of Jack Smith, Tom Murrin—The Alien Comic, Ethyl Eichelberger, and the Split Breeches Company," dissertation, New York University, 1988. Parnes's work contains excellent material on Jack Smith and on the East Village low-grade 1980s pop performance which Smith's model largely inspired. See also the special issue of *Drama Review* on East Village performance edited by Michael Kirby, vol. 29, no. 1 (Spring 1985), particularly Uzi Parnes's own "Pop Performance in East Village Clubs," pp. 5–16.

36. Carel Rowe, *The Baudelairean Cinema* (Ann Arbor: University of Michigan Research Press, 1983), p. xiv.

37. The notion of reification originally appeared in Karl Marx's *Capital* to refer to the instrumentalism that defined human relations mediated by profit, an instrumentalism that resulted in conceptualizing relations between people as relations between things. George Lukács gave the concept wider philosophical currency in his *History and Class Consciousness* by adapting it to his critique of bourgeois historical and social discourse. Reification, in this context, was the reduction of historical—hence contingent, dialectical, internally split—phenomena to univocal, self-identical formulations. Reification partook of a scientifically clad passion for closure, for formalizing phenomena that were particularly difficult to formalize, yet once codified could be regarded as operative tools for analysis. Failure to account for dialectics was for Lukács the result of class position. Unable to adopt a perspective from outside their own class, bourgeois researchers and writers mystified as permanent and stable what actually were provisional social relations. See Georg Lukács, *History and Class Consciousness* (Cambridge, MA: MIT Press, 1971). Freed from its class-determinism, which itself reified and idealized the proletariat as the class with the right point of view on social relations, Lukács's concept can be used, in its broadest sense, to designate the simplification of cultural products with the purpose of facilitating their cultural and economic exchange. This is the sense in which T. W. Adorno adapted the concept in his formulation of the "fetish character of music." Adorno's version of the concept underlies my analysis in the following pages. See Adorno, "The Fetish Character

of Music and the Regression of Listening," and Eike Gebhardt's Introduction in *The Essential Frankfurt School Reader,* ed. A. Arato and E. Gebhardt (New York: Continuum, 1982).

38. Jack Smith, "The Perfect Film Appositeness of María Montez," *Film Culture,* no. 27 (Winter 1962–63).

39. Ronald Tavel, "The Theater of the Ridiculous," *Tri-Quarterly,* no. 6 (1966), p. 93.

40. For the unstable conceptual binaries that accrue around the closet, see Eve Sedgwick, *Epistemology of the Closet* (Berkeley: University of California Press, 1990). Michael Moon also mentions the trope of the closet in Jack Smith's work, not in terms of secrecy and guilt, but at the intersection of a secluded (private) space "in front of the mirror" and the fascinating (public) film sets in which Smith locates María Montez. "Flaming Closets," p. 43.

41. "Question: 'Who in the New American Cinema do you like?' Warhol: 'Jaaaaack Smiiiiith. . . . When I was little I always thought he was my best director . . . I mean, just the only person I would ever try to copy, and just . . . so terrific, and now since I'm grown up, I just think he makes the best movies.' Q: 'What particularly do you like about his movies?' Warhol: 'He's the only one who uses color backwards.'" David Ehrenstein and Andy Warhol, "An Interview with Andy Warhol," *Film Culture,* no. 40 (Spring 1966), pp. 41–42.

42. In his words: "My lack of visibility was my own fault. I haven't been organized properly. I have made it idiotically easy for everyone to put me where I could be ignored." Jack Smith, *Historical Treasures,* p. 126.

6. The Artist as Advertiser

1. Oscar Wilde, "Pen, Pencil, and Poison: A Study in Green." *The Works of Oscar Wilde* (London: Collins, 1948), p. 995.

2. Andy Warhol, *THE Philosophy of Andy Warhol: From A to B and Back Again* (New York: Harcourt, 1975), pp. 133–34.

3. A few sample opinions on Warhol: For a neo-formalist "Greenbergian" like Hilton Kramer, Warhol, with the whole of pop art, was "indistinguishable from advertisement, art assimilated to the dishonesties of contrived public symbols and pretentious commerce." (Cited in Benjamin H. D. Buchloch, "The Andy Warhol Line," in *The Work of Andy Warhol,* ed. Gary Garrells [Seattle: Bay, 1989].) A leftist critic like Max Kozloff denounces Warhol on similar grounds in "Pop Art: Metaphysical Disgust or the New Vulgarians," *Art International,* March 6, 1962. More recently, Fredric Jameson has recast these negative views in his influential critique of postmodernism: "Andy Warhol's work indeed turns centrally around commodification, and the great billboard images

of the Coca-Cola bottle or the Campbell's soup can, which explicitly foreground the commodity fetishism of a transition to late capital, *ought* to be powerful and critical political statements. If they are not one would surely want to know why, and one would want to begin to wonder a little more seriously about the possibilities of political or critical art in the postmodern period of late capital." "Postmodernism, or the Cultural Logic of Late Capitalism," *New Left Review* 146 (July–August 1984), p. 60.

Others gave a more positive assessment of the collapse of art into commodity form that Warhol and the whole of pop art enacted. In their accounts, Warhol (and pop) were the latest of a series of stages in the history of the avant-garde that brought art and everyday life closer to each other. See in this line, Allan Kaprow's "Pop Art: Past, Present, and Future," in which he signaled that pop had a double goal: the aestheticization of the everyday and the creation of an art of immediate impact among the larger public. "A Coke bottle may be more mysterious than we thought." And further, "How can we understand Leonardo's pin-up without understanding the Coke bottle?" *Malahat Review* (July 1967). See also his earlier "The Legacy of Jackson Pollock," *ARTnews* (October 1958), which can almost be considered an avant-la-lettre pop art manifesto and an attempt to synthesize found imagery art with abstract expressionism. American critics Alan Salomon, Barbara Rose, and Henry Geldzahler defended Warhol and pop art along the lines Kaprow had staked out. See *Pop Art,* ed. Carol Anne Mahsun (Ann Arbor: University of Michigan Research Press, 1983). These critiques emerged independently from the ones developed since the late 1950s by the British International Group, led by Lawrence Alloway and institutionally linked to the London Institute of Contemporary Art. This group extolled the artistic values to be found in industrial design. For a sample of their attitudes, see John Russell and Suzi Gablick, eds., *Pop Art Redefined* (New York: Praeger, 1970). For a study on Warhol in relation to British pop, see Andrew Ross, "The Uses of Camp," in *No Respect* (New York: Routledge, 1989) and Dick Hebdige, "In Poor Taste," *Post-Pop Art,* ed. Paul Taylor (Cambridge, MA: MIT Press, 1989).

See also Rainer Crone's Brechtian interpretation of Warhol, *Andy Warhol* (New York: Praeger, 1970). For him, Warhol's manipulation of found commercial imagery in the context of avant-garde art served to demystify both the art institutions and banal commercial mythologies.

4. This formula is indebted to the semiotic approaches to Warhol: Umberto Eco states that "Pop is a metalanguage on everyday culture, since its main themes are image about the

image, language about the language. Hence, the words on a Warhol's Campbell's soup cans are a comment on the words on the real soup cans." In Mahsun, *Pop Art: The Critical Dialogue,* p. 226.

Along similar lines, Roland Barthes wrote "Pop cleanses the image of everything in it that is not rhetoric. . . . The philosophical meaning of these labors is that things have no essence other than the social code which manifests them, so that ultimately, they are no longer ever produced (by Nature), but immediately 're-produced': reproduction is the very meaning of modernity." In Mahsun, *Pop Art: The Critical Dialogue,* p. 239. While wholly agreeing with these judgments, I am proposing that the ultimate semiotic level for Warhol is not language but capital.

5. The classical formulation of commodity fetishism and the operations of monetary value is Karl Marx, "The Fetishism of Commodities and the Secret Thereof," in *Capital: A Critique of Political Economy,* vol. 1 (New York: International, 1961).

6. Warhol, *THE Philosophy,* p. 92.

7. Warhol himself differentiated between the phase when he *did* things and the one when he *produced* them. See *THE Philosophy,* p. 180. For an excellent reading of Warhol along this line, see David James, "The Producer as Artist," *Allegories of Cinema* (Princeton: Princeton University Press, 1989).

8. I borrow this phrase from David James: "How can a line be drawn to distinguish artist from advertiser in the myriad of later roles including self-portraitist, society painter, television producer, actor, model (Warhol registered both with the Ford and Zoli agencies), and ad designer?" "The Unsecret Life: A Warhol Advertisement," *October* (Spring 1991), p. 30.

9. Warhol himself glibly described his trajectory as follows: "I started as a commercial artist, and I want to finish as a business artist. After I did the thing called 'art' or whatever it's called, I went into business art." *THE Philosophy,* p. 92.

10. Thierry De Duve, "Andy Warhol, or the Machine Perfected," *October,* no. 48 (Spring 1989), p. 9.

11. Thomas Crow, "Saturday Disasters: Trace and Reference in Early Warhol," in *Reconstructing Modernism: Art in New York, Paris, Montreal, 1945–1964,* ed. Serge Guilbaut (Cambridge, MA: MIT Press, 1990), pp. 311–31.

12. Warhol's biographical circumstances reinforce the myth: during the 1960s he surrounded himself mostly with an underground bohemian entourage; in the 1970s and 1980s, with politicians, aristocrats, financiers, and socialites.

13. "Art wasn't fun for me any more; it was people who were fascinating and I wanted to spend all my time being around them

and making movies of them." Andy Warhol and Pat Hackett, *POPism: The Warhol Sixties* (New York: Harcourt, 1980), p. 113. See Warhol's comments on the transition from painting to film, "Nothing to Lose: Interview with Andy Warhol," Gretchen Berg, *The Andy Warhol Film Factory,* ed. Michael O'Pray (London: British Film Institute, 1989) and "So He Stopped Painting Brillo Boxes and Bought a Movie Camera," *New York Times,* December 11, 1966.

14. For David James, the continuity between them resides in "the investigation of subjectivity and self-consciousness in a media-saturated environment" and in "the permeation of all artistic activity by the culture industries." "The Unsecret Life: A Warhol Advertisement," *October,* no. 59 (Spring 1991), p. 22. While in full agreement with the former, I am, on the other hand, recasting the latter to propose that what is at stake in Warhol is not just "permeation" of art by the culture industry, but a demonstration of the actual homology of two semiotics: art and money.

15. Warhol and Hackett, *POPism,* 46.

16. Such interest in stardom also shows in Warhol's courting of fame and the famous and in his becoming a celebrity himself. Already in the early 1960s he was often written up in the society sections of the *New York Times, Time,* and *Newsweek,* as a companion of such socialites as Baby Jane Holzer, Babe Pailey, Cristina Paolozzi, or Wendy Vanderbilt. See, for example, "Edie and Andy," *Time,* August 27, 1965; and "Saint Andy," *Newsweek,* December 7, 1964.

17. Warhol and Hackett, *POPism,* p. 28.

18. Jonas Mekas, *Movie Journal* (New York: Macmillan, 1972), p. 109.

19. Interview with Tavel, in Patrick Smith, *Warhol: Conversations about the Artist* (Ann Arbor: University of Michigan Research Press, 1988), p. 324.

20. Stanley Aronowitz, "When the Left Was New," in *The 60s without Apology,* ed S. Sayres, S. Aronowitz, A. Stephanson, F. Jameson, et al. (Minneapolis: University of Minnesota Press, 1984), p. 18. For a survey of the relation between the underground film ideology and the social activism of the time, see Paul Arthur, "Routines of Emancipation: Alternative Cinema in the Ideology and Politics of the Sixties," in *To Free the Cinema,* ed. David James (Princeton: Princeton University Press, 1992).

21. Mekas, *Movie Journal,* p. 110.

22. Ibid., p. 131.

23. "The Independent Film Award," *Film Culture Reader,* ed. P. Adams Sitney (New York: Praeger, 1970), p. 427.

24. Jonas Mekas, "Notes on Reseeing the Movies of Andy Warhol," in *Andy Warhol,* ed. John Coplans (New York: New York Graphic Society, 1971), p. 32.

25. *Film Culture,* no. 30 (Fall 1963).

26. On expanded cinema generally, see Gene Youngblood, *Expanded Cinema* (New York: Dutton, 1970); Mekas, *Movie Journal,* especially the reviews of 1965, passim; David James, *Allegories of Cinema,* pp. 127–37. On the Velvets, see Victor Bockris and Gerard Malanga, *Up-Tight: The Velvet Underground Story* (London: Chimera, 1984); Warhol and Hackett, *POPism,* pp. 162–64; and Patrick Smith's interview with Gerard Malanga in *Warhol: Conversations about the Artist* (Ann Arbor: University of Michigan Research Press, 1988).

27. In an interview with Gretchen Berg, Warhol went so far as to connect his Marilyns to his "Disaster Series"—also called "Death in America." Gretchen Berg, "Nothing to Lose," pp. 54–56.

28. Warhol and Hackett, *POPism,* p. 89.

29. Ibid, 31.

30. By stressing amateurism, Warhol underscored one of the fundamental ideological values that stardom plays out: normalcy. Normalcy brings stars close to audiences and promotes the sort of democratic populism traditionally fostered by American mass culture. As an example of this, almost contemporaneously with Warhol, *Playboy* tycoon Hugh Hefner stated that "potential playmates [*Playboy* models] are all around you: the new secretary at your office, the doe-eyed beauty who sat opposite you at lunch yesterday, the girl who sells you shirts and ties at your favorite store." Hefner's attitude eroticized all spaces, infusing normalcy with a sense of possibility and sexual *frisson.* Cited in John D'Emilio and Estelle Freedman, *Intimate Matters* (New York: Harper and Row, 1989), p. 303. For Horkheimer and Adorno, "star normalcy" is a spectacularized disavowal of the lack of real options in social life. *The Dialectic of Enlightenment,* trans. John Cumming (New York: Continuum, 1972).

31. Cited in Smith, *Andy Warhol's Art and Films,* p. 243.

32. For Benjamin, this sort of aura has to do not so much with the authenticity of the person as with "the spell of the personality," the phony spell of a commodity. "The Work of Art in the Age of Mechanical Reproduction," in *Illuminations,* trans. Harry Zohn (New York: Schocken, 1969), p. 231; see also Benjamin's "A Short History of Photography," *Screen* 13, no. 1 (Spring 1972).

33. Interview with Ronald Tavel in Smith, *Andy Warhol: Conversations about the Artist,* p. 378.

34. Warhol and Hackett, *POPism,* pp. 55–56.

35. H. M. Koutoukas, "Papal References," *Film Culture,* no. 45 (Summer 1967), p. 22.

36. Tom Wolfe, "Pariah Styles: The New Chic," *Harper's Bazaar* (April 1965); and "Radical Chic," *Radical Chic and Mau-Mauing the Flak-Catchers* (New York: Bantam, 1971).

37. Warhol and Hackett, *POPism,* p. 195.

38. Peter Wollen, "Raiding the Icebox," in *Andy Warhol Film Factory,* ed. O'Pray, pp. 6–29. For further background on the mixture of avant-garde aesthetics from which Warhol's work emerged, see Barbara Haskell, *Blam! The Explosion of Pop, Minimalism, and Performance* (New York: Whitney, 1977), and Calvin Tomkins, *The Bride and the Bachelors* (New York: Viking, 1965), esp. the sections on John Cage, Merce Cunningham, and Robert Rauschenberg.

39. See the pieces on the fiftieth anniversary of the 1913 Armory Show—homage presided over by Marcel Duchamp—and on a Paul Cézanne exhibit at the Knoedler Gallery, both in *Vogue,* June 1963. On the latter, the writer reported: "Many guests came from dinner parties, many women wore long dresses, everybody looked especially effective against the dark walls and the soft painting-directed light of the galleries."

40. Tom Wolfe, *The Kandy-Kolored Tangerine-Flake Streamline Baby* (New York: Noonday, 1965), p. 240. See also his "Bob and Spike" (originally titled "Upward with the Arts") in *The Pump-House Gang* (New York: Noonday, 1987).

41. Walter Benjamin, "The Work of Art in the Age of Mechanical Reproduction," p. 237.

42. See Gerard Malanga's interview in Smith, *Andy Warhol's Art and Films,* p. 412.

43. Andy Warhol, *THE Philosophy,* p. 51.

44. Andrew Sarris, "The Chelsea Girls," *Village Voice,* Dec. 15, 1966.

45. Warhol and Hackett, *POPism,* p. 110.

46. Cited in Simon Frith and Howard Horne, *Art into Pop* (London: Methuen, 1987), pp. 141–43.

47. Warhol and Hackett, *POPism,* pp. 186–87. For an excellent description and analysis of Max's Kansas City, see Ronald Sukenick, *Down and In* (New York: Beech Tree, 1988).

48. See, for example, Georges Bataille, "The concept of *dépense,*" *The Accursed Share,* vol. 1, trans. Alan Stoekl (Minneapolis: University of Minnesota Press, 1989).

49. Edgar Morin, *Stars,* trans. Richard Howard (New York: Grove, 1961), p. 137.

50. *THE Philosophy,* p. 86.

51. On tie-ups and showcasing during the 1930s, see Charles Eckert, "The Carole Lombard in Macy's Window," *Quarterly*

Review of Film Studies 3, no. 1 (Winter 1978). For the beginnings of the tie-up industry, see George Mitchell, "The Consolidation of the Hollywood Film Industry," *Cine-Tracts* 6, 7, and 8 (1979), and Miriam Hansen, *Babel in Babylon* (Cambridge, MA: Harvard University Press, 1990).

52. Cited in Patrick Smith, *Andy Warhol's Art and Films,* p. 167.

53. Bob Colacello, *Holy Terror* (New York: Random, 1991), pp. 23–24.

54. Richard Dyer, *Heavenly Bodies* (New York: St. Martin's, 1986); see esp. the Introduction.

55. Cited in Stephen Koch, *Stargazer* (New York: Praeger, 1973), p. 121.

56. Warhol and Hackett, *POPism,* pp. 132–33. Bob Colacello, *Interview* editor and Factory worker throughout the 1970s, writes in his excellent biography: "When he got bored at a restaurant or was trying to charm a potential client, he did what he called 'my Duchamp number'—and signed spoons, forks, knives, plates, ashtrays, and gave them away." *Holy Terror,* p. 170.

57. Colacello, *Holy Terror,* p. 168.

58. Stephen Koch, *Stargazer,* pp. 7, 13.

59. Jean Baudrillard, "Fetishism and Ideology: The Semiological Reduction," in *For a Critique of the Political Economy of the Sign,* trans. Charles Levin (St. Louis: Telos, 1981), pp. 89–101.

60. Warhol, *THE Philosophy,* pp. 63, 159.

61. Warhol and Hackett, *POPism,* p. 128.

62. Warhol, *THE Philosophy,* p. 148.

63. Jean Baudrillard, *For a Critique of the Political Economy of the Sign,* pp. 92–93.

64. This concept of melancholia is taken from Walter Benjamin, *The Origin of German Tragic Drama,* trans. John Osborne (London: Verso, 1982). For the relevance of Benjamin's writings on melancholia in Baroque drama to his analysis of modernity, see Susan Buck-Morss, *The Dialectics of Seeing* (Cambridge, MA: MIT Press, 1989), esp. pp. 159–201.

65. Warhol, *THE Philosophy,* p. 44.

66. Ibid., pp. 52–53. For a reading of this paragraph in relation to the gay clone phenomenon, see Richard Meyer, "Warhol's Clones," *Yale Journal of Criticism* 7, no. 1 (1994), p. 97ff.

67. Dick Hebdige, "The Bottom Line on Planet One: Squaring Up to *The Face,*" in *Hidden in the Light* (London: Routledge, 1988), p. 170.

68. Jean Baudrillard, *For a Critique of the Political Economy,* p. 207.

69. Colacello, *Holy Terror,* p. 140.

70. Gretchen Berg, "Nothing to Lose," p. 56.

Anger, Kenneth (b. 1930)
 Fireworks (1947) 16mm, 15 min.
 Puce Moment (1949) 16mm, 8 min.
 Rabbit's Moon (1950) 35mm, 5 min.
 Eaux d'artifice (1953) 16mm, 13 min.
 Inauguration of the Pleasure Dome (1954) 16mm, 39 min.
 Thelema Abbey (1955) 16mm, 10 min.
 Scorpio Rising (1963) 16mm, 31 min.
 Kustom Kar Kommandos (1965) 16mm, 3 min.
 Invocation of My Demon Brother (1966-69) 16mm, 11 min.
 Lucifer Rising (1972) 16mm, 45 min.

In the filmography Anger wrote and published in *Film Culture,* no. 31 (Winter 1963-64), he appended the following note: "Kenneth Anger has worked on a number of film projects not completed due to lack of funds, notably: *Puce Women* ('49); *The Love That Whirls* ('49); *Maldoror* ('51–52); *Eros Eidolon* ('53); *Histoire d'O* (1959-60)." This filmography also mentions six short films, all in 16mm, made by Anger between 1941 and 1947; the titles are: *Who Has Been Rocking My Dream* (1941); *Tinsel Tree* (1941–42); *Prisoner of Mars* (1942); *The Nest* (1943); *Escape Episode* (silent version, 1944; sound version 1946); *Drastic Demise* (1945). The filmography in Robert Haller's *Kenneth Anger* reports that *The Love That Whirls* was destroyed by the laboratory. This and other filmographies also mention *Le Jeunne homme et la mort,* based on a ballet by Cocteau, choreographed by Roland Petit.

Smith, Jack (1932–1989)

Scotchtape (1962) 8mm, 3 min.

Little Stabs at Happiness (1958–63) (with Ken Jacobs) 16mm, 10 min.

Blonde Cobra (1959–62) (Bob Fleischner, Ken Jacobs, and Jack Smith) 16mm, 28 min.

Flaming Creatures (1963) 16mm, 60 min.

Normal Love (aka *The Great Pasty Triumph*) (1964) 16mm, 40 minutes in the cut currently in distribution by Anthology Film Archives.

No More President (1964–65) 16mm, 100 min.

Warhol, Andy (1928–1987)

Unless otherwise indicated, all the following films are in 16mm. For more detailed filmographies of Warhol, see Stephen Koch, *Stargazer: Andy Warhol's World and His Films* (1973); Jonas Mekas's "Andy Warhol Filmography," in John Coplans, ed. *Andy Warhol* (1970); and more recently, the Whitney Museum's catalog, *The Films of Andy Warhol* (1988).

Tarzan and Jane Regained . . . Sort of (1963) 120 min.

Andy Warhol Films Jack Smith Filming 'Normal Love' (1963) 3 min.

Kiss (1963) 50 min.

Sleep (1963) 6 hours.

Eat (1963) 45 min.

Haircut (1963) 33 min.

Salome and Delilah (1963) 30 min.

Dance Movie (1963) 45 min.

Blow Job (1964) 45 min.

Batman Dracula (1964) 120 min. (with Jack Smith as Dracula)

Empire (1964) 8 hours.

Mario Eats a Banana (aka *Mario Banana*) (1964) 4 min.

Soap Opera (aka *The Lester Persky Story*) (1964) 70 min.

Harlot (1964) 70 min.

Henry Geldzahler (1964) 100 min.

Couch (1964) 40 min. (A twenty-four-hour version of this movie is also mentioned in some filmographies.)

Shoulder (1964) 4 min.

The Thirteen Most Beautiful Women (1964) 40 min.

Taylor Mead's Ass (1964) 70 min.

The Thirteen Most Beautiful Boys (1965) 40 min.

Fifty Fantastics and Fifty Personalities (1965) 45 min.

Ivy and John (1965) 35 min.

Suicide (1965) 70 min.

Screen Test #1 (1965) 70 min.

Screen Test #2 (1965) 70 min.

The Life of Juanita Castro (1965) 70 min.

Horse (1965) 105 min.

Poor Little Rich Girl (1965) 70 min.

Vinyl (1965) 70 min.

Bitch (1965) 70 min.

Restaurant (1965) 35 min.

Kitchen (1965) 70 min.

Beauty #2 (1965) 70 min.

Prison (1965) 70 min.

Face (1965) 70 min.

Afternoon (1965) 105 min.

Outer and Inner Space (1965) 70 min.

Paul Swan (1965) 70 min.

Space (1965) 70 min.

My Hustler (1965) 70 min.

Camp (1965) 70 min. (with Jack Smith).

Hedy (1965) 70 min.

More Milk Yvette (1965) 70 min.

Lupe (1965) 70 min.

The Velvet Underground and Nico (1966) 70 min.

Bufferin (1966) 35 min.

The Chelsea Girls (1966) 3 hours, 15 min.

**** (aka *Four Stars,* aka *The Twenty-Four Hour Movie*) (1966–67) 25 hours (gathers material shot during 1966 and 1967).

The Loves of Ondine (1967) 86 min.

I, A Man (1967) 100 min.

Bike Boy (1967) 96 min.

Nude Restaurant (1967) 96 min.

Lonesome Cowboys (1967) 110 min.

Blue Movie (1968) 90 min.

Flesh (1968) 35mm, 105 min. Dir: Paul Morrissey.

Trash (1970) 35mm, 104 min. Dir: Paul Morrissey.

Heat (1972) 35mm, 118 min. Dir: Paul Morrissey.

(The trilogy *Flesh, Trash,* and *Heat* was produced by Andy Warhol and, according to film credits, written and directed by Paul Morrissey. However, it is included in all Warhol filmographies.)

Women in Revolt (1972) 35mm, 98 min.

L'Amour (1973) 35mm, 90 min.

Bad (1976) 35mm, 109 min.

BIBLIOGRAPHY

Aaron, Daniel. *Writers on the Left.* New York: Oxford University Press, 1961.

Abel, Richard. *French Cinema: The First Wave, 1919–1929.* Princeton: Princeton University Press, 1983.

Ades, Dawn. *Photomontage.* London: Thames and Hudson, 1986.

Adorno, Theodor W. *Aesthetic Theory.* Trans. C. Lenhardt. Boston: Routledge and Kegan Paul, 1984.

———. "The Culture Industry Reconsidered." Trans. Anson G. Rabinbach. *New German Critique* (Fall 1975), pp. 12–19.

———. "The Fetish Character of Music and the Regression of Listening." In *The Essential Frankfurt School Reader,* ed. A. Arato and E. Gebhardt. New York: Continuum, 1982.

———. "Freudian Theory and the Pattern of Fascist Propaganda." In *The Essential Frankfurt School Reader,* ed. A. Arato and E. Gebhardt. New York: Continuum, 1982.

———. *Prisms.* Trans. Samuel and Sherry Weber. Cambridge, MA: MIT Press, 1967.

Agee, James. *Agee on Film: Collected Essays and Reviews,* vol. 1. Boston: Beacon, 1968.

Bibliography

Albert, Judith, and Steward Edward Albert, eds. *The Sixties Papers: Documents of a Rebellious Decade.* New York: Praeger, 1984.

Alexander, William. *Film on the Left: American Documentary Film from 1931 to 1942.* Princeton: Princeton University Press, 1983.

Allen, Blaine. "The Hip, the Beat, and the Square." *Film Reader,* no. 5 (1982).

Alloway, Lawrence. "The Long Front of Culture." In *Pop Art Redefined,* ed. J. Russell and S. Gablick. New York: Praeger, 1970.

———. "Soho as Bohemia." In *New York, Downtown Manhattan, Soho: Ausstellungen, Theater, Musik, Performance, Video, Film,* ed. R. Block. Berlin: Akademie der Kunste, 1976.

Althusser, Louis. *Lenin and Philosophy.* Trans. Ben Brewster. New York: Monthly Review, 1971.

Altman, Dennis. *The Homosexualization of America.* Boston: Beacon, 1983 [St. Martin's, 1982].

Anderson, Christopher. "Hollywood in the Home: Television and the End of the Studio System." In *Modernity and Mass Culture,* ed. J. Naremore and P. Brantlinger. Bloomington: Indiana University Press, 1991.

Andy Warhol. Stockholm: Modern Museet, 1968. Exhibition catalogue.

Anger, Kenneth. "Filmography." *Film Culture,* no. 31 (Winter 1963–64).

———. *Hollywood Babylon.* San Francisco: Straight Arrow, 1975 [Paris: J. J. Pauvert, 1960].

Aragon, Louis. *Paris Peasant.* Trans. Simon Watson Taylor. London: Cape, 1971.

Arthur, Paul. "History and Crass Consciousness: George Kuchar's Fantasies of Un-Power." *Millennium Film Journal,* nos. 20/21 (Fall–Winter 1988–89).

———. "Last of the Last Machine." *Millennium Film Journal,* nos. 16/17/18 (Fall–Winter 1986–87).

———. "Routines of Emancipation: Alternative Cinema in the Ideology and Politics of the Sixties." In *To Free the Cinema: Jonas Mekas and the New York Underground,* ed. David James. Princeton: Princeton University Press, 1992.

Babuscio, Jack. "Camp and the Gay Sensibility." In *Gays and Film,* ed. Richard Dyer. London: British Film Institute, 1978.

Baker, Robb. "The Trials of Lucifer: An Interview with Kenneth Anger." *Soho Weekly News,* October 28, 1976, pp. 16–17.

Balakian, Anna. *Surrealism: The Road to the Absolute.* Chicago: University of Chicago Press, 1986 [1970].

Balsey, Gene. "The Hot Rod Culture." *American Quarterly* (Winter 1950), pp. 353–58.

Barnouw, Eric. *Tube of Plenty: The Evolution of American Television.* New York: Oxford University Press, 1975.

Barthes, Roland. *Image-Music-Text.* Ed. and trans. Stephen Heath. New York: Hill and Wang, 1978.

———. *Mythologies.* Trans. Annette Lavers. London: Cape, 1972.

———. *S/Z: An Essay.* Trans. Richard Miller. New York: Hill and Wang, 1974.

Battcock, Gregory, ed. *The New American Cinema.* New York: Dutton, 1967.

Baudelaire, Charles. *The Mirror of Art.* Trans. Jonathan Mayne. New York: Phaidon, 1955.

Baudrillard, Jean. *For a Critique of the Political Economy of the Sign.* Trans. Charles Levin. St. Louis: Telos, 1981.

———. *Simulations.* Trans. Paul Foss, Paul Patton, and Philip Beitchman. New York: Semiotext(e), 1983.

Bazin, André. *What Is Cinema?,* vol. 1. Trans. Hugh Grey. Berkeley: University of California Press, 1971.

Beaver, Harold. "Homosexual Signs." *Critical Inquiry* (Autumn 1981).

Becker, Howard S. *Outsiders: Studies in the Sociology of Deviance.* New York: Free Press, 1963.

Benjamin, Walter. "The Author as Producer." In *The Essential Frankfurt School Reader,* ed. Andrew Arato and Eike Gebhardt. New York: Continuum, 1982.

———. *Charles Baudelaire: A Lyric Poet in the Era of High Capitalism.* Trans. Harry Zohn. London: New Left, 1973.

———. *Illuminations.* Trans. Harry Zohn. New York: Schocken, 1969.

———. *The Origin of German Tragic Drama.* Trans. John Osborne. London: Verso, 1982.

———. "A Short History of Photography." Trans. Stanley Mitchell, *Screen* 13, no. 1 (Spring 1972), pp. 5–26.

Berg, Gretchen. "Nothing to Lose: Interview with Andy Warhol." In *The Andy Warhol Film Factory,* ed. Michael O'Pray. London: British Film Institute, 1989.

Bergman, David, ed. *Camp Grounds: Style and Homosexuality.* Amherst: University of Massachusetts Press, 1993.

Berlin, Brigid. "Factory Days." *Interview* (February 1989).

Bersani, Leo. *The Freudian Body: Psychoanalysis and Art.* New York: Columbia University Press, 1986.

———. "Is the Rectum a Grave?" *October,* no. 43 (1987).

Block, René, ed. *New York, Downtown Manhattan, Soho: Ausstellungen, Theater, Musik, Performance, Video, Film.* Berlin: Akademie der Kunste, 1976.

Bockris, Victor, and Gerard Malanga. *Up-Tight: The Velvet Underground Story.* London: Chimera, 1984.

Bogdanovich, Peter. "Bogie in Excelsis." *Esquire* (September 1965).

Booth, Michael. *Camp.* New York: Quartet, 1983.

Bordwell, David, Kristin Thompson, and Janet Steiger. *The Classical Hollywood Cinema: Film Style and Modes of Production to 1960.* New York: Columbia University Press, 1985.

Bowlt, John E. "A Brazen Can-Can in the Temple of Art." In *Modern Art and Popular Culture,* ed. Kirk Varnedoe and Adam Gopnick. New York: Museum of Modern Art, 1990.

Bradbury, Malcolm, and James McFarlane, eds. *Modernism.* Harmondsworth: Penguin, 1976.

Brakhage, Stan. *Brakhage Scrapbook: Collected Writings 1964–1980.* Ed. Robert Haller. New Paltz, New York: Documented, 1982.

———. *Metaphors of Vision. Film Culture,* no. 30 (Fall 1963). Special issue on Brakhage's writings.

Brantlinger, Patrick. *Bread and Circuses: Theories of Mass Culture as Social Decay.* Ithaca, NY: Cornell University Press, 1983.

Brasell, R. Bruce. "My Hustler: Gay Spectatorship as Cruising." *Wide Angle* (Summer 1992), pp. 55–64.

Brecht, Bertolt. *Brecht on Brecht.* Ed. John Willet. New York: Hill and Wang, 1964.

Brecht, Stephan. *Queer Theater.* Frankfurt: Suhrkamp, 1979.

Brenkman, John. "Mass Culture: From Collective Experience to the Culture of Privatization." *Social Text* 1, no. 1 (Winter 1979).

Breton, André. *Nadja.* Trans. Richard Howard. New York: Grove, 1960.

Bronski, Michael. *Culture Clash: The Making of Gay Sensibility.* Boston: South End, 1984.

Buchloch, Benjamin H. D. "The Andy Warhol Line." In *The Work of Andy Warhol,* ed. Gary Garrells. Seattle: Bay, 1989.

Buck-Morss, Susan. *The Dialectics of Seeing: Walter Benjamin and the Arcades Project.* Cambridge, MA: MIT Press, 1989.

———. *The Origin of Negative Dialectics: Theodor Adorno, Walter Benjamin, and the Frankfurt Institute.* New York: Free Press, 1977.

———. "Walter Benjamin's *Passagenwerk:* Redeeming Mass Culture for the Revolution." *New German Critique* (Spring–Summer 1983), pp. 211–40.

Buñuel, Luis. *Mon dernier soupir.* Paris: Gallimard, 1981.

———. "Variations on the Moustache of Menjou," in "Appendix: Buñuel's Film Criticism." In *Luis Buñuel: A Critical Biography,* by Francisco Aranda. Trans. David Robinson. New York: Da Capo, 1976, pp. 271–73.

Bürger, Peter. *Theory of the Avant-Garde.* Trans. Michael Shaw. Minneapolis: University of Minnesota Press, 1984 [1974].

Butler, Judith. *Gender Trouble.* New York: Routledge, 1990.

———. "Imitation and Gender Insubordination." In *Inside/Out: Lesbian Theories, Gay Theories,* ed. Diana Fuss. New York: Routledge, 1991.

Cagle, Robert L. "Auto-Eroticism: Narcissism, Fetishism, and Consumer Culture." *Cinema Journal* 33, no. 4 (Summer 1994).

Calinescu, Matei. *Five Faces of Modernity: Modernism, Avant-Garde, Decadence, Kitsch, Postmodernism.* Durham, NC: Duke University Press, 1987.

Castiglia, Christopher. "Rebel without a Closet." In *Engendering Men: The Question of Male Feminist Criticism,* ed. Joseph Boone and Michael Cadden. New York: Routledge, 1990.

Chambers, Iain. *Popular Culture: The Metropolitan Experience.* New York: Routledge, 1986.

Christgau, Robert. "Will Art Spoil the Kuchar Brothers?" *New York World Journal Tribune,* November 20, 1966.

"Cinema Underground." *New Yorker,* July 13, 1963.

Clark, T. J. "Clement Greenberg's Theory of Art." *Critical Inquiry* 9, no. 1 (September 1982). Reprinted in F. Frascina, ed. *Pollock and After.* New York: Harper and Row, 1985.

———. *Image of the People: Gustave Courbet and the Second French Republic, 1848–1851.* Greenwich, CT: New York Graphic Society, 1973.

———. *The Painting of Modern Life: Paris in the Art of Manet and His Followers.* Princeton: Princeton University Press, 1984.

Clarke, Shirley, Amos Vogel, Bill Kenly, et al. "The Expensive Art—A Discussion on Independent Film Distribution and Exhibition in the United States." *Film Quarterly* 13, no. 4 (Summer 1960).

Cockcroft, Eva. "Abstract Expressionism: Weapon of the Cold War." *Artforum* 12 (June 1974), pp. 49–51.

Colacello, Bob. *Holy Terror: Andy Warhol Up Close.* New York: Random, 1991.

Collins, Jim. *Uncommon Cultures.* New York: Routledge, 1989.

Comolli, Jean-Luc, and Paul Narboni. "Cinema/Ideology/Criticism." *Screen* 12, no. 1 (Spring 1971). Reprinted in *Movies and Methods,* vol. 1, ed. Bill Nichols. Berkeley: University of California Press, 1976.

Coplans, John, ed. *Andy Warhol.* New York: New York Graphic Society, 1970.

Core, Philip. *Camp: The Lie That Tells the Truth.* New York: Delilah, 1984.

Cosgrove, Stuart. "The Zoot Suit and Style Warfare." *History Workshop* 18 (Autumn 1984).

Crane, Diana. *The Transformation of the Avant-Garde: The New York Art World, 1940–1985.* Chicago: University of Chicago Press, 1987.

Croce, Arlene. "New York Letter." *Sight and Sound* (Spring 1962).

Crone, Rainer. *Andy Warhol.* New York: Praeger, 1970.

Crow, Thomas. "Modernism and Mass Culture in the Visual Arts." In *Pollock and After,* ed. Francis Frascina. New York: Harper and Row, 1985, pp. 21–33.

———. "Saturday Disasters: Trace and Reference in Early Warhol." In *Reconstructing Modernism: Art in New York, Paris, Montreal, 1945–1964,* ed. Serge Guilbaut. Cambridge: MIT Press, 1990, pp. 311–31.

Curtis, David. *Experimental Cinema.* New York: Universe, 1971.

Dalí, Salvador. *Oui 1: La Révolution paranoïaque-critique.* Paris: Gonthier-Noël, 1971.

d'Aurevilly, Jules Barbey. *Dandyism.* Trans. Douglas Ainslie. New York: PAJ Publications, 1988 [1845].

D'Emilio, John. *Sexual Politics, Sexual Communities: The Making of the Homosexual Minority in the United States, 1940–1970.* Chicago: University of Chicago Press, 1983.

D'Emilio, John, and Estelle Freedman. *Intimate Matters: A History of Sexuality in America.* New York: Harper and Row, 1989.

DeBrier, Samson. "On the Filming of *Inauguration of the Pleasure Dome.*" *Film Culture,* nos. 67/68/69 (1979).

de Certeau, Michel. *The Practice of Everyday Life.* Trans. Steven Rendall. Berkeley: University of California Press, 1986.

De Duve, Thierry. "Andy Warhol, or the Machine Perfected." *October,* no. 48 (Spring 1989).

De Salvo, Donna, ed. *Success Is a Job in New York.* New York: Grey Art Gallery and Studio Center, 1989.

Deren, Maya. *An Anagram of Ideas on Art, Form, and Film.* New York: Arno, 1946.

———. "Cinematography: The Creative Use of Reality." *Daedalus,* 1960.

Deutsche, R., and C. Ryan. "The Fine Art of Gentrification." *October,* no. 31 (Winter 1984), pp. 91–111.

Dickstein, Morris. *Gates of Eden: American Culture in the 1960s.* New York: Penguin, 1989 [1977].

Dobi, Stephen. "Cinema 16: The Largest Film Society in America." Dissertation, New York University, 1983.

Dollimore, Jonathan. "Different Desires: Subjectivity and Transgression in Wilde and Gide." *Genders 2* (Summer 1988).

—————. *Sexual Dissidence: Augustine to Wilde, Freud to Foucault.* New York: Oxford University Press, 1991.

Duberman, Martin. *Cures: A Gay Man's Odyssey.* New York: Plume, 1994.

—————. *Stonewall.* New York: Plume, 1994.

Duchamp, Marcel. *Marchand du sel. Ecrits de Marcel Duchamp,* ed. Michel Sanouillet. Paris: Terrain Vague, 1958.

Duchamp, Marcel, and Pierre Cabanne. *Conversations with Marcel Duchamp.* New York: Da Capo, 1982.

Dwoskin, Stephen. *Film Is: The International Free Cinema.* Woodstock, NY: Overlook, 1975.

Dyer, Richard. "Entertainment and Utopia." In *Genre: The Musical,* ed. Rick Altman. New York: Routledge, 1981.

—————. *Heavenly Bodies.* New York: St. Martin's, 1986.

—————. *Now You See It: Studies in Gay and Lesbian Film.* New York: Routledge, 1990.

—————. "Seen to Be Believed: Some Problems in the Representation of Gay as Typical." *Studies in Visual Communication* 9, no. 2 (Spring 1983), pp. 2–19.

Eckert, Charles. "The Carole Lombard in Macy's Window." *Quarterly Review of Film Studies* 3, no. 1 (Winter 1978).

Eco, Umberto. *Apocalitticci e integrati.* Milan: Bompiani, 1961.

—————. "*Casablanca:* Cult Movies and Intertextual Collage." *SubStance,* no. 57 (1985).

"Edie and Andy." *Time,* August 27, 1965.

Egbert, Donald D. *Social Radicalism and the Arts.* Princeton: Princeton University Press, 1970.

Ehrenstein, David. *Film: The Front Line. 1984.* Denver: Arden, 1984.

Enzensberger, Hans Magnus. "The Aporias of the Avant-Garde." In *The Consciousness Industry.* New York: Seabury, 1974, pp. 22–48.

Erb, Cynthia. "Film and Reception: A Contextual and Reading Formation Study of *King-Kong* (1933)." Dissertation, Indiana University, 1991.

Ester, Mark. *A History of the Underground Comic Books.* San Francisco: Straight Arrow, 1974.

Farber, Manny. *Negative Space.* New York: Praeger, 1971.

Feingold, Michael. "Caffé Cino: Twenty Years after Magic Time." *Village Voice,* May 14, 1985.

Fiedler, Leslie. *Collected Essays of Leslie Fiedler,* vols. 1 and 2. New York: Stein and Day, 1971.

—————. *Love and Death in the American Novel.* New York: Dell, 1966.

Bibliography

Fiske, John. "Popular Discrimination." In *Modernity and Mass Culture,* ed. J. Naremore and P. Brantlinger. Bloomington: Indiana University Press, 1991.

———. *Television Culture.* London: Methuen, 1988.

Ford, Charles Henri, ed. *Parade of the Avant-Garde: An Anthology of* View *Magazine.* New York: Thunder's Mouth, 1991.

Ford, Charles Henri, and Parker Tyler. *The Young and Evil.* London: GMP, 1989 [1933].

Foster, Stephen, and Rudolf Kuenzli, eds. *Dada-Spectrum: The Dialectics of Revolt.* Madison, WI: Coda, 1979.

Foucault, Michel. *History of Sexuality,* vol. 1. Trans. Robert Hurley. New York: Vintage, 1980.

———. *Madness and Civilization.* Trans. Richard Howard. New York: Random, 1976.

Frascina, Francis, ed. *Pollock and After.* New York: Harper and Row, 1985.

Freud, Sigmund. "The Economical Problem of Masochism (1924)." *Standard Edition,* vol. XIX. Trans. James Strachey. London: Hogarth, 1948.

———. "Three Essays on the Theory of Sexuality (1905)." *Standard Edition,* vol. VII.

Frith, Simon. "Rock and the Politics of Memory." In *The 60s without Apology,* ed. S. Aronovitz, F. Jameson, S. Sayres, A. Stephanson. Minneapolis: University of Minnesota Press, 1984.

———. *Sound Effects: Youth, Leisure, and the Politics of Rock 'n' Roll.* New York: Pantheon, 1981.

Frith, Simon, and Howard Horne. *Art into Pop.* London: Methuen, 1987.

Fryer, Ellen. "Formalist Cinema: Artistic Suicide in the Avant-Garde." *The Velvet Light-Trap,* no. 13 (Fall 1974), pp. 47–49.

Fuss, Diana. *Essentially Speaking: Feminism, Nature, and Difference.* New York: Routledge, 1989.

Garrells, Gary, ed. *The Work of Andy Warhol.* Seattle: Bay, 1989.

Gendron, Bernard. "Jamming at Le Boeuf: Jazz and the Paris Avant-Garde." *Discourse* 12, no. 1 (Fall–Winter 1989–90), pp. 3–27.

Genet, Jean. *Our Lady of the Flowers.* Trans. Bernard Frechtman. New York: Grove, 1963.

———. *The Thief's Journal.* Trans. Bernard Frechtman. New York: Grove, 1964.

Gidal, Peter. *Andy Warhol: Films and Paintings.* London: Studio Vista/Dutton, 1971.

Gilbert, James Burkhardt. *Cycle of Outrage: America's Reaction to the Juvenile Delinquent in the 1950s.* New York: Oxford University Press, 1986.

————. *Writers and Partisans: A History of Literary Radicalism in America.* New York: Wiley, 1968.

Gilman, Richard. "The Idea of the Avant-Garde." *Partisan Review* 39, no. 3 (1972), pp. 383–97.

Ginsberg, Allen. *Howl and Other Poems.* San Francisco: City Lights, 1962.

Gitlin, Todd. *The Sixties: Years of Hope, Days of Rage.* New York: Bantam, 1987.

————. *The Whole World Is Watching: Mass Media in the Making and Unmaking of the New Left.* Berkeley: University of California Press, 1980.

Goffman, Irving. *Stigma: Notes on the Management of Spoiled Identity.* Englewood Cliffs, NJ: Prentice-Hall, 1963.

Gomery, Douglas. *The Hollywood Studio System.* London: Macmillan, 1985.

Goodman, Ezra. *The Fifty Year Decline and Fall of Hollywood.* New York: Macfadden, 1962.

Gorbman, Claudia. *Unheard Melodies: Narrative Film Music.* Bloomington: Indiana University Press, 1987.

Greenberg, Clement. *Art and Culture.* Boston: Beacon, 1961.

————. "Avant-Garde and Kitsch." *Partisan Review* 6, no. 5 (Fall 1939), pp. 34–49.

————. "Towards a Newer Laocoon." *Partisan Review* 7, no. 4 (July–August 1940), pp. 296–310.

Grosz, George. *A Little Yes and a Big No.* Trans. Lola Sachs. New York: Dial, 1947.

Guilbaut, Serge. *How New York Stole the Idea of Modern Art.* Trans. Arthur Goldhammer. Chicago: University of Chicago Press, 1983.

Habermas, Jürgen. "Modernity and Postmodernity." *New German Critique* (Winter 1981) pp. 3–14.

————. *The Philosophical Discourse of Modernity.* Trans. Frederick Lawrence. Cambridge, MA: MIT Press, 1987.

————. "The Public Sphere." *New German Critique* (Fall 1974).

————. *The Structural Transformation of the Public Sphere.* Cambridge, MA: MIT Press, 1989 [1969].

Hahn, P. *Nos ancêtres les pervers. La vie des homosexuelles sous le second empire.* Paris: Olivier Orban, 1979.

Hall, Stuart. "Encoding/Decoding." In *Culture, Media, Language,* ed. Stuart Hall et al. London: New Left Review, 1979.

————. "Notes on Deconstructing the Popular." In *People's History and Socialist Theory,* ed. Raphael Samuel. London: Routledge and Kegan Paul, 1981, pp. 227–39.

Haller, Robert. *Kenneth Anger.* Minneapolis: Walker Art Center, 1980.

Hamill, Peter. "Explosion in the Movie Underground." *Saturday Evening Post,* September 28, 1963.

Hammond, Paul, ed. *The Shadow and Its Shadow: Surrealist Writings on Cinema.* London: British Film Institute, 1978.

Hanlon, Lindley, and Tony Pipolo. "Interview with Ken and Flo Jacobs." *Millennium Film Journal,* nos. 16/17/18 (Fall–Winter 1986–87).

Hansen, Miriam. *Babel in Babylon.* Cambridge, MA: Harvard University Press, 1990.

Harvey, David. *The Condition of Postmodernity.* Oxford: Blackwell, 1989.

Harvey, Sylvia. *May '68 and Film Culture.* London: British Film Institute, 1978.

Haskell, Barbara. *Blam! The Explosion of Pop, Minimalism, and Performance.* New York: Whitney, 1977.

Hassan, Ihab. *The Dismemberment of Orpheus.* Madison: University of Wisconsin, 1982 [1971].

Hausmann, Richard. *Courier Dada.* Paris: Terrain Vague, 1958.

Heath, Stephen. *Questions of Cinema.* Bloomington: Indiana University Press, 1981.

———. "Screen Images, Film Memory." *Edinburgh Magazine* 1 (1976), pp. 33–42.

Hebdige, Dick. "The Bottom Line on Planet One." In *Hidden in the Light: Essays on Images and Things.* London: Routledge, 1988.

———. *Subculture: The Meaning of Style.* London: Methuen, 1979.

Heide, Robert. "Magic Time at the Caffé Cino." *New York Native,* May 6, 1985.

Hillier, Jim, ed. *Cahiers du Cinéma, The 1950s: Neo-Realism, Hollywood, New Wave.* Cambridge, MA: Harvard University Press, 1985.

Hoberman, J. "After the Orgy." *Village Voice,* December 3, 1991.

———. "The Big Heat." *Village Voice,* November 12, 1991.

———. "Desire under the El: How the Kuchar Brothers Discovered Hollywood in the Bronx." *Village Voice,* December 8, 1975.

———. "No Wavelength: The Parapunk Underground." *Village Voice,* May 21, 1979.

———. "Once More with Anger." *Village Voice,* August 13, 1980.

———. "The Short Happy Life of the Charles." *American Film* (March 1982).

———. "The Theater of Jack Smith." *Drama Review* 23, no. 1 (1979).

———. *Vulgar Modernism*. Philadelphia: Temple University Press, 1991.

Hoberman, J., and Jonathan Rosenbaum. *Midnight Movies*. New York: Harper and Row, 1983.

Hoffman, Abbie. *The Best of Abbie Hoffman*. New York: Four Walls, Eight Windows, 1988.

Horkheimer, Max. "Authoritarianism and the Family." In *Critical Theory*. New York: Continuum, 1981.

———. "The End of Reason." In *The Essential Frankfurt School Reader*, ed. A. Arato and E. Gebhardt. New York: Continuum, 1982.

Horkheimer, Max, and Theodor W. Adorno. *The Dialectic of Enlightenment*. Trans. John Cumming. New York: Continuum, 1972.

Howard, Richard. "Homosexuality as a Vehicle for Masochism Symbolized in the Film *Fireworks*." *Mattachine Review* 7, no. 7 (July 1961), pp. 6–9.

Howe, Irving, ed. *Literary Modernism*. New York: Farrell, 1957.

———. "Mass Society and Postmodern Fiction." *Partisan Review* 26, no. 3 (Summer 1959).

———. "The New York Intellectuals." *Commentary* 46, no. 4 (October 1968). Reprinted in I. Howe, *Selected Writings 1950–1990*. New York: Harcourt, Brace, Jovanovich, 1990.

Huelsenbeck, Richard. "En Avant-Dada." In *The Dada Painters and Poets*, ed. Robert Motherwell. Cambridge, MA: Belknap, 1972.

———. *Memoirs of a Dada Drummer*. New York: Viking, 1974.

Huysmans, Joris Karl. *Against the Grain*. New York: Dover, 1969.

Huyssen, Andreas. *After the Great Divide: Modernism, Avant-Garde, Postmodernism*. Bloomington: Indiana University Press, 1986.

Jacobs, Lewis. "The Experimental Cinema in America." *The Rise of the American Cinema*. New York: Teachers' College Press, 1968.

James, David E. *Allegories of Cinema: American Film in the 1960s*. Princeton: Princeton University Press, 1989.

———, ed. *To Free the Cinema: Jonas Mekas and the New York Underground*. Princeton: Princeton University Press, 1992.

———. "The Unsecret Life: A Warhol Advertisement." *October*, no. 59 (Spring 1991).

Jameson, Fredric. *Marxism and Form*. Princeton: Princeton University Press, 1974.

———. "Periodizing the 60s." In *The 60s without Apology*, ed. S. Aronowitz, F. Jameson, S. Sayres, A. Stephanson. Minneapolis: University of Minnesota Press, 1984.

———. *The Political Unconscious.* Ithaca, NY: Cornell University Press, 1981.

———. "Postmodernism and Consumer Society." In *The Anti-Aesthetic: Essays in Postmodern Culture,* ed. Hal Foster. Port Townsend, WA: Bay, 1983.

———. "Postmodernism, or the Cultural Logic of Late Capitalism." *New Left Review,* no. 146 (July–August 1984).

———. *Postmodernism, or the Cultural Logic of Late Capitalism.* Durham, NC: Duke University Press, 1991.

———. "Reification and Utopia in Mass Culture." *Social Text* 1, no. 1 (1979), pp. 120–47.

Jay, Martin. *The Dialectical Imagination: A History of the Frankfurt School and the Institute of Social Research.* Boston: Little Brown, 1973.

Jean, Marcel, ed. *The Autobiography of Surrealism.* New York: Viking, 1982.

Jenkins, Bruce, and Melinda Ward, eds. *The American New Wave, 1958–1967.* Minneapolis: Walker Art Center, 1982.

Jenkins, Henry. *Textual Poachers: Television Fans and Participatory Culture.* New York: Routledge, 1992.

Jenkyns, R. *The Victorians and Ancient Greece.* Oxford: Blackwell, 1981.

Josephson, Matthew. *Life among the Surrealists.* New York: Holt, Rinehart, and Winston, 1962.

———. "The Rise of the Little Cinemas." In *Spellbound in Darkness,* ed. George C. Pratt. Greenwich, CT: New York Graphic Society, 1973.

Kael, Pauline. "The Glamour of Delinquency." In *I Lost It at the Movies.* Boston: Little Brown, 1962.

Kahn, Douglas. *John Heartfield: Art and Mass Media.* New York: Tanam, 1985.

Kaprow, Alan. "The Legacy of Jackson Pollock." *ARTnews* (October 1958).

———. "Pop Art: Past, Present and Future." *Malahat Review* (July 1967).

Kelman, Ken. "Anticipation of the Light." *Nation,* May 11, 1964.

———. "Smith Myth." *Film Culture,* no. 29 (Summer 1963).

———. "Thanatos in Chrome." *Film Culture,* no. 31 (Winter 1963–64).

Kern, Stephen. *The Culture of Time and Space: 1880–1918.* Cambridge, MA: Harvard University Press, 1983.

Kerouac, Jack. *The Subterraneans.* New York: Grove, 1979 [1958].

Kirby, Lynne. "From Marinetti to Vertov: Women on the Track of Avant-Garde Representation." *Quarterly Review of Film Studies* 10 (1989), pp. 309–29.

Kirby, Michael. *Futurist Performance.* New York: Dutton, 1971.

Kleinschmidt, Hans J. "Berlin Dada." In *Dada-Spectrum: The Dialectics of Revolt,* ed. Stephen Foster and Rudolf Kuenzli. Madison, WI: Coda, 1979.

Knödler-Bunte, Eberhardt. "The Proletarian Public Sphere and Political Organization." Trans. Sara and Frank Lennox. *New German Critique* (Summer 1973), pp. 51–75.

Koch, Stephen. "Reflections on Soho." In *New York, Downtown Manhattan, Soho: Ausstellungen, Theater, Musik, Performance, Video, Film,* ed. R. Block. Berlin: Akademie der Kunste, 1976.

————. *Stargazer: Andy Warhol's World and His Films.* New York: Praeger, 1973.

Koutoukas, H. M. "Papal References." *Film Culture,* no. 45 (Summer 1967).

Kozloff, Max. "American Painting during the Cold War." *Artforum* 13 (May 1973), pp. 43–54.

————. "Pop Art: Metaphysical Disgust, or the New Vulgarians." *Art International,* March 6, 1962.

Krauss, Rosalind. *The Originality of the Avant-Garde and Other Modernist Myths.* Cambridge, MA: MIT Press, 1986.

Kuenzli, Rudolf, ed. *New York Dada.* New York: Willis, Locker, and Owens, 1986.

Laing, Dave. *One-Chord Wonders.* Milton Keynes: Open University Press, 1985.

Lawder, Standish. *The Cubist Cinema.* New York: New York University Press, 1975.

LeGrice, Malcolm, ed. *Abstract Film and Beyond.* Cambridge, MA: MIT Press, 1977.

Léger, Fernand. "The Machine Aesthetic: The Manufactured Object, the Artisan, and the Artist." In *The Function of Painting.* Trans. Alexandra Anderson. New York: Viking, 1973.

Lehman, Peter. "The Avant-Garde: Power, Change, and the Power to Change." *Cinema Histories / Cinema Practices,* ed. Patricia Mellencamp and Robert Rosen. Frederick, MD: University Publications of America, 1984.

Lester, Eleanore. "The Final Decline and Total Collapse of the American Avant-Garde." *Esquire* (May 1969).

Levin, Harry. "What Was Modernism?" *Massachusetts Review* 1, no. 4 (August 1960).

Lewis, Felice Flannery. *Literature, Obscenity, and the Law.* Carbondale: Southern Illinois University Press, 1976.

Lewis, Helena. *The Politics of Surrealism.* New York: Paragon, 1988.

Lewis, Timothy. *Physique: A Pictorial History of the Athletic Model Guild.* San Francisco: Gay Sunshine, 1983.

Liebman, Stuart. "The Contribution of the French Literary Avant-Garde to Film Theory and Criticism (1907–1924)." *Quarterly Review of Film Studies* (Winter 1983).

Lipsitz, George. *A Rainbow at Midnight: Class and Culture in Post-War America.* New York: Praeger, 1981.

———. *Time Passages: Collective Memory and American Popular Culture.* Minneapolis: University of Minnesota Press, 1987.

Loos, Adolf. "Ornament and Crime [1908]." In *Programs and Manifestos on Twentieth-Century Architecture,* ed. Ulrich Conrads, trans. Michael Bullock. Cambridge, MA: MIT Press, 1970.

Lowenthal, Leo. *Literature, Popular Culture, and Society.* Englewood Cliffs, NJ: Prentice-Hall, 1961.

Lowry, Ed. "The Appropriation of Signs in *Scorpio Rising.*" *The Velvet Light Trap,* no. 20 (1983), pp. 41–47.

Lüdke, W. M., ed. *Theorie der Avant-Garde: Antworten auf Peter Bürgers Bestimmung von Kunst und Bürgerlicher Gesellschaft.* Frankfurt: Suhrkamp, 1976.

Lukács, Georg. *History and Class Consciousness.* Trans. Rodney Livingstone. Cambridge, MA: MIT Press, 1971 [1923; first English edition: Merlin, 1971].

Lyotard, Jean-François. *The Postmodern Condition.* Trans. Geoffrey Bennington and Brian Massumi. Minneapolis: University of Minnesota Press, 1984.

MacCabe, Colin. "Realism and the Cinema: Notes on Some Brechtian Theses." *Screen* 15, no. 2 (Summer 1974), pp. 7–27. Reprinted in C. MacCabe, *Theoretical Essays.* Manchester, U.K.: Manchester University Press, 1985.

Macdonald, Dwight. *Against the American Grain.* New York: Random, 1962.

———. *On Movies.* New York: Da Capo, 1981.

———. "A Theory of Mass Culture." In *Mass Culture: The Popular Arts in America,* ed. Rosenberg and White. Glencoe, IL: Free Press, 1958, pp. 59–73.

MacDonald, Scott. "Amos Vogel and Cinema 16." *Wide Angle* 9, no. 3 (1987).

———. *Avant-Garde Film: Motion Studies.* New York: Cambridge University Press, 1993.

———. "Cinema 16: Interview with Amos Vogel." *Film Quarterly* (Summer 1984).

———. *A Critical Cinema: Interviews with Independent Filmmakers.* Berkeley: University of California Press, 1988.

———. "Interview with Jonas Mekas." *October,* no. 29 (Summer 1984), pp. 82–116.

———. "The 'Millennium' after Twenty Years: Interview with Howard Guttenplan." *Millennium Film Journal,* nos. 16/17/18 (Fall–Winter 1986–87).

Mahsun, Carol Anne. *Pop Art: The Critical Dialogue.* Ann Arbor: University of Michigan Research Press, 1983.

Mailer, Norman. *The Armies of the Night.* New York: New American Library, 1968.

———. *Of a Fire on the Moon.* Boston: Little Brown, 1970.

———. "The White Negro." In *Advertisements for Myself.* New York: Putnam, 1959.

Malanga, Gerard, and Jack Smith. "Interview with Jack Smith." *Film Culture,* no. 45 (Summer 1967).

Mamiya, Christin J. *Pop Art and Consumer Culture: The American Supermarket.* Austin: University of Texas Press, 1992.

Man Ray. *Self-Portrait.* Boston: Little Brown, 1963.

Marcus, Eric. *Making History: The Struggle for Gay and Lesbian Equal Rights.* An Oral History. New York: Harper/Collins, 1992.

Marcus, Greil. "The Dance That Everybody Forgot." *New Formations* 1, no. 2 (Summer 1987), pp. 37–50.

———. "'Hollywood-Babylon' on the Road." *Village Voice,* October 13, 1975.

———. *Lipstick Traces: A Secret History of the Twentieth Century.* Cambridge, MA: Harvard University Press, 1989.

———. *Mystery Train: Images of America in Rock 'n' Roll Music.* New York: Dutton, 1976.

Marcuse, Herbert. "The Affirmative Character of Culture." In *Negations.* Boston: Beacon, 1968.

———. *Eros and Civilization.* Boston: Beacon, 1952.

———. *One-Dimensional Man.* Boston: Beacon, 1964.

Marinetti, Filippo Tommaso. *Selected Writings.* Ed. and trans. R. W. Flint. New York: Farrar, Straus, and Giroux, 1971.

Markman, Joel. "Some Thoughts about Jack Smith," *Film Culture,* no. 32 (Spring 1964).

Markopoulos, Gregory. "Innocent Revellers." *Film Culture,* no. 33 (Summer 1964).

———. "*Scorpio Rising.* First Impressions after a First Viewing, 10/29/63." *Film Culture,* no. 31 (Winter 1963–64).

Marotta, Toby. *The Politics of Homosexuality.* New York: Houghton Mifflin, 1981.

Marx, Karl. "The Fetishism of Commodities and the Secret Thereof." In *Capital: A Critique of Political Economy,* vol. 1. New York: International, 1961.

———. *The Marx-Engels Reader,* ed. Robert Tucker. New York: Norton, 1978.

Matthews, Jane De Hart. "Art and Politics in Cold War America." *American Historical Review,* no. 81 (1976).

McCann, Graham. *Rebel Males: Clift, Brando, and Dean.* New Brunswick, NJ: Rutgers University Press, 1992.

McCarthy, Todd, and Charles Flynn, eds. *Kings of the Bs.* New York: Dutton, 1975.

McLuhan, Marshall. *Understanding Media: The Extensions of Man.* New York: Signet, 1964.

McLuhan, Marshall, and Quentin Fiore. *The Medium Is the Massage: An Inventory of Effects.* New York: Bantam, 1967.

McNeill, Don. *Moving through Here.* New York: Knopf, 1970.

Mekas, Jonas. "Call for a New Generation of Filmmakers." *Film Culture,* no. 19 (1959).

———. "The Cinema of the New Generation." *Film Culture,* no. 21 (Summer 1960), pp. 1–20.

———. "Editorial Statement on Censorship." *Film Culture,* no. 32 (Spring 1964), p. 3.

———, et al. "Film Unions and the Low-Budget Independent Film Production—An Exploratory Discussion." *Film Culture,* nos. 22/23 (Summer 1962), pp. 134–50.

———. *Movie Journal: The Rise of The New American Cinema, 1959–1971.* New York: Macmillan, 1972.

———. "New York Letter: Towards a Spontaneous Cinema." *Sight and Sound* 28, nos. 3/4, pp. 118–22.

———. "Notes on the New American Cinema." *Film Culture,* no. 24 (Spring 1962), pp. 6–16.

———. "Notes on Reseeing the Movies of Andy Warhol." In *Andy Warhol,* ed. John Coplans. New York: New York Graphic Society, 1970.

Mellencamp, Patricia. "Receivable Texts: U.S. Avant-Garde Cinema, 1960–1980." *Wide Angle* 7, no. 1, pp. 74–91.

Meyer, Moe, ed. *The Politics and Poetics of Camp.* New York: Routledge, 1993.

Meyer, Richard. "Warhol's Clones." *Yale Journal of Criticism* 7, no. 1 (1994).

Michaelson, Annette. "Film and the Radical Aspiration." *Artforum* 5 (1967).

———. "Screen/Surface: The Politics of Illusionism." *Artforum* 11 (1973).

———. "Toward Snow." *Artforum* 9 (June 1971).

Michelson, Peter. "The Pop Scene and the Theater of the Ridiculous." *Tri-Quarterly,* no. 6 (1967).

Miller, Michael. *The Bon-Marché.* Princeton: Princeton University Press, 1981.

Mitchell, George. "The Consolidation of the Hollywood Film Industry." *Cine-Tracts* 6 (Spring 1979); and *Cine-Tracts* 7/8 (Summer–Fall 1979).

Modleski, Tania. *Loving with a Vengeance.* Greenwich, CT: Archon, 1981.

Moon, Michael. "Flaming Closets." *October,* no. 51 (Winter 1989).

―――. "A Small Boy and Others: Sexual Disorientation in Henry James, Kenneth Anger, and David Lynch." In *Comparative American Identities,* ed. Hortense Spillers. New York: Routledge, 1991.

Morin, Edgar. *The Stars.* Trans. Richard Howard. New York: Grove, 1961.

Mulvey, Laura. "Visual Pleasure and Narrative Cinema." *Screen* 16, no. 3 (Autumn 1975).

Mussman, Toby. "The Chelsea Girls." *Film Culture,* no. 46 (Summer 1967).

Naremore, James. "Authorship and the Cultural Politics of Film Criticism." *Film Quarterly,* vol. 44 (Fall 1990).

Naremore, James, and Patrick Brantlinger, eds. *Modernity and Mass Culture.* Bloomington: Indiana University Press, 1991.

Negt, Oscar, and Alexander Kluge. *Öffentlichkeit und Erfahrung.* Frankfurt: Verlag, 1972.

―――. "The Public Sphere and Experience." Trans. Peter Labanyi. *October,* no. 46 (Fall 1988), pp. 60–82. Special issue devoted to Alexander Klüge's films and critical writings.

Netzer, Dick. *The Subsidized Muse: Public Support for the Arts in the U.S.* New York: Cambridge University Press, 1978.

New American Cinema Group. "First Statement of the New American Cinema Goup." *Film Culture,* nos. 22/23 (Summer 1961), pp. 131–33.

Noguez, Dominique. *Une renaissance du cinéma: le cinéma "underground" américain.* Paris: Klincksieck, 1985.

―――. "Towards Irreference: American Avant-Garde Film of the Sixties—From the Triumph of the Signified to the Rise of the Signifier." *Millennium Film Journal,* no. 19 (1987), pp. 23–37.

Obst, Lynda Rosen, ed. *The Sixties.* New York: Random House/Rolling Stone, 1977.

Oglesby, Carl, ed. *New Left Reader.* New York: Grove, 1969.

Olalquiaga, Celeste. *Megalopolis: Contemporary Cultural Sensibilities.* Minneapolis: University of Minnesota Press, 1991.

O'Neill, William L. *Coming Apart: An Informal History of the Sixties.* Chicago: Quadrangle, 1971.

Ostrow, Stephen. *Raid the Icebox 1 with Andy Warhol.* Providence: Museum of Art, Rhode Island School of Design, 1969.

Parnes, Uzi, "Pop Performance, Four Seminal Influences: The Work of Jack Smith, Tom Murrin—The Alien Comic, Ethyl Eichelberger, and the Split Breeches Company." Dissertation, New York University, 1988.

———. "Pop Performance in East Village Clubs." *Drama Review* 29, no. 1 (Spring 1985).

Peck, Abe. *Uncovering the Sixties: The Life and Times of the Underground Press.* New York: Pantheon, 1985.

Penley, Constance. "The Avant-Garde: Histories and Theories." In *The Future of an Illusion: Film, Feminism, Psychoanalysis.* Minneapolis: University of Minnesota Press, 1989.

———. "Brownian Motion: Women, Tactics, and Technology." In *Technoculture,* ed. C. Penley and A. Ross. Minneapolis: University of Minnesota Press, 1991.

Penley, Constance, and Janet Bergstrom. "The Avant-Garde: History and Theories." In *Movies and Methods,* ed. Bill Nichols. Vol. 2. Berkeley: University of California Press, 1985.

Poirier, Richard. *The Performing Self.* New York: Oxford University Press, 1970.

Polan, Dana. *The Political Language of Film and the Avant-Garde.* Ann Arbor: University of Michigan Research Press, 1985.

———. *Power and Paranoia: History, Narrative, and the American Cinema, 1940–1950.* New York: Columbia University Press, 1986.

Polsky, Ned. "The Village Beat Scene." *Dissent* 8, no. 3 (Summer 1961), pp. 339–59.

Potamkin, Harry Alan. *The Compound Cinema.* New York: Columbia Teachers' College, 1977.

Praz, Mario. *The Romantic Agony.* New York: Oxford University Press, 1970 [1951].

Proust, Marcel. *Cities of the Plain* and *Time Regained,* in *Remembrance of Things Past,* vols. 2 and 3. Trans. C. K. Scott Moncrieff and Terence Kilmartin. New York: Random, 1982.

Rabinovitz, Lauren. *Points of Resistance: Women, Power, and Politics in the New York Avant-Garde Cinema, 1943–1971.* Urbana: University of Illinois Press, 1991.

Ray, Robert. *A Certain Tendency of the Hollywood Cinema, 1930–1980.* Princeton: Princeton University Press, 1985.

Regelson, Rosalyn. "Where Are 'The Chelsea Girls' Taking Us?" *New York Times,* September 24, 1967.

Rembar, Charles. *The End of Obscenity: The Trials of "Lady Chatterley," "Tropic of Cancer," and "Fanny Hill."* New York: Leslie B. Adams, 1991 [Random: 1968].

Renan, Sheldon. *An Introduction to the American Underground Film.* New York: Dutton, 1967.

Richards, I. A. *Principles of Literary Criticism.* New York: Harcourt, Brace, Jovanovich, 1981 [1930].

Richter, Hans. *Dada: Art and Anti-Art.* New York: Oxford University Press, 1964.

Riesman, David. *The Lonely Crowd.* New Haven: Yale University Press, 1968 [1950].

Rimbaud, Arthur. "The Alchemy of the Word." In *Complete Works,* trans. Wallace Fowlie. Chicago: University of Chicago Press, 1970.

Robinson, Mark. "*View:* Parade of the Avant-Garde." *Village Voice Literary Supplement,* February 11, 1992, p. 5.

Rodowick, David. *The Crisis of Political Modernism.* Urbana: University of Illinois Press, 1988.

Rosenbaum, Jonathan. "*The Savage Eye, Shadows.*" In *The American New Wave, 1958–1967,* ed. Bruce Jenkins and Melinda Ward. Minneapolis: Walker Art Center, 1982.

Rosenberg, Bernard, and David Manning White, eds. *Mass Culture: The Popular Arts in America.* Glencoe, IL: Free Press, 1957.

Rosenblum, Robert. "Cubism and Pop Art." In *Modern Art and Popular Culture,* ed. Kirk Varnedoe and Adam Gopnick. New York: Museum of Modern Art, 1990.

Ross, Andrew. *No Respect: Intellectuals and Popular Culture.* New York: Routledge, 1989.

Rowe, Carel. *The Baudelairean Cinema: A Trend within the American Avant-Garde.* Ann Arbor: University of Michigan Research Press, 1983.

Russell, Bruce. "Wilhelm von Pluschow and Wilhelm von Gloeden." *Studies in Visual Communication* 9, no. 2 (Spring 1983), pp. 57–80.

Russell, John, and Suzi Gablick, eds. *Pop Art Redefined.* New York: Praeger, 1970.

Russo, Vito. *The Celluloid Closet: Homosexuality in the Movies.* New York: Harper and Row, 1981.

"Saint Andy." *Newsweek,* December 7, 1964.

Sarris, Andrew. *The American Cinema.* New York: Dutton, 1968.

———. *Confessions of a Cultist.* New York: Simon and Schuster, 1970.

———. "The Independent Cinema." *Motive,* November 1966. Reprinted in *The New American Cinema,* ed. G. Battcock. New York: Dutton, 1967.

Sayres, Sohnya. *Susan Sontag: The Elegiac Modernist.* New York: Routledge, 1990.

Schapiro, Barbara Stern, ed. *Paris Pleasures: From Daumier to Picasso.* Boston: Museum of Fine Arts/David Godine, 1991.

Schapiro, Meyer. "The Social Bases of Art" and "The Nature of Abstract Art." In *Modern Art: The Nineteenth and Twentieth Centuries.* New York: Braziller, 1978.

Schatz, Thomas. *The Genius of the System.* New York: Pantheon, 1988.

Schickel, Richard. "The Movies Are Now High Art." *New York Times,* January 5, 1969.

Schwartz, Arturo, ed. *New York Dada: Duchamp, Man Ray, Picabia.* Munich: Prestel Verlag, 1974.

Sedgwick, Eve K. *Epistemology of the Closet.* Berkeley: University of California Press, 1990.

Seigel, Jerry. *Bohemian Paris: Culture, Politics and the Limits of Bourgeois Life.* New York: Viking, 1986.

Shklovsky, Victor. "Art as Technique." In *Russian Formalist Criticism: Four Essays,* ed. Lee T. Lemon and Marion J. Reis. Lincoln: University of Nebraska Press, 1965.

Simmel, George. "The Metropolis and Mental Life." In *On Individuality and Social Forms,* ed. David Levine. Chicago: University of Chicago Press, 1970.

Sitney, P. Adams. *The Avant-Garde Film: A Reader in Theory and Criticism.* New York: New York University Press, 1978.

―――. "Autobiography in Avant-Garde Film." *Millennium Film Journal* 1, no. 1 (Winter 1977).

―――. *The "Film Culture" Reader.* New York: Praeger, 1970.

―――. *Visionary Film: The American Avant-Garde.* New York: Oxford University Press, 1979 [1974].

Smith, Jack. *Historical Treasures.* New York: Hanuman, 1990.

―――. "The Memoirs of María Montez, or Wait for Me at the Bottom of the Pool." *Film Culture,* no. 31 (Winter 1963–64).

―――. "The Moldy Hell of Men and Women." *Film Culture,* no. 31 (Winter 1963–64).

―――. "The Perfect Film Appositeness of María Montez." *Film Culture,* no. 27 (Fall–Winter 1962).

―――. "*Pink Flamingoes:* Formulas in Focus." *Village Voice,* July 19, 1973.

―――. "Taboo of Jingola: The Art of the Audience." *Village Voice,* December 21, 1972.

Smith, Jack, and Sylvère Lotringer. "Uncle Fishook and the Sacred Baby Poo Poo of Art." *Semiotext(e)* 1, no. 2 (1978).

Smith, Patrick. *Andy Warhol's Art and Films.* Ann Arbor: University of Michigan Research Press, 1987.

―――. *Warhol: Conversations about the Artist.* Ann Arbor: University of Michigan Research Press, 1988.

"So He Stopped Painting Brillo Boxes and Bought a Movie Camera." *New York Times,* December 11, 1966.

Sontag, Susan. *Against Interpretation.* New York: Farrar, Straus, and Giroux, 1966.

―――. *Styles of Radical Will.* New York: Farrar, Straus, and Giroux, 1968.

SPIDER magazine. "An Interview with Kenneth Anger." *Film Culture,* no. 40 (Winter 1966).

Staehling, Richard. "From *Rock around the Clock* to *The Trip:* The Truth about Teen Movies." *Rolling Stone,* December 27, 1969.

Starr, Cecile. "Independents of New York." *Sight and Sound* (Winter 1960–61), pp. 22–24.

Stauffacher, Frank, ed. *Art in Cinema.* New York: Arno, 1947.

Stein, Jean, and George Plimpton. *Edie: An American Biography.* New York: Knopf, 1982.

Steiner, George. "Eros and Idiom." In *On Difficulty and Other Essays.* New York: Oxford University Press, 1982.

Sukenick, Ronald. *Down and In: Life in the Underground.* New York: Beech Tree, 1988.

Synger, Marilyn, ed. *A History of the American Avant-Garde Cinema.* New York: American Federation of Arts, 1976.

Tartaglia, Jerry. "The Gay Sensibility in American Avant-Garde Film." *Millennium Film Journal* 2, no. 1 (1977).

Tavel, Ronald. "The Banana Diary." *Film Culture,* no. 40 (Spring 1966).

———. "The Theater of the Ridiculous." *Tri-Quarterly,* no. 6 (1966).

Taylor, Christina. *Futurism: Politics, Painting, and Performance.* Ann Arbor: University of Michigan Research Press, 1979.

Taylor, Paul, ed. *Post-Pop Art.* Cambridge, MA: MIT Press, 1989.

Taylor, Ronald, ed. *Aesthetics and Politics.* London: New Left Review, 1979.

Terdiman, Richard. "Newspaper Culture." In *Discourse/Counter-Discourse: The Theory and Practice of Symbolic Resistance in Nineteenth-Century France.* Ithaca, NY: Cornell University Press, 1985, pp. 117–46.

Thompson, Hunter S. *Hell's Angels: The Strange and Terrible Saga of the Outlaw Motorcycle Gangs.* New York: Ballantine, 1981 [1966].

Timmons, Stuart. "Wanted: Athletic Models." *The Advocate,* July 30, 1992.

Tomkins, Calvin. "All Pockets Open." *New Yorker,* January 6, 1973.

———. *The Bride and the Bachelors. Six Masters of the Avant-Garde: Duchamp, Cage, Tinguely, Rauschenberg, Cunningham.* New York: Viking, 1965.

Traub, Stuart H., and Craig B. Little, eds. *Theories of Deviance.* Itasca, IL: S. E. Peacock, 1975.

Trilling, Lionel. *Freud and the Crisis of Our Culture.* Boston: Beacon, 1955.

Trishjian, Dickran. *Skyscraper Primitives.* Middletown, CT: Wesleyan University Press, 1975.

Truffaut, François. "A Certain Tendency of the French Cinema." In *Movies and Methods,* ed. Bill Nichols, vol. 1. Berkeley: University of California Press, 1976.

Tyler, Parker. *The Hollywood Hallucination.* New York: Simon and Schuster, 1970.

———. "Is Film Criticism Only Propaganda?" In *The New American Cinema,* ed. Gregory Battcock. New York: Dutton, 1967.

———. *Underground Film: A Critical History.* New York: Grove, 1969.

Van Der Beek, Stan. "The Cinema Delimina." *Film Quarterly* (Summer 1961).

Varnedoe, Kirk, and Adam Gopnick, eds. *Modern Art and Popular Culture.* New York: Museum of Modern Art, 1990.

Vincendeau, Ginette. "France 1945–1965 and Hollywood: The *Policier* as International Text." *Screen* (Spring 1992), pp. 50–79.

Virmaux, Alain, and Odette Virmaux. *Les Surréalistes et le cinéma.* Paris: Seghers, 1976.

Vogel, Amos "Thirteen Confusions." *Evergreen Review* (Summer 1966). Reprinted in *The New American Cinema,* ed. G. Battcock. New York: Dutton, 1967.

Warhol, Andy. *a.* New York: Grove, 1967.

———. *THE Philosophy of Andy Warhol: From A to B and Back Again.* New York: Harcourt, Brace, Jovanovich, 1975.

———. *The Warhol Diaries,* ed. Pat Hackett. New York: Harcourt, Brace, Jovanovich, 1989.

Warhol, Andy, and Pat Hackett. *POPism: The Warhol Sixties.* New York: Harcourt, 1980.

Warshaw, Robert. "Paul, the Horror Comics, and Dr. Wertham." In *The Immediate Experience.* Garden City, NY: Doubleday, 1962.

Waugh, Tom. "A Heritage of Pornography." *Body Politic,* no. 90 (January–February 1983).

———. "Homoerotic Representation in the Stag Film, 1920–1940. Imagining an Audience." *Wide Angle* (Summer 1992).

———. "Photography: Passion and Power." *Body Politic,* no. 101 (February 1984).

Weiss, Jeffrey S. "Picasso, Collage, and the Music Hall." In *Modern Art and Popular Culture,* ed. Kirk Varnedoe and Adam Gopnick. New York: Museum of Modern Art, 1990.

Wellington, Fred. "Liberalism, Subversion, and Evangelism." In *The New American Cinema,* ed. G. Battcock. New York: Dutton, 1967.

Whitman, Walt. *Leaves of Grass,* ed. Malcolm Cowley. New York: Penguin, 1959.

Wilcock, John. *The Autobiography and Sex Life of Andy Warhol.* New York: Other Scenes, 1971.

Wilde, Oscar. *The Artist as Critic: The Critical Writings of Oscar Wilde,* ed. Richard Ellmann. New York: Vintage, 1970.

———. *The Decorative Arts in America.* New York: Brentano, 1909.

———. "Pen, Pencil, and Poison: A Study in Green." In *The Works of Oscar Wilde.* London: Collins, 1948.

Williams, Raymond. *Culture.* London: Fontana, 1981.

———. *Marxism and Literature.* London: Oxford University Press, 1977.

Williams, Rosalind. *Dream Worlds: Mass Consumption in Late Nineteenth-Century France.* Berkeley: University of California Press, 1982.

Willis, Paul. *Profane Cultures.* London: Routledge, 1978.

Wolfe, Tom. "Bob and Spike." In *The Pump-House Gang.* New York: Noonday, 1987.

———. *The Electric Kool-Aid Acid Test.* New York: Bantam, 1969.

———. *The Kandy-Kolored Tangerine-Flake Streamline Baby.* New York: Farrar, Straus, and Giroux, 1965.

———. "Pariah Styles: The New Chic." *Harper's* (April 1965).

———. *Radical Chic and Mau-Mauing the Flak-Catchers.* New York: Bantam, 1971.

Wollen, Peter. "Cinema/Americanism/The Robot." In *Modernity and Mass Culture,* ed. J. Naremore and P. Brantlinger. Bloomington: Indiana University Press, 1991, pp. 43–70.

———. "Fashion/Orientalism/The Body." *New Formations* 1, no. 1 (Fall 1988), pp. 5–35.

———. "Raiding the Icebox." In *Andy Warhol Film Factory,* ed. Michael O'Pray. London: British Film Institute, 1989.

———. *Raiding the Icebox: Reflections on Twentieth-Century Culture.* Bloomington: Indiana University Press, 1993.

———. *Readings and Writings: Semiotic Counter-Strategies.* London: Verso, 1983.

Yablonsky, Lewis. "The Violent Gang." *Commentary,* no. 30 (August 1960), pp. 125–30.

York, Peter. *Style Wars.* London: Sedgwick and Jackson, 1980.

Young, Colin, and Gideon Bachman. "New Wave or Gesture?" *Film Quarterly* 14, no. 3 (Spring 1961).

Youngblood, Eugene. *Expanded Cinema.* New York: Dutton, 1970.

Zecevic, Bodizar. "The First of the Independents, or How 'A Hollywood Extra' Was Made." *Framework,* no. 21 (Summer 1983).

Zukin, Sharon. *Landscapes of Power: From Detroit to Disney World.* Berkeley: University of California Press, 1992.

———. *Loft Living.* Baltimore: Johns Hopkins University Press, 1982.

INDEX

ACT UP, 178
Adorno, Theodor W: and Max Horkheimer's criticism of mass culture, xii, 1, 7, 28, 35, 166–71; on aesthetic experience, 19–21; on fetish character of listening, 174–75; mentioned, 2, 88
aestheticism, 15–16
Agee, James, 73, 74, 77, 91
Althusser, Louis: definition of ideology, xxiii–xxiv
Anger, Kenneth: and gay culture, xvii–xviii, 98, 128–30, 155–60, 171–74, 175, 178–80; machine culture, 47; *Kustom Kar Kommandoes* (film), 47; as film poet, 78; as "Baudelairean" filmmaker, 99–100 *passim;* and film cultism, 122–25 *passim; Hollywood Babylon*, 123, 147–48; *Fireworks* (film), 128–30, 134, 143–44, 147, 191; early films, 141–49; *Puce Moment* (film), 145; *Rabbitt Moon* (film), 145, 148; *Inauguration of the Pleasure Dome* (film), 145–46, 148; *Waterworks* (*Eaux d'artifice*) (film), 145–46, 148; mentioned, xi, xxvii, xxviii, 54, 55, 60, 61, 68, 89, 95, 221, 223, 255. *See also Scorpio Rising*
Anthology Film Archives, 66, 199, 207, 209
Apollinaire, Guillaume, 71, 115
Aragon, Louis, 29, 30, 32, 38
Aronowitz, Stanley, 223
Artaud, Antonin, 116
Athletic Model Guild, 156–59
Audio-Film Collective, 263

B., Scott and Beth, 257
Baillie, Bruce, 55, 78

Bakhtin, Mikhail, 131
Bakunin, Mikhail A., 27
Balla, Giacomo, 38
Ballet mécanique (film), 47, 49, 50, 62
Balsey, Gene, 153–54
Barry, Iris, 63
Battleship Potemkin (film), 177
Baudelaire, Charles: and aestheticism, 17; studied by Walter Benjamin, 19, 99; defense of "low" culture, 40; and dandyism, 42, 44
Baudelairean cinema, 98–100, 186–87, 223
Baudrillard, Jean: on capital overcoding, 248–50; mentioned, 215, 228, 255
Bauhaus, xiv, xv, 90
Bazin, André, 119, 223
Belson, Jordan, 116
Benjamin, Walter: on aestheticism, 16; on experience, 19–20, 21–22; on reception of mass culture, 36; on Charles Baudelaire, 99; on *faccies hippocratica* of the commodity, 125–26; on author as producer, 217–18; on star aura, 229; on photography, 235
Benning, Sadie: *Jollies,* 179
Bersani, Leo, 135
Bertolucci, Bernardo: *Il Conformista,* 164
Beuys, Joseph, xiii
Bieber, Irving: homosexuality as illness, 137–38
Biker subculture: in postwar America, 150–60; and S&M, 156; mentioned, 148
Blackboard Jungle, The (film), 155
Blitz (magazine), 258
Bogart, Humphrey, 123
Bogdanovich, Peter, 77, 79
Bonnie and Clyde (film), 166–67, 232
Boultenhouse, Charles, 96
Bourdieu, Pierre, xii, 239
Brakhage, Stanley: as film poet, 77–78; *Anticipation of the Night,* 96; *Window Water Baby Moving,* 96; *Dog Star Man,* 97–99 *passim;* on Warhol, 224–26; *Metaphors*

on Vision, 226; mentioned, xvi, xxi, 60, 61, 68, 73, 74, 129, 221
Brando, Marlon: camp object, 132; in *Scorpio Rising,* 142, 162, 168, 170, 173
Breathless (A Bout de souffle) (film), 177
Brecht, Bertolt, 2, 8, 45
Brecht, Stephan, 200–201, 206
Breer, Robert, 61
Breton, André, xvi, 30, 38, 120. *See also* Surrealism
Broom (journal), 4, 91
Broughton, James, 63, 129, 191
Brown, Kenneth: *The Brig,* 79
Buchloch, Benjamin H. D., 215
Buñuel, Luis: *L'Age d'or,* 3, 60; *Un Chien andalou,* 50, 60; film cultist, 120; mentioned, xv, xvi, 59, 62, 142
Bürger, Peter: on the historical avant-garde, xiii, 9–18 *passim,* 268n4
Burton, Michael and Philip: *Wasn't That a Time,* 73
Butler, Judith: gay subjectivity, 135, 194–95

Cabinet of Dr. Caligari (film), 63
Caffé Cino, 133–34, 230
Cahiers du cinéma: and auteurism, 118–20; and cultism, 118, 119
Calinescu, Matei, 39, 271n47
Camp: as dandyism, 44; and the gay sensibility, xviii, 232
Carruthers, Ben, 77
Cassavetes, John: *Shadows,* 54, 64, 74–75, 79, 80; and the New American Cinema, 74–80 *passim*
Chomont, Tom, 66
Cinema clubs: avant-garde film venues, 65; little cinemas, 123
Cinema 16, 64–68 *passim,* 130
Clark, T. J., 8, 12, 31
Clarke, Shirley: *The Cool World,* 61; and the New American Cinema, 74–77 *passim,* 80; *The Connection,* 80, 184
Cocteau, Jean: *Sang d'un poète,* 60, 129; in relation to Kenneth Anger, 144, 146
Colacello, Bob, 247, 257

Comic books: as deviant youth culture, 110–14; Comic Book Code Authority, 111; influence on underground film, 113–14

Conner, Bruce, xvii, 122, 222

Conrad, Tony: *The Flicker* (film), 55, 261

Cooper, Gary, 163, 168

Cornell, Joseph: individual film production, 60; film poet, 78, 224; *Rose Hobart* (film), 120–22

Courbet, Gustave, 13

Creative Film Foundation, 61, 77

Crone, Rainer, 215, 256, 257

Crow, Thomas, 15, 28, 218

Cubism, xiv, 18

Cultism: and auteurism, 118–20; and the surrealists, 120–21; in Jack Smith, 122; in Andy Warhol, 122–23; in Kenneth Anger, 122–23; and cultural recycling, 123–25; and necrophilia, 125–26; and camp, 132–34

Curtis, David, 68, 77

Curtis, Jackie, 231, 242

Dada: use of technology, 21; and the cabaret, 29; contesting urban space, 30, 31; championing "low" culture, 37, 38; and subcultural style, 43, 116–17; mentioned, xiv

Dalí, Salvador: and mass-produced objects, 37–38; mentioned, 60

Dallessandro, Joe, 229, 238, 242

Dandyism: as deviant style, 41–44, 278–79nn104,106

Darling, Candy, 122, 231, 242

D'Avino, Carmen, 56, 61, 222

Dean, James: as gay icon, 173; mentioned, 142, 162, 168, 170, 251

De Antonio, Emile: independent film producer, 61; and the New American Cinema, 77, 80; *In the Year of the Pig* (film), 178; *Milhouse* (film), 178

de Duve, Thierry, 218

Deren, Maya: independent film funding efforts, 61; Creative Film Award, 64; Film Artists' Society, 76; film poet, 77–78

passim; modernist interiority, 83; modernist film psychodrama, 129; mentioned, 68

Dial, The (journal), 4, 92

Dick, Vivienne, 257

Dine, Jim, 202

Dollimore, Jonathan, 135, 194

Duchamp, Marcel: and the historical avant-garde, xiii, xv, 17; and machine culture, 46–47; individual film production, 60; and term "underground," 81; compared with Andy Warhol, 215–17; mentioned, 62

Dupree, William, 91

Dyer, Richard, 131, 158, 246

E.C. Comics, 110–14

Easy Rider (film), 176–77, 261

Eggeling, Viking, 49

Eisenstein, Sergei: use of technology, 45; influence on Kenneth Anger, 142, 168; mentioned, xv, xxv, 62

Eliot, T. S., 18, 83, 93, 116

Engel, Morris, 73, 74, 77

Eyen, Tom, 133

The Face (magazine), 258

Farber, Manny: on underground film venues, 66; on "underground cinema" (term), 85–86

Fascism: and the avant-garde, 22, 273n58; and mass culture, 164–71

Fiedler, Leslie: and "the new sensibility," xxv, 5, 89, 103, 104, 106, 109, 111

Film Artists Society, 76, 83

Film Culture (journal), 58, 72, 96, 198, 210, 224, 230

Filmmakers' Cinematheque, 66, 198, 237

Filmmakers' Cooperative, 67–68, 141

Fischinger, Oskar, 49, 59

Fiske, John, 162, 175

Flaming Creatures (film): use of rock and roll music in, 117–18; influence of *Rose Hobart* on, 122; prosecution of, 139, 181–86; criticism on, 186–87; description of, 188–93;

portrayal of subjectivity,
193–97; mentioned, 199
Fleischner, Bob, 98, 135
Fluxus, 30, 206, 226
Ford, Charles Henri, 4, 91
Foster, Richard, 63
Foucault, Michel, 194
Fourier, Charles, 27, 29
Frank, Robert: *Pull My Daisy,*
64, 74, 80; *Sins of Jesus,*
79; mentioned, 77, 222
Freud, Sigmund, 103, 235
Fung, Richard, 179, 263
Fuss, Diana, 135
Futurism: and the cabaret
tradition, 29; subversion of
city spaces, 30, 31; on anti-
neutral clothing, 38; and
design, 43; and machine
culture, 46–47, 48–49;
mentioned, xiv, xv

Gaines, Joseph: founder of
E.C. Comics, 110
Garbo, Greta, 122, 226, 245
Garland, Judy, 131
Gay: the "gay sensibility" and
the underground, xvii–xviii,
126, 266n3; gayness in
post-war experimental
cinema, 128–31; camp,
132–34; reception of mass
culture, 131–37; models of
subjectivity 134–35,
193–96; in Anger, xvii–xviii,
98, 128–30, 155–60,
171–74, 175, 178–80; in
Smith, xvii, xviii, 184–96
passim, 203, 211–23
passim; in Warhol, 135, 239,
252–53
Gay Liberation Front, 196, 260
Gendron, Bernard, 41
Genet, Jean: and rough
homoeroticism, 157; *Un Chant
d'amour,* 182
Gitlin, Todd, 178
Gloeden, Wilhelm von, 157
Godard, Jean-Luc: auteur critic,
119; and Jean-Pierre Gorin,
Dziga Vertov group, 178;
mentioned, xxii, xxv, 102
Goffman, Irving, 159, 251
Goss, John, 179

Greenberg, Clement: on avant-
garde and kitsch, 1–10, 25,
39, 84, 88, 165, 175, 215,
264; modern art and
bourgeoisie, 12, 14; on
aestheticism, 15; and
Theodor W. Adorno, 20; and
Walter Benjamin, 22;
mentioned, 28
Greyson, John, 179, 263
Grosz, George, 43, 116–17. *See
also* Dada
Guggenheim, Peggy: Art of This
Century Gallery, 108

Habermas, Jürgen: definition of
the public sphere, 14–15, 23
Hair (film), 261
Harlow, Jean, 90, 122, 123, 132
Harper's Bazaar: and Andy
Warhol's underground films,
233–39 *passim*
Harrington, Curtis: *Fragment of
Seeking,* 128, 191
Hausmann, Raoul, 38
Haussmann, Baron Georges-
Eugène de, 25, 31, 206
Hawks, Howard, 85
Heartfield, John, 17
Heath, Stephen: and *Screen*
criticism, xix, xxii,
284–85n26
Hebdige, Dick, xii, 254
Heide, Robert, 133
Herko, Freddie, 226, 230
High School Confidential (film),
155
Hill, Jerome, 224
Hillyard, Roger, 116
Hoberman, J., 55, 65, 68, 209
Hockney, David, 156
Hoffman, Abbie, 105, 298n80
Horkheimer, Max: and Theodor
Adorno's criticism of mass
culture, xii, 1, 7, 28, 166–71,
175
Hot Rods, 107
Howe, Irving, 100–103 *passim*
Huelsenbeck, Richard, 37, 115
Huysman, Joris-Karl, 42
Huyssen, Andreas, 41

Ibsen, Henrik, 200
i.d. (magazine), 258

In the Street (film), 74
Independent Filmmakers'
    Association, 78
Indiana, Robert, 236

Jacobs, Ken: and Millennium
    Film Workshop, 66;
    Baudelairean Capers, 98;
    collaborations with Jack Smith,
    135, 199–201; mentioned,
    xvii, 56, 95, 182
James, David E., xvi, 54, 86, 215,
    311*n8,* 312*n14*
Jameson, Fredric, xxvi, 215
Johns, Jasper, 38, 102, 237
Johnson, Philip, 236
Jost, Jon, 178
Judson Church Performances,
    230

Kant, Immanuel, 10, 104, 166
Kaprow, Alan, 202
Kelman, Ken, 58, 66, 95–96, 98
Kennedy, John F., 204
Kennedy, Robert, 176
Kerouac, Jack, 75, 82
Keynes, Maynard: keynesianism
    in 1960s America, 161–62
Kieghley, William, 85, 119
King, Martin Luther, 176
Klüge, Alexander: and Oscar
    Negt on the public sphere,
    23–26, 33–35
Koch, Stephen, 247–48
Kootz, Samuel, 84
Koutukas, H. M., 230
Kramer, Robert, 178
Krazy Kat, 113
Kropotkin, Piotr, 27
Kruger, Barbara, 257
Kubelka, Peter, 66, 78
Kuchar, George and Mike, xvii,
    56, 80, 95, 96, 113–14

La Bruce, Bruce, 179
Lacan, Jacques, 251
Larionov, Mikhail, 47
Lawder, Standish, 49
Léger, Fernand: on window
    displays, 38; *Ballet
    mécanique,* 47, 49, 50, 62
Leslie, Alfred: *Pull My Daisy,* 64,
    74; mentioned, 77
Levine, Sherry, 257

Levitt, Helen: *In the Street* (film),
    74
Light Shows (and Trip Festivals),
    116, 227
Lindner, Robert, 151, 165
Liotard, Jean-Etienne, 234
Lipsitz, George, 152
Little cinemas, 123
Little Review (journal), 92
Loeb, Janice, 74
Loos, Adolf, 90
Lost in Space (TV series), 204
Lowry, Ed, 174
Ludlam, Charles, 231
Lukács, Georg, 2, 308*n37*
Lyon, Ninette, 236

Maas, Willard: *Geography of the
    Body,* 78; *Images in the Snow,*
    128; mentioned, 191
MacCabe, Colin, xxii
McClard, Michael, 257
Macdonald, Dwight: critic of mass
    culture, 28, 84, 165, 175; on
    1960s American film, 89–91;
    critic of underground film,
    91–94 *passim*
MacDonald, Scott, 49, 64
Maciunas, George, 225
McLuhan, Marshall, 5, 102, 104,
    105, 227
Mad (comic book magazine), 111
Maddow, Ben: *The Savage Eye,* 74
Mailer, Norman, 101
Malanga, Gerard, 225, 227, 229,
    238, 241, 252
Mallarmé, Stéphane, xiii, 37
Mann, Thomas, xiii, 17
Marcus, Greil, 115
Marcuse, Herbert: on affirmative
    character of culture, 11–12;
    and the "new sensibility," 102,
    290*n22;* mentioned, 1
Marinetti, F. T., 30
Marker, Chris, 178
Markopoulos, Gregory, 56, 60, 77,
    96, 128, 177, 191
Marx, Karl: on the 18th Brumaire,
    14; on social monism, 26; on
    commodity fetishism, 216–17;
    mentioned, 103
Mass culture: definition, xii–xiii;
    relations with the avant-garde,
    xiv–xv, 1–51; and modernism,

xiii, 7–8, 20–21, 83–84, 175; utopian potential of, 32–44, 171–75; gay reception of, 131–37, 138–40 *passim;* as totalitarianism, 165–71

Matisse, Henri, xiii, 83

Mekas, Adolfas, 60, 64, 72, 76

Mekas, Jonas: underground film promoter, xvi, 58, 60; and the term "underground film," 55, 81–82; underground exhibitor and programmer, 64–66, 68; *Guns of the Trees* (film), 64, 79; underground distributor, 67–68; editor of *Film Culture,* 72–73; and the New American Cinema, 74–79 *passim;* film poet, 78; *The Brig* (film), 79; *Lost, Lost, Lost* (film), 79; *Notes, Diaries, and Sketches* (film), 79; *Reminiscences of a Journey to Lithuania* (film), 79; criticized, 92–95 *passim;* Baudelairean cinema, 98–99; on gay component in underground film, 126; on *Flaming Creatures,* 181–87, 196; falling-out with Jack Smith, 198–99, 207–209, 307*n25;* on Warhol, 221–26; mentioned, 106, 227

Menken, Marie, 55, 56, 60, 78, 224

Mettrie, Julien Offrey de la, 45–46

Meyerhold, Vsevolod, xv

Meyers, Sidney, 73, 74, 77

Midnight Cowboy (film), 261

Millennium Film Workshop, 66

Mitchell, Eric, 257

Mizer, Bob, 98, 156–58

Modernism: different from the avant-garde, xiii, 9–18 *passim,* 268*n4;* and avant-gardism in cinema, 49–50, 54; cultural politics of, 82–85; and the critical reception of the underground, 91–94; and the new sensibility, 100–104; exhaustion of, 107–109; in post-war gay cinema, 128–30

Moholy-Nagy, Laszlo, xv

Monroe, Marilyn, 191, 192, 215, 228

Montez, María, 122, 132, 193, 203, 210

Montez, Mario, 122, 193, 226, 231

Moon, Michael, 187

Morin, Edgar, 243

Morrissey, Paul, 55, 56, 242

Moses, Robert, 206

MTV, xxvi, 258

Mulvey, Laura, xix, xxii, 160

Museum of Modern Art: circulating film library, 66; promoter of modernism, 108

Naremore, James, 268*n10,* 293*n41*

Negt, Oskar: and Alexander Klüge on the public sphere, 23–25, 26, 33–35

Neue Sachlichkeit, xiv

New American Cinema, 74–81

New York Times, The, 137–38

New York World's Fair (1964), 203–204

Newsreel units, 178, 261

Newsweek, 137

Noailles, Charles de, 60

Noguez, Dominique, 54

off-off-Broadway: part of 1960s gay culture, 133–34; and Warhol's performers, 230, 237

Olalquiaga, Celeste, 204

Oldenburg, Claes, 202

Ondine (Robert Olivio), xix, 134, 226, 229, 230, 231, 238, 239

Oshima, Nagisha, xxii

Owen, Robert, 27, 29

Partisan Review, 4, 9, 82, 84, 93

Patrick, Robert, 133

Peterson, Sidney, 62, 129

Phillips, William, 82, 83, 91

Physique Pictorial (magazine), 156–59 *passim*

Picabia, Francis, 30, 47

Picasso, Pablo, 17, 83, 115

Piscator, Erwin, 45

Pluschow, Wilhelm von, 157

Poiret, Paul, 38

Polan, Dana, xx

Polk, Brigid, 123, 229, 238

Popova, Liubov, 38, 47
Popular Front, 81, 84, 92
Postmodernism: and the avant-garde, xiv–xv; postmodern cultural criticism, 5–6, 89, 100–106 *passim*, 291*n25*; the 1960s underground as, 53–54, 87–140; inflected by gay culture, 131–40
Potamkin, Harry Alan, 125
Presley, Elvis, 115, 162, 172, 215
Prince, Richard, 257
Proust, Marcel, xiii, 157
Public Sphere: theory, 14–15, 23–25
Pull My Daisy (film), 54, 64, 74–75
Punk, 128, 257

Queer Nation, 178, 213

Rabinovitz, Lauren, xxv
Radical Drag, 213
Rauschenberg, Robert, 38, 101, 202
Ray, Man, xv, xvi, 30, 38, 60, 62, 115
Ray, Nicholas, 119, 173
Ray, Robert, 124, 155
Rebel without a Cause (film), 155, 173
Reich, Wilhelm, 164
Rhav, Philip, 82, 83, 91
Rice, Ron, 80, 98, 222
Richter, Hans, xv, 46, 49, 62, 67, 72
Riesman, David, 104, 154
Rigaut, Jacques, 120
Riggs, Marlon, 179, 263
Rimbaud, Arthur, 40, 44, 99, 116
Rock and roll, 114–18
Rock around the Clock (film), 155
Rocky Horror Picture Show (musical), 119
Rodowick, David, xxiii
Rodríguez-Soltero, José, xvii, 95
Rogosin, Lionel, 74, 76, 78
Rosenbaum, Jonathan, 55, 75
Ross, Andrew, 82, 215
Rowe, Carel, 209, 289–90*n17*
Rubin, Barbara: *Christmas on Earth*, 80, 184
Rubin, Jerry, 105
Rubnitz, Tom, 179

Ruttman, Walter: *Berlin: Symphony of a Great City*, xv, 59; mentioned, 49

Sade, Marquis de, 99, 166
S&M: and biker style, 156, 157; in *Scorpio Rising*, 169–71; in Andy Warhol's films, 252–53
Saint-Simon, Henri de, 27, 44–45
San Remo Bar, 229, 230, 231
Sankofa, 263
Sarris, Andrew: on the underground, 94; on auteurism, 118–19; on gay element in the underground, 126; mentioned, 72, 239
Sartre, Jean-Paul, 224
Schapiro, Meyer, 1, 13–14
Schiller, Johann Christoph Friedrich, 10–11, 12, 20
Schneemann, Carolee: *Fuses*, 184
Schönberg, Arnold, xiii, 17, 83
Scorpio Rising: and machine culture, 47; reception of, 96–99 *passim*, 299*nn4,5*, 303*n35*; comic book imagery in, 114; pop music in, 117, 171–75; and youth styles, 150–55; and critiques of mass culture, 160–76; after-effects of, 176–80; prosecution of, 184; mentioned, 56, 61, 80, 95
Screen (journal): criticism of avant-garde cinema, xii–xxvii
Sedgwick, Edie, 122, 226, 227, 229, 230, 238, 239, 244, 249
Sedgwick, Eve, xviii, 309*n40*
Shadows (film), 54, 64, 74–75, 80
Sherman, Cindy, 257
Simmel, Georg, 26
Sims, Jerry, 135
Sitney, P. Adams: characterization of avant-garde cinema, xix–xxii, xxv; characterization of the underground, 96–98; mythopoetic film, 145–46; mentioned, 55, 58, 72
Smith, Harry, xvi, 222
Smith, Jack: and gay culture, xvii, xviii, 184–96 *passim*, 203, 211–23 *passim*; and the cabaret tradition, 29, 199; *Normal Love* (film), 80, 114;

Little Stabs at Happiness, 80; as "Baudelairean filmmaker," 98, 99, 186–87, 223; and cultism, 121–22, 124, 125; and drag, 134, 136, 192, 195–96; *Blonde Cobra* (film), 135–37; performances, 196–211 *passim; No More President* (film), 197; *Scotch Tape* (film), 199; *Human Wreckage Review* (cabaret act), 199; urban space in Jack Smith's work, 203–11 *passim;* compared with Warhol, 212–13, 221, 228, 255; performer in Warhol's films, 230; mentioned, xi, xxvii, xxviii, 54, 60, 89, 95, 143, 226. *See also Flaming Creatures*

Snow, Michael, 261
Socarides, Charles, 138
Solanas, Valerie, 218
Sonbert, Warren, xvii, 95, 117, 134
Sontag, Susan: on the "new sensibility," xvii, xxvii, 5, 89, 100–102, 104–105, 106; on camp, 44; on *Flaming Creatures,* 186, 189, 196–97
Sound of Music, The (film), 90
Speaking Directly (film), 178
Star Trek (TV series), 204
Stauffacher, Frank, 63
Stein, Gertrude, xiii, 83
Sternberg, Josef von, 193
Stijl, De, 90
Stonewall Inn, The: riots, 260
Straub, Jean-Marie, xxii, xxv
Strick, Joseph, 74
Sunset Boulevard (film), 145
Supremes, The, 101, 105
Surfaris, The, 171
Surrealism: and the cabaret tradition, 29; subversion of urban space, 30, 31, 32; fascination with mass-produced objects, 37, 38, 40; and dandyism, 43–44; and film cultism, 120–22; mentioned, xiv, xv, xvi, 2

Taller de Arte Fronterizo, 263
Tallmer, Jerry, 133

Tatlin, Vladimir, xv, 47
Tavel, Ronald, 122, 133–34, 211, 222, 229, 231, 244, 252
Theater of the Ridiculous, 134, 198, 231
Thompson, Hunter, 150, 156
Time (magazine), 137
Tom of Finland, 157
Tönnier, Fernand, 26
Trilling, Lionel, 85
Trotsky, Leon, 8
Tyler, Parker: criticism of the underground, 91, 92, 93; mentioned, 4, 68
Tzara, Tristan, xiii, 17

Urban, Al, 157
Urban renewal: and Jack Smith's work, 205–207

Vaccaro, John, 198, 231
Van Der Beek, Stan, 56, 61, 83–85 *passim*
Van Meter, Ben, 116
Vehr, Bill, xvii, 95, 134
Velvet Underground, The, 117, 227, 241
Vertov, Dziga, xv, xvi, 45, 47, 62
Victim (film), 158
View (magazine), 4, 91
Village Voice, The, 58, 59, 209, 239, 245
Visconti, Luchino: *La caduta degli dei,* 164
Vogel, Amos: alternative film programmer, 64, 68; critic of the underground, 91–94 *passim;* mentioned, 130. *See also* Cinema 16
Vogel, Marsha: alternative film programmer, 64, 68. *See also* Cinema 16
Vogue: and Andy Warhol's underground cinema, 232–41 *passim*

Waldman, Bernard: Modern Merchandising Bureau, 244
Walsh, Raoul, 85, 119
Warhol, Andy: contesting urban space, 39; subcultural style, 41, 231–32, 237–41; is a machine, 47, 247–48; *Harlot* (film) 90, 91, 94; and cultism,

123–25 *passim;* compared
with Jack Smith, 212–13, 221,
228, 255; critical reception
of, 214–15, 309–11*nn3,4;*
compared with Duchamp,
215–17; and art as business,
214–21; and the underground,
221–25; and superstars,
225–31; style and fashion
in, 231–41; and
commodification, 241–48;
and capital overcoding,
248–50; melancholia and
mediation in, 250–52; S&M in,
252–53; death in Warhol's
films, 253–54; influence of,
255–59; mentioned, xi, xiii,
xvii, xviii, xix, xxi, xxvii, xxviii,
54, 56, 60, 69, 89, 95, 106,
139, 143

Warshaw, Robert: responses to
E.C. Comics, 111–12
Warwick, Dionne, 101, 105
Waugh, Tom, 157
Weber, Max, 26, 248
Wein, Chuck, 230
Wertham, Frederic, 110, 111, 166
Whitman, Walt, 157
Whitney Museum of American
Art, 66

Wild Bunch, The (film), 176
Wild One, The (film), 155, 162,
173
Wilde, Oscar, 17, 34, 42, 116, 214
Williams, Raymond: cultural
formations, 27–28, 52–54;
mentioned, xii
Wilson, Landford, 133
Wiseman, Frederick, 61
Wolfe, Tom: and postmodern
cultural criticism, 5, 89, 104;
on 1960s youth style,
106–107, 113; on "low style,"
231; art in New York society,
234; mentioned, 176
Wollen, Peter: criticism of avant-
garde cinema, xix, xxii,
xxiv–xxv; mentioned, 232
Woronov, Mary, 227, 231

Yippie movement, 105, 298*n80*
Youth styles: and the pop
sensibility, 109–18; in post-war
America, 150–55; in Warhol's
films, 231–32, 237–41. *See
also* Punk

Zando, Julie, 179
Zoot suit riots, 151–52
Zukin, Sharon, 205

Juan A. Suárez
is an assistant professor of English
at the Universidad de Murcia, Spain.